THE SUPREME COURT

AND THE AMERICAN ELITE,

1789–2008

THE SUPREME COURT
AND THE AMERICAN ELITE,
1789–2008

Lucas A. Powe, Jr.

HARVARD UNIVERSITY PRESS

Cambridge, Massachusetts, and London, England

For
Tom Krattenmaker
and
Sandy Levinson

First Harvard University Press paperback edition, 2011

Publication of this book has been supported through the generous provisions of
the Maurice and Lula Bradley Smith Memorial Fund.

Library of Congress Cataloging-in-Publication Data

Powe, L. A. Scot.
The Supreme Court and the American elite, 1789–2008 / Lucas A. Powe Jr.
p. cm.
Includes bibliographical references and index.
ISBN 978-0-674-03267-5 (cloth : alk. paper)
ISBN 978-0-674-06041-8 (pbk.)
1. United States. Supreme Court—History. 2. Constitutional history—United
States. 3. Law—Political aspects. I. Title.
KF8742.P683 2009
347.73'26—dc22   2008036606

Contents

X.

XI.

Preface

SINCE THE 1984 ELECTION the Supreme Court has been front and center in presidential politics. Each party's candidate warns of dire consequences should his opponent prevail and be afforded the opportunity to appoint new justices, thereby impacting the future well after the president leaves office. Today the Supreme Court is confident and powerful (enough so to enter without hesitation the 2000 presidential contest). It did not begin this way. Nor did it have to end up this way. The Court's history, like all histories, is contingent.

While Americans are more aware of the Court than before, it has always been a player, if for the most part a lesser one, in American history. Jeffersonians and Jacksonians scrutinized opinions for evidence that the Court might be engaging in "consolidation," which they deemed the constitutional heresy of a national government that could act. During the Civil War and Reconstruction, Republicans watched lest the Court undo their plans to remake the South. Then for decades into the New Deal, the Court policed the boundaries of state and nation and the permissible and impermissible uses of the police power. In both cases the underlying issue was the ability to regulate economic affairs. Following the New Deal, the Court began the process of ending segregation and supervising state criminal procedure as well as addressing constitutional issues arising out of World War II and the cold war. Then, in an extraordinary burst of activity, the Court nationalized liberal values and took on all outliers. Thereafter, right up until the present, Americans have debated whether the Court should go further or retreat.

This book is a history of the Supreme Court, placed within the context of a broader history of the United States and its politics. In a typical book on American history, the Supreme Court appears, if at all, as an interruption here and there. Thus there is the controversy between Thomas Jefferson and the outgoing Federalists that leads to the establishment of judicial review, *Dred Scott* and the run-up to the Civil War, the enshrining of separate but equal, the Court versus the New Deal, *Brown v. Board of Education,* and *Roe v. Wade,* but not much else. Conversely, in a history of the Supreme Court, political events intrude occasionally, but the Court is so busy that there is no chance for a sustained narrative of that history. *The Supreme Court and the American Elite, 1789–2008* situates the Court and its work within a broad narrative of American history.

This is a law professor's book enlightened by political science and history. That is, I have written it in the context of history with the insights of political science but remaining true to the ways the justices perceived their own work. Doctrine may be driven by events and the intellectual currents of the times, but nevertheless the justices, for the most part, take it seriously.

I have attempted to avoid taking sides in any of the controversies of historical interpretation. But as to the Court itself I have made judgments, based on four decades of study, about how the events and decisions should be understood. The best single volume on the Court and American history is Robert McCloskey's study *The American Supreme Court* (updated wonderfully by my friend and colleague Sandy

Levinson), but McCloskey's masterpiece was written when the New Deal dominated thinking about the functions of the judiciary. As the New Deal has receded into history, the Court's performances before, after, and during that era take on different meanings. Instead of viewing the Court as an enemy or competitor of the other two branches of government (though occasionally it is), I see it as a part of a ruling regime doing its bit to implement the regime's policies. Some of its most historically controversial decisions seem far less controversial when set within the politics of the time. Justices are, after all, subject to the same economic, social, and intellectual currents as other upper-middle-class professional elites.

Several themes run throughout the book, some highlighted explicitly, others implicit. The dominant theme is that the Court is a majoritarian institution. That is, it identifies with and serves ruling political coalitions. It is staffed by men (and in recent years a few women) who for the most part are in tune with their times. Relatedly, changes in personnel matter. Lucky presidents who are able to appoint several justices can—and do—change the direction of the Court. That helps explain why the Court and its decisions at the beginning of the twenty-first century are a part of presidential politics and the country's ongoing history. It is also a testament to how far the Supreme Court and the nation have come from the time when the Court's first major decision was immediately reversed by constitutional amendment.

Law school friends, as always, provided assistance and encouragement. Tom Krattenmaker and Sandy Levinson read the entire manuscript, while Doug Laycock, H. W. Perry, Jordan Steiker, and Keith Whittington each read parts of the manuscript. All offered helpful suggestions.

Monika Powe Nelson, an English major turned chef turned restaurant reviewer, and Jason Steed, a former English professor and a member of the University of Texas Law School's class of 2009, both read the manuscript with an eye to seeing that it would be accessible to those who were neither lawyers nor historians.

Marlyn Robinson, of the reference department of the University of Texas Law Library, performed wonders, as she always has. Barbara Bridges, the government documents librarian at the law school, found everything I needed. Their help was indispensable.

Finally, Patrick Luff, a student of mine as an undergraduate and a member of the University of Michigan Law School's class of 2009, aided with checking nineteenth-century footnotes and did much of the work in preparing the index.

Very Modest Beginnings

BY 1787 THERE WAS GENERAL AGREEMENT among American leaders that the Articles of Confederation, the constitution of the newly independent republics in North America, had proven a failure. The Articles created a unicameral legislature but neither an executive nor a judiciary, and the legislature was impotent. From the Constitutional Convention in Philadelphia, George Washington wrote to Thomas Jefferson in Paris, where the former Virginia governor was serving as the American ambassador: "That something is necessary, none will deny; for the situation of the general government, if it can be called a government, is shaken to its foundation . . . [U]nless a remedy is soon applied, anarchy and confusion will inevitably ensue."[1] That remedy was a new constitution creating a stronger central government.

The Articles of Confederation

The Articles made explicit that each state retained its sovereignty as well as every power "not by this confederation expressly delegated to the United States, in Congress assembled."[2] The Articles created among the states less a nation than "a firm league of friendship with each other"[3] that nevertheless was to be "perpetual."[4] Each state got a single, equal vote on each issue, and the issues of war, treaties, borrowing, and appropriation required a positive vote of nine states.

In practice the Articles left Congress helpless to deal with either economic or military matters. The first problem was money. Congress lacked the powers of taxation. It issued too much paper money—thus the phrase "as worthless as a Continental"—and it successfully negotiated several foreign loans (for which further loans would be necessary to pay them off) and requisitioned the states for money. In 1786 Congress requisitioned $3.8 million to make current payments on the debt. The thirteen states responded to congressional begging by anteing up a total of $663.

The second defect lay in the lack of enforcement powers in Congress. The Treaty of Paris granted American independence but stipulated that prewar debts be paid to British creditors. Virginia and, to a lesser extent, Maryland balked. Forgetting that the war had been about taxation and for independence, Virginians asked, "If we are now to pay the debts due the British merchants, what have we been fighting for all this while?"[5] Later, after the Constitution replaced the Articles of Confederation and the Supreme Court was established, Chief Justice John Marshall observed that the "fact was notorious that it was the general opinion of [Virginians], and of the juries that a British debt could not be recovered."[6]

Because the Americans were not complying with parts of the treaty, the British refused to evacuate their string of northern forts running from Lake Champlain to the Straits of Mackinac as they had pledged to do "with all convenient speed."[7] This created ample opportunities to foment hostilities between settlers and the native Indians. Furthermore, because Congress lacked money to pay for an army, there was no way to dislodge the British. As one Englishman aptly noted: "What can the Americans do? They have neither government nor power."[8] The same held true with the Barbary pirates' captures of American shipping. Americans rotted in jail or slavery because their government had neither the funds nor the will to support a navy.

The final defect was within the Articles themselves. They could be amended only with the unanimous consent of all the states. In 1782 Finance Minister Robert Morris proposed a 5 percent duty on imports in order to pay off the foreign debt run up during the war. Rhode Island—not so fondly known as Rogue Island—voted no, claiming that such a tax "derogated from the Sovereignty and Independence of the State."[9] In 1783 it offered Congress the helpful advice that it should borrow any needed funds in Europe—as if the Europeans would keep the new government afloat financially when the Americans had no means of repaying the loans. Four years later that state positively refused to send delegates to the Philadelphia Convention. Meanwhile, Rhode Island took the lead in issuing paper money, coupled with draconian steps to force its acceptance as legal tender.

States, free under the Articles to act as sovereigns, did so in ways that harmed their neighbors or undermined economic stability. Those with ports imposed varying tariffs on imported goods to raise revenues. In operation, that allowed New York to tax Connecticut and New Jersey residents. With New York City to its north and Philadelphia to the south, New Jersey was, to James Madison's mind, like "a cask tapped at both ends."[10]

States issuing paper money typically engaged in other forms of debtor relief. *The Federalist*, the eighty-five brilliant propaganda essays on the Constitution designed to sway the New York convention, condemned the "rage for paper money, for an abolition of debt, for an equal division of property [i.e., confiscation], or for any other improper or wicked project."[11] Rhode Island again was the leader, but North Carolina, too, was aggressive. In western Massachusetts, where high property taxes and the lack of gold and silver coins were sending farmers into bankruptcy, a rebellion under Daniel Shays, a veteran of the Revolutionary War battles of Bunker Hill and Saratoga, closed courts to prevent foreclosures on property. Massachusetts appealed to Congress for help, but as always, Congress was without funds and unable to assist. Instead, men of property loaned money to pay for an army of four thousand that easily routed the rebels. Still, the commonwealth capitulated to the debtors by passing debt relief legislation. Washington lamented the events, writing, "To be more exposed in the eyes of the world, and more contemptible than we already are, is hardly possible."[12]

From the Articles to the Constitution

James Madison, the best political thinker among the Virginians, had already begun to conceptualize a better structure for the new republic. The diminutive Madison was only in his mid-thirties, yet he was in the first rank of the commonwealth's politicians, having served on the Council of State (where he commenced his lifelong friendship with Jefferson), in the Continental Congress, and in the Virginia House of Delegates. He was especially influential in guaranteeing religious liberty in the commonwealth. Shortly he would be the most important architect of the Constitution at the Philadelphia Convention and, along with Alexander Hamilton, one of the two prime authors of *The Federalist.*

By the time of Shays's Rebellion, Madison had persuaded the Virginia legislature to call for the states to meet in Annapolis to discuss commercial problems. Maryland balked on the ground that such a meeting might weaken Congress—as if that were possible. Indeed, five states sent but twelve delegates, who could only talk about what might be done. The outgrowth of the meeting, however, was a call for a further convention in Philadelphia to again consider granting Congress powers over trade. The call for a new convention, too, might have failed but for the fact that in February 1787 the Confederation Congress backed up the call "for the sole and express purpose of revising the Articles of Confederation and reporting to Congress and the several legislatures such alterations and provisions therein as shall when agreed to in Congress and confirmed by the states render the federal constitution adequate to the exigencies of Government."[13]

At the beginning of the convention, Edmund Randolph introduced the Virginia Plan, envisioning a strong new national government with a bicameral legislature where representation in both houses was proportional to population. The Virginia Plan made it apparent that the delegates from the largest state were ready to scrap the limiting instructions of the Confederation Congress. Randolph, who would later be Washington's attorney general, explained that "[t]here are great seasons when persons with limited powers are justified in exceeding them, and a person would be contemptible not to risk it."[14] These great men were not contemptible, and with Washington presiding, they were going to risk it. Thus by an overwhelming vote on May 30 the delegates agreed "that a national Govern[men]t ought to be established consisting of a supreme Legislative, Executive & Judiciary."[15]

There were, of course, compromises to be made, because for some states certain issues were potential deal breakers. The small states were not willing to leave themselves to the tender mercies of their more populous neighbors Massachusetts, Pennsylvania, and Virginia. The small states liked the one-state, one-vote formula of the Articles, while the large states wished representation to be apportioned according to population, as the Virginia Plan proposed. Roger Sherman, with the support of his Connecticut colleagues, proposed that the House be elected on a population basis while in the Senate there would be equality of states. This "Grand Compromise" was demanded by the smaller states, but would lead to future trouble when the admission of new states became intertwined with the other deal-breaking issue: slavery.

While all the states had countenanced slavery, it was on its way to extinction in the North. Indeed, a number of statesmen saw abolition of slavery as an imperative moral issue. In the plantation economy

South, however, slavery was an economic issue. John Rutledge, a future Supreme Court justice, stated that the Southerners would never "be such fools as to agree to a plan of union [unless] the right to import slaves were untouched."[16] A series of compromises gave the South the right to count slaves as three-fifths of a person for representation in the House and a clause requiring the return of runaway slaves, but Congress could end the international slave trade after 1807 if it wished. Perhaps as a sop to the North, the word "slave" does not appear in the document; instead slaves are "all other persons," "such persons," and "person[s] held to Service." Madison "thought it wrong to admit in the Constitution the idea that there could be property in men," but only the blind could fail to see it was there.[17]

There was never any doubt that the new government was going to have "energy"[18]—meaning a lot more power than the Confederation Congress. The only question was how much more power. It could raise taxes, levy duties on imports, and regulate both foreign and interstate commerce by acting on individuals and not merely the states (as the Articles required). There was even a power to make laws "necessary and proper for carrying into Execution all . . . Powers vested by this Constitution in the Government." The meaning of this clause was undetermined; potentially it left the extent of the new Congress's powers open-ended.

The one power that Madison deemed essential, but which was denied, was a congressional veto of state laws deemed inimical to the general welfare of the republic. That was going too far for the majority, although the Constitution did forbid the states to pass debtor relief or to make anything except gold and silver legal tender, as well as proscribing ex post facto laws (that is, making innocent conduct retroactively criminal).

When the veto over state laws failed, it became necessary to make clear that in cases of conflict between national and state laws, national law would prevail. Thus the delegates immediately adopted the Supremacy Clause, Article VI of the Constitution, which declares, "This Constitution, and the Laws of the United States which shall be made in Pursuance thereof; and all Treaties made, or which shall be made, under Authority of the United States, shall be the supreme Law of the Land."

Article III and the Judiciary

With the veto of state laws dead and the supremacy of the Constitution, federal laws, and treaties agreed to, the judiciary became important as an enforcement mechanism, although far less time was devoted to it than to the legislature and the executive. The delegates agreed that there would be a Supreme Court and there could be inferior federal courts, but whether the latter would come into existence was left to Congress. Judges would be nominated by the president and confirmed by the Senate. Thereafter they would have life tenure with a guaranteed salary and were subject to removal only by impeachment. No state constitution gave judges such independence.

Surprisingly, judicial review—the power to decide the constitutionality of statutes, especially congressional enactments—was not mentioned in the text and was hardly discussed at the convention. Judicial review of state statutes did gain some textual support in the Supremacy Clause, with its statement that "[j]udges in every State shall be bound thereby, any Thing in the Constitution or Laws of any State to the Contrary notwithstanding," but there is nothing about judicial review of federal statutes.

There seem to be somewhat contradictory reasons why judicial review was not mentioned in the text. Perhaps it simply slipped the delegates' minds. Judicial review in 1787 was such a novelty that there was not much to say about it. Thus John Dickinson said that "no such power ought to exist [but] he was at the same time at a loss what expedient to substitute."[19] There were but a handful of supporting references,[20] such as Gouverneur Morris's noting that a "law that ought to be negatived will be set aside in the Judiciary department," but the strongest statement about judicial review came from Elbridge Gerry, who refused to sign the Constitution.[21] The fact that members of the First Congress readily assumed that their work was subject to judicial review offers clear evidence that such review was deemed implicit in the Constitution.

The delegates were realists with sufficient experience to know that humans misuse power. They recognized that in creating a government, "[y]ou must first enable the government to control the governed; and in the next place, oblige it to control itself. A dependence on the people is no doubt the primary control on the government; but experience has taught mankind the necessity of auxiliary precautions."[22] To create those auxiliary precautions, the Constitution separated power in the three branches and offered ample checks to ensure that no branch would dominate (although the implicit view was that the legislative branch would be the strongest). Despite the paucity of statements about judicial review, from Alexander Hamilton's perspective in *The Federalist* No. 78 it offered one of the checks on the legislature.

The Constitution began with the preamble announcing that "We the People of the United States" were the ones bringing the document to life. It ended by explicitly ignoring the Confederation Congress's call in creating the convention, as Article VII states that the Constitution would come into effect when nine states ratified it. Because the articles required unanimity for change, this meant that when conventions of the people in nine states seceded from the "perpetual" union under the articles, there would be a different union. Furthermore, Article VII bypassed the bodies that had sent delegates to Philadelphia by stating that the Constitution must be ratified by conventions and not by the state legislatures (on the assumption that existing legislatures would not be as welcoming as new conventions). It was all patently illegal under the Articles of Confederation. James Wilson, in the Pennsylvania convention, deflected this charge by arguing that he had "never heard, before, that to make a proposal was an exercise of power."[23] Madison finessed the point in *The Federalist* when he wrote that the delegates "must have borne in mind, that as the plan to be framed and proposed, was to be submitted *to the people themselves,* the disapprobation of this supreme authority would destroy it for ever; its approbation would blot out all antecedent errors and irregularities."[24]

Ratification

Thirty-nine delegates signed the document. Edmund Randolph, George Mason, and Elbridge Gerry did not, and returned to their important states, Virginia and Massachusetts, to work against ratification (although Randolph later changed his mind). They would have ample support, because the document bristled with powers for the new government that set many Americans on edge: taxation, a standing army, the potentially elastic Necessary and Proper Clause. To put it succinctly, the Constitution created a real government and subordinated the (formerly) sovereign states to it. Those opposing ratification, successfully dubbed with the oxymoronic name "Anti-Federalists," viewed the Necessary and Proper Clause as authorizing federal authority everywhere: "[T]o almost every thing about which any legislative power can be employed . . . nothing can stand before it."[25] Washington's transmittal letter to Congress had stated that one purpose of the Constitution was the "consolidation of our Union," and the Anti-Federalists picked up on this to claim that the Constitution established a consolidated government at the expense of the states.[26] Furthermore, there was no bill of rights like those found in most of the post-Independence state constitutions. Could there be any doubt that the new government would abuse those powers and exceed the limits, just as the Philadelphia Convention had? The Federalist response that the people wouldn't allow this to happen rang hollow to Anti-Federalists. So did the Federalist argument that to have a bill of rights would imply the existence of power to violate those rights in the first place and that no such powers had been delegated to the new government. That argument, moreover, was flatly inconsistent with written limitations on federal power—such as prohibiting bills of attainder or titles of nobility—found in Article I, Section 9.

The Constitution received five quick ratifications. Three of them, Delaware, New Jersey, and Georgia, were unanimous, and a fourth, Connecticut, was overwhelming. In each case these were states that would benefit from a stronger nation. Georgia needed protection from the Indians; the other three could count on economic advantages (or the lack of disadvantages) under the new government. They all had got the best deal they could in the Senate.

The fifth state was Pennsylvania, where the two-to-one margin of ratification masked a deeper preexisting division. Supporters of the Constitution had control of the legislature, and they sought an immediate election for the convention to meet barely two months after the Constitutional Convention had ended. Opponents absented themselves to deny a quorum, only to have a Philadelphia mob carry two of them to the legislative floor to create the necessary quorum. The rush to ratify was maintained throughout: early election, limited debate, a refusal to countenance amendments. It was not a pretty process.

The easy ratifications were over, and in the three large states remaining, Massachusetts, Virginia, and New York, Anti-Federalists appear to have had the majority at the beginning of each convention. Lack of a bill of rights was an issue in each state. If the states ratified, the important issue was whether the ratification would be conditional on the adoption of proposed amendments, or amendments would be recommended but ratification was unconditional. In Massachusetts, John Hancock and Samuel Adams, both of whom thought the Constitution too consolidating, nevertheless supported it and offered the compromise of proposing amendments to it. The result was a 187–168 vote for unconditional ratification.

Before New York and Virginia could act, Maryland, South Carolina, and New Hampshire ratified, thereby creating the requisite nine states to bring the Constitution into being. Only in New Hampshire was ratification difficult as the convention once adjourned before reconvening and proposing amendments. South Carolina also offered suggested amendments, again rather than making ratification conditional on adopting them. Nine ratifications or not, however, a "United States" without New York and Virginia would have been unstable at best and perhaps unthinkable.

Virginia was by far the largest state (encompassing present-day West Virginia and Kentucky) and the leader of the South. Its planter elites were deeply divided on ratification, but Madison was able to argue convincingly that the strengthened government would assure the free flow of goods down the Mississippi River. The Mississippi was a divisive issue, one far more important to the South than to the North. A stronger government would work to the benefit of the South because the mouth of the river was controlled by Spain. Madison also asserted that Virginia would be the leader of the new government. He was strongly aided by Governor Edmund Randolph, who switched positions again, this time arguing that the Constitution would preserve the Union. By an 89–79 vote the Federalists prevailed. New York was even closer, following Virginia with a 30–27 vote. Both states recommended amendments and unsuccessfully proposed a second convention after ratification was final.

The North Carolina convention rejected the Constitution and did not ratify until the new government was up and running. Rhode Island refused even to call a convention; it joined the Union in 1790 only after the Senate passed a bill that would prohibit Rhode Island ships in American ports and American ships in Rhode Island ports, Providence and Newport threatened to secede from the state, and George Washington informed the state legislature that it could expect hostile actions from the new government.

Meeting in Philadelphia for three and a half months, America's natural aristocracy (Benjamin Franklin called it "the most august and respectable assembly" he had ever been in)[27] produced a document that, while hardly perfect, was vastly better than the existing Articles of Confederation constitution. Yet in retrospect, the amount of opposition to the Constitution is truly surprising given the status of the men at the convention. Indeed the opposition was probably sufficient to have blocked the new constitution if only those opposing it had behaved differently.

The Federalists wanted a government with "energy," and with ratification they succeeded. Obviously their own energy—especially that of Madison and Hamilton—played a vital role. So did the lack of energy in support of some form of the status quo shown by the Anti-Federalists both before and after the convention. Opponents of a stronger government were largely absent from Philadelphia. Rhode Island boycotted. The demagogic Patrick Henry, having "smelt a rat," stayed in Virginia.[28] So did Richard Henry Lee; Willie Jones, who led the opposition in the North Carolina convention, also stayed home. John Lansing Jr. and Robert Yates abandoned the convention for New York once its direction became clear. Two Maryland delegates went home for the same reason. Had the Anti-Federalists participated more fully, the premise that the Articles should be scrapped could have been contested, and perhaps compromises could have been made more difficult to reach. Furthermore, by absenting themselves, the Anti-Federalists let the convention meet in secrecy. Madison later noted that "no Constitution would ever have been adopted by the convention if the debates had been public."[29]

The Constitution still could have been defeated. The Anti-Federalists in New York and Virginia had solid majorities in both states, which they used to delay convening ratifying conventions. If instead they had called the conventions quickly and then rejected the Constitution, it is unlikely that nine states would have brought the new government into existence. Intensity matters; so does luck. So did the fact that the press, being based in urban centers, where support for the Constitution was by far the stronger, favored ratification.

Judicial Review and the Bill of Rights

As at the Philadelphia Convention, there was little mention in the state conventions of the powers of the federal judiciary to declare statutes, both state and federal, unconstitutional. Interestingly, however, two future chief justices offered their opinions. Oliver Ellsworth told the Connecticut convention that courts could strike down acts that exceeded the powers delegated to the government. Later, in Virginia, John Marshall explained that Congress could not exceed its powers because "[i]f they [the representatives] were to make a law not warranted by any of the powers enumerated, it would be considered by the Judges as an infringement of the Constitution which they are to guard . . . They would declare it void."[30] Hamilton concurred in *The Federalist,* where he stated that a "constitution is in fact, and must be, regarded by the judges as a fundamental law. It therefore belongs to them to ascertain its meaning as well as the meaning of any particular act proceeding from the legislative body. If there should happen to be an irreconcileable variance between the two, that which has the superior obligation and validity ought of course to be preferred; or in other words, the constitution ought to be preferred to the statute."[31]

Statements by Ellsworth, Marshall, and Hamilton show that the idea of judicial review was in the air, but they also virtually exhaust the number of references to it. One additional, perhaps prescient, statement came from the New York Anti-Federalist "Brutus," who saw the potential of judicial review as meaning that "[t]here is no power above [the justices] to controul their decisions." They "are independent of the people, of the legislature, and of every power under heaven. Men placed in this situation will generally soon feel themselves independent of heaven itself."[32] In essence, these two sides of the debate on judicial independence and judicial review survive to this day.

In contrast to judicial review, other aspects of the new federal judiciary were much discussed, and they proved quite controversial in the state conventions. Almost one-fifth of the proposed amendments to the Constitution dealt with the judiciary, especially the omission of jury trials in civil cases.

After receiving and studying the Constitution in Paris, Thomas Jefferson wrote Madison with his thoughts. He claimed to find considerable merit in the document, but "[I] will now add what I do not like. First the omission of a bill of rights . . . [which is] what the people are entitled to against every government on earth, general or particular, and what no just government should refuse, or rest on inference."[33] Jefferson's rebuke was the initial spur that caused Madison to switch from believing a bill of rights unnecessary and unwise to becoming the father of the Bill of Rights.

The Anti-Federalists had attempted to turn the lack of a bill of rights into a deal breaker. Therefore Federalists questioned whether their opponents actually wanted a bill of rights, believing instead that what the Anti-Federalists really sought was a second convention that would undo the work at Philadelphia. But some of the advocates of a bill of rights, such as Jefferson, were sincere. Furthermore, Madison acquired political reasons for supporting one. He had opposed a bill of rights at the Virginia ratifying convention, but then reluctantly agreed to suggesting amendments in order to head off making ratification conditional on amendments. When he ran for the First Congress, his Baptist constituents made clear their concern about the absence of guarantees of religious liberty, and he promised that he would introduce amendments. He was prodded again by Jefferson, who offered an idea he never would entertain as president. A bill of rights would provide "the legal check . . . [put] into the hands of the judiciary."[34]

Washington, too, now wanted a bill of rights and recommended in his inaugural address that the Constitution be amended to guarantee that "the characteristic rights of freemen [be] more impregnably fortified."[35] Some Federalists thought that there was more important business at hand. The new government, like the old one, needed money. Unlike the old one, it also needed to get both the executive and the judiciary up and running. In fact, the first substantive act under the Constitution was the passage of a 5 percent impost (nearly identical to the one Rhode Island vetoed in 1783) to fund payment of the war debts. Thereafter the Senate worked on the judiciary, while Madison tried to prod the House into creating a bill of rights.

Madison introduced his amendments in a lengthy speech which began by recognizing that the House would rather be doing something else. Nevertheless, Madison stated in a couple of ways that some changes to the Constitution could be "ingrafted so as to give satisfaction to the doubting part of our fellow citizens." A great number were "dissatisfied," and "it will be practicable . . . to obviate the objection, so far as to satisfy the public mind that their liberties will be perpetual, and this without endangering any part of the constitution."[36] In other words, a bill of rights could still any lingering opposition to the Constitution and government.

The state conventions had suggested two types of changes to the Constitution: protecting the citizen from the federal government and weakening that government (the latter stemming from Anti-Federalist concerns over consolidation and the potential of the government to create an aristocracy). Madison's proposals ignored the latter and are easily recognized as Amendments I through X, although they underwent changes in both the House and Senate. He guaranteed freedom of religion, the press, and speech. Should the government truly overreach, he protected the citizen by guaranteeing a right to keep and bear arms. To cure the supposed defects in the judiciary, he demanded procedural fairness in criminal trials and a right to juries in civil ones. In two feints toward the Anti-Federalists, he offered (in what became the ninth and tenth amendments) clauses stating that the Constitution should "not be construed to deny or disparage [rights] retained by the people" and that powers not delegated were "reserved to the States or to the people." On the basis of his observations over the previous decade, however, he believed that the states were a greater threat to liberties than the federal government. Therefore his favorite proposal denied the states the power to "violate the equal rights of conscience, or the freedom of the press, or the trial by jury in criminal cases."[37] The proposal did not survive the Senate, and these propositions would not be recognized for almost a century and a half.

Twelve amendments were eventually passed by the House and Senate and sent to the states. Numbers three through twelve were ratified in 1791 and became the Bill of Rights. The two that failed dealt with the numbers of representatives (responding to the Anti-Federalist concern that the House was too small) and congressional pay (the latter being added to the Constitution two hundred years later). The immediate impact of the Bill of Rights was to facilitate North Carolina's ratification of the Constitution.

Like the Constitution, the Bill of Rights needed luck to come into existence. After failing to prevent Virginia's ratification of the Constitution, Patrick Henry, who controlled the state legislature, searched for ways to undermine the new government, and a prime one was to keep Madison out of Congress. First he blocked Madison's election as a senator, and two Anti-Federalists were selected instead. Then he placed Madison's Orange County in a congressional district with a solid Anti-Federalist majority and a very attractive Anti-Federalist candidate in James Monroe. But Madison promised a bill of rights and squeaked to victory, and thus went on to force the reluctant First Congress to face the issue of a bill of rights. Henry was unmollified, fearing that ratification would "tend to injure rather than serve the Cause of Liberty."[38] His reason was the absence of a provision destroying Congress's power to tax, but in 1791, after new state elections, Virginia became the necessary final state to ratify the amendments. This ended, as both Madison and Henry knew it would, the possibility of calling for a second convention. Opposition to the new Constitution evaporated thereafter.

The First Judiciary Act

In the Senate, Oliver Ellsworth and William Paterson, both signers of the Constitution and future Washington appointees to the Supreme Court, were fashioning a judiciary act as part of a committee consisting of one senator from each state. As the proposed amendments had illustrated, the judiciary was a controversial subject, and it remained so in the creation of the Judiciary Act of 1789. As at the convention, the dominant questions regarded the lower federal courts (how many?) and their jurisdiction (how much?). The answers were "few" and "not much." Senator Richard Henry Lee—the Anti-Federalist "Federal Farmer"—stated that he had "endeavored successfully in the Judiciary bill to remedy, so far a law can remedy the defects in the Constitution in that line."[39] The Judiciary Act, when combined with the Bill of Rights, finished pulling the teeth from the opposition to the new federal government.

Judges would draw a salary for life, and in a debt-strapped republic, Congress wished to keep expenses to a minimum. This meant that there would be as few judges as possible. Nevertheless, federal courts were seen as important because they were the best way to show national authority on the local level. As Paterson explained, federal courts would "carry Law to [the People's] Homes, Courts to their Doors."[40]

A three-tier court system was authorized: district courts with original jurisdiction, circuit courts with both original and appellate jurisdiction, and a Supreme Court with both original and appellate jurisdiction. Only the district courts and Supreme Court were independently staffed. The Supreme Court had a chief justice and five associate justices. Circuit courts consisted of the district judge and two Supreme Court justices (and after 1793 one justice and a district judge). Having two of the highest-ranking federal officials traveling to so many communities both personalized and dignified the new government.

The most important aspect of the Supreme Court's appellate jurisdiction was Section 25, whereby the Court could review the judgments of the highest state courts when the state court decided against the validity of a treaty, when a state statute was challenged as unconstitutional and the state court found the statute valid, and when any construction of federal law went against the claimed federal right. Interestingly, the Court's appellate jurisdiction did not extend to cases where state courts upheld a federal claim.

The Judiciary Act mandated that both the Supreme Court and the circuit courts hold two terms per year. Although the judges initially had little to do, these requirements meant that they would be traveling a lot, often in the worst conditions. Circuit riding was the bane of every justice's existence. Several nominees to the Supreme Court declined in order to avoid its hardships. Furthermore, there was no provision for reimbursing justices for their expenses away from home.

Initial Appointments

Washington wrote that "the selection of the fittest characters to expound the laws, and dispense justice, has been an invariable subject of my anxious concern."[41] He nominated his justices on the same day he signed the Judiciary Act, for he had been thinking of the appointments for months. He wanted justices who were prominent men of the Revolution and staunch supporters of the new government (albeit in one case there is no extant evidence on the nominee's views during ratification). They also should also be geographically dispersed among the republic's three regions.

Foremost among the nominees was the chief justice, John Jay of New York. In 1789 Jay was, after Washington, Franklin, and John Adams, the most accomplished statesman of the founding generation. He had been a delegate to the first two Continental Congresses, president of the Continental Congress in 1778, then unacknowledged commissioner to Spain before joining Adams and Franklin to negotiate the Treaty of Paris. On returning home, he became the secretary of foreign affairs until his appointment to the Court. He wanted the appointment and expected the first years of the Court to be filled with cases dealing with international issues, especially debt payment under the Treaty of Paris.

James Wilson had the best mind of the early appointees. He had been a delegate to the Philadelphia Convention, and after Madison, he had played the most significant role in the convention by explicating separation of powers and sovereignty of the people. The best lawyer, James Iredell, came in the second round of Washington appointments. He replaced a nominee who fell ill on the road to New York, declined his commission, and died within three months. Iredell was only thirty-nine, and yet he had been both a justice on the North Carolina Supreme Court and that state's attorney general during the war, and was a towering figure for ratification in the state's two conventions.

Circuit Riding and Grand Jury Charges

Initially the Supreme Court had nothing to do but meet the required two times a year and admit attorneys. But that does not mean the justices were not busy. In fact they were the hardest-working members of the government (after Hamilton) because their job truly was full-time and vastly different from that of their successors two hundred years later. Circuit riding was time-consuming and arduous. Horses ran away, carriages overturned, nights spent in far-flung taverns were often crowded and unpleasant. The middle circuit of New Jersey, Pennsylvania, Delaware, Maryland, and Virginia was the easiest because there were reasonable accommodations. Nevertheless, the coach of one justice went through the ice while crossing the Susquehanna River, and only through the efforts of his son was his almost lifeless body recovered.[42] The northern circuit was longer than the middle circuit, and winter snows often brought travel to a halt. Jay's cryptic descriptions of inns on one trip included "pretty good," "tolerably clean," "*bad,*" "tolerable," and "dirty."[43]

The southern circuit was all but impossible. It took 1,800 miles to complete a single circuit. Iredell constantly complained: "I scarcely thought there had been so much barren land in all America as I have passed through."[44]

Owing to either illness or impossible conditions, justices too often could not make it to their circuit duties. Iredell noted that a Georgia grand jury was unhappy because Thomas Johnson (who would resign after two years on account of circuit riding) was ill and did not attend the court. A few years later Iredell himself "was prevented [from] reaching Savannah by one of the greatest floods of rain ever known in this State . . . all the bridges almost being broke up in every direction."[45] He almost drowned; yet that would have shortened his life by only a year. Iredell was dead before turning fifty.

The principal way that the justices brought law to everyman's home was the grand jury charge delivered in every courthouse and often reprinted in local newspapers. We know that opposition to the new government largely vanished, but at the time the justices could not know that this would be the outcome. Furthermore, given their background in the Revolution and ratification controversies, they would naturally want to share their views about what the new government meant to its citizens. The justices used the opportunity to charge the grand juries, that is, to lecture them. The charges were designed to promote respect for the new government and to inculcate the duty to obey its laws.

A prime facet of the grand jury charge was that it celebrated the accomplishments of putting the new government into place and creating a reverence for the Constitution itself. In his first grand jury address Jay noted that the remarks might not seem pertinent to the occasion, but spreading truths to the citizens shouldn't be slighted: "Whether any People can long govern themselves in an equal uniform & orderly manner, is a Question . . . exceedingly important to the Cause of Liberty." The new government "already affords advantages," but it was not perfect, and so "the good Sense of the People will be enabled by Experience to discover and correct its Imperfections."[46] A wise government must consider the virtues of its citizens as well as the vices inherent in human nature: "It is pleasing to remark, that the national laws appear to have been mindful of both; for while they meet transgression with punishment, their mildness manifests much confidence in the reason and virtue of the people."[47]

The justices thought it was important that the principles underlying the Constitution be understood, because they believed that the greater the understanding, the firmer the support for it. In extolling the new government, the justices spoke of the need for citizens to obey the laws, since the laws are the product of the people. Wilson, like other justices, combined self-government and the duty to obey the laws by intertwining them with liberty, security, and dignity. Therefore citizens "cannot be true and faithful, unless they *obey* as well as *make* the laws—unless in the terms . . . they partake of *subordination* as well as *power*."[48] In a charge in Richmond, Jay informed the Virginians that the Treaty of Paris required paying their British creditors: "Justice and Policy unite in declaring that Debts fairly contracted should be honestly paid."[49]

Somewhat later the charges began to reflect a fear of anarchy resulting from the French Revolution abroad and resentment over the excise tax on liquor at home. Iredell asked a grand jury: "If you suffer this government to be destroyed, what chance have you for any other? A scene of the most dreadful confusion must ensure. Anarchy will ride triumphant, and all lovers of order, decency, truth and justice be trampled under foot."[50]

Late in the 1790s, after the emergence of a two-party system, the grand jury charges acquired the potential to be politically explosive. But in the initial years of circuit riding they were accomplishing just what the drafters of the Judiciary Act wished: bringing law and justice to community after community.

Initial Decisions

The ever cash-starved Congress thought it had found another way to economize while carrying justice to the people's homes when it passed a pension program for those who had been injured in the Revolutionary War. The Invalid Pensions Act of 1792 advised veterans to submit applications and proof to a federal circuit court. The court would then determine the applicant's eligibility and the amount owed him. That decision, in turn, would go to the secretary of war, who, upon checking the records, could approve or reject it. All the justices believed that the measure was unconstitutional (without mentioning the word) because it required them to perform an act that could then be overturned by a nonjudicial officer. Jay and William Cushing perceived the secretary of war as sitting "as a court of errors on the judicial acts or opinions of this court."[51] There had been no application for Jay and Cushing to consider, so they wrote their conclusion in a letter to President Washington, who in turn forwarded it to Congress.

Madison applauded the justices for pronouncing the act "unconstitutional and void—perhaps they may be wrong in the execution of their power—but such an evidence of its existence gives inquietude to those who do not wish Congress to be controllable or doubted whilst proceedings correspond with their views."[52] It is interesting that Madison, but not the justices, used the word "unconstitutional," but then Madison had his eyes on bigger game; perhaps the justices could rein in Hamilton's ambitious fiscal programs, to which Madison had led the opposition.

Jay and two others were nonetheless reluctant to kill a worthy and popular statute, so instead of rejecting it outright, they grossly misconstrued it and concluded that the act made them commissioners, and that this was a nonjudicial office that they were free to accept or reject, but two other justices refused to go along. Shortly Congress modified the law and replaced the justices with real commissioners. A year later, in *United States v. Yale Todd,* the Court held that an award that had been granted by a judge under the statute was invalid. We know the result of *Yale Todd* but not the reasoning, because the justices gave no reasons. Indeed the decision wasn't even reported.

As the justices' willingness to take on the job of commissioners and to write letters to the president show, they perceived no separation of powers problems with taking on extrajudicial activities. The justices had been advising Washington and Congress on the defects of the Judiciary Act—especially the hardships of circuit riding and the need for true circuit judges—from the beginning.

Jay went far beyond the judiciary in his advice to Washington. He helped with the president's annual message to Congress and, as an ex–foreign minister, he responded to requests for advice on foreign policy. Later, in 1794, he would accept Washington's offer of serving as an special envoy to Great Britain, over objections both that he was too pro-British and that such an appointment violated the Constitution. In England he negotiated the treaty that bears his name, which he believed avoided another war between the two countries.

The execution of Louis XVI and Marie Antoinette, the Reign of Terror, and the general European war shattered the strong American enthusiasm for the French Revolution. The war pitted America's ally and former benefactor France (with which the United States had a Treaty of Alliance) against its largest commercial partner, Great Britain. Both sides wanted the United States to cease trading with the other, and both attacked shipping to enforce that policy. No American leader wished to be dragged into a war which the country was wholly unprepared to finance or fight. The only available option was neutrality. But could it be neutrality with a preference, since France symbolized the march of liberty and equality?

In April 1793 Hamilton wrote Jay asking him to draft a declaration of neutrality, and Jay responded with one just two days later. Meanwhile, Washington had Randolph draft one as well, with Secretary of State Jefferson's contribution being that the word "neutrality" was not to appear in the document. Some statement of the American position was essential because the newly arrived French ambassador, Edmond Genet, was bringing America to the French side by outfitting privateers in American ports and soliciting American seamen to man them. On circuit in Richmond, Jay delivered a grand jury charge that praised Washington's neutrality policy; indeed it quoted the entire proclamation, and stated that it was consistent with the law of nations. He also argued that the United States should prosecute and punish those who violated the republic's neutrality.

Given Jay's grand jury charge on neutrality and the willingness of justices to offer advice on prior occasions, it is surprising that when Jefferson, on Washington's behalf, asked the Court for answers to twenty-nine specific questions dealing with the Treaty of Alliance, international law, and neutrality, the justices balked. In a letter to Washington drafted by Jay, they stated that the "lines of separation drawn by the Constitution between the three branches of government . . . being in certain respects checks on each other, and our being judges of a court in the last resort, are consideration which afford strong arguments against the propriety of our extra-judicially deciding the questions alluded to."[53] Perhaps the justices did not wish to be placed in a position where a president could treat them like cabinet members and require them to answer. Perhaps Hamilton, having the votes in the cabinet, urged the justices not to respond because he feared that on some points they might side with Jefferson. Whatever the reason, with this refusal there emerged the rule against issuing advisory opinions, which the Court has endorsed ever since.

Some of the questions asked by Washington were answered a year later in the normal routine of litigation. The *Betsey* had been captured by a French privateer and taken to Baltimore, where the French consul declared that the ship and its cargo were British and thus a legitimate prize. A man claiming to be the true owner of the cargo sued in federal court alleging that the *Betsey* had been seized in American waters. The courts below held, in accordance with the accepted view of international law, that only the consul or court of the captors' nation could decide the fate of the prize. In *Glass v. The Sloop Betsey* the Court reversed, holding that the district court should decide the case "consistently with the laws of nations and the treaties and laws of the *United States*" and that "no foreign power can of right institute or erect any court of judicature of any kind within the United States" unless authorized by the United States.[54] That was one aspect of American sovereignty that could be imposed on the two belligerents.

When Jay called for the prosecution and conviction of anyone violating American neutrality, he knew that Congress had passed no such criminal laws. Rather Jay assumed that the federal courts had inherent authority to prosecute conduct deemed so clearly criminal that no prior statute need exist for everyone to understand its criminality. This was highly controversial, and opposition was immediate.

An initial prosecution for violation of the neutrality proclamation involved Gideon Henfield, who had sailed from Charlestown on one of the first privateers commissioned by Genet. Henfield subsequently brought a French prize into Philadelphia and was arrested and indicted for violating American neutrality. Washington's cabinet as well as Jay, Iredell, and Wilson believed that Henfield should be convicted for violating the law of nations, which was deemed to be part of the common law. Henfield's defense, mounted by well-known Jeffersonians, questioned the court's jurisdiction as well as the idea that courts could prosecute where Congress had not acted. The judges thought that Henfield was guilty, but the jury did not—to the applause of Jeffersonians (though not Jefferson himself) all throughout the country. The *National Gazette,* the paper Jefferson subsidized to oppose the policies of Hamilton (and Washington), praised the jury for upholding the Constitution, stated that the case established the right of Americans to man French privateers, and concluded that "our posterity will, probably, venerate this [verdict] . . . for adding to the security of the rights and liberties of mankind."[55]

The First Major Case: *Chisholm v. Georgia*

Possibly the reason why the Court proved so reluctant to write opinions was the 1793 decision in *Chisholm v. Georgia,* where its written opinions proved a disaster that crossed political lines. Chisholm was the executor of the estate of a South Carolinian who had sold Georgia some 64,000 (English) pounds of goods during the Revolutionary War, and the state, with its empty treasury, never had paid for them. Georgia claimed it was a sovereign state and was therefore immune from suit without its consent. *The Federalist* supported Georgia's position: "[C]ontracts between a nation and individuals are only binding on the conscience of the sovereign, and have no pretensions to a compulsive force."[56] Madison and John Marshall had assured the Virginia convention that nothing in the Constitution would allow states to be sued without their consent.

Chisholm filed suit in circuit court, and Iredell dismissed it for want of jurisdiction. Chisholm then refiled, this time with the Supreme

Court, with Attorney General Randolph as his private lawyer, relying on the Judiciary Act, which gave the Court jurisdiction over all cases in which a "state shall be a party."

In the biggest case of the Court's first decade, Georgia declined to argue. Unrebutted arguments have a way of prevailing, and the justices ruled for Chisholm. Unlike some of the later cases in which no opinion was issued, the Court followed the British practice whereby each justice offered his own views of the case seriatim.

The most important was that of Jay, who issued a lengthy opinion, reasoning that because of the Revolution, sovereignty passed from the Crown to the people of the United States, a point confirmed by the preamble to the Constitution. A European government might be above its subjects, but not so an American one. When Jay turned to the Constitution, he found that the natural language of Article III indicated a state was amenable to suit: "If the Constitution really meant to extend these powers only to cases in which a State might be a Plaintiff, to the exclusion of those in which citizens had demands against a State, it is inconceivable that it should have attempted to convey that meaning in words, not only so incompetent, but also repugnant to it."[57] That the judicial power extended to suits between states and citizens of other states "appears to me to be *wise,* because it is *honest,* and because it is *useful.*"[58]

Neither Federalists nor Jeffersonians agreed with Jay's warm sentiments. A Boston paper saw the decision as yet another step toward "the absorption of state governments [that] has long been a matter determined on by certain influential characters in this country who are aiming gradually at monarchy."[59] States, it seemed agreed, should enjoy the same sovereign immunity in federal courts that they enjoyed in their own courts. There were immediate proposals for amendment in both the House and the Senate, but the Second Congress was near its end, and it would be the Third Congress that sent what would become the Eleventh Amendment to the states, one denying federal courts jurisdiction over suits against a state initiated by citizens of another state or country. Ten months after the amendment went to the states, it received the necessary three-quarters approval when North Carolina ratified in January 1795. No one in the Washington administration announced that the amendment was part of the Constitution, and President John Adams waited until January 1798 to do so.

Exit Jay

Washington could not have picked a more qualified man than Jay to head the Court. Indeed, it would be well into the twentieth century before any president chose a man of such accomplishments. But the reaction to *Chisholm* had been a stunning rebuke to Jay and the Court, and Jay accepted a diplomatic mission to Great Britain over political (he was accused of being pro-British) and constitutional (compromising the independence of the judiciary) objections. He averted a potential war with England by negotiating the commercial treaty that bears his name. Afterward, while still in England, he was elected governor of New York. Believing that the Court lacked "energy, weight and dignity," he resigned.[60]

The evidence suggested that Jay was right. Maybe the Court wasn't an important place for constitutional interpretation, even though members of Congress routinely asserted that their actions would be subject to judicial review. The main venues for the exploration of constitutional issues were in pseudonymous newspaper essays, in Washington's cabinet, and on the floor of the Congress, where statesmen had debated the constitutionality of chartering a bank, the assumption of state debts, prescribing the oath to be taken by state officers, presidential succession, employment of the militia, neutrality, and numerous other minor issues.

· II ·

The Court in a Two-Party Republic

SHORTLY AFTER THE ESTABLISHMENT of the new government under the Constitution, Americans split over Alexander Hamilton's fiscal policy in creating a national bank and having the government assume the existing state Revolutionary War debts. This split initiated the movement toward political parties as Southerners led by Thomas Jefferson saw the new government as too energetic and too mercantile. When foreign policy, war, and the meaning of neutrality were added to the mix, two political parties emerged in the republic in which everyone appeared to agree that parties should not exist. Jefferson thought that those opposing the French Revolution were monocrats and, with James Madison, called them "Anglomen." Despite official neutrality, Jefferson and his Republican followers believed that France was following in America's republican footsteps. Hamilton and other Federalists, who supported strong commercial ties with England, thought that those opposing their policies were radicals, or worse, Jacobins.

Writing his biography of George Washington during Jefferson's presidency, John Marshall looked back on the era and saw two parties, "one of which [Federalists] contemplated America as a nation, and laboured incessantly to invest the federal head with powers competent to [its] preservation . . . The other [Republicans] attached itself to the state authorities, [and] viewed all the powers of congress with jealousy." According to Marshall, "[m]en of enlarged and liberal minds" aligned themselves with the former.[1] Jefferson, by contrast, saw the distinction as between one party "which fears the people most [Federalists], [and] the other [Republicans] the government."[2] Marshall echoed the prevailing sentiment of the republic's founding, Jefferson the mid-1790s reality. With the exception of Marshall's obviously biased conclusion about men with liberal minds, both assessments were fundamentally correct. The Federalists did see America as a nation and did fear the people. The Republicans did attach themselves to their states and did fear the powers of the new national government. There was, however, another divide. Federalist leaders—Washington, Hamilton, and Marshall—had suffered through the winter of 1778 with the ill-clad, freezing, starving troops at Valley Forge, where the inadequacies of a state-dominated confederation surfaced. (Pennsylvania, for example, ignored Washington's call for provisions while simultaneously denouncing his decision to go into winter quarters.) Jefferson and Madison, the Republican leaders, had spent that winter at home in Virginia.

The Federalists were less a party than friends of the government. The Republicans were former Anti-Federalists joined by those who were repelled by Hamilton's aggressive fiscal program, which needed an interpretation of the Constitution emphasizing implied powers. They feared an energized, consolidated government that could use the army against citizens as Washington did to suppress the Whiskey Rebellion, a tax revolt in western Pennsylvania. They coupled those concerns with an understandable Anglophobia, which put them at odds with Washington over the commercial treaty John Jay negotiated with Great Britain.

Revenue Cases

In two important mid-decade cases Daniel Hylton, a Richmond merchant, brought John Marshall and Alexander Hamilton to the Court, each in his sole appearance there as an advocate. The first was a battle over British debts, the second over whether a tax on carriages, which hit the less populous South especially hard, was a "direct tax" that had to be apportioned according to the population of each state (that is, if a state has 8 percent of the republic's population, its inhabitants pay 8 percent of the total tax). In the former the Court held that the Treaty of Paris superseded a Virginia law allowing its citizens to pay the debt to the state government (with devalued currency) and receive a certificate of discharge. In the latter the Court held that the tax was constitutional because it was not a direct one and therefore need not have been apportioned.

Marshall represented Hylton in his efforts to avoid paying his British creditor. He argued that the debt had been extinguished prior to the Treaty of Paris by a lawful action of a state at war with Great Britain, and therefore Article IV of the treaty on repayment of debts did not apply. In the course of his argument he disparaged "those, who wish to impair the sovereignty of Virginia,"[3] a highly ironic statement in light of what he would accomplish later as chief justice. The Court held that there was a conflict between the Virginia law and the treaty, and that accordingly the Supremacy Clause of the Constitution gave the treaty precedence. (While the British creditor prevailed in this instance, both the severe limitations on federal jurisdiction stemming from the requirement that a substantial amount of money be at issue in the case and the reluctance of juries to hold against their countrymen resulted in the Convention of 1802, whereby the United States paid a lump sum to Great Britain to settle all Article IV claims.)

A day later Hylton lost his conjured lawsuit against the carriage tax that had been enacted to help defer defense costs during the war scare with Britain. Hamilton, representing the government (which also paid Hylton's counsel), argued that the tax was an excise that need not be apportioned. Hylton's counsel asserted that the justices could declare a statute unconstitutional because such a power was "[n]ecessar[il]y incident to a limited Constitution."[4] Hamilton, in turn, conceded that "a Law inconsistent with the Constitution [was] void," but also that the power to declare a law unconstitutional had "to be exercised with great moderation."[5]

James Iredell concluded that direct taxes were exclusively those that could be apportioned by a census. Since there was no reason to believe that the number of carriages in a state was proportional to population (the South having far more need of them), the carriage tax was an excise and not a direct tax. Samuel Chase and William Paterson, the only others participating,[6] both emphasized the fact that the "great object of the Constitution was, to give Congress a power to lay taxes, adequate to the exigencies of government."[7] *Hylton* implicated judicial review—for implicit in the decision upholding the tax was its converse: the justices had the option and therefore the power to find the law unconstitutional. In supporting the government in raising revenue, the justices were in their natural position as friends of the government. But with the Quasi-War with France, the government's actions became controversial.

The Quasi-War at Home

The Jay Treaty and adversity in its war with England caused France to begin attacking American ships trading with Britain and then to refuse to accept the appointment of a new ambassador. Adams learned these facts three days after assuming the presidency in March 1797. Events both at home and abroad were to become worse.

At a special session of Congress, Adams called for arming American merchant ships, bolstering harbor defenses, and speeding construction of a navy. He justified the requests on the ground that France had treated the Americans "neither as allies nor as friends, nor as a sovereign state."[8] Republicans thought that Adams was heading for war and limited his measures to some strengthening of coastal defenses and completing the construction of three already authorized frigates (one of which was "Old Ironsides"). Adams repeated his requests for a naval buildup six months later, during the regular session, and the Republicans in the House rejected them again as unnecessarily warlike. Republicans were not even bothered when a French privateer attacked a British merchant ship inside Charleston harbor.

Adams had also dispatched three envoys—Elbridge Gerry, Charles Pinckney, and John Marshall—to France to negotiate a settlement without a war. Their mission, which became known as the XYZ Affair (after the codenames for French intermediaries), was rebuffed by persistent demands for a substantial bribe to the French foreign minister, Talleyrand, as well as a sizable loan to France, and an American apology for Adams's speech to Congress. Adams received notification of the XYZ Affair in the spring of 1798.

Adams informed Congress of the failure of the mission and reiterated his requests for a naval and military buildup as well as "such efficient revenue as will be necessary to defray extraordinary expenses." He concluded with the hope that Congress would act with "zeal, vigor, and concert in defense of the national rights proportioned to the danger with which they are threatened."[9] Jefferson thought that the message was "insane,"[10] and the House demanded to see the dispatches from the envoys. Adams readily complied. One of the dispatches detailed Y's boast that the envoys must accede to the French demands because "the diplomatic skill of France and the means she possesses in your country, are sufficient to enable her, with the French party in America, to throw the blame which will attend the rupture of the negotiations on the Federalists."[11] Implying that the Republicans would put loyalty to France above loyalty to America had an explosive effect.

Opposition to the defense buildup dissolved, and Congress gave Adams everything he asked for (and considerably more for the army). The Federalists weren't entirely sure what they intended the army for; it was more the case that they simply wanted one. While an army might be necessary if there were a threat of war, once that passed, a standing army contravened the Founding's republican principles, especially with a man like Hamilton at its head. An army also needed taxation for its support, and as both the American Revolution and the Whiskey Rebellion showed, Americans were not keen on being taxed.

With the military buildup, the Quasi-War was unofficially declared. Unfortunately for the Federalists, and ultimately for the Court, the Federalists, in an effort to create what Hamilton called "national unanimity," decided to use the war hysteria to rid themselves of Republican newspapers, which they perceived as traitorous.[12] Thus Congress, in 1798, also gave Adams things he hadn't asked for: the Alien Act and the Sedition Act.

The Alien Act authorized the president, without hearings or stated reasons, to order the deportation of any nonnaturalized person born abroad, if the president judged the person "dangerous to the peace and safety of the United States."[13] If the person ordered deported did not leave, he could be imprisoned for three years and permanently barred from citizenship. Adams signed only three warrants under the act, each for a French citizen who had already fled the country.

The Sedition Act prohibited uttering or publishing "any false, scandalous and malicious writing" against the government of the United States, or either house of Congress, or the president with intent to defame or bring them "into contempt or disrepute."[14] With this language the partisan nature of the act was thus apparent on its face: falsely defaming the vice president—Jefferson—was not a crime. Yet the act was far more liberal than that of Great Britain because it recognized truth as a defense. Nevertheless, Republicans were sure that the act was doubly unconstitutional. First, Congress lacked the power to pass such a law since there was nothing in Article I about regulation of the press. Second, even if Congress had such a power, the First Amendment negated it. Hamilton seemingly had agreed; in *The Federalist* No. 84 he stated that only "men disposed to usurp" would contend that there was a power granted to restrict the press.[15] But that was then, when ratification of the Constitution was in doubt, and this was now, when fortune offered the opportunity to deal a knockout blow to the Republicans and entrench Federalist dominance by going after those treasonous Republicans who were undermining public confidence in the government of the republic.

The Federalists had little trouble dismissing the First Amendment claim. It was "never understood to give the right of publishing falsehoods and slanders, nor of exciting sedition, insurrection, and slaughter, with impunity. A man was always answerable for the malicious publication of falsehood."[16] The First Amendment could hardly "guarantee, as a sacred principle, the liberty of lying against the Government."[17]

As for the claim that Congress lacked the power, Federalists located three sometimes overlapping sources of power authorizing the Sedition Act. First, they claimed that the power was inherent in all governments: "Every independent Government has a right to preserve and defend itself."[18] Second, the power was necessary: "[C]an the powers of a Government be carried into execution, if sedition for opposing its laws, and libels against its officers, itself, and its proceedings, are to pass unpunished?"[19] Third, the common law carried over from the Revolution was the law of the land, and there was no doubt that seditious libel was a common law crime. What courts could reach under the common law, Congress could reach by statute, and the Sedition Act ameliorated the common law by making truth a defense and giving all issues to the jury. Republican objections on both policy and constitutional grounds were overridden in a party-line vote.

The first prosecution under the law was against Congressmen Matthew Lyon of Vermont, a Republican whom Federalists despised. William Paterson, one of Washington's second round of appointments to the Court, presided and charged the grand jury to pay attention "to the seditious attempts of disaffected persons to disturb the government."[20] Lyon had charged that, under Adams, "every consideration of the public welfare [had been] swallowed up in a continual grasp for power."[21] Paterson rejected Lyon's claim that the Sedition Act was unconstitutional and instructed the jurors that they must find Lyon guilty if his statements were made with the intent to bring Adams into disrepute. The jury so found.

Jefferson reacted to Lyon's case by stating that federal judges were now "objects of rational fear."[22] He and Madison meanwhile were working on a new constitutional theory that could cut federal courts out of constitutional interpretation and offer a way for the Republicans to survive politically. While the Federalists walked away from their claims at the Founding that Congress lacked any powers over the press, Jefferson and Madison returned to the ideas of the Confederation. The Constitution was a compact—that is, a contract—among the several states, and therefore there is no neutral arbiter to interpret the Constitution when there are disputes between states and the federal government. Certainly the federal courts could not hold the ultimate authority, for they were part of the federal government itself. Therefore the dispute must be resolved by the parties to the compact.

Jefferson and Madison drafted resolutions adopted respectively by the Kentucky and Virginia legislatures. The Kentucky and Virginia Resolutions demanded a very strict construction of any federal power, and the Kentucky Resolutions indicated that if states believed that the federal government had exceeded its limited powers, they could nullify the offending law. The Kentucky Resolutions, in fact, proclaimed the Sedition Act "void and of no effect."[23] The resolutions were sent to the other parties to the compact—that is, the fourteen other states—and were rejected by nine and ignored by four, with only North Carolina agreeing that the Sedition Act was unconstitutional but disagreeing on remedy. Despite the fact that the resolutions were resoundingly rejected, this effort to rewrite the constitutional upheaval of 1787 that replaced the Articles of Confederation would create enormous intellectual and political mischief in the decades that followed.

There were fifteen indictments under the Sedition Act; the ten cases that went to trial resulted in convictions. All five of the leading Republican newspapers were prosecuted, and three were forced to close, two of which never resumed publication. Albert Gallatin, the Republican House leader, subsequently observed: "How has it been executed? Only by punishing persons of politics different from those of the administration."[24]

Justices Iredell, Paterson, and Chase, who presided at trials, all believed that the act was constitutional. Iredell's views were fully representative: if you "take away from a Republic the confidence of the people . . . [,] the whole fabric crumbles into dust."[25]

The justices were enthusiastic about applying the Sedition Act—Chase, another of Washington's later appointees, too much so. He handled two trials, those of James Callender and Thomas Cooper, as though he were part of the prosecution team. He informed the defendant that writing about the president was risky business, and in instructing the jury he went through Cooper's handbill line by line to explain why it violated the act. To Cooper's statement that Adams had called for a standing army, Chase noted that this was impossible because the Constitution limited an appropriation for the army to two years. Thus there could be no standing army unless "the Constitution is first destroyed."[26] In Callender's trial Chase refused to see a distinction between statements of fact and statements of opinion and was so abusive that Callender's attorneys withdrew, knowing their efforts would be futile. The little remaining Republican press quite properly found his conduct outrageous.

Coterminous with the Sedition Act prosecutions, Chief Justice Oliver Ellsworth, whom Washington appointed on John Jay's resignation, concluded on circuit that federal jurisdiction extended to the prosecution of common law crimes—that is, acts that no statute has criminalized. The particular case involved an America sailor who had joined the French navy and was fighting against the British. In an injudicious statement Ellsworth claimed that "[t]he common law of this country remains the same as it was before the Revolution."[27] Taken seriously, he was claiming that the federal government had the power to reach everything that the common law reached—and the common law reaches everything! If accurate, such a claim perfectly validated the Republicans' fears about the federal government. An editorial responded that "by the Chief Justice's opinion, we are still the subjects of Great Britain; we are so by this principle, her common law."[28] A correspondent of the *Virginia Argus* wrote that "it has long been feared the the government of the United States tended to a consolidation . . . [and] nothing can so soon produce [it] as the establishment of the doctrine that the common law of England is the law of the United States."[29]

Ellsworth had managed to tie a controversy over common law crimes (which emerged in the unsuccessful prosecution of Gideon Henfield) into the controversy surrounding the Sedition Act. Because the Sedition Act was defended as reforming the common law, it then became an article of faith for Republicans that prosecutions for common law crimes were unconstitutional.

In *The Federalist* No. 80 Hamilton wrote of the "political axiom" of "the judicial power of a government being coextensive with its legislative" power.[30] Both Republicans and Federalists believed the axiom, and that is what made the issue of common law crimes so inflammatory. If the judiciary could apply the common law, then it followed that Congress could legislate on all subjects of the common law, and thus Congress was not bound by either the limitations of Article I or the Tenth Amendment's statement that powers not delegated were reserved to the states. For Jefferson this was intolerable: "[I]f the principle were to prevail of a common law being in force in the US (which principle possesses the general government at one of all the powers of state governments, and reduces us to a single consolidated government) it would become the most corrupt government on the face of the earth."[31] St. George Tucker, the great legal synthesizer of the era, observed that the common law had unlimited reach; this meant that the powers of the federal government, too, would be unlimited.[32] Republicans were both angry and frightened.

While the Sedition Act was being turned against prominent Republicans, the French signaled that they wished for an end to the Quasi-War. Federalists, especially Hamilton, who was in actual command of the new army, liked the Quasi-War both because it pitted America against France rather than Great Britain and because it justified an army. The Federalists didn't want it put to an end. Nevertheless, copying Washington's example of sending Chief Justice John Jay to Great Britain to negotiate a treaty, Adams asked Ellsworth to head a mission to France to end the Quasi-War. Jefferson fumed that the judiciary was being annexed to the executive: the executive "has been able to draw into this vortex the Judiciary branch of the Government, and by their expectancy of sharing the other offices in the Executive gift to make them auxiliary to the Executive in all its views."[33] Jefferson's vexation may have been justified on other grounds as well. Justice Bushrod Washington, the former president's nephew, appointed to the Court in 1798 by Adams, and Chase, a signer of the Declaration of Independence who had opposed ratification of the Constitution and then turned fiercely Federalist, both campaigned actively for Adams's reelection in 1800.

The Election of 1800

Ellsworth's mission to France, like Jay's to England, resulted in a treaty, and it ended the Quasi-War. Adams had already suspended enlistments in the army and asked Congress to reduce the relevant expenditures, but it was too late. With the national emergency in the past, taxes in the present, and the Federalists perceived as having overreached, Jefferson bested Adams in their rematch for the presidency, and the Republicans took control of the incoming Congress (with a two-to-one margin in the House). Counting slaves as three-fifths of a person for voting purposes in the Electoral College gave Jefferson his margin; had they not been counted, Adams would have squeaked through to a second term.

Stunningly, because of a huge defect of not separating the presidential and vice presidential balloting in the Electoral College, Jefferson and his vice presidential running mate, Aaron Burr, tied in their number of votes. This threw the decision regarding the presidency into the House of Representatives, where the congressional delegation of each state had a single vote. Because of another provision of the Constitution (bringing a new Congress into session in December, thirteen months after an election), the lame-duck Federalist Congress would decide between Jefferson and Burr—or perhaps not choose either. A further defect in the Constitution was thus exposed: Who would be president if the House deadlocked? Then there was yet another problem: the unanticipated scenario of an opposition party ousting the ruling party.

From the Federalists' perspective, all options were open, from supporting either Jefferson or Burr to creating an interim president pending a new election. From Jefferson's perspective only one option was legitimate: selecting him. And the Republican governors of both Pennsylvania and Virginia were willing to back up Jefferson's opinion with their militias. With the new army dissolved and the Federalist militias too far away in New England, the Republicans would prevail if there was a resort to arms. If it became necessary, Jefferson, never a fan of the Constitution, was ready to call a second convention. But before the balloting in the House could take place, there was considerable change in the judiciary.

The Judiciary and the Events of 1801

The change involved the creation and staffing of new courts, plus the filling of a vacancy created by Ellsworth's resignation. Initially the two events were separate, but then they became intertwined.

Ellsworth's letter of resignation arrived from France, citing ill health as a reason. Adams received it the same day he learned that he would be a one-term president. He immediately nominated Jay to return to the Court, and the Senate confirmed him a day later. Thinking of the change in administrations, Adams explained to Jay that "the firmest security we can have against the effects of visionary schemes or fluctuating theories, will be in a solid judiciary."[34] Unwilling to resume circuit riding, and believing that the Court would not amount to much of anything, Jay declined, his letter arriving on January 19, 1801. Jay did not know that the House was taking up a proposal by Adams to eliminate circuit riding by creating real circuit courts with their own judges.

Adams's second choice was to promote Paterson to chief justice and replace him with Jared Ingersoll of Philadelphia, since Pennsylvania had been unrepresented following James Wilson's death. But Adams could not be sure of Ingersoll's response, and a pending statute would reduce the six-member Court to five justices at the earliest vacancy. If Adams did not act quickly, that vacancy would be Ellsworth's.

When John Marshall, the forty-five-year-old secretary of state, told Adams of Jay's refusal, Adams concluded that the chief justiceship should go to Marshall. Because of his moderate views, his service in the Continental Army, and his having been the first diplomat home from the XYZ Affair, Marshall was the republic's most popular Federalist. He was a natural in small groups, having been elected to Congress in 1799 from Republican Richmond, and virtually everyone who met this fun-loving and unpretentious man liked him.

One person who did not like him, however, was his distant cousin Thomas Jefferson; the two detested and fundamentally distrusted each other. Their mutual antipathy may have stemmed from the Revolution, when Marshall had been at Valley Forge and thought Jefferson was a shirker. Whatever its cause, there was no mistaking their dislike by the time the French Revolution turned violent and Marshall offered criticism. Jefferson, writing to Madison, thought that Marshall should be retired from politics; "nothing better could be done than to make him a judge."[35] If only Jefferson had a sense of irony.

Marshall was not that politically popular with fellow Federalist politicians in Washington, who wanted Paterson in the center seat. Marshall had strayed off their reservation in questioning the wisdom of the Alien and Sedition Acts and not supporting a war with France. The Senate thus delayed his confirmation for a week, hoping in vain that Adams would withdraw the nomination.

Marshall took the oath of office February 4, 1801, but Adams asked him to continue as secretary of state for the month remaining in his presidency. During that month Marshall was busy, partisan, and uncharacteristically sloppy.

The new judiciary bill had Jefferson worried: "I dread [it] above all the measures meditated, because appointments in the nature of freehold render it difficult to undo what is done."[36] Indeed the bill would create sixteen life-tenured circuit judges, eliminate circuit riding by the Supreme Court justices, and reduce the Court from six justices to five. The House passed the bill on a party-line vote on January 20. To avoid delays, the Senate passed the bill without amendment, again by a strict party-line vote, on February 11, the very day that the House began voting to break the tie between Jefferson and Burr. It took six days and thirty-six ballots before the Federalists caved and allowed Jefferson what was rightly his, thereby paving the way for a peaceful handover of power to an opposition party.

Adams had been searching for his new circuit judges even before the Judiciary Act reached his desk. Because March 4 loomed as the deadline, he could not afford to wait for nominees to decline via the mail if he was to fill all sixteen positions. The result was that the willingness to say yes predominated over competence. Oliver Wolcott, who had been admitted to the bar in 1781 but never practiced law and who had recently been forced to resign as secretary of the treasury, got a judgeship. Two of Marshall's brothers-in-law received appointments, too. Edward Tilgham was to be nominated, but upon being informed that he would decline, Adams had his first name stricken and that of William, Edward's cousin, inserted. Six district judges, including one Republican, were promoted, thereby creating vacancies below to be filled. A district court position went to Senator Ray Green of Rhode Island, but after confirmation Marshall filled out a commission designating Green as a circuit judge. Green did not notice until after he resigned his Senate seat and prepared to assume judicial duties. He then sent the commission to the new secretary of state, James Madison, asking for a corrected one. Madison refused.

Congress also passed two statutes for the District of Columbia. One created a three-judge court, possessing the powers of a circuit court. Marshall's brother and Adams's nephew both got jobs. There were also forty-two justices of the peace—a huge number for such a sparsely settled area—who were confirmed March 2. Marshall, however, did not deliver four of the commissions before the March 4 deadline, a failure he would have to address shortly.

Everyone understood what was happening. As Gouverneur Morris observed of his party, "[T]hey are about to experience a heavy gale of adverse wind; can they be blamed for casting many anchors to hold their ship through the storm?"[37] Marshall concurred: "Of the importance of the judiciary at all times, but more especially the present I am fully impressed & I shall endeavor in the new office to which I am called not to disappoint my friends."[38] Meanwhile Jefferson seethed. The Federalists "had retired into the judiciary, in a strong body where it lives on the treasury, & therefore cannot be starved out. While in possession of that ground it can check the popular current which runs against them, & seize the favorable occasion to promote reaction."[39]

Jefferson and the Judiciary

Once in office Jefferson told his acting secretary of state not to deliver the unsent commissions, and then Madison didn't correct that of hapless Ray Green, now out of two jobs, either. In the meantime, Jefferson had nine months before the new Congress convened to decide what to do. His domestic program was to reduce the debt, eliminate all internal taxes, and cut federal spending.

Roughly $30,000 a year would be saved by eliminating the sixteen new circuit judges, and that is what Jefferson proposed to do. Republicans claimed that the dockets of the circuit courts were decreasing and therefore the new judges were an unnecessary expense. Privately, as usual, Jefferson was candid: "lopping off the parasitical plant engrafted at the last session on the judiciary body" would be controversial,[40] but necessary because "from that battery all the works of Republicanism are to be beaten down and erased."[41] Federalists saw through the thin guise and claimed that it was unconstitutional because of life tenure for federal judges. The Republicans conceded that they could not take the judge from the office, but they claimed they could take the office from the judge. No Federalist could fall for such sophistry, but all the Federalists could do was wail at the supposed demise of judicial independence.

Republicans answered the Federalist assertion of life tenure by claiming that the power to create implies the power to abolish. Since the Constitution provides for salaries "during their continuance in office," stripping the judges of their office ended the need to pay them.

The Repeal Act of 1802, eliminating the Judiciary Act of 1801, barely passed the Senate but was solidly supported in the House. The votes, 16–15 and 59–32, reflected the partisan balances in the Seventh Congress. The Republican *National Intelligencer* exulted: "Judges created for political purposes, and for the worst of purposes under a republican government, for the purpose of opposing the national will, from this day cease to exist."[42] The Republicans could claim that the repeal did not affect judicial independence because they had eliminated positions rather than replacing the judges with their own. Nevertheless, in a widely republished editorial in the Federalist press, the repeal was seen as the end: "The fatal bill has passed. Our Constitution is no more."[43] Congressman Charles Matoon called the repeal "the death of the Constitution" and "anticipate[d] all the horrors of a French Revolution."[44]

What would the judges and justices do? The new circuit judges could hold court and see if anyone came. The justices could refuse to ride circuit. A congressman who talked with Marshall in Richmond reported his assurance "that the firmness of the Supreme Court may be depended on should the business be brought before 'em."[45] But first the justices needed to work things out among themselves, most likely at their June term.

In that term they would also hear an action by William Marbury, one of the four Adams appointees as justices of the peace whose commission Marshall had failed to deliver. In December 1801 Marbury had brought an action against Secretary of State Madison for his commission. That action was a request to the Court that Madison be required to show cause why the commission should not be delivered. Madison had declined to appear, and Attorney General Levi Lincoln informed the justices that he had no instructions. The Court agreed to hear argument in its June 1802 term on whether to issue the necessary writ.

In order to forestall the justices from meeting, the Republicans rushed through another judiciary act, this one eliminating the June term and setting a single February term for the Court to sit each year. Federalists chided the Republicans for being afraid that the justices would pronounce the repeal void, but lost in the party-line vote.

With no chance to meet and talk, the justices corresponded largely through Marshall. He wrote to Paterson stating an unconquerable belief that circuit riding was unconstitutional, combined with a willingness to be bound by a majority decision. After all, the other five had ridden circuit in the past, and if it was valid then, it was valid now. Chase, too, had received a letter from Marshall, and he quickly responded with a memorandum arguing that the Repeal Act was unconstitutional. He believed that the justices should refuse to ride circuit. Bushrod Washington responded unequivocally that he would ride circuit. Paterson came to the same position: "Practic[e] has fixed construction; which it is too late to disturb."[46] Once a single justice made it clear that he would ride, the others had no option but to follow suit. Thus the justices would ride circuit and then meet in Washington in February 1803.

The Cases of 1803

When they did meet, they had Marbury's action against Madison as well as a case challenging the repeal. The latter, *Stuart v. Laird,* involved a case transferred from a repealed circuit court to one revived by the 1802 Repeal Act. Lawyers argued that the receiving court lacked jurisdiction because the Repeal Act was unconstitutional. Marshall, on circuit, held that the court did have jurisdiction and thus implicitly sustained the Repeal Act as it related to circuit riding.

The possibility of a constitutional crisis hovered over *Marbury v. Madison* and *Stuart,* with the latter being by far the more explosive. The justices could decide against the Republicans in both cases, thereby giving the more extreme Republicans the fight they were looking for. Alternatively, the justices could try to split the difference by deciding for Marbury while approving the Repeal Act, or by deciding against Marbury while invalidating the Repeal Act. In either of these cases they could expect a strong response from the Republicans. No one doubted that Jefferson, having tipped his hand by refusing to contest *Marbury,* would refuse to obey any order. The best option for avoiding a confrontation was to rule twice in favor of the Republicans.

The Court had been dealt a terrible hand, one in which the Republicans held all the trumps. The justices had already agreed, over Chase's objections and Marshall's now conquered belief, to ride circuit again. Treasury Secretary Albert Gallatin had zero-budgeted the circuit judges, and even if the Court ordered them paid, the House would not appropriate funds. Similarly, if the Court ordered Madison to give Marbury his commission, Madison would refuse, and the Court's impotence would be exposed for all to see. Finally, the Republicans had the votes to initiate the ace of trumps—impeachment of the justices in the House, to be followed by conviction in the Senate and their replacement by Republican loyalists.

Marshall's genius—and make no mistake, it was genius—was that he found cards to play in such a losing hand. To be sure, he had to cheat, but he was neither the first nor the last great politician to do so in the service of a higher cause.

Marbury came down first. But before we turn to Marshall's famous opinion, it is worth noting that he had no business participating in the decision. Functionally, *Marbury* was an appeal of his own actions as secretary of state whereby he had not arranged for prompt delivery of Marbury's commission, and the key affidavit had to be provided by Marshall's brother, the new circuit judge. None of this was mentioned.

Marshall's opinion in *Marbury* simultaneously rebuked Jefferson for not following the law, affirmed a judicial power to declare congressional statutes unconstitutional, and avoided Jefferson's ignoring any order by holding that the Court had no jurisdiction over the case. Initially Marshall found that Marbury's commission was complete when the seal of the United States was affixed, and hence delivery was unnecessary to create "a vested legal right."[47] After that he asked whether, since Marbury's rights had been violated, "the laws of this country afford him a remedy?"[48] In answering the question affirmatively, Marshall distinguished between political actions, where he suggested the executive was supreme, and legal rights, where the executive is answerable to the law—and therefore the judiciary. In the process he gave Jefferson a lecture on the rule of law: "The government of the United States has been emphatically termed a government of laws, not of men. It will certainly cease to deserve this high appellation if the laws furnish no remedy for the violation of a vested legal right."[49] So there must be a remedy.

Marbury then gets interesting. After Marshall declares that there must be a remedy, he goes on to say that the Court can grant no relief because it has no jurisdiction over Marbury's action (and thus everything Marshall previously said was unnecessary). The Court held that Section 13 of the Judiciary Act of 1789 was unconstitutional insofar as it added to the Court's original jurisdiction. There are three steps here, with one obviously being that the Court has the power to declare a federal statute unconstitutional. That point, for which *Marbury* is famous, was hardly in contention. The justices had implicitly held so on circuit in the Invalid Pension Act cases. *Hylton v. United States* had sustained the excise tax on carriages, with the clear implication that the Court could have voided the tax. Republicans themselves had unsuccessfully argued that the Sedition Act was unconstitutional. With regard to judicial review, *Marbury* only confirmed what members of Congress had acknowledged from the beginning: that their actions would be subject to judicial review.

Leading up to the finding of unconstitutionality, the Court found that Section 13 vested it with original jurisdiction in Marbury's action against the secretary of state. In fact the statute did not do so; Marshall misconstrued it to confer jurisdiction.[50] Then he held that the ambiguous language of Article III[51] necessarily precluded adding to the Court's original jurisdiction. Once Marshall asserted a conflict between a statute and the Constitution, the outcome could only be that the Constitution was superior and controlled. The statute that purported to vest jurisdiction was unconstitutional, so there was no jurisdiction to decide the case.

What seems so easy really wasn't. The case could have come out differently in a number of ways. Marshall could have found that receipt of the commission was necessary to create a vested legal right; but he didn't. He could have construed Section 13 correctly—it was, after all, drafted by his predecessor Ellsworth—and found that it authorized issuing writs only when the Court otherwise had jurisdiction; but he didn't. He could have started with the lack of jurisdiction and not lectured Jefferson about his duties; but he didn't. By doing it the way Marshall did it, he made *Marbury* a magnificent declaration of judicial power, complete with its slap at Jefferson, and it left no opportunity for Jefferson and Madison to thwart the decree. But that's not the end of the story.

Marbury also shouts twice at *Stuart v. Laird* and the Repeal Act. First, if *Marbury*'s undelivered commission to a five-year post as a justice of the peace is legally vested, then the delivered (and acted upon) commissions for life-tenured positions as circuit judges were at least equally legally vested (although no displaced judge had filed suit because the government wouldn't pay in any case). Second, if it is unconstitutional for Congress to add to the Court's original jurisdiction, then it should be unconstitutional to send the Court's justices all over the country to exercise original jurisdiction (as circuit judges without a commission as such). In other words, the logical implications of *Marbury* would place the Court at direct odds with Jefferson and the Republican Congress over the Repeal Act.

To avoid the confrontation that Marshall had worked so hard in *Marbury* to defuse, Marshall needed *Stuart* to vanish. Although there was no invariable rule, Marshall recused himself from *Stuart* because he had decided the case on circuit. Paterson then wrote but three paragraphs to dispose of the questions whether Congress could move cases from a nonexistent court to a current one and whether justices could be made to ride circuit. On the latter point the Court tersely noted, "[T]he question is at rest and ought not now to be disturbed."[52] On the former, Paterson noted that Congress has "constitutional authority to establish from time to time such inferior tribunals as they may think proper; and to transfer a cause from one such tribunal to another. In this last particular, there are no words in the constitution to prohibit or restrain the exercise of legislative power."[53] With Marshall out and Chase leaving his quill dry, no one pointed out the inconsistencies between *Marbury* and *Stuart.*

The justices in *Stuart* had known better; they just realized that there was nothing else to do, and by writing the opinion as he did, Paterson made sure *Marbury* was not implicated and therefore not undermined. Thus the Court had skillfully maneuvered through a dangerous political situation. Placed in a no-win position, the Court had asserted power in a way that could not be confronted without threatening either the Republicans or itself. Jefferson did not like the lecture in *Marbury,* but he accepted his two victories in silence, as did the Republican press.

Because of the way it was written, *Stuart,* the only case between 1801 and 1804 for which Marshall did not write the opinion of the Court, dropped from view.[54] *Marbury* itself did not achieve iconic status until the twentieth century. Nor was *Marbury* the most important constitutional decision of 1803. That honor fell to Jefferson's doubling the size of the United States with the Louisiana Purchase—the only decision he made as chief magistrate where he acknowledged constitutional qualms (because the Constitution does not explicitly authorize the acquisition of additional territory). Heretofore the Court's docket had looked east, with prize and maritime cases dominating; soon it would look west.

Still looking east, Jefferson's two victories had come on the heels of a third, *United States v. The Schooner Peggy.* The *Peggy* had been captured during the Quasi-War and had been condemned at trial and therefore sold. As part of Ellsworth's negotiations with France, vessels not yet condemned were to be returned to their original owner. The treaty was finalized after the sale. After taking office, Jefferson ordered the proceeds paid to the French owner. The clerk of the court refused, but Marshall reversed, finding that the proceedings were not final until appeals were exhausted. During the appeal, if the law "changes the rule which governs, the law must be obeyed."[55] Most likely Marshall misconstrued the treaty, but he gave Jefferson a victory he wanted and simultaneously exercised a power to interpret treaties. Like *Stuart* and *Marbury, The Schooner Peggy* was a conscious choice not to confront the president.

Impeachment

The détente between the Court and the Republicans was decisively breached just two months after *Stuart* because Chase couldn't leave well enough alone. He may have been able to hold his quill, but he couldn't hold his tongue.

Chase gave a grand jury charge in Baltimore that assailed Republicans on both the state and national level. He asserted that the Repeal Act had been an unconstitutional assault on an independent judiciary: "The independence of the national Judiciary is already shaken to its foundation."[56] He then asserted that "our Republican Constitution will sink into a mobocracy, the worst of all governments."[57] The charge was reprinted in a Baltimore newspaper, which was then forwarded to Jefferson, who wrote immediately to Joseph Nicholson, one of the Republican leaders in the House: "[O]ught this seditious & official attack on the principles of our constitution . . . to go unpunished?"[58] Judge John Pickering of New Hampshire, who was a senile drunk, had just been impeached in the House earlier in 1803, even though, despite one politically charged decision against the administration, everyone knew that his real crime was continuing in office while "insane." His conviction in the Senate the next year caused Federalist senator William

Plummer to observe how far the precedent of removal without finding high crimes and misdemeanors "time alone can develop."[59] Chase's impeachment would go a long way toward answering that question.

There was a delay in waiting for the next Congress to convene, but in January 1804 John Randolph demanded an investigation of Chase by the House. Two months later the House voted 73–32 to impeach without articulating why. The articles of impeachment were supplied later. When finally settled upon, the charges dealt with Chase's conduct during James Callender's Sedition Act trial, his conduct during a trial for treason, and the Baltimore grand jury charge with its direct assault on Republicans.

If the Senate broke along party lines, the Republicans had more than enough votes to convict, as they enjoyed a 25–9 advantage, well over the two-thirds necessary. Chase believed that the Pickering precedent would be used to remove him. Marshall feared the same and wrote to Chase suggesting that in exchange for the Republicans' dropping political impeachments, the Court's supposedly erroneous decisions could be appealed to Congress for a legislative override.[60] The suggestion never saw the light of day because the Senate didn't convict. Needing three Republicans to vote with them, the Federalists always got at least six. The only charge that garnered a majority was the grand jury address, in which the vote was 19–15. With his sweeping victory for a second term Jefferson might have been able to move four of the six Republicans to the other side, but he did not try. Although he kept a vote tally, Jefferson remained silent throughout. If Chase's political overreaching couldn't cause his conviction before a Republican Senate, then no one could be removed. With the failure to remove Chase, political impeachment of justices was dead, and would not be attempted again until Richard Nixon and Gerald Ford moved against the liberal William O. Douglas in 1970. Political charges to grand juries, like the one Chase had given, were equally dead.

Just before Chase's impeachment in the House, Jefferson's first appointment to the Court, thirty-two-year-old William Johnson of the South Carolina Supreme Court, was confirmed. Johnson was a Republican from a solidly Republican state who was young enough to withstand any of the rigors of circuit riding. He was not, however, anywhere near as ideologically rigid as a number of the Virginia Republicans. Neither were Jefferson's two second-term appointments, Brockholst Livingston from the New York dynasty in 1806 and Thomas Todd of Kentucky a year later. The former replaced Paterson, who never fully recovered from an accident in which his coach went over a ten-foot precipice. The latter filled a new vacancy when Congress created a new circuit for the West.

The Embargo

Philip Barton Key referred to the "storm that is gathering" around the judiciary in early 1808, but in fact the crisis had passed.[61] Foreign affairs, stemming from the unprovoked attack the previous June by a British warship on the navy frigate *Chesapeake,* pushed Marshall and the recent acquittal of Aaron Burr on treason charges to the sidelines (in much the same way that the Iraqi invasion of Kuwait ended the controversy over the nomination of David Souter to the Court 183 years later).

Like his predecessors, Jefferson wished to avoid a war for which the United States still remained wholly unprepared. He also believed he had a win-win policy. He could avoid a military buildup and war by having the United States impose an embargo that would bring Britain to its knees. In a matter of months Congress passed four implementing statutes, each more draconian that the last. Somewhat ironically, Jefferson had created a more intrusive government than his Federalist predecessors. In words similar to those Marshall would eventually use, Jefferson wrote to Gallatin that "Congress must legalize all *means* which may be necessary to obtain its *end.*"[62] The embargo may have avoided war for the moment, but it operated exactly opposite to Jefferson's prediction: it brought the American economy, especially in New England, to its knees while simultaneously expanding the British carrying trade. As a result, the embargo was unpopular—some claimed unconstitutional—and openly defied, especially in New England.

The embargo produced three interesting decisions in trial courts. On the one hand, a Federalist judge in Massachusetts sustained its constitutionality under both the Commerce Clause and the war power in an expansive recognition of national power that Jefferson would have hated had it been delivered a decade earlier. On the other hand, his appointees Johnson and Livingston each delivered rebukes to his implementation.

The fourth Embargo Act gave collectors of customs the authority to detain any vessel whenever they believed its cargo was intended to violate the embargo. The ship could then be held "until the decision of the President of the United States be had thereupon."[63] Jefferson interceded and had his treasury secretary alert every collector "to consider every shipment of provisions, lumber, flaxseed, tar, cotton, tobacco, &c., enumerating the articles, as sufficiently suspicious for detention and reference here."[64] The Charleston collector, following Jefferson's directive, detained the *Gilchrist,* even though he believed that the ship was actually headed to Baltimore. The owners of the *Gilchrist* sued, and Johnson ruled for them that the act gave discretion in the first instance to the collector, and therefore Jefferson's blanket order was not authorized by the statute. Jefferson's attorney general, Caesar Rodney, opined that "[y]ou can scarcely elevate a man to a seat in a Court of Justice before he catches the leprosy of the Bench."[65] He also wrote an opinion, which the Republican press reprinted, attacking Johnson's decision.

Meanwhile, smuggling in New England was so prevalent that Jefferson declared a state of insurrection, and several perpetrators were charged with treason. Livingston would have none of it: "No single act in opposition to or in evasion of a law, however violent or flagrant when the object is private gain, can be construed as levying war on the United States."[66]

National Republicans on the Court

The end of Jefferson's presidency brought the end of the embargo as well as the end of hostility between the executive and the judiciary. The idea that a part of government could be independent of the will of the people was anathema to Jefferson's way of thinking.[67] Thus he bemoaned the "original error of establishing a judiciary independent of the nation."[68] His hatred for the federal judiciary was visceral. In contrast, Madison, who lacked Jefferson's ideological edge and was at home with a Constitution that he more than anyone else had forged, had no trouble with the judiciary.

The end of Jefferson's presidency was close to the end of partisan politics as well, for despite the embargo, Republicans had become a huge-tent party, known as National Republicans, ranging from unreconstructed Anti-Federalists in the South to middle-of-the-road former Federalists, such as John Quincy Adams, in New England. The Federalists, who as a party had been dying only to gain a respite in New England because of the embargo, would commit political suicide by toying with secession at the Hartford Convention exactly as the War of 1812 was ending. Whether or not this was an "era of good feelings," a one-party republic, with dissenters largely being Virginia ideologues whose thinking was frozen in 1798 (if not 1786), existed until the mid-1820s.

Madison gained the opportunity that Jefferson had so strongly desired: to transform the Court from a Federalist institution to one with a majority of Republicans. When the Massachusetts justice died in September 1810, Jefferson figuratively danced on his grave as he contemplated the naming of a Republican justice from New England as well as a Republican majority on the Court. But Madison, over the course of the next fourteen months, had to send four nominees to the Senate before it confirmed his seventh preference for the job, thirty-two-year-old Joseph Story. Story became—and remains—the youngest justice in history. Jefferson had tried to head off this nomination, unsuccessfully asserting to Madison that Story had "deserted us" on the embargo and was "unquestionably a tory."[69] But during Madison's struggle to get a new justice from New England, the hated Chase also died, and replacing a justice from the middle states with a good Republican was easy. So even if Story was a "tory," there was nevertheless a Republican majority on the Court.

An immediate dividend from the Republican majority was *United States v. Hudson and Goodwin*, where the Court held that federal courts had no jurisdiction over common law crimes. The case was a common law prosecution for seditious libel against the editors of a Federalist newspaper in Connecticut. Ironically Jefferson had tried unsuccessfully to derail the prosecution. In the end a unanimous Court, through Johnson, ended the practice that the Republicans had believed was so serious and objectionable when the Federalists controlled the legislature and executive. Johnson delivered a very Jeffersonian opinion. First he stated that the issue had "been long since settled in public opinion."[70] He then echoed the Kentucky and Virginia Resolutions in concluding that the "powers of the general Government are made up of concessions from the several states."[71] Marshall's abhorrence of dissent must have been sorely taxed when he read those words, but to judge on the basis of results alone, Marshall had never denied Jefferson anything he wanted—except Burr hanging by a noose (when an unhappy jury followed Marshall's instructions and ruled that Burr was "not proved to be guilty under this indictment by any evidence submitted to us").[72]

Jefferson worried about finding a justice who had "a character of firmness enough to preserve his independence on the same bench with Marshall."[73] This was an apt concern. When the justices met in the capital, they always boarded together, took meals together, drank together, and discussed their cases in the evening. In such a setting Marshall could shine. Despite being a towering intellect, Marshall wore his robes lightly. He was a modest human being; abandoning the scarlet and ermine, he was the first justice to wear a simple black robe. He loved to talk and joke. Dissent among the justices had been rare once Marshall took his seat and remained that way even after Republicans gained a majority of the seats, as *Hudson and Goodwin* illustrates (where Marshall and Story suppressed their disagreement with the majority).

Unanimity did not mean everyone agreed; it meant only that no one recorded a dissent. Johnson subsequently explained to Jefferson that after he had "remonstrated in vain" at Marshall's practice of writing a single opinion for the Court, he "heard nothing but lectures on the indecency of judges cutting at each other."[74] Story explained the rationale for the Court's habit of issuing a single opinion: "Judge Washington thinks (and very correctly) that the habit of delivering dissenting opinions on ordinary occasions weakens the authority of the Court, and is of no public benefit."[75] Thus the good feelings the justices had toward their chief, coupled with peer pressure, kept separate opinions to an absolute minimum. As a result, Marshall wrote the opinion for over 80 percent of the cases decided during his first decade. Jefferson's claim in his first inaugural address that "[w]e are all Republicans, we are all Federalists" fully described the Court.[76]

· III ·

The States and the Republic

HAVING SURVIVED THE SERIOUS ATTACK on its independence, the Court returned to an issue that sparked the Congress and states to overturn its decision in *Chisholm v. Georgia:* the relationship of the states to the republic through the vehicle of the federal judiciary. The Constitution had not solved this issue, leaving it to other days, and during James Madison's presidency the first of those days arrived. The relationship between state and nation was defined in two ways, first by restrictions found in the Constitution and second, more important, by the powers granted the federal government. In both circumstances the Court was nationalistic, circumscribing the states while untethering the federal government. This created a Jefferson-like hostility to the Court in Southern states that subsided only when John Marshall passed from the scene at the end of Andrew Jackson's presidency.

Yazoo

In 1795 the Georgia legislature sold Yazoo, some 35 million acres consisting of much of what is now Alabama and Mississippi, for a cent and a half an acre, netting $500,000. The price may seem low, but it wasn't a bad deal since Yazoo was claimed by both the United States and Spain in addition to Georgia. And of course it was dominated by its initial inhabitants, the Cherokee, Creek, Choctaw, and Chickasaw tribes. So Georgia was selling what it did not control and what it may not have owned at a time when its treasury was empty and its militia unpaid. Still, the transaction reeked of fraud, as all but one of the legislators voting in favor of the sale had been bribed. After an intervening election in which the incumbents were routed, a new legislature passed a rescinding law declaring the earlier statute authorizing the sale fraudulent and void. All documents concerning the sale were ordered destroyed, and the original act was burned in a public ceremony.

In the meantime, the various initial purchasers sold Yazoo at a 650 percent profit to a new set of speculators, mainly residing in New England. For most of the next two decades a battle over Yazoo focused on whether the federal government, to which Georgia sold Yazoo in 1802, this time for $1.25 million, would compensate those whose title claims stemmed from the original Georgia transaction. (Those secondary purchasers asserted that they had not known of any fraud and thus were bona fide.)

Yazoo interacts with many of the events and people from the previous chapter. When the Jay Treaty was ratified, Senator James Gunn, a Georgia Federalist and a prominent figure among the Yazoo speculators, stuck with his party despite the unpopularity of the treaty in Georgia, thereby securing its ratification by a 20–10 vote. It appears that in exchange for his vote, any chance of a federal investigation into the legality of the first sale was killed. The speculators obtained an opinion from Alexander Hamilton, arguing that the rescission of the first sale was "a contravention of the first principles of natural justice and social policy,"[1] as well as a violation of Article I, Section 10, of the Constitution by impairing the obligation of contract: "[T]aking the terms of the constitution in their large sense, and giving them effect according to the general spirit and policy of the provisions, the revocation of the grant ... may justly be considered as contrary to the constitution of the United States, and, therefore null; and . . . the courts of the United States, in cases within their jurisdiction will be likely to pronounce it so."[2] As usual, prescient.

When the Yazoo issue moved into Congress, then-congressman John Marshall both spoke in favor of and voted for compensation for the New England purchasers. As part of the transfer to the federal government, Georgia's second sale of Yazoo, a report by Secretary of State James Madison, Treasury Secretary Albert Gallatin, and Attorney General Levi Lincoln stated that "the title of the claimants [under the first sale] cannot be supported" but nevertheless recommended seeking a compromise (something Madison would champion for a decade). Congress then set aside 5 million acres to settle claims "derived from any act or pretended act of the state of Georgia, which Congress may hereafter think fit to provide for."[3]

Federalists typically supported the Yazoo speculators, while Republicans were split. The Senate was more willing than the House to offer compensation. The Republican House leader, John Randolph, was implacably opposed and was prepared to go against the administration. Randolph was also the floor leader at the Senate impeachment trial of Samuel Chase. A common explanation for Chase's acquittal is that some senators were intent on cutting Randolph down to size for his opposition to the Yazoo settlement. But Randolph remained adamant, and the settlement remained blocked.

The Yazoo speculators then followed Hamilton's advice and went to court. Robert Fletcher of New Hampshire sued John Peck of Massachusetts in federal court to recover money paid for Yazoo land. Fletcher claimed breach of warranty of title because of the repealing act. Everyone would benefit if Peck, a seasoned speculator, prevailed. Fletcher would have good title to his land; Peck would have good title to his remaining land; all Yazoo claimants would have the imprimatur of a Supreme Court decision. With so much at stake, Fletcher and

Peck had concocted a collusive case. The pleadings reflect that initially Fletcher claimed one thousand acres and $250; then those figures were crossed out and fifteen thousand acres and $3,000 written in. The Supreme Court could hear an appeal only if the amount in controversy exceeded $2,000, and the speculators wanted a Supreme Court decision that the rescinding act was void in order to bolster their claim for congressional relief.

At the Supreme Court, Joseph Story, a year before his appointment to the Court, argued for Peck and the speculators. Fletcher, who only in theory was defending Georgia's right to repeal, was represented not by a Republican lawyer but instead by Luther Martin, the "Federalist bulldog," who previously had defended Samuel Chase and Aaron Burr. Martin was drunk at oral argument, and Marshall adjourned the Court until he could sober up. Then Martin offered a perfunctory argument that neither supported the repeal nor challenged the initial act on grounds of its fraudulence.

As Hamilton had predicted, the Court sided with the speculators. Marshall's opinion in *Fletcher v. Peck*, like that in *Marbury v. Madison*, began with a disclaimer to create the appropriate veneer of judicial humility, then spoke in the language of vested rights. The lands were "vested absolutely" in the original grantees, who in turn sold to purchasers who had no knowledge of the original fraud.[4] Marshall claimed that the issue presented was that of a legislature's power to "devest the vested estate of any man whatever, for reasons which shall, by itself, be deemed sufficient."[5] In other words, Marshall interpreted Georgia's actions as representing a power to extinguish a good land title simply because the state wished to do so. Marshall was able to place the issue at such a high level of generality because he disclaimed any judicial power to inquire into the workings of the legislature. It would be "indecent, in the extreme . . . to enter into an inquiry respecting the corruption of the sovereign power of a state."[6] Thus if Georgia could divest innocent purchasers here, then "[a]ll titles would be insecure."[7]

Georgia was absolving itself "from those rules of property which are common to all citizens."[8] The first legislative act vested rights, and if an act can be done under an existing law, a new legislature "cannot undo it. The past cannot be recalled by the most absolute power."[9] Once title vested, the state's power was at an end.

Marshall then spent considerable space concluding that a land grant executed a contract so that the prohibition on states impairing the obligation of contract in Article I, Section 10, came into play. At no point did he write explicitly about his implicit assumption that a federal court had the power to strike down a state statute. The Supremacy Clause could easily have been trotted out, but Marshall apparently saw no necessity to do so.

Justice William Johnson agreed that the rescission was void, but for different reasons: Georgia's action had transgressed "a principle which will impose laws even on the deity."[10] Johnson was on to something fundamental. If he had found a principle that binds "the deity," then surely that same principle would bind both Georgia and the United States Supreme Court. It was best to get right with it.

Just as *Marbury* marked the first time a federal statute was found unconstitutional, *Fletcher* marked the first time a state statute was held to violate the Constitution. *Fletcher*, like *Marbury*, emphasized the importance of vested rights, and it offered a tentative beginning for use of the Contracts Clause to protect those rights. Interestingly, Marshall assumed instead of showing that a contract between a state and a private party, rather than just contracts between private parties, was governed by the Contracts Clause. He thus returned to a related point from *Chisholm*—that a state was bound by its contracts. Finally, the most important vested rights were property rights, as Johnson's law binding the deity illustrated, and the Court was protecting them against precipitate state action.

Events were making it imperative to settle the Yazoo claims because settlers were moving into Mississippi and Alabama, the territories were clamoring for statehood, and there was a huge cloud over the land titles within Yazoo. Furthermore, Randolph was no longer there to fight; he had been defeated by a Jefferson son-in-law in 1812. In 1814 Congress appropriated $5 million to settle the outstanding claims. Everyone who had touched Yazoo made a profit—except, of course, the Cherokee, Creek, Choctaw, and Chickasaw tribes, and they were destined to suffer far more grievous loses in the future.

Elaborating on the Contracts Clause

In 1812, two years after *Fletcher,* Marshall clarified the case's reasoning in *New Jersey v. Wilson.* Colonial New Jersey agreed with the Delaware Indian tribe that the latter would cede lands and move to a reservation, but that the reservation would be tax exempt. The Delaware subsequently decided to move to New York and obtained a statute from New Jersey allowing them to sell reservation land, which they did in 1803. The state then imposed taxes on the land held by the purchasers. The latter claimed that the tax exemption was a contract that stayed with the land. The Court agreed. New Jersey might have bargained for removal of the exemption when the Delaware tribe sought permission to sell the land, but the state had not done so; therefore the exemption continued, and its existence enhanced the value of the land when the Delaware sold it. The purchasers, standing in the place of the tribe, were entitled to the benefits of the contract with New Jersey. Accordingly, the tax violated the Contracts Clause. Anticipating what would be a typical response to being ordered by the Court to do something, New Jersey kept right on taxing the land.

Two quite distinct economic matters became Contracts Clause issues. Because of the depression at the end of the 1810s, states had to decide what to do about insolvent debtors (Congress had not passed a bankruptcy act), and in many states the old law held that those who could not repay their debts were to be imprisoned. Additionally corporations were emerging, and how they fit into the legal world had to be determined. Two cases, both decided in 1819, offered some, but hardly complete, insight.

In *Dartmouth College v. Woodward* the Court entered into a political dispute in New Hampshire, where the Republicans had asserted control over Dartmouth by appointing new (Republican) public trustees. The former trustees sued. Marshall held that corporate charters were contracts to which the state was bound—even in this case, to colonial charters for nonprofit institutions. He acknowledged that the Framers did not contemplate such a case, but "[i]t is necessary . . . to say that, had this particular case been suggested, the language would have been so varied, as to exclude it, or it would have been made a special exception."[11] It's pretty hard to meet that standard; still, holding that a state-granted franchise was a contract that could not be impaired, while novel, was not controversial within the legal profession. As a result, the private trustees regained control of Dartmouth.

Unlike *Dartmouth* and *Fletcher v. Peck, Sturges v. Crowninshield* dealt with a problem that the Contracts Clause was actually designed for, namely, a contract between private parties. New York's 1811 insolvency law allowed debtors to be discharged from their contractual obligations by assigning their property to their creditors whether or not the value of the property covered the debt. The justices were divided on the outcome, but Marshall orchestrated a consensus that retroactive application of the law to contracts in existence prior to its enactment was unconstitutional. Prospective application of insolvency laws to contracts made after the law was on the books was left for another day (when, over Marshall's only dissent in a constitutional case, the Court upheld application of the bankruptcy law).

Virginia v. the Court: Jurisdiction

Until the controversy with South Carolina over the Tariff of 1828, Virginia, where Jefferson's and Madison's ideas from the Kentucky and

Virginia Resolutions were held as religious truths, was in the lead in theorizing on the relationship between the states and the national government. Virginia dogma held that the Constitution was a compact among sovereign states to create a nominal federal government, which would be kept in its place by the various (and vigorous) states. The beginning of Virginia's disputes with the Court came in yet another application of the Treaty of Paris to Virginia's Revolutionary War decrees.

Virginia had confiscated Lord Thomas Fairfax's 300,000-acre estate during the Revolutionary War, and part was granted by the commonwealth to David Hunter a decade later. Meanwhile a syndicate that included John Marshall and his brother James purchased the land from Fairfax's heir, Denny Martin. Reversing a decision in favor of Hunter, the Court through Story (Marshall having recused himself) held that the Treaty of Paris controlled, and so the syndicate rather than Hunter owned the land. In the process Story delivered an unwanted lecture on Virginia land law.

The Virginia court, outraged by the holding and Story's lecture, reverted to the Kentucky and Virginia Resolutions: "It must have been foreseen that controversies would sometimes arise as to the boundaries of the two jurisdictions. Yet the constitution has provided no umpire."[12] The Virginia court ruled that the Supreme Court had no power under the Constitution to hear and decide appeals from state courts. It therefore held that Section 25 of the Judiciary Act of 1789 authorizing appellate review of state court judgments was unconstitutional. The court acknowledged that it was bound by the Constitution and treaties; it was just that its decisions were not subject to review. To back this up, it refused to cooperate further—meaning that no judge would sign the papers to authorize additional review by the justices in Washington.[13] This effectively declared war on the Supreme Court (and, by implication, on the national government).

In *Martin v. Hunter's Lessee* in 1816 the Court again reversed. Story began by rejecting Virginia's compact theory. The Constitution "was ordained and established, not by the states in their sovereign capacities, but emphatically, as the preamble of the constitution declares, by 'the people of the United States.'"[14] Article III on the judiciary was intended "to act not merely upon individuals, but upon states; and to deprive them altogether of the exercise of some powers of sovereignty, and to refrain and regulate them in the exercise of others."[15] Story concluded with a strong point on policy. Supreme Court review of state decisions on federal law made sense. The Framers expected some state recalcitrance, and federal judicial supremacy was a chosen means to deal with it. Furthermore, even in perfect good faith, two state courts might reach differing conclusions on federal law. Supreme Court review provided uniformity, always a value in a legal system.

Johnson concurred, and while he indicated some sympathy for the compact theory, there was nothing separating him from Story on the validity of Section 25. There could not be an "endless . . . diversity of decisions throughout the union upon the constitution, treaties, and laws of the United States; a subject on which the tranquility of the union . . . may materially depend."[16]

Rather than allow the Virginia Court of Appeals a chance to initiate a further fight, the Court issued its mandate directly to the Virginia trial court, which had originally rejected Hunter's claim. The nationalism of the Court meshed with the euphoric nationalism that burst forth at the end of the War of 1812. The best the Virginians could do in response came from the *Richmond Enquirer,* which reprinted Johnson's opinion in full while simultaneously ignoring Story's.

McCulloch v. Maryland

Virginia's next attack on the Court was spurred by Maryland's tax on the second Bank of the United States. The first bank had been chartered in 1791 after a major battle over its constitutionality in which Madison had led the opposition in the House of Representatives by asserting that there was no power in the federal government to charter a bank. To the claims that it facilitated powers of taxation or borrowing money, he noted that a law chartering a bank "laid no taxes" and "does not borrow a shilling."[17] His strong textual analysis rejected reliance on the Necessary and Proper Clause, finding the bank "at most . . . convenient."[18] Seven members of the Philadelphia Convention were in the House, and they voted 4–3 in favor of the bank.

Once the bill had passed, Washington asked his cabinet for constitutional advice. Here Jefferson led the opposition, relying on the language of the yet to be ratified Tenth Amendment as expressing "the foundation of the Constitution."[19] Prior to his presidency, Jefferson was always concerned about the slippery slope: "To take a single step beyond the boundaries thus specifically drawn around the powers of Congress is to take possession of a boundless field of power, no longer susceptible of any definition."[20] Opposing an effort to charter a company to mine copper, Jefferson turned to sarcasm to illustrate the lack of congressional power: "Congress are authorized to defend the country: ships are necessary for that defence; copper is necessary for ships: mines are necessary for copper: a company necessary to work mines: and who can distrust this reasoning who has ever played at 'this is the house that Jack built'?"[21]

Hamilton, the bank's chief sponsor, wrote a lengthy defense of the constitutionality and joined issue with Madison. The bank was a convenient means to the constitutional ends of facilitating borrowing and collecting taxes; the Constitution required nothing more. Washington then signed the bill.

There never was a court challenge to the bank. Instead its charter expired in 1811. In the debates over renewal some members of Congress expressed constitutional qualms, but Jefferson had switched and now supported rechartering. Secretary of the Treasury Albert Gallatin, on whom the consequences of not having a bank would largely fall, was also an enthusiastic backer of rechartering. Nevertheless, probably because of opposition from other banks, the charter was not renewed. This caused serious problems during the War of 1812, and in 1815 a second bank charter passed Congress. Madison vetoed the bill, but on policy—not constitutional—grounds. He thought that the constitutional question had been settled "by repeated recognitions under varied circumstances of the validity of such an institution."[22] Congress soon passed a bill that met with his approval.

The second bank was chartered because experience showed it was valuable, and it initially enjoyed the postwar prosperity. But the bank overexpanded credit and then sharply reduced it when the economy slackened (because of the improved situation in Europe), exacerbating a panic, especially in the South and West. This in turn led Ohio, Kentucky, and Tennessee to pass measures designed to cripple the bank. Yet however controversial the Bank was in some parts of the country, it had solid support in Washington, D.C., where both President James Monroe and an overwhelming majority of congressmen were on record supporting it.

The first case involving the rechartered bank, *McCulloch v. Maryland*, involved a nondiscriminatory revenue measure, commensurate with the bank's booming business in the state, requiring the bank to pay an annual tax of $15,000. The bank didn't want to pay, and Maryland agreed to a quick lawsuit to allow the Court to settle the issue. What a contrast to Virginia!

McCulloch, in 1819, was Marshall's most important opinion because he used the opportunity to write as strongly nationalist an opinion as possible. He began by summarizing the prior history: "After being resisted, first in the fair and open field of debate, and afterwards in the executive cabinet, with as much persevering talent as any measure has ever experienced, and being supported by arguments which convinced minds as pure and as intelligent as this country can boast, it became law."[23] Like Hamilton, Marshall recognized that there were national powers beyond those explicitly mentioned in the Constitution;

the question was how vast was the scope of implied powers. Because each member of the Virginia dynasty—Washington, Jefferson, Madison, and Monroe—believed that implied powers authorized chartering a bank, it was totally unreasonable to think that the justices would come to the opposite conclusion. Indeed that was not the true issue in the case, although Marshall wrote as if it were. Maryland didn't object to the federally chartered bank profiting in Baltimore. Having borne the brunt of the war on land in 1814, Maryland knew that taxing the bank would help replenish its depleted treasury.

What made *McCulloch* so important was not what the Court did but what it said. It reflected Marshall's usual approach of writing at a high level of abstraction, tying an unassailable general principle into constitutional text, intertwining a dash of history, if available, while avoiding mention of judicial precedents. In *McCulloch* he wove all these together to write an opinion that went far beyond the facts of the case into the realm of supposedly forbidden (because unconstitutional) advisory opinions.

McCulloch's significance rests on three pillars: first, what it said about the nature of the Constitution; second, what it said about congressional power; and finally, its conclusion that the Court was the proper forum for determining the scope of implied federal powers. Marshall made no real argument on this last point. He acknowledged the "deep sense of importance" of the questions and the "awful responsibility" of decision, but if a decision was necessary, "by this tribunal alone can the decision be made. On the Supreme Court of the United States has the constitution of our country devolved this important duty."[24] That was that; the Court and no one else could determine the boundaries of federal power—a leap from *Marbury*'s holding that the Court could determine whether its own original jurisdiction could be expanded.

Marshall intended to use the case to slay the Virginia theology that the Constitution was just a compact among sovereign states. While noting that Maryland was "a sovereign state,"[25] he then immediately began to pull the teeth out of state sovereignty. According to Marshall, as the preamble declares, the Constitution was "ordained and established" by "We the People." To be sure, the ratifying conventions were held in the separate states, but where else could they have been? That the conventions were local did not make the measures any less those of the people, nor did they become measures of state governments. The assent of the states was required to call conventions, but thereafter the state was irrelevant: "The people were at perfect liberty to accept or reject it; and their act was final."[26] States retain sovereignty, but within its own sphere of action, the federal government is supreme.

At this point, Marshall turned to constitutional interpretation. A bank is not mentioned, but "great powers" such as declaring and waging war, taxing and borrowing, and regulating commerce are. A "government, entrusted with such ample powers, on the due execution of which the happiness and prosperity of the nation so vitally depends, must also be entrusted with ample means for their execution. The power being given, it is in the interest of the nation to facilitate its execution."[27] "Necessary and proper" meant convenient; in response to the argument that "necessary" meant absolutely necessary, Marshall noted that the Framers knew about absolute necessity and placed that language elsewhere (in part of Article I, Section 10). The Court would not second-guess whether the means were necessary; unlike the boundaries of national power, that was purely a legislative decision.

Marshall then presented his test for the limits of federal power: "Let the end be legitimate, let it be within the scope of the constitution, and all means which are appropriate, which are plainly adapted to that end, which are not prohibited, but consist with the letter and spirit of the constitution, are constitutional."[28] Marshall offered one caveat in addition to recognizing that if the actions were specifically prohibited, then the Court would void them. If, "under the pretext of executing its powers, [Congress should] pass laws for the accomplishment of objects not entrusted to the government, it would become the painful duty" of the Court to declare them void.[29] All in all, the opinion came quite close to saying that if Congress pursues a legitimate end, then it can do as it pleases unless the Constitution specifically forbids the means, something Madison easily grasped: Marshall had granted the legislature a discretion as to means "to which no practical limit can be assigned."[30] Yet a majority of the Court—five of seven—were Republican appointees.

Marshall claimed that there was no specific text covering state taxation of a federal creation. Yet the Constitution expressly limits state taxation only on imports and exports. From that one could infer that any other nondiscriminatory tax was valid. Instead, following Daniel Webster's argument for the bank, Marshall asserted that no state can destroy a federal entity, and "the power to tax is the power to destroy."[31] With this statement Marshall equated Maryland's fair tax with the Western states' taxes to exclude or expel the bank. As with necessity, the judicial power did not encompass questions of degree.

As in *Marbury*, the bulk of what Marshall wrote was unnecessary to the decision in the case, and he created a lot of constitutional law to hold that a state could not nondiscriminatorily tax a federally chartered private corporation when the federal statute was silent on the issue of taxation. Rather than wait for a case out of the West where the state might attempt to defy an order, the Court used *McCulloch*, where Maryland would acquiesce in a judgment, to rule on taxing the bank.

Virginia v. the Court: Reaction to *McCulloch*

Timing is everything, and *McCulloch*'s timing was bad. The burst of nationalism that followed the War of 1812, so well reflected in Marshall's opinion, was waning, in no small part because the Panic of 1819 catapulted the country into a depression. There had been a chance for the federal government to help build roads and canals to better tie the country and the economy together, but Madison had vetoed an internal improvements bill on the constitutional ground that the power to build infrastructure remained with the states.[32] James Monroe felt similarly, and Henry Clay, an enthusiastic supporter of internal improvements, would never gain the presidency. *McCulloch* offered an answer to the internal improvements issue that Southerners did not wish to hear and one that, by their control of the presidency (with the exception of the Adamses), they could ignore.

More ominously, slavery, long submerged as an issue, had burst onto the scene in arguments over whether Missouri would be admitted as a state only with conditions placed on slavery. The only part of the Constitution that expressly limited federal power over slavery was the now dead prohibition on banning the international slave trade before 1808. Under *McCulloch's* reasoning, Congress could have authority to legislate with respect to slavery as an incident of some expressly granted power. Indeed, part of the settlement over whether Missouri would be admitted as a slave state was that slavery was "forever prohibited" north and west of Missouri.[33] Every Southerner in Congress who spoke on the issue believed that the ban was unconstitutional. Spencer Roane, chief justice of the Virginia Supreme Court of Appeals and son-in-law to the demagogic Patrick Henry (himself an implacable foe of the Constitution), was sure that *McCulloch* spoke to congressional power and slavery, and he readied his denunciation.

Two weeks after *McCulloch,* Marshall wrote to Story and Bushrod Washington that the case "has roused the sleeping spirit of Virginia."[34] He accurately predicted that "[w]e shall be denounced bitterly in the papers & . . . undoubtedly be condemned as a pack of consolidating aristocratics."[35] Marshall knew his neighbors. Two Virginia judges, Roane and William Brockenbrough, led the intellectual attack. The latter turned to Madison's Virginia *Report,* written to amplify on the Kentucky and Virginia Resolutions, to claim that the Court, as part of the national government, had a conflict of interest, and therefor the states never would have consented to let it umpire their disputes with the national government. Roane took on Marshall's interpretation of federal power (while never questioning the bank itself, which Virginians found quite well run). He deemed *McCulloch* "a judicial *coup de main*" which portended the destruction of the liberties of the people.[36] He argued that there was no difference between an unlimited grant of power and a limited grant accompanied by unlimited means of execution. The Virginia House of Delegates then protested against *McCulloch* and recommended creating a new court to decide questions involving the powers of the general and state governments under the compact. Jefferson, in turn, bemoaned the Court's "construing our constitution from a co-ordination of a general and special government to a general and supreme one alone."[37]

McCulloch's green light for internal improvements helped with passage of funds for the Cumberland Road. Monroe then vetoed the act, adding a lengthy pamphlet which stated his general views on the limitations on federal power. He sent the pamphlet to each of the justices. Johnson, after consultation with the others, replied with an advisory letter that the justices "are all of the opinion that the decision on the Bank question completely commits them on the subject of internal improvements, as applied to Postroads and Military Roads."[38] The justices may have been committed, but Monroe was unmoved.

Virginia v. the Court: Jurisdiction Again

Martin v. Hunter's Lessee was then revisited in 1821 in *Cohens v. Virginia*. Philip and Mendes Cohen were convicted and fined $100 for violating a Virginia law prohibiting the sale of out-of-state lottery tickets. The tickets they sold were for a Washington, D.C., lottery, established by congressional statute, to effect improvements to the city. There is little doubt that Congress intended the tickets to be sold elsewhere, because Washington lacked a sufficient population to make the lottery a success. The Court agreed to review the Cohens' conviction, and the state legislature ordered Virginia's lawyers to limit their argument to the fact that the Court did not have jurisdiction under the Constitution. Because it was a criminal case involving a statute designed to protect the state's economic interest, *Cohens* could readily be deemed a more fundamental intrusion of the Court into state affairs than that in *Martin*. Virginia's lawyers argued, again, that Section 25 was unconstitutional, and in any event, that the Eleventh Amendment precluded taking Virginia into any federal court—the Supreme Court included.

Virginia's arguments were weak. *Martin* had already decided that Section 25 was constitutional, and while the Eleventh Amendment limited federal jurisdiction, its text spoke only to suits "commenced" against (not by) a state. The Court, through Marshall, again reaffirmed that Section 25 was constitutional and held that the Eleventh Amendment was inapplicable because Virginia had commenced the case against the Cohens, not vice versa, and besides, they were citizens of Virginia. On the merits the Cohens' attorney argued that since Congress had the right to raise revenue for any national purpose, it "had a right to establish this lottery, and no State law can defeat this, any more than the exercise of any other national power."[39] The reasoning flowed directly from *McCulloch*. Marshall nevertheless held that Congress had not intended to require states to allow lottery sales. Given that without sales in the states the lottery would fail, Marshall's construction is implausible. But given that Virginia had signaled it would not comply with a decision requiring it to allow sales, Marshall was shrewd. Like *Marbury, Cohens* asserted a jurisdiction and then wisely chose not to exercise it.

Roane was not mollified. Writing in the *Enquirer,* he found *Cohens* a product of "that love of power, which all history informs us infects and corrupts all who possess it, and from which even the high and ermined judges, themselves, are not exempted."[40] Virginia had won the case against the Cohens, but despite Roane's escalated rhetoric, the Court won the principle.

Steamboat Monopolies

By a series of statutes culminating in 1808, New York had granted Robert Livingston and Robert Fulton an exclusive right to operate steamboats on its waterways for thirty years. Rather than exercising their monopoly personally, Livingston and Fulton franchised it. Aaron Ogden got the rights to operate steamboats between New York City and points in New Jersey. The monopoly was unpopular, especially given New York City's exponential growth, and entrepreneurs challenged it. One was Thomas Gibbons, who created an unauthorized ferry service between New York City and Elizabethtown, New Jersey, piloted by the future railroad magnate Cornelius Vanderbilt. When Ogden sued, Gibbons defended that he was licensed under a 1793 act of Congress enrolling vessels that traded along the seaboard, and therefore a state could not interfere with his business. The New York courts were unimpressed, concluding that the licensing statute was designed to raise revenue and favor American vessels in the coasting trade and therefore had nothing to do with the matter.

The steamboat case, *Gibbons v. Ogden,* presented a fundamental issue looking to the future of the republic, which still remained more an association of states than a nation. If New York could grant a monopoly on the Hudson River, could not Louisiana, where Livingston and Fulton had also secured a steamboat monopoly, do the same on the Mississippi? Monopolies being monopolies, commerce could be throttled, or at least rendered expensive. Some states granted monopolies, while others retaliated and forbade steamboats licensed in New York to operate in their waters.

Marshall found the case covered by the Commerce Clause, which grants Congress the power to regulate commerce "among the several states." He quickly noted, "All America understands, and has uniformly understood, the word 'commerce' to comprehend navigation."[41] Marshall then concluded that he could "restrict" the Commerce Clause to apply only "to that commerce which concerns more States than one."[42] It would therefore not reach commercial activities "completely within a particular State, which do not affect other States, and with which it is not necessary to interfere."[43] Some restriction!

The commerce power, according to Marshall, "is complete in itself, may be exercised to its utmost extent, and acknowledges no limitations, other than are prescribed in the constitution," and was "vested in Congress as absolutely as it would be in a single government."[44] That was big, but Marshall next wrote as if Congress had not yet exercised the power. Did the very existence in Congress of the power to regulate commerce deny a state the right to exercise a like power? Marshall spent considerable time flirting with the possibility, intimating that the power in Congress was indeed exclusive (even though, in two unmentioned contemporaneous cases, the Court had found that the "mere" grant of power to Congress did not preclude a similar one in the state).[45] Finally, at the very end of his opinion, he switched and found that the 1793 act was not merely a licensing statute but also one that granted a substantive right to engage the coasting trade. Therefore the monopoly was contrary to congressional policy and invalid.

The demise of the monopoly was celebrated almost everywhere, regardless of what people otherwise thought about the Court, although Jefferson smarted at the opinion because of its expansive treatment of federal power. The fare to Connecticut dropped by 40 percent. The number of steamboats in New York State's waters jumped from six to forty-three within a year. Coinciding with the opening of the Erie Canal, the decision set New York City on course to become dominant in the republic's commerce.

The demise of the monopoly also coincided with the demise of the Virginia opposition. There were extensive congressional debates on the judiciary in 1825–26 involving enlarging the Court, circuit riding duties, and jurisdiction to review judgments of state courts. The debates revealed varieties of views on the judiciary, some quite harsh, but no legislation emerged. Even Philip Barbour, a states' rights Virginian who had argued against finding jurisdiction in *Cohens,* pronounced the Court a "deposit[ory of] 'the peace and tranquility of the Union.'"[46] Barbour's statement, coupled with the deaths of Roane in 1822 and Jefferson four years later, signaled the end of Virginia's era as chief opposition to the Court's jurisprudence.

The *Cherokee Cases*

Three days after his inauguration in 1829, President Andrew Jackson used his first appointment to move his inherited postmaster general, John McLean, out of the cabinet and onto the Court. McLean had been in the cabinet for six years (beginning under Monroe). Married and used to living in the capital, he chose not to change these arrangements. This marked the end of all the justices boarding, eating, and socializing together during the Court's term, as Johnson, too, resolved to live separately. The result was a waning of Marshall's influence, although that was not immediately apparent.

Jackson's states' rights ideology could not have been to Marshall's liking. A little over a year into his presidency Jackson vetoed funds for the Maysville Road, a project entirely within Kentucky though reaching to the Ohio River. Jackson believed that internal improvements could be funded only if they aided national defense or were otherwise of a national benefit. In his notes about the bill, which would have allowed the federal government to own stock in the corporation, he wrote that this was "corrupting and must destroy the purity of our govt . . . [and] it must lead to consolidation and the destruction of state rights."[47] Like Monroe before him, Jackson rejected *McCulloch's* invitation to extend federal action as an improper interpretation of the Constitution. Indeed it would turn out that Jackson rejected *McCulloch* right down to its narrowest holding.

As Marshall passed his seventy-fifth birthday in 1830, the Court and

Georgia tangled again, and this time the president was not looking for the settlement the Court offered. As part of the federal purchase of Yazoo from Georgia, the government promised to extinguish all tribal land titles (to some 4 million acres) within the state. But despite years of complaining by Georgia, nothing yet had been done. The Cherokee declared themselves an independent nation and adopted a constitution in 1827, but in the same year gold was discovered on their land. From Madison on, all presidents had believed that the Indians, no matter how Americanized, had to move west of the Mississippi River both to provide lands for whites and to separate settlers from Indians (and thus save the Indians from extermination). But Andrew Jackson was a doer, and with four-fifths Southern support besting two-thirds Northern opposition, the Removal Act of 1830 made emigration the republic's official policy, whatever the Indians' feelings.

Georgia's first step toward acquiring the Cherokee's land was to assert jurisdiction over it; Jackson refused to intervene, claiming that he lacked "power to protect [the Cherokees] against the laws of Georgia."[48] After Georgia's assertion of jurisdiction, the state tried an Indian, Corn Tassel, for the murder of another Indian on reservation land. Corn Tassel obtained a writ so that the Court could hear his case. Georgia did not bother to argue its own or the Court's jurisdiction; it hanged him immediately. Instead of expressing outrage, the House of Representatives considered repealing Section 25 of the Judiciary Act, causing Story to despair that if it were repealed, "the Constitution is practically gone."[49] The Judiciary Committee reported favorably on repeal, but the House refused to go along.

Having been beaten politically at all levels, the Cherokee saw that their last, albeit faint, hope was the federal judiciary. Continuing its assertion that it was an independent nation (and therefore able to invoke the Court's original jurisdiction), the tribe sought an injunction against Georgia. Again Georgia quickly tipped its hand. It made no appearance, and governments that refuse to appear before the Court will also refuse to abide by an adverse judicial ruling. The Court ducked, with Marshall ruling for himself and McLean that the Indians were not an independent nation but instead a "domestic dependent nation"[50]— a phrase and concept created especially for the case. Therefore there was no original jurisdiction for the Court to hear the case. But as in *Marbury,* Marshall had something to say before dismissing the case, namely, that the Cherokee were right: "If courts were permitted to indulge their sympathies, a case better calculated to excite them can scarcely be imagined."[51] The relationship of the Indians to the federal government was like "that of a ward to a guardian."[52] The Indians "look to our government for protection; rely upon its kindness and its power; appeal to it for relief to their wants; and address the president as their great father."[53] A lot of good that did them. In an acid concurring opinion Johnson expressed the Jacksonian view that the Cherokee, being Indians, got what they deserved.

By chance, the Cherokee got one more shot, and again Georgia not only refused to appear but also announced in advance that it would ignore any adverse decision. One of Georgia's laws required a license for whites to enter onto Indian land. When missionaries were convicted under it and sentenced to four years at hard labor, Marshall for the Court overturned the convictions, concluding that the "whole intercourse between the United States and this nation is, by our constitution and laws, vested in the government of the United States."[54] Therefore Georgia's law was invalid. Story exulted, "Thanks be to God, the Court can wash their hands clean of the iniquity of oppressing the Indians, and disregarding their rights."[55] Nevertheless, the missionaries remained in prison since Georgia, as promised, ignored the decision. Jackson agreeably observed that the decision "fell stillborne."[56] He was entitled to his opinion and that result because, happily for him, the Court's judgment did not require the executive to do anything.

Jackson's opinion of Marshall's handiwork was transparent in his message accompanying his veto of the rechartering of the Bank of the

United States in 1832. The veto message pronounced the bill unconstitutional and brushed aside *McCulloch*. The Court, declared Jackson, "ought not control the coordinate authorities of this Government . . . The authority of the Supreme Court must not, therefore, be permitted to control the Congress or the Executive when acting in their legislative capacities." The Court should "have only such influence as the force of their reasoning may deserve."[57] And that, he soon made clear, was not much. Implicitly this applied to Marshall's holding in the missionaries' case, too.

Marshall had much to despair of in 1832. His health was failing; his beloved wife, Polly, had died several months previously; and with states' rights in the ascendant, he could wonder if his actions to promote a stronger Union had been in vain: "I yield slowly and reluctantly to the conviction that the Constitution cannot last. The Union has been prolonged thus far by miracles. I fear they cannot last."[58] The newly formed Whig Party under Henry Clay, supporting both the bank and internal improvements, was defeated by Jackson, who carried a majority of the states in both the North and the South.

Nullification

South Carolina then proceeded to fashion a miracle for Marshall. For four years, led by John C. Calhoun, Jackson's estranged vice president, South Carolina had been talking like the Jefferson and Madison of 1798. Outraged by the 1828 "Tariff of Abominations," which protected Northern manufacturers but did nothing for the agrarian South, South Carolina revived the issue of nullification. The state's leaders claimed that the tariff was unconstitutional because it protected Northern industry rather than raising revenue. As articulated by Calhoun, a state convention could declare a federal law void, and afterwards that law could be enforced within the state only if it were legitimated by an

Article V constitutional amendment. South Carolina's new governor, Robert Hayne, of the 1830 Webster-Hayne debates on the nature of the Union, intended to lead the nullification of the lower but still protective Tariff of 1832. In late November 1832 a newly elected state convention nullified the tariffs of both 1828 and 1832 and forbade taking an appeal of its decision from the South Carolina courts to the Supreme Court.

Nullification placed Jackson in an uncomfortable position. How could he support Georgia's flouting the Court while opposing South Carolina (as he intended to do)? First, he acted on the latter. Less than three weeks after South Carolina made its move, Jackson responded with a Nullification Proclamation that put the state on notice that he would use the military to enforce federal law. If he found it necessary to take such action, in its aftermath some traitors would be hanged. He also requested a Force Act to deal with the recalcitrant state.

Realizing that Jackson was serious, Calhoun, with an assist from Henry Clay, backed down. Congress in turn passed both the Force Act and a lowered schedule of tariffs. South Carolina stood down, but not before nullifying the Force Act (which gave federal district courts the right to issue writs of habeas corpus on behalf of prisoners who were held in state custody because they had enforced federal law) a purely symbolic action.

Jackson's performance was all Marshall and Story could have wanted. After a dinner at the White House, Story wrote that "the Chief Justice and myself have become his [Jackson's] warmest supporters, and shall continue so just as long as he maintains the principles contained in them. Who would have dreamed of such an occurrence?"[59] Nullification had managed simultaneously to make the Court's jurisprudence look good and to draw a states' rights president into supporting it. It was a double miracle.

Meanwhile, before Jackson asked for the Force Act, the problem with Georgia had dissipated. The two missionaries agreed to accept a pardon, and the governor immediately issued one. The missionaries were freed, so that problem was solved, though the Indians had obtained no real assistance from the Court. Whereas Yazoo had produced some winners, the *Cherokee Cases* did not. Presently, the Trail of Tears to Oklahoma would commence.

The End of an Era

Barron v. Baltimore in 1833 was Marshall's last constitutional case. It involved a deep-water wharf in Baltimore whose value was destroyed when the city paved streets, graded hills, and diverted streams, resulting in soil deposits in the harbor that rendered the wharf useless. The plaintiffs claimed that the city had taken their property for public use without just compensation, in violation of the Fifth Amendment. A jury awarded the plaintiffs $4,500, but a state appellate court reversed.

In language reminiscent of *Marbury*'s discussion of whether an act repugnant to the Constitution can become law, Marshall stated that the issue in *Barron* was important but not difficult. The Constitution was adopted by the people "for themselves, for their own government, and not for the government of the individual states."[60] Textually the amendments apply to the federal government. Furthermore, "[s]erious fears were extensively entertained that those powers which the patriot statesmen, who then watched over the interests of our country, deemed essential to union, and to the attainment of those invaluable objects for which union was sought, might be exercised in a manner dangerous to liberty."[61] Relying on this understanding of the Founding, Marshall correctly held that the Bill of Rights did not bind the states. Like all of Marshall's opinions that upheld state powers, *Barron* was short.

Marshall, now with but two years left to live, was presiding over a Court that could no longer issue constitutional decisions. The justices had agreed that no constitutional rulings would come down unless there were four votes in the majority (so as to guarantee that the full seven-justice Court could not overrule a decision). But with absences due to ill health, an increasingly divided Court could not find four justices who agreed on constitutional issues, and three important constitutional cases were left to be decided in 1837, after the composition of the Court dramatically changed. Johnson missed the entire 1834 term and died that summer. Gabriel Duval, already deaf, also missed much of that term and resigned before the 1835 term, leaving just five justices, and only Marshall and Story from before the 1820s.

Because of nullification, Jackson did not fill Johnson's seat with a South Carolinian. Instead he nominated James Wayne of Georgia, a staunch Unionist, who had been a state supreme court judge for five years as well as a Democratic congressman. His main qualifications were geography and the fact that he loyally supported Jackson on the bank and had opposed nullification.

To replace Duval, Jackson turned to Roger B. Taney, a superb lawyer from an aristocratic Maryland family who had freed the slaves he inherited. Taney had been Jackson's attorney general and had assisted with the message vetoing the bank. But when Jackson's secretary of the treasury refused an order to remove federal deposits from the bank, Jackson fired him and substituted Taney, who happily moved the federal funds to "pet" state banks. When Jackson finally submitted Taney's name to the Senate for confirmation to Treasury, he was instantly rejected. The same fate befell Taney's nomination to be Duval's replacement. Then Marshall died, opening a second vacancy.

Jackson, now in his last year as president, nominated Taney for chief justice, coupling him with Virginian Philip Barbour, another bank opponent, for Duval's seat. A new Senate, this time controlled by Democrats, confirmed both men. There was gloom among the Whigs. Daniel Webster reported that Story "thinks the Supreme Court is gone, and I think so too; and almost everything is gone or seems rapidly going."[62] Indeed Story thought that the Court "began with first-rate men for judicial trusts, and we have now got down to the thirdrate."[63] Seemingly it would get worse. Martin Van Buren succeeded Jackson, and Congress added two Western circuits, bringing the Court up to nine justices. All but Story were Democrats.[64]

· IV ·

The Sectional Crisis and the

Jacksonian Court

"SCARCELY ANY POLITICAL QUESTION arises in the United States that is not resolved, sooner or later, into a judicial question."[1] Alexis de Tocqueville's statement, however often quoted, is demonstrably false. In Jacksonian America the Supreme Court was not invited to participate in the great constitutional debates of the times. This is not to say it did nothing, for it announced constitutional limits on Congress a dozen times and struck down almost two dozen state statutes. The areas in which the Court acted were not that important—with the glaring exception of slavery, where Congress encouraged the Court to act. The Founding generation had put off the slavery question for their descendants. Thomas Jefferson had compounded the issue with the Louisiana Purchase. The Court fared badly as well.

Congress itself was not doing much outside of dealing with slavery, especially after the Mexican War. Again there was a single exception: in 1841 the Whig Congress twice passed bills creating a new national bank. A hostile Supreme Court, where by this time seven of the nine justices had been appointed by Andrew Jackson and Martin Van Buren, was waiting. Several justices had declared the bank unconstitutional before coming on the Court, and Daniel Webster for the Whigs and

Reverdy Johnson for the Democrats, both leading advocates at the Supreme Court bar, were convinced that the Court would overrule *McCulloch v. Maryland* and constitutionalize the small-government policies of Jefferson and Jackson. Joseph Story, the lone holdover from *McCulloch*, had already observed that "I am the last of the old race of Judges. I stand their solitary representative, with a pained heart, and a subdued confidence."[2] Worn out and intending to retire, he died shortly thereafter in 1845.

One of those who would have voted to overrule was Peter V. Daniel. Neither Jefferson nor Madison nor Monroe had placed a Virginia ideologue on the Court. But Van Buren did, with but a week left in his presidency, when he selected Daniel, a Richmond aristocrat who easily became the most ardent states' rights justice in the republic's history. Daniel and the others never got their chance at *McCulloch,* though. When William Henry Harrison died just a month after his inauguration as president, John Tyler assumed the presidency. More Virginian than Whig, he twice vetoed the rechartering of the bank, thereby preventing the matter from going before the Court.

With the exception of Story and, in the 1850s, Benjamin Curtis, all of the justices of the era were Jacksonian Democrats and believers in a limited federal government. Because of the geography of the circuit system, five were from slave states. But Southern control did not fully set the Court apart from the other branches of government. Between the Three-fifths Clause on representation and the internal rules of the Democratic Party, it was impossible to nominate a Democrat for president who was not acceptable to the South. (The Whigs won the presidency only twice, when they ran a war hero.) Still, the Missouri Compromise line, forbidding slavery in any new states above 36°30″ north latitude, created a long-term problem for the South. Arkansas had just gained statehood, and that exhausted the slave territory of the Louisiana Purchase; the only Southern territory was Florida, and once it was admitted, there would be no future slave states—unless the United

States acquired new territory or the Missouri Compromise line was repealed. Because of Northern population growth from immigration, the South, even with the Three-fifths Clause, had lost its grip on the House, and its hold on the Electoral College was therefore insecure. As slavery eroded in the border states and upper South and new states were carved out of the Louisiana Purchase, the Senate too would be in jeopardy.

Charles River Bridge

The Jacksonian Court had announced itself immediately when, in 1837, it decided the three constitutional cases that the Marshall Court could not. The form of announcement was through Story; he dissented in all three cases and twice claimed that the deceased Marshall had agreed with him. All three cases pointed toward future problems—banking and corporate rights, internal and external immigrations and state and national power, and contracts and transportation—but by far the most important was *Charles River Bridge v. Warren Bridge Company.*

Charles River Bridge involved several issues: corporate charters, the Contract Clause, and transportation. In 1785 the Charles River Bridge had been chartered to connect Boston with Charlestown. In 1792 the charter was extended until 1856, at which time the bridge would revert to the state. Decades of growth had left the bridge inadequate to handle the volume of traffic; they had also left it extremely profitable. The Massachusetts legislature in 1828 chartered a second bridge to be built less than a quarter of a mile from the existing structure—one that would become toll free in six years or earlier if costs were covered. (By the time of oral argument the Court was informed that the bridge had been paid off.)

The owners of the Charles River Bridge sued to prevent the competition, arguing that their charter created vested rights and that the commonwealth was impairing an implied condition that the state would not authorize a competing structure in close proximity. Otherwise, they claimed, investors would not be willing to put their money at risk in a project when the state could so readily sap its value. The Court was told that the value of the old bridge had been destroyed.

Charles River Bridge illuminated transportation changes in the young republic. First there were turnpikes, then canals, and soon railroads. Each new technology had the capacity to destroy (or at least diminish) the value of preexisting technologies. *Charles River Bridge* also exposed different property rights. The Charles River Bridge Company spoke of vested rights, although they were rights that were initially given by the government. The Warren Bridge represented entrepreneurial property, the gamble that enough money could be made in six years to justify the investment. In simple terms the case pitted stability against change. And Jacksonian America was about change. So, too, was the Court, through an opinion by Chief Justice Roger Taney.

There were two strands to Taney's opinion: "While the rights of private property are sacredly guarded, we must not forget that the community also have rights; and that the happiness and well-being of every citizen depends on their faithful preservation."[3] First, just as Marshall's opinion in *Providence Bank v. Billings* had held that an exemption from taxation would not be inferred in a corporate charter, so here an exemption from competition would not be inferred. Taney also noted that this was the English rule as well, and if the mother country was against monopolies, how could the more free and open United States support them? Second, there were policy implications to consider. To rule for the Charles River Bridge Company would retard progress, because what was truly at stake was whether railroad corporations would have to compensate turnpike companies.

Story wrote a long dissent, filled with discussion of English cases and concluding, "I stand upon the old law."[4] He too looked at policy implications, but his mercantilist beliefs assumed that investors had to be assured of enjoying the rewards of their success. This was the sole case in which Story did not invoke Marshall, although in a letter he lamented that "the future cannot be as the past."[5]

The losers raised the draw on the Charles River Bridge and let it stand idle. Then in 1841 the legislature paid $25,000 for the bridge (whose capitalized value had been ten times that twenty years earlier). Owning two bridges, the commonwealth imposed tolls on each.

Political Questions

A prime example of the Court not entering a political controversy without an invitation came in the aftermath of the Dorr Rebellion in Rhode Island. That state, along with Connecticut, had not drafted a constitution after Independence. Connecticut relented in 1818, but Rhode Island continued through the Jackson and Van Buren presidencies under its 1663 Charter, which not surprisingly limited suffrage to freeholders. When in 1841 a legislative effort at reform failed, Thomas Dorr, who had actively been seeking reform, called for a convention to draft a new constitution. That constitution was then ratified by a majority vote of all adult males, although supporters of the existing Charter Government boycotted the election. Dorr was subsequently elected governor under the freshly minted constitution. John Locke had defended, and the American revolutionaries had accepted, the idea of rejecting illegitimate authority and appealing to heaven by way of overthrowing it. But of course such appeals must be won, since the losers can never expect those they deemed illegitimate to accept the legitimacy of the losers' insurrectionary conduct. Dorr was to learn this lesson.

The Charter Government, controlled by Whigs, did not sit idly by as Dorr led his revolution. Naturally it refused to acknowledge the legitimacy of the new constitution or government and made participation in the new government illegal. After Dorr failed in an attempt to seize an arsenal in Providence, he fled the state. Rumors abounded that he would attempt to return with a military contingent. Thus the Charter governor asked President Tyler for troops to put down the likely insurrection. Tyler replied that if there was an insurrection, he would come to the government's aid, but until then it was the Charter Government's problem. The Charter Government completed Dorr's collapse by declaring martial law and arresting several participants in the rebellion.

Dorr was tried for treason against the state, convicted, and sentenced to life at hard labor. He sought habeas corpus from the Court, but was unanimously rebuffed by an opinion stating that the Court lacked jurisdiction to release a state prisoner held in state custody. Perhaps Dorr could take some solace from the fact that the Charter Government later allowed for the creation of a new constitution.

In a final attempt to win a judicial victory for the people who believed in the political theory that they could change their government as needed, a Dorrite sued for trespass a member of the militia who, acting on orders, had broken into his home without a search warrant. If the Charter Government had been superseded by Dorr's government, then those orders were of no effect. But what about all the other actions in the subsequent years?

Seven years after the ratification of Dorr's constitution and six after the demise of the Charter Government, the Court decided *Luther v. Borden*. Or rather it decided that it was improper to decide the case.

Taney's opinion began by announcing that all that had occurred in Rhode Island under its post-Charter constitution was at risk: "its taxes wrongfully collected; its salaries and compensation to its officers illegal paid; its public accounts improperly settled; and the judgments and sentences of its courts in civil and criminal cases null and void, and the officers who carried their decisions into operation answerable as trespassers, if not in some cases as criminals."[6]

"When a decision of this court might lead to such results, it becomes its duty to examine very carefully its own powers before it undertakes to exercise jurisdiction."[7] At this point, the answer became clear: the Dorrites had lost yet again.

The holding of *Luther v. Borden* was that there are some questions that a court just can't decide. Under Article IV, Congress is charged with guaranteeing to each state a republican form of government. To enforce that guarantee, Congress must necessarily decide whether the government is legitimate. Similarly, the president has statutory authority to direct military aid to suppress an insurrection. He, too, must make the decision that the government he is supporting is legitimate. To be sure, the people have the right to change their government at their pleasure. "But whether they have changed it or not by abolishing an old government, and establishing a new one in its place, is a question to be settled by the political power."[8] There are therefore some areas, dealing with questions deemed political, where for their own sake courts cannot tread. *Luther v. Borden* is exemplary of the modest judicial role of the era—slavery excepted. (Dorr was freed in 1845 after twenty months in jail; nine years later the legislature annulled his conviction, but he died that year at the age of forty-nine, his health having been broken during incarceration.)

Slavery Prior to the Jacksonian Court

For the Constitution's first three decades slavery was a dormant issue, with Congress easily outlawing the horrific international slave trade effective in 1808, as soon as the Constitution allowed. But the controversy commenced over Missouri's bid for statehood in 1819 when a provision was quickly offered to prohibit the further introduction of slaves into Missouri and subsequently to free all slaves born after statehood when they reached age twenty-five. Suddenly slavery stood center stage. Northerners saw the issue as tied into the Three-fifths Clause, whereby any new slave state would add to the South's numbers in both the House and the Electoral College. Rufus King wrote that if the

North lost on this issue, it would "[settle] forever the dominion of the Union. Not only the presidency, but the Supreme Judiciary, at least a majority of its members, will forever hereafter come from the Slave region. This is as fully understood, and almost avowed, as any future purpose."[9]

Northerners prevailed in the House but failed in the Senate, where the Southern-sympathizing (and slaveholding) Illinois senators voted with the South. The next year, Speaker of the House Henry Clay made admission of Maine as a Free State conditional on the admission of Missouri as a slave state. When this failed, the Missouri Compromise was offered: Missouri and Maine could be admitted, the former as a slave state, but only if slavery were "forever prohibited" in all other lands of the Louisiana Purchase north and west of Missouri.[10] Although the Missouri Compromise passed, both North and South had snarled at each other for well over a year, and all congressmen from the future Confederacy who spoke on the issue declared that banning slavery from any part of the Louisiana Purchase prior to its achieving statehood was unconstitutional. Northerners, by contrast, mistakenly saw the Missouri Compromise as a Southern victory. The intensity of the debate caused one congressman to opine that "[s]o eager has been the competition to obtain the floor that a modest man would hardly dare to rise among such a mob."[11] In such an overheated atmosphere, *McCulloch v. Maryland*'s recent offer of extensive federal power was an unwanted gift.

Subsequent to the Missouri Compromise, John Marshall, Story, and William Johnson on circuit had decided cases with implications for slavery. Most Southern states enacted a law providing for the jailing of any free Negro sailor while his ship was in port. The fear of another Santo Domingo, site of the only successful slave revolt (which had entailed extraordinary butchery), haunted Southern slaveholders, and immediately after crushing Denmark Vesey's plot for a slave uprising, South Carolina decided to protect itself against any future uprising by locking up Negro sailors until their ship departed lest they foment insurrection while in port. The master of the vessel was to pay for their keep, and if he did not, they would be sold into slavery to cover the humanitarian cost of feeding them. This was a blatant interference with commerce, which Great Britain protested again and again because it also violated treaties between the countries.

Johnson believed that the power to regulate commerce rested exclusively in the federal government, and hence the South Carolina law was unconstitutional. [12] His opinion caused a predictable uproar in South Carolina. The *Niles Register,* the South's leading newspaper, stated that the negative reaction was "no wonder; for self-preservation is said to be the be the first principle of law."[13] Disregarding Johnson's decision, South Carolina continued to jail any Negro seaman aboard a ship in its ports. Marshall was unsurprised. He would have expected the same from Virginia when he faced a similar issue, but he chose to duck the constitutional question, explaining to Story that "I am not fond of butting against a wall in sport."[14]

Monroe's attorney general William Wirt wrote an opinion agreeing that the South Carolina law was unconstitutional, but that was hardly the last word. Taney, while Jackson's attorney general, drafted an opinion declaring that the states had reserved to themselves the power to exclude people who posed a danger to their security; hence neither the commerce nor treaty powers could limit the states. Eventually James Buchanan, as James Polk's secretary of state, informed Great Britain that it should stop its incessant protesting, because any corrective actions were beyond federal power, and if the federal government did act, the Union would be dissolved.

Story's Boston was more sympathetic to attacks on slavery, and Story himself was an ardent enemy of the institution. He had publicly denounced extending slavery anywhere during the debates over Missouri statehood, but accepted the compromise after the fact. Sitting on a case involving the international slave trade, he condemned it as "repugnant to the great principles of Christian duty, the dictates of natural religion, the obligations of good faith and morality, and the eternal maxims of social justice."[15]

Yet in 1825, when the Marshall Court decided its most significant slavery case, not only did Marshall's caution prevail, but also Story and Johnson remained mute. The ship *Antelope* was captured off the Florida coast on suspicion of violating the prohibition against engaging in the slave trade. There were 280 Africans on board. Both Spain and Portugal claimed the Africans on behalf of their citizens, arguing that the American prohibition of the slave trade did not apply to them. The United States was a party to the case claiming freedom for the Africans.

Marshall found slavery contrary to natural law. Indeed, he wrote, this "will scarcely be denied. That every man has a natural right to the fruits of his own labour, is generally admitted; and that no other person can rightfully deprive him of those fruits, and appropriate them against his will, seems the necessary result of this admission."[16] But not all nations had outlawed the slave trade, and international law recognizes "the perfect equality of nations."[17] Therefore, Spanish and Portuguese allowance of the slave trade was on par with the American prohibition. Then Marshall ruled that international law controlled (to the decided detriment of the Africans). The reason for such a conclusion was that if positive law did not trump natural law, then all the slaves in the South would be free—an unthinkable conclusion prior to the Civil War.

Johnson joined the opinion, even though in *Fletcher v. Peck* he had observed that natural law would bind even the deity. It turned out, however, that natural law bound the deity and white men only when they were dealing with other white men. When they turned on Africans or Indians, natural law did not bind state governments.

The Court had given the Spanish and Portuguese governments everything they could have wanted and more on the law. But when it turned to the facts, the justices reverted to their hostility to slavery and awarded every African they could to the United States, since that meant they would be returned to Africa rather than dying as slaves.

With *The Antelope*, the Marshall Court justices bequeathed deference to slavery to their successors, because if slavery could trump natural law, it could trump anything. Furthermore, the Jacksonian justices, McLean and Curtis excepted, lacked their predecessors' moral revulsion to slavery. The change in the attitudes of the justices reflected a more general social change. Slavery was no longer defended as an inherent evil; rather, Southerners were beginning to defend it as a positive good, and they were tired of Northern complaints. In 1836 Southerners, with the aid of their three-fifths boost and a majority of Northern Democrats, imposed a gag rule in the House whereby all antislavery petitions were automatically tabled. The gag rule was then tightened four years later, by the same Southern votes, this time joined by a minority of Northern Democrats, to preclude even receiving an antislavery petition. The ostensible justification for overriding the Petition Clause of the First Amendment was that Congress lacked any power over slavery in the states. This consciously ignored the fact that most petitions dealt with the District of Columbia, where congressional power was express and exclusive (even if many Southerners would have held to the contrary).

Slavery Prior to the Mexican War

In the Jacksonian era, *United States v. Schooner Amistad* involved a captured ship with enslaved Africans aboard. The *Amistad* had been traveling from Havana to another port in Cuba when its slaves mutinied and killed several whites, leaving two alive to steer the ship back to Africa. After two months of sailing east by day and north and west by night, the ship was taken by the U.S. Navy off Long Island. At this point litigation commenced to determine the status of the Africans and the ship. Were they pirates and murderers, free men, or slaves? (And if slaves, who would get the proceeds from any sale?) Representing the Africans, John Quincy Adams made his first court appearance in thirty-two years, while his co-counsel argued that the United States lacked power to enslave anyone. In a noninflammatory opinion, intentionally ducking that argument, Story held that the Africans were free because they had been illegally kidnapped and taken to Cuba. This answered the question of piracy, since free men, fighting to regain their freedom, are not criminals.

The Amistad was a propaganda coup for abolitionists, who eventually raised the money to send the Africans home. Meanwhile, during their several administrations, presidents Tyler, Polk, Pierce, and Buchanan tried to wring compensation from Congress, which the Spanish government demanded. The Senate once voted the money; but a dying Adams, "pale and trembling . . . his voice . . . so weak" that he could barely be heard, condemned the appropriation, and at least in part because of this, the House refused to join the Senate.[18]

Alongside *The Amistad*, the Court had to decide the potentially explosive issue of how the interstate slave trade fit into the constitutional scheme. Robert Slaughter had entered Mississippi with a number of slaves, whom he then sold. This was in violation of Mississippi's new constitution, which prohibited the introduction of slaves into the state for sale. Mississippi may have been trying to maintain the value of slaves already there; more likely it was concerned about the practice of troublemaking slaves being "sold South." The Panic of 1837 ("panic" being the nineteenth-century name for an economic depression) made debt collection difficult, and Slaughter sued a defaulting buyer, who defended by arguing that the transaction was illegal and therefore he did not need to pay. In the not distant background were issues of congressional power over interstate commerce as well as state power to preclude commerce in slaves.

The majority finessed all the issues by concluding that the Mississippi constitutional provision was not self-executing, and without implementing legislation was unenforceable. Writing separately and reaching the constitutional issues, McLean and Taney—though they represented opposite wings on slavery—nevertheless wound up in the same place. McLean denied that slaves were an item of commerce; therefore the states were free to regulate slavery as they pleased. From his Northern perspective this meant that states could protect themselves "against the avarice and intrusion of the slave dealer [and] guard . . . against the inconveniences and dangers of a slave population." These rights of "self-preservation" were "higher and deeper than the Constitution."[19] From the Southern perspective, Taney agreed with McLean that Congress could not touch the interstate slave trade. The power was "exclusively with the several states [and] cannot be controlled by Congress either by virtue of its power to regulate commerce, or by virtue of any other power."[20]

Despite his moral revulsion to slavery, Story's last major opinion, *Prigg v. Pennsylvania* in 1842, ranks with Marshall's trumping of natural law in *The Antelope,* and just behind Taney's *Dred Scott* decision, as a major victory for the South in slavery cases. Edward Prigg was convicted under an 1826 Personal Liberty Law enacted to protect Negroes residing in Pennsylvania. Claiming that a mother and her children were runaway slaves, Prigg took them out of the state and into Maryland, where they were sold. Story held that Prigg was within his rights.

First, the Court found that the Fugitive Slave Clause was "fundamental."[21] Story thus gave the clause added stature among the provisions of the Constitution. He claimed (perhaps wrongly) that without the Fugitive Slave Clause, the South would not have ratified the Constitution, and that the clause must be interpreted with this in mind. He concluded that the clause clothed the slave owner with a right of self-help—that is, the right to abduct the fugitives and return them to the

South—that could be exercised in the North, as long as the slave catcher engaged in no "illegal violence."[22] In effect this legalized kidnapping Negroes at gunpoint.

Second, Story held that the Fugitive Slave Clause authorized Congress to pass implementing legislation. This was a leap, because the enumerated powers of Congress are in Article I and the Fugitive Slave Clause is in Article IV. Its language—"shall be delivered up on Claim"—implies action by states and says nothing about congressional authority, in contrast to all other sections in Article IV, which expressly authorize congressional action. The Court then held that states were barred from passing any laws on the subject of fugitive slaves whether such laws aided or hindered recapture. Finally, Story indicated that state officials could, if they wished, act in assistance to the federal law, but Northern opinion precluded such aid.

The consequences of *Prigg* were potentially enormous. All Negroes in the North, whether free or escaped, were placed at risk of being taken South. By authorizing self-help, the Court eliminated any hearing whereby the supposed runaways could prove mistaken identity or give other evidence that they were free. The facts of *Prigg*, which Story elided, offer sad commentary on its implications. There is no doubt that the mother, Margaret Morgan, had been born a slave. But there was considerable evidence that she was free when captured, and there is no doubt that at least one and perhaps all of her children were born free. Yet they were taken from their home, transported across a state line, and with their sale passed from the record of history. Pennsylvania's Personal Liberty Law had been enacted to deal with just such circumstances, yet the Court left the state and the free Negroes helpless.

There were more separate opinions in *Prigg* than in any other case up to the time, but again, those of Taney and McLean offer the starkest contrasts. Taney took issue with Story's conclusion that states could not pass statutes to aid recapture. He found no textual authorization for that interpretation and concluded that "on the contrary, it is enjoined upon them as a duty to protect and support the owner."[23] McLean rested on different text, the Fifth Amendment's guarantee of liberty: "[I]n a non-slave-holding state every person is presumed to be free, without regard of colour."[24] There had to be a judicial hearing to rebut that presumption. Therefore, according to McLean, self-help was unconstitutional.

Taney showed that the South did not get all it could have asked for, but it certainly got a lot. Story had feared the disruptive force of abolitionism more than he hated slavery, and *Prigg* was applauded a year later when the *North American Review* could speak of "the beneficial action of the Judiciary in quieting public contests and maintaining unruffled the majesty of the law."[25]

That was a snapshot of a social and legal landscape that was changing. *Prigg* exacerbated sectional feelings by making Northerners feel part of a dirty process. Northern courts became less willing to extend comity to Southerners in transit or sojourning with their slaves. Southerners, in turn, saw the North as unwilling to fulfill a constitutional duty.

Texas and Mexico

A major constitutional issue of the 1840s was the power to annex Texas. Slavery was the driving force behind the issue, and it caused people to flip constitutional positions. Democrats, especially Southern Democrats, who were skeptical of expanded federal powers, favored annexation, while Whigs, like Story himself, who had always supported the exercise of federal powers, believed that annexation was unconstitutional.[26] Story did not explain why or how he reconciled his position with Marshall's conclusion in *American Insurance v. Cantor* that the Constitution "confers absolutely on the government of the Union . . . the power of acquiring territory, either by conquest or by treaty."[27] He probably couldn't. The United States had previously acquired Louisiana, West Florida, and East Florida. Either those acquisitions were unconstitutional (as Jefferson had initially thought with Louisiana) or Story believed that their precedent did not extend to acquiring an independent nation. Daniel Webster, who had supported the earlier acquisitions but opposed annexation, unpersuasively explained that the former were driven by national necessity, while "[n]o such necessity" existed with Texas.[28]

President Tyler sent a treaty of annexation to the Senate in April 1844. Van Buren and Henry Clay, the likely presidential candidates, came out against it, and John Calhoun, Tyler's secretary of state, did it no good by defending it on proslavery grounds. Needing a two-thirds vote in the Senate, it could not even get one-third and went down 16–35. Tyler immediately proposed an end run around the Treaty Clause: "[T]he power of Congress is . . . fully competent in some other form of proceeding to accomplish everything that a formal ratification of the treaty could have accomplished."[29]

James Polk, an ardent expansionist, gained the Democratic nomination instead of Van Buren, and when he bested Clay, Tyler interpreted the election as validating his position on annexation. He again proposed avoiding the Treaty Clause by admitting Texas as a state by joint resolution (a real extension of Marshall's *Cantor* opinion). Whigs and antislavery Democrats were aghast, with some Whigs claiming that even if it passed, the joint resolution would be null and void. But after some modifications the resolution passed, 27–25 in the Senate (with three Southern Whigs joining the Democrats to form a majority), and 132–76 in the House. The Missouri Compromise line was extended to cover the northernmost part of Texas, but most important, by agreement between Texas and the United States, Texas had the right to divide itself in the future into five states, thereby potentially increasing the South's power.

The South had jumped its territorial limits. And because the president of Mexico had already informed the United States that annex-

ation would be the equivalent of a declaration of war, military hostilities were to be expected. That suited the slaveholding Polk just fine, for
he wanted to expand the South westward to California.

As a province of Mexico, Texas had its southern border at the
Nueces River (near present-day Corpus Christi). But the Republic of
Texas claimed the Rio Grande as its border with Mexico. Polk guaranteed his war when he ordered General Zachary Taylor to post his
troops just north of the Rio Grande. After Mexican troops attacked a
party of dragoons, Polk sent Congress a message declaring that as
"Mexico has passed the boundary of the United States, has invaded our
territory and shed American blood on American soil . . . war exists . . .
by an act of Mexico herself."[30]

Although some Northern Whigs, like Abraham Lincoln, believed
the war unconstitutional (because Polk's orders to Taylor were deemed
to have started the war), Congress voted the necessary authorization.
Then, just three months later, the House voted to adopt an amendment offered by Pennsylvania Democrat David Wilmot that would
ban slavery from any territories acquired from Mexico. No Southern
Democrat voted favorably on the measure, and only two Southern
Whigs did. The Wilmot Proviso arrived at the Senate just before ad-
journment, and no vote was taken. But slavery in the territories was on
the table. In an era marked by fairly strict party discipline, the Wilmot
Proviso had shattered it. The parties were created to argue economic
issues—the national bank, internal improvements, the tariff. Slavery,
or slavery in the territories, was sectional, and the parties were not
equipped to deal with it.

Both parties were national, but the Whigs were proportionately
stronger in the North than in the South, while the situation was reversed with the Democrats. Democrats were proslavery at heart, but
quietly so in order to accommodate their Northern brethren. The
Whigs had repressed discussions of slavery in hopes of growing their
Southern wing.

Over the course of the Mexican War the Wilmot Proviso was but one of several options articulated to deal with slavery in the territories. James Buchanan placed his presidential hopes on extending the Missouri Compromise line to the Pacific. With the Mexican Cession, extension would largely benefit the South. Lewis Cass, who won the Democratic nomination in 1848, articulated "popular sovereignty," whereby settlers would decide. John Calhoun claimed that the territories were held in trust for all Americans, and slavery could not be excluded prior to statehood. Each idea had a constitutional basis, and all but Calhoun's assumed that Congress had the power to determine the matter.

Slavery in the Territories

A possible compromise on the expansion of slavery into the territories was offered by Senator John M. Clayton of Delaware: say nothing, but allow any slave brought into a territory access to the federal courts, which would then determine the legal status of slavery. Clayton's idea was simple. By asking the federal courts to decide, Congress would be saved the incessant political fighting over an issue it seemed incapable of resolving, since the House, with its Northern tilt, supported the Wilmot Proviso while the more evenly balanced Senate rejected it. If the Court could take slavery off the political table, then the parties could resume their disputes over traditional economic issues. Moving slavery out of politics and into the courts prevailed in the Compromise of 1850 (admitting California as a Free State, organizing the New Mexico and Utah territories without reference to slavery, banning public slave trading in the District of Columbia, and creating a draconian Fugitive Slave Act). It was carried over into the Kansas-Nebraska Act of 1854 (leaving the question of territorial slavery to the settlers).

Turning slavery in the territories into a judicial matter offered something for everyone: ambiguity that sustained the hope of judicial victory and the opportunity to right the political system so that economic issues would determine elections. Moreover, the Jacksonian Court that would decide the question was a fully representative national institution. Of the nine justices, only two, Daniel and McLean, could be labeled extremists, the former rabidly proslavery, the latter adamantly antislavery.

The various parts of the Compromise of 1850 were hardly compromises. The South had given in on its hopes of extending the Missouri Compromise line to the Pacific and maintaining the slave trade in the District of Columbia, but in return got a new, more severe Fugitive Slave Act, which denied an alleged fugitive a jury trial and instead placed the claim before a commissioner who was afforded $10 if the fugitive was given to the claimant but only $5 if he was found to be free. As if that didn't stack the odds enough, the act also denied the fugitive the right to testify. The new act exposed free Negroes to kidnapping and slavery, and many Northern whites were outraged. Not coincidentally, *Uncle Tom's Cabin* sold 300,000 copies in 1852, one for every four votes president-elect Franklin Pierce received.

The Compromise of 1850 was an armistice, as most representatives and Senators voted strictly along sectional lines on each of the measures, with a small number voting for most of the measures. Nevertheless, there were celebrations, and in their 1852 platforms both the Democrats and the Whigs declared the Compromise of 1850 to be the final solution to slavery in the territories.

President Millard Fillmore, who had taken office on Zachary Taylor's death, had signed the compromise measures, and the Whigs denied him their nomination in 1852. Yet Winfield Scott, the candidate imposed by the Northern Whigs, could not even carry the North. As a result, Southern Whigs deserted the party, and this paved the way to its death in the 1854 elections after passage of the Kansas-Nebraska Act, when Southern Whigs again backed section over party. That law, organizing two new territories, repealed the Missouri Compromise line and instead substituted popular sovereignty, whereby the settlers would decide whether the future state would be slave or free. Pierce gave his benediction by noting that the Missouri Compromise line was part of a statute, "standing open to repeal, like any other act of doubtful constitutionality, subject to be pronounced null and void."[31]

Northerners were outraged by the repeal. They had come to believe that the line was sacrosanct; after all, the law stated that slavery was "forever prohibited" north of the line.[32] Northerners had accepted the Compromise of 1850 as a final solution and were decidedly unpersuaded by the Southern assertion that the Missouri line somehow violated the spirit of the more recent Compromise of 1850. First it was Texas, then the Compromise of 1850, and now Kansas-Nebraska. The Slave Power demanded, and Congress and the president gave.

Kansas-Nebraska, plus anti-Catholicism, resulted in Northern Democrats' being decisively defeated in the 1854 elections, where they lost sixty-six of their ninety-one House seats (and only seven of the forty-four who had voted for Kansas-Nebraska were reelected). Already in the 1840s both the Baptists and the Methodists had split along sectional lines because of disputes over slavery. The republic was dividing into two sections without national mediating institutions.

The Kansas-Nebraska Act also bequeathed the republic "Bleeding Kansas," where border ruffians from Missouri sacked the Free State stronghold of Lawrence, and then John Brown entered American history by leading his sons at Pottawatomie Creek, where they brutally murdered five proslavery settlers in retaliation. The South won the initial territorial legislature, but the North won the propaganda war. The same day as the sack of Lawrence, Representative Preston Brooks of South Carolina entered the Senate chamber and nearly smashed to death Massachusetts senator Charles Sumner for the latter's hostile criticisms of the South. "Bleeding Kansas" and "Bully Brooks" symbolized how the South viewed the North and made further Northern accommodation of the South impossible.

Democrats enjoyed a comeback in 1856 with the effective death of the Whigs, gaining control over both Houses as well as the presidency by nominating James Buchanan, who had been out of the country as ambassador to Great Britain. But the balance of the party shifted decisively to the South. In 1852 Franklin Pierce, like all presidents since Jackson's second term, had won a majority of states in both the North and the South. Buchanan, however, carried only five of the sixteen Free States. Together the Compromise of 1850 and the Kansas-Nebraska Act had killed the bisectional structure of political parties. The 1856 election saw the rise in the North of the Republican Party. Like the Democrats, the Republicans were racist, but they were adamantly against the extension of slavery both on moral grounds and because they did not believe that free whites should have to compete against slave labor. Unlike the Democrats (and the now deceased Whigs), the Republicans were purely sectional and therefore had a strong political interest in seeing that the controversy over slavery persisted.

The *Dred Scott* Decision

It was against the background of the disintegration of national institutions that the Court considered *Dred Scott v. Sandford*. Seemingly everyone thought that a judicial decision on slavery in the territories offered the best opportunity for the republic. Politicians as diverse as James Polk, Stephen Douglas, Jefferson Davis, and Henry Clay had favored it. Even the Whig-turned-Republican Abraham Lincoln did, publicly stating to an audience in Galena in the summer of 1856 that "the Supreme Court of the United States is the tribunal to decide such questions, and we will submit to its decisions; and if you do also, there will be an end of the matter."[33] Before his inauguration Buchanan encouraged Justices Robert Grier and John Catron to seek a broad ruling. When informed that an opinion holding the Missouri Compromise line "of non-effect" would be forthcoming,[34] he gladly bowed to the Court in his inaugural address, saying that slavery in the territories was "a judicial question which legitimately belongs to the Supreme Court of the United States, before whom it is now pending, and will, it is understood, be speedily and finally settled. To their decision, in common with all good citizens, I shall cheerfully submit, whatever this may be."[35]

Dred Scott was a slave who claimed his freedom on the basis of having lived with his master first in Illinois, where slavery was prohibited under the state constitution, and then in the Wisconsin territory, where slavery was prohibited by the Missouri Compromise. While there were several concurring opinions, the key was Taney's, and it decided three major constitutional issues, the last two being interrelated. First, Taney held that a descendant of African slaves could never become a citizen of the United States. Therefore Scott could not invoke diversity jurisdiction, where under Article III federal courts may hear suits between "citizens of different states." Taney effectively changed that language into "citizens of the United States residing in different states." Second, the Court determined that the territories were held in common for all Americans, and Congress lacked power to ban slavery in the territories. Therefore the Missouri Compromise line was unconstitutional. Third, *Dred Scott* held that if slaves were freed by operation of territorial law, this would effect a taking of the masters' property without due process of law. Taney also rejected Scott's time in Illinois on the established doctrine that the state of residence—Missouri—determined his status. The Free Soiler McLean and the Whig Curtis dissented on all points (and assumed that Taney spoke for a majority on citizenship even though only two others explicitly agreed). Although it is only speculation, it is likely that, just as in *Bush v. Gore* a century and a half later, the justices voted in the case as they voted for president.

History is written by winners, and Taney's result and his reasoning have been condemned by history. But at the time and until the

Civil War, Southerners had been winners, and Taney was busy writing Southern history. Believing that the question must be answered "according to [the Constitution's] true intent and meaning when it was adopted," Taney wrote that the Framers never intended that descendants of slaves could become citizens.[36] He was certain that all citizens had the right to arm themselves and was equally sure that the South would never allow free Negroes to do so. Ergo, Negroes could not be citizens. Thus, he asserted, when the Declaration of Independence invoked the inalienable rights of life, liberty, and the pursuit of happiness, it was "too clear for dispute that the enslaved African race were not intended to be included, and formed no part of the people who framed and adopted this declaration."[37] While seemingly true on its face, this was hardly dispositive; Taney ignored the fact that there were free Negroes who were citizens of at least five states between 1781 and 1787 under the Articles of Confederation.

Referring to all descendants of Africans, Taney stated that "they had no rights which the white man was bound to respect."[38] While Taney purported to be talking about the state of affairs in 1787, the language he used seemed to indicate the status of Negroes in 1857. Taney's theory stripped them of their citizenship from the moment the Constitution was ratified—hardly a likely outcome without express language to that effect. Taney's claim that this was all "[t]oo clear for dispute" was a gratuitous conclusion, and it went beyond what was necessary to hold the Missouri Compromise line unconstitutional.

Having concluded that Scott was not a citizen, the Court could have ended the case right there. But following Buchanan's desire for a broad ruling, Taney turned to the Missouri Compromise line. Banning slavery could be justified under Article IV, Section 3, giving Congress the power to "make all needful Rules and Regulations respecting the Territory" of the United States, or as attached to the war-making or treaty powers. Taney instead found them all inapplicable, arguing that "Territory" meant the territory that the United States already owned in 1787, not that which was acquired later. To remedy the defect he had just created, Taney held that a different part of Article IV, Section 3—the ability to admit new states—governed. The United States, he concluded, could not be like Great Britain. Having escaped colonial bondage, the country could not hold colonies. The United States was a trustee, "charged with the duty of promoting the interests of the whole people of the Union."[39] This meant that all the people of the country were free to bring their property and settle. Once settlers could govern themselves, they must be allowed to do so, but with a proviso: Congress could not authorize a territorial government to exercise powers that Congress did not have.

Taney offered little reasoning on the due process issue. He simply asserted that a statute that deprives a citizen of property "merely because he came or brought his property into a particular Territory . . . could hardly be dignified with the name of due process of law."[40] A law taking property from A (the master) and giving it to B (the slave) was the quintessential constitutional violation in antebellum America. The point was so obvious that Taney offered little reasoning beyond the fact that the federal government could not violate the Bill of Rights. If Congress could not do this, could a territorial government created by Congress? No again, Taney said. Then what about a state? Could a slave owner take his slaves into a Free State and live there? The question was not presented, and Taney did not answer it. In such a case Taney could fall back on *Barron v. Baltimore* and note that the Due Process Clause applies only to the federal government. But what if he did not? Lincoln would always stoke Republican fears about a *Dred Scott II* wherein the Court would declare that a slave owner could take and use his property in any state.[41] Harking back to Andrew Jackson, Republicans protested against any claim that the Court could bind other branches of government.

If Taney's reasoning in *Dred Scott* was not his best, holding the recently repealed Missouri Compromise line unconstitutional was nevertheless defensible. With so many responsible politicians pushing the justices to act because politicians no longer could, it would have been irresponsible for the justices to announce that it wasn't really their problem. To have done so would have been abdication. And once they were going to reach the merits, only one outcome was possible, because the justices were Democrats and because the Democrats' solution was the only viable national political solution (even though it might make future sectional compromises extraordinarily difficult).

The Court has been roundly condemned for 150 years. But to appease its subsequent critics, the Court would have had to sustain the Missouri Compromise line and free the Scotts. That would be conceivable only if the four Northern justices were joined by the Georgia nationalist James M. Wayne. As a result of that hypothetical 5–4 decision, the South would likely have abandoned the Union under Buchanan— and with impunity. Although Buchanan believed that secession was illegal, he also believed that the national government could not prevent it by force. If *Dred Scott* had been decided the other way and the South seceded, the United States as we know it would not exist.

Taney clearly overreached twice. Once was his absurd holding that no descendant of slaves could ever be a citizen, however well that played to racism in America. The other was in his dictum that a territorial legislature could not forbid the importation of slaves. This was Calhoun's position in his later years, but not that of Douglas and Cass, speaking for the party's Northern wing. Taney was a moderate from Maryland who had years before freed his own slaves and was proud of their accomplishments in freedom. But Northern holier-than-thous repelled him (as they repelled other Southern moderates) into the embrace of the doctrine of the Southern fire-eaters.

The Aftermath to *Dred Scott*

Despite the fact that it meant siding with the Southern wing, all Democrats embraced *Dred Scott*. It took slavery off the table and placed it under the Constitution, where they thought it belonged. Most Northern Democrats, delighted that the Court had validated the Kansas-Nebraska Act, simply ignored Taney's dictum on the powers of a territorial legislature. One who didn't was Stephen Douglas, who squared *Dred Scott* with his notion of popular sovereignty by noting that the right to import slaves would be "barren and worthless . . . unless sustained, protected and enforced" by laws that "must necessarily depend upon the will and wishes of the people of the Territory."[42] This was the Freeport Doctrine articulated by Douglas so as to reconcile *Dred Scott* with the squatter sovereignty of the Kansas-Nebraska Act. By 1860 it was anathema in the South, but in 1857 Douglas's speech was favorably received there; indeed, several prominent Southern Democrats, including soon-to-be House Speaker James L. Orr of South Carolina, had offered similar thoughts in 1856. Although the implications of *Dred Scott* would split the Democratic Party, that was in the future. In 1857 Democrats rallied around *Dred Scott* in the face of Republican attacks on the Court. Perhaps surprisingly, *Dred Scott* gave the Republicans no converts. In Northern state elections in the fall, Democrats gained votes in every state and reversed their losses from the previous year.

Dred Scott was a direct attack on the existence of the Republican Party. The only position uniting Republicans was the belief that slavery must be contained by banning it in the territories. After *Dred Scott* the Republicans could achieve their goal only by constitutional amendment, an impossibility because of the requirement of ratification by three-quarters of the states. Not surprisingly, the Republicans took the Court's order badly; instead of surrendering, they chose to fight, with party leader William Seward calling *Dred Scott* a "judicial usurpation [that] is more odious and intolerable than any other among the manifold practices of tyranny."[43] Yet even Susan B. Anthony acknowledged the opinion's merit, albeit in a backhanded way: "Judge Taney's decision, infamous as it is, is but a reflection of the spirit and practice of the American people, North as well as South."[44] She understood well the racism endemic in the North, where four Free States went so far as to ban Negroes from residence.

Republicans saw *Dred Scott* as intertwined with the annexation of Texas, the war with Mexico, the Fugitive Slave Act, and the Kansas-Nebraska Act. Southerners—once it was clear that the Republicans were not going to disband—saw Republican opposition to *Dred Scott* as treasonous, nothing less than a frontal attack on the Constitution. Yet as a practical matter, *Dred Scott* did nothing for slavery and much against it. Unless some Caribbean island was annexed, Kansas was the last possible slave state. And in the months following the decision, the slave population of Kansas declined.

Nevertheless, Southern Democrats wanted proof of the fealty of the Northern wing of the party, and statehood for Kansas was it. Proslavery legislators in Kansas, who themselves had been elected when Missourians flooded across the border to vote, overrode the governor's veto and authorized both a census and an election for a constitutional convention. Sensing a fix, Free State settlers boycotted. The predictable result was a fraud, and one giving a solid majority to proslavery delegates. Meeting at Lecompton, they produced a constitution that protected slavery and forbade any amendment of the slaveholding clause for seven years. They then authorized a referendum that allowed voters only the choice between that constitution and one that would bar the future introduction of additional slaves. Thus the voters were offered no vote against slavery. Furthermore, the election would be supervised by the same officials who had supervised the rigged vote for the convention. The governor, a Southerner who believed Kansas was inevitably to be free, headed for Washington to oppose the constitution.

Before the referendum, elections for the territorial legislature were held, and Free Staters prevailed. Nevertheless, the Free Staters boycotted the vote on Lecompton, and the slavery version of the proposed constitution prevailed with six thousand votes, while there were fewer than six hundred for no importation. The new antislavery territorial legislature called for its own vote, a simple up or down, on Lecompton, and with proslavery voters abstaining, the constitution was defeated by over ten thousand votes.

Amazingly, President Buchanan announced that Kansas was as much a slave state as South Carolina. Reneging on an earlier commitment to support a referendum on the constitution, he recommended admission under Lecompton, demonstrating *The Federalist*'s observation that "[e]nlightened statesmen will not always be at the helm."[45] Buchanan had the votes in the Senate, but it was too much for Northern Democrats in the House to stomach. If Lecompton was the price to be paid for staying in the Democratic Party, Northern Democrats could not pay it and survive. Lecompton had to be resubmitted to the Kansas voters, where it was finally defeated by a six-to-one margin.

Lecompton left everyone angry. Southerners felt that they had been cheated out of a slave state by the deserting Northern Democrats. Some, like James H. Hammond of South Carolina, expressed the view that if Lecompton was rejected, "let it [the Union] perish in blood and fire."[46] John P. Hale of New Hampshire had used similar language— "resist to blood and to death"—but he was talking of carrying out *Dred Scott* by forcing Lecompton on Kansas.[47] The administration newspaper labeled Douglas, who led the opposition to Lecompton, a traitor. Northern Democrats in turn were furious at being pushed so hard to validate a fraud when retribution at the polls would surely follow. And it did. Republicans routed Democrats in the North, reducing them to just thirty-two House members and demonstrating as well how a Republican could win the presidency in 1860 without the South.

That summer Lincoln and Douglas engaged in the most famous debates in American history as each tried to secure one of Illinois's seats in the Senate. The debates centered on popular sovereignty, the meaning of *Dred Scott*, the role of the Court, and the morality of slavery. Lincoln bettered Douglas on the former. Popular sovereignty was unconstitutional under *Dred Scott;* it may have been dictum, but the opinion's logic offered no alternative. Only with the achievement of statehood—if even then—could a legislature forbid slavery. Douglas's answer, which he had given the year before, was the so-called Freeport Doctrine: "Those police regulations [necessary to protect slavery] can only be established by the local legislature, and if the people are opposed to slavery, they will elect representatives to that body who will by unfriendly legislation effectually prevent the introduction of it into their midst."[48]

The debates followed Lincoln's "House Divided" speech, and Lincoln continued with that conspiracy theme, as well as Douglas's moral indifference to slavery. According to Lincoln, "Stephen [Douglas], Franklin [Pierce], Roger [Taney], and James [Buchanan]" were conspiring together to nationalize slavery.[49] Because slavery was evil, it must be headed for "ultimate extinction."[50] But the conspirators had another idea. "We shall lie down pleasantly dreaming that the people of Missouri are on the verge of making their state free; and we shall awake to the reality, instead, that the Supreme Court has made Illinois a slave state."[51] Lincoln spelled out the bleak future he foresaw. States, like territories, had to respect private property. Therefore, under *Dred Scott,* as to be extended in an anticipated *Dred Scott II,* slaveholders would have the right to take their slaves into Free States and reside therein.

In an ironic reversal of positions, Lincoln sounded like the descendant of Jefferson and Jackson, while Douglas embraced the judiciary like a Federalist. Douglas asserted that Lincoln wanted to take an appeal from the Supreme Court to "a Republican caucus sitting in the country," and that this would put everyone's property or personal rights in jeopardy.[52] Lincoln responded that he would not take Dred Scott from his master, but he would vote in favor of prohibiting slavery in the territory if he had the chance.

Dred Scott removed Lincoln from his prior "cheerfully submit" mode to one of rule or ruin: "We will try to reverse that decision . . . Somebody has to reverse that decision, since it is made, and we mean to reverse it."[53] But that was Douglas's point; how could it be reversed except by appointing new judges? "Well let us see how that is going to be done . . . Why, the Republican President is to call up the candidates and catechize them, and ask them, 'How will you decide this case if I appoint you judge?'"[54] Lincoln had no answer except to explain again that he would "respect . . . judicial" authority, but would not follow *Dred Scott* as a political rule.[55] Whatever political power was available would be used to reverse the case, and he quoted Jefferson on the dangers of setting judges as the "ultimate arbiters of all constitutional questions."[56] That would place Americans under "the despotism of an oligarchy . . . in office for life, and not responsible . . . to the elective control."[57] Douglas worried about confidence in the courts if there was a policy of political overruling. Lincoln, like Republicans a century and a half later, cared more about actual results (which is not to imply that Democrats do not).

Slavery drove everything before it. Lincoln and Douglas were not the only ones reversing intellectual positions. Some Northerners were now advocating nullification of the Fugitive Slave Act of 1850. In a pair of cases involving the abolitionist editor Sherman Booth, who led a mob that rescued a runaway slave from jail and then aided his escape to Canada, the Wisconsin Supreme Court held the Fugitive Slave Act unconstitutional and issued writs of habeas corpus that released Booth from custody—the second writ being issued after Booth had already been convicted. What Wisconsin did was truly extraordinary; after all, the Court itself had stated in Dorr's case that it lacked jurisdiction to free a state prisoner. Yet the Wisconsin court claimed it could free a federal prisoner. And in one sense it was right, because doing so was easy. There was no federal jail in Wisconsin, and Booth was being held in a state jail.

When the United States appealed to the Supreme Court, the clerk of the Wisconsin court was ordered to forward no papers to Washington, and Booth ignored the Court as well. That did not deter a unanimous Court from reversing. Taney noted that if Wisconsin's judges possessed the jurisdiction the state claimed, then it had to come from either the federal government or the state, and "it certainly has not been conferred upon them [the states] by the United States."[58] Wisconsin was sovereign within its own territory "to a certain limited extent, yet that sovereignty is limited and restricted by the Constitution."[59] To rule otherwise would "subvert the very foundations of this government."[60] To prevent settlement "by force of arms," it was necessary to have a tribunal with the power of authoritative settlement.[61] The Wisconsin judges had sounded like Calhoun, while Taney, in another reversal, now echoed Marshall and Story.

Despite the fervent hopes of politicians of all stripes during the first half of the 1850s, there was no judicial solution available for the slavery problem. Taney had failed; if Marshall had been alive, he would have failed. Slavery had passed out of politics and could not find a home in constitutional jurisprudence, so the country lurched into nation destroying and creating—and war.

In late 1859, in the wake of John Brown's raid at Harper's Ferry, Buchanan delivered his State of the Union message. He expressed fear over the North-South split and congratulated the Court on its "final settlement" to the slavery conflict.[62] As usual, he was wrong. The final settlement would not come for another six years, to be preceded by a forthcoming split at the Democratic Convention that would lead to two Democratic candidates running for president and the consequent victory of Lincoln, which in turn would be followed by civil war. The final settlement of the slavery issue came with Secretary of State William Seward's announcement that the Thirteenth Amendment—abolishing slavery everywhere—had been ratified.

· V ·

Civil War and Reconstruction

THE SOUTH CONTINUED with its Lecompton no-compromise mode. It refused to accept Stephen Douglas as the Democratic nominee for the presidency. Thus in 1860 there were two elections for the republic's 303 electoral votes: one in the South that was irrelevant because it lacked a majority of electoral votes and another in the North for 169 electoral votes and the presidency. Abraham Lincoln, the sectional candidate of a sectional party, won the Northern election handily while receiving less than 40 percent of the national popular vote. The two Democrats, Douglas and the Southern candidate John Breckinridge, running independently of each other, won a higher percentage of the popular vote than James Buchanan had four years earlier, but the votes for Douglas, the only national candidate, were too dispersed. Hence Lincoln prevailed in the Electoral College.

Previously both the Democrats and Whigs, as national parties, had to take account of Southern interests; the Republicans, as a Northern party, did not. Lincoln was expressly committed to overruling *Dred Scott* by appointing only justices likewise committed to doing so. Under Lincoln's view the South was destined for permanent minority status. His recent Cooper Union address had made this clear; the North would tolerate and protect slavery in states where it already existed, but it could not be expanded.[1]

The Deep South had had it with the North and refused to accept Lincoln as president (even though its actions in splitting the Democrats had made him president). It did not wait for his inauguration before seceding. The lame-duck president James Buchanan believed that secession was unconstitutional; paradoxically, he claimed that he was powerless to do anything more than hold two forts that could be provisioned by sea, even though he had acted with dispatch to put down John Brown's raid on the arsenal at Harper's Ferry. The contrast with Andrew Jackson's forceful stand against nullification could not have been starker. William Seward aptly characterized Buchanan's position as "no state has the right to go out of the Union—unless it wants to."[2]

Lincoln also believed that secession was unconstitutional, because the Articles of Confederation had created a "perpetual" Union that the Constitution made "more perfect."[3] Unlike his predecessor, Lincoln maintained that he had a duty to act, for "if destruction of the Union by one or by a part only of the States be lawfully possible, the Union is less perfect than before the Constitution, having lost the vital element of perpetuity."[4] Lincoln's views, combined with South Carolina's actions at Fort Sumter, led the upper South to join the lower in the Confederacy.

The South had ready answers to Lincoln. First, the Declaration of Independence enshrined the inherent right of the people to alter or abolish their government. Second, as Senator Judah Benjamin of Louisiana noted in his farewell speech to the Senate, through Article VII the Constitution had come into existence when nine states seceded from the Articles of Confederation. Third, the Virginia and Kentucky Resolutions of 1798 held that the Constitution was a compact among sovereign states which every state must construe for itself. The North had breached the compact by undoing the constitutional understanding not only that slavery must be tolerated but also that decisions on slavery could not be made without Southern acquiescence. Worse, the new president was committed to changing the Constitution by packing the Court with yes-men. It was time to go.

Secession left the Republicans in charge of both the House and the Senate. Just as the South had had it with the North, some Republicans in turn had had it with the Court; as one of them explained, while the Constitution says there must be one Supreme Court, it does not say that it must be this one. But there was little need for dramatic measures, as Lincoln could begin the transformation through new appointments. Peter Daniel had died in 1860, and Buchanan had delayed too long in naming a successor; his nominee had failed by a single vote. Then, in the spring of 1861, John Campbell resigned to return to Alabama, and John McLean died. Moreover, three elderly Southern justices—Roger Taney at eighty-four, William Catron a year younger, and James Wayne at seventy-one—were still on the Court but offered the promise of vacancies in the near future. For the present, after Lincoln filled the three existing vacancies, there would be, for the first time, a Northern majority on the Court. His three appointees were Midwest Republicans: Noah Swayne, David Davis, and the first judge from west of the Mississippi, Samuel Miller from Keokuk, Iowa.

Constitutional Questions of the War

Taney had stayed on the Court because there was no place for him to go. In 1861 he wrote to Franklin Pierce and expressed his hopes for a quick and reasonably peaceful separation.[5] He also did his part to promote that separation. The quickest possible solution to the war was for the South to capture Washington, D.C., and the government officials therein, and to that end, Marylanders sympathetic to the South blew up railroad bridges to prevent the movement of troops and supplies into the capital. One was John Merryman, a prominent farmer, state legislator, officer in the state militia, and ardent secessionist. Lincoln had quickly declared martial law in Maryland, and at 2 o'clock one May night Merryman was arrested, taken to Fort McHenry, and charged with treason for participating in the destruction of railroad bridges.

Because of his social and political standing, Merryman had immediate access to counsel, and his attorney petitioned for a writ of habeas corpus from Taney. When General George Cadwalader ignored the writ, Taney sat down and wrote an opinion in the case for delivery to Lincoln.[6] The strongest part of Taney's opinion was the claim that Lincoln was exercising a power that even George III had not had and never claimed. When the mayor of Baltimore congratulated him on preserving the integrity of the writ, Taney responded, "I am an old man, a very old man, but perhaps I was preserved for this occasion."[7] His opinion was applauded by Democrats in the North, loved by secessionists, and ignored by Lincoln. (Merryman was subsequently indicted on charges of treason by a grand jury, released on bail, and never tried. Late in the war, Merryman's wife gave birth to a boy whom they named Roger Brooke Taney Merryman.)

The Confederacy's failure to capture Washington as well as thoroughly defeat the Union army quickly meant that an easy ending to the war would not be achieved. To prepare for a longer war, the government abandoned Jacksonian notions of limited government. By 1865 the Union would do what the federal government had never done before: impose courts-martial for civilians, employ large-scale conscription, emancipate slaves, adopt an income tax, and print paper money ("greenbacks"). All of these actions raised constitutional questions.

Yet only one constitutional question about wartime policies was decided by the Court during the war itself. In the *Prize Cases,*[8] the Court ruled that Lincoln had acted constitutionally by immediately blockading Southern ports and capturing ships trying to run the blockade. Faced with arguments that there was no power to declare war on a state and that, in any event, the war powers rested in Congress, the majority announced that the "President was bound to meet [the war] in the shape it presented itself, without waiting for Congress to baptize it with a name; and no name given to it by him or them could change the fact."[9] Ominously, the vote was 5–4, with Taney and Catron being joined by two doughfaces—a label first used during the debates over Missouri's statehood that signified Northern men of Southern principles—in dissent.

Taney believed that all the Union actions to win the war were unconstitutional. In his conclusion that the Emancipation Proclamation was unconstitutional Taney had company: retired justice Benjamin Curtis, the principal *Dred Scott* dissenter, agreed with him, as did Samuel Nelson and Nathan Clifford, the doughface dissenters in the *Prize Cases.* Taney wrote draft opinions holding both conscription and paper money unconstitutional, too, but never had the opportunity to deliver any of them. When Congress passed the income tax and 3 percent of his salary was withheld, Taney wrote a letter to Secretary of the Treasury Salmon Chase protesting that the tax was unconstitutional. He received no reply. Rather than impeach Taney, as Jeffersonians might have, the Republicans made a conscious decision to ignore him. This would leave the Court intact when the Republicans took control—which would be soon if they prevailed in the 1864 elections.

Between argument and decision in the *Prize Cases,* Congress added California and Oregon to the circuit system and thus created the need for a tenth justice. In keeping with his policy of offering high positions to War Democrats, Lincoln selected Stephen J. Field, a transplanted New Yorker who was chief justice of the California Supreme Court. Then, just three weeks before the 1864 election, the eighty-seven-year-old Taney died. Antislavery Republicans wanted Salmon Chase named to the position, and even though Chase had thought he could wrest the presidential nomination from Lincoln—and had been shocked when Lincoln accepted his resignation from the Treasury—

Lincoln acceded to the views of the antislavery wing of his party. Furthermore, Chase, the "abolitionist attorney general," fit Lincoln's expressed desire for a "Chief Justice who will sustain what has been done in regard to emancipation and the legal tenders."[10] Chase's appointment left the ten-person Court evenly split between appointees of Lincoln and those of his Democratic predecessors, although six of the justices were Democrats (because of Lincoln's appointment of Field). Chase's was the last appointment for five years, as Congress in 1866, with the Court's support, reduced the number of justices to seven as future vacancies occurred.

After the *Prize Cases* the Court found that it lacked jurisdiction with regard to courts-martial of civilians and legal tender, areas that offered an opportunity to decide wartime issues while the war was still on. Clement Vallandigham, the most prominent Northern Democrat supporting the Confederacy, had denounced the "unnecessary" war and urged resistance to the use of courts-martial. The Union's commanding general in southern Ohio ordered Vallandigham arrested and tried by court-martial for aiding the enemy. After conviction Vallandigham was sentenced to detention for the remainder of the war. Lincoln instead ordered him released behind Confederate lines. An effort at habeas failed because he was no longer in custody (and habeas, a writ requiring those detaining someone to justify the detention, necessarily demands custody);[11] and a subsequent effort to have the Court review the record failed because there was no jurisdictional statute authorizing it.[12]

Where there was a statute authorizing jurisdiction, the Court misconstrued it. In *Roosevelt v. Meyer* the Court claimed that because a New York state court had sustained the Legal Tender Act, the Court had no jurisdiction to review. It was true that one part of Section 25 of the Judiciary Act limited jurisdiction to cases where a federal statute was invalidated, but another part authorized jurisdiction in cases such as this, a decision against a right claimed under the Constitution. Roosevelt, a prewar power in Tammany Hall and Teddy's great-uncle, claimed that the Constitution allowed him to refuse payment in paper money, but that claim was rejected. The Court ducked because the justices would have found paper money unconstitutional, and the Republicans would have, at best, ignored the decision.

After Lincoln

Once the war was over, the dominant question was what to do about the South. For eight months after Lincoln's assassination, Andrew Johnson, a War Democrat from Tennessee, was fully in charge. His policy was the Constitution of 1860, minus slavery. But once the Thirty-ninth Congress, elected with Lincoln in November 1864, met for the first time in December 1865, there were competing ideas. Ready to participate in that session were generals and congressmen from the Confederacy; Alexander Stephens, the vice president of the Confederacy, had been elected to the Senate. Johnson was uneasy, noting that there was "something like defiance, which is all out of place at this time."[13]

Because of the Thirteenth Amendment, ex-slaves would be counted as full persons, and the South stood to gain thirteen additional seats in the House. The *Richmond Examiner* cooed that with the next census "political power of the country will pass into the hands of the South, aided, as it will be, by Northern alliances."[14] The Republicans, however, would not cede power any sooner than necessary. The names of the Southern representatives were not even read, and thus they were not seated. As a result, Republicans had a veto-proof majority, should it prove necessary, in both Houses. It did in fact prove necessary, as Johnson believed that the Southern states, having been restored by presidential policies with the requirement that they ratify the Thirteenth Amendment, were entitled to equal status within the postwar Union. After all, their participation in the ratification of the amendment had been essential to getting the requisite three-quarters of the states (because of slavery in the border states that remained in the Union). But as Ohio's John Bingham declaimed, the Democrats gave "aid and comfort to the rebellion," and now "the Republic, sir, is in the hands of its friends, and its only safety is in the hands of its friends."[15] That meant Southern Democrats would be excluded indefinitely from Congress.

While Congress convened, so did a majority of Southern legislatures, and their first order of business was the question of what to do about the freed slaves. The universal answer was to adopt "Black Codes," sets of statutes systematically regulating employment. Freedmen were required by law to obtain labor contracts and to fulfill them or be subject to criminal penalties. In practice, wages were not negotiated but set by the employer. Those who did not have contracts were deemed "vagrants" and could be sold as contract laborers to whites, who would pay their fine. When authorities believed that parents could not support their children, the children could be forced into apprenticeships. All in all, the Black Codes created serfdom by another name.

Republicans wanted proof that Southerners accepted the results of the war. Instead there were tales of the South's unwillingness to protect the freedmen as well as dispatches from a correspondent from the *Nation* reporting on an unrepentant South willing to accept only that the North had prevailed by superior force. If there had been doubts about the need for the North to impose terms for the settlement of the war, the Black Codes, illustrating the white South's unwillingness to acknowledge defeat, eliminated them.

Congress responded to the situation in the South by extending the Freedmen's Bureau and passing the Civil Rights Act of 1866, guaranteeing the freed slaves the same civil rights that whites enjoyed in their respective states. In 1862, despite *Dred Scott*, Congress had outlawed slavery in the territories; the Civil Rights Act continued the legislative gutting of *Dred Scott* by declaring the freed slaves to be citizens of the

United States. Johnson vetoed both acts on constitutional grounds, concluding that they were illegitimate because of the exclusion of the South. The Senate did not override on the Freedmen's Bureau, but both Houses overrode the second veto. With that override Congress signaled its intent to shape Reconstruction in the South.

The Fourteenth Amendment

Although the Civil Rights Act had been passed pursuant to the Thirteenth Amendment, a number of Republicans, not to mention Democrats, were uneasy with its constitutional underpinnings and believed that another constitutional amendment was necessary to put congressional power beyond question. Furthermore, there were other important questions from the war that needed resolution. The newly formed Joint Committee on Reconstruction drafted the Fourteenth Amendment to place the results of the war beyond ordinary politics (and a potential future Democratic Party majority).

The proposed amendment came in five sections. The first overturned *Dred Scott* by declaring that all persons born in the United States were citizens. It then went on, in its most portentous clause, to forbid the states from abridging the privileges and immunities of United States citizens. It also copied the Fifth Amendment's Due Process Clause and borrowed from Andrew Jackson's bank veto message to forbid the states from denying to any person equal protection of the laws. Section 2 dealt with the end of the Three-fifths Clause by providing that should states not enfranchise adult males, their representation would be reduced accordingly. Section 3 disqualified former members of Congress from holding office if they had participated in the rebellion, although Congress could lift the ban by a two-thirds vote. Section 4 guaranteed the Union debt and voided that of the Confederacy. Finally, Section 5 gave Congress the power to enforce all of the other provisions. Eventually the ex-Confederates accepted the Fourteenth

Amendment as willingly as the Germans would agree to the Treaty of Versailles fifty years later.

The amendment received the necessary two-thirds votes in each House in June 1866 and went to the states. Because a number of Northern states were unwilling to permit Negroes to vote, Section 2 would affect those states adversely. Thus gaining the necessary three-fourths for ratification in the North alone (and deeming the South an irrelevancy) was a political impossibility. To be ratified, the amendment—which in effect was the peace treaty ending the war—needed solid Southern support.

Johnson told the unreconstructed South what it wanted to hear: do not ratify; the process is unconstitutional. Only Tennessee rejected his advice, and was rewarded with the seating of its congressmen. The rest of the South was contemptuous, and by February 1867 all other Southern states had rejected it by votes that were virtually unanimous. The outcome was often justified by the fact that a state's representatives had been unconstitutionally excluded from the congressional process. After all, Article V, on amending the Constitution, provides "that no State, without its Consent, shall be deprived of its equal Suffrage in the Senate."

Johnson nationalized the 1866 elections, embarking on a "swing around the circle" in the North, slamming the Republican Congress, and turning the electorate completely against him because of his demagoguery and lack of decorum. Republicans had to win at least 122 Northern seats to have the necessary majority in the House (counting the South) to continue the policy of not counting the South (until Southerners behaved better). If the Republicans had fewer than 122 seats and nevertheless still used their Northern majority to exclude the Southern Democrats, Johnson might recognize the Northern Democrats and their Southern compatriots as the true Congress. Yet a mere 122 seats would mean stalemate, for it would give the president more than enough Northern Democrats to sustain his vetoes through the life of the Fortieth Congress. No stalemate occurred, however, because the 1866 elections were a spectacular Republican triumph. Republicans carried the House by 144–49 and won every Northern legislature and every contested gubernatorial race. By winning in the states that counted, the Republicans made them the states that were allowed to count. The South was out until the Republicans allowed it in. Nevertheless, a Democratic leader in Ohio advised the Georgia governor to "let the Jacobins run their course, spurn and indignantly reject all their degrading and humiliating terms of constitutional amendment and universal or impartial suffrage."[16]

The Supreme Court then complicated things. Lampdin Milligan, an Indiana Peace Democrat like Vallandigham, had been convicted by a court martial and had been sentenced to hang for antiwar activities. In April 1866 the Court ordered him released on habeas with opinions to follow. In December the Court issued its opinions in the case. Four justices through Chase held that Congress had not authorized courts-martial in circumstances like Milligan's. Davis, joined by four Democrats, agreed but went further and answered a question no one had asked, saying, "Martial rule can never exist where the courts are open."[17] Privately he asserted the need to combat "the prevalent idea, that the legislative dept of the govt can override everything."[18] The *Nation* accurately noted that *Milligan* "arouses a suspicion that the Court is anxious to express its views upon these great questions before they are legitimately presented to it."[19]

Next the Court invalidated both state and federal loyalty oaths to the Union as bills of attainder and ex post facto laws.[20] The 5–4 division was strictly along party lines, with the Democrats signifying judicial hostility to Republican policies, while the Republicans thought that the laws helped protect the Union against disloyal men. Democrats were heartened because, as a decided minority in the Congress, they were publicly placing their hopes on the Court to end what they believed were unconstitutional policies of Reconstruction.

Meanwhile, Johnson clung to his opposition to congressional Reconstruction and his hope, encouraged by advisors and Northern Democrats, for a different outcome in the 1868 elections, when Negro suffrage would surely be an issue. The lame-duck Thirty-ninth, however, saw the elections that had created the Fortieth as strengthening its own mandate. The result, after three months of intense debate, was the (First) Reconstruction Act of 1867, establishing military rule in the South in order to create better-behaved governments that would ratify the Fourteenth Amendment. The act explicitly stated that the newly constituted governments would be readmitted to Congress only when the Fourteenth Amendment received the necessary twenty-seven ratifications. One congressman characterized the policy as returning to "the point where [General] Grant left off work, at Appomattox Court-House."[21]

Forcing states to ratify an amendment while excluding those which had not, until three-quarters of the states had ratified, hardly looks like the constitutional process created by the Framers; it looked more like ratification at the point of a bayonet. But returning to the 1860 constitution minus slavery as Johnson and the Democrats desired—that is, leaving all issues of civil rights to state governments, with enhanced Southern influence in the House and the Electoral College (because the freedmen would be counted as five-fifths and not three-fifths of a person)—was unacceptable to the Republicans. To preclude a political and legal vacuum favoring Johnson, the Thirty-ninth Congress also passed a statute bringing the Fortieth into session immediately after the Thirty-ninth expired. The Fortieth followed quickly with a Second Reconstruction Act tasking the military to register the voters, black and white, whom Congress deemed eligible. When secessionists boycotted the subsequent elections, the results were sealed.

Worried generally about how Johnson might interpret their handiwork, the Republicans arranged for a special summer session if necessary. It was. Attorney General Henry Stanbery issued an opinion, agreed to by the cabinet, gutting military Reconstruction. The Republicans came into the summer session and passed a Third Reconstruction Act, overruling Stanbery's restrictive interpretation.

McCardle and Impeachment

There were, however, other means by which the Democrats might prevail. Military Reconstruction relied on courts-martial. If a case could be brought quickly enough, *Milligan* suggested that the Court would void the procedure and perhaps go further and void Reconstruction before the reorganized Southern states ratified the Fourteenth Amendment. But to do so quickly enough meant that the Court would have to decide during its December 1867 term. Shortly after that term commenced, *Ex parte McCardle* was docketed. McCardle, the editor of the *Vicksburg Times,* had advocated forcible resistance to Reconstruction, had been convicted by a court-martial, and was now seeking habeas. Normally it took two years to get from docketing to decision, but the Court granted a motion to advance, and the case was argued in early March.

McCardle's counsel were swinging for the fences: a decision that military Reconstruction was unconstitutional. Afraid that the Supreme Court would agree, the Republicans passed a statute stripping the Court of jurisdiction in the case. Democrats bewailed taking the Constitution from the Court, but as was the case in all Reconstruction measures, the Democrats' objections were to no avail. In *Milligan* the Court had announced, "We're players again." With its jurisdiction stripping (and impeachment of Johnson), the Republicans responded, "At your peril." Senator James Wilson, an Iowa Republican, asserted that it was "our duty to intervene . . . and prevent the threatened calamity [from] falling upon the country."[22]

Meanwhile, afraid that Johnson would use his commander in chief powers to thwart military Reconstruction, Congress passed the Tenure in Offices Act, and then in February 1868 the House proceeded to impeach Johnson, in part for violating that act by attempting to remove Secretary of War Edwin Stanton from office without congressional approval. The underlying reason for Johnson's impeachment, of course, was that he was attempting to thwart congressional Reconstruction and thereby block ratification of the Fourteenth Amendment. Had Johnson been successful, neither the Fourteenth nor the Fifteen Amendment would likely ever have been adopted.

The same numerical logic that had been operating to exclude the South in Congress was driving these events. If Johnson and the Democrats could successfully hold out, they could turn the 1868 elections into a battle over whether to adopt the Fourteenth Amendment (and whether to seat the South without it). This was hardly an idle hope. Northern citizens would eventually tire of the constant political battles, and some form of normalcy was sure to reassert itself. The question was when. Because it might be in 1868, the Republicans wanted the Fourteenth Amendment on the books before the elections.

With Johnson being tried in the Senate, the Supreme Court yielded by doing nothing in *McCardle* prior to the election. It could have handed down an opinion, as Robert Grier and Stephen Field desired, in the period between passage of the jurisdiction-stripping bill and the override of Johnson's inevitable veto, or it could have held that the statute could not bar a decision in a case that had already been argued. But it did neither. Instead it waited to hear arguments about the statute's effect at its December 1868 term, thereby withholding its (probably negative) views on the constitutionality of Reconstruction.

After the Senate heard one of the House managers argue that Johnson could be convicted not only for actual crimes but also if his actions were subversive of some fundamental principle of government, or just highly prejudicial to the public interest, Johnson switched. He assured moderate Republicans that he would do nothing to violate the laws or the Constitution if acquitted. But more important, he ceased his obstruction of congressional Reconstruction in the South. The Senate nevertheless came within a single vote of removing him and establishing the precedent that a president who seeks to nullify an important congressional policy can be ousted from office.

Next Seward issued a noncommittal proclamation noting the ratifications of the Fourteenth Amendment by six newly formed Southern governments "avowing themselves to be and acting as" real legislatures.[23] A day later the House and the Senate passed a concurrent resolution declaring the Fourteenth Amendment duly ratified. Seward then issued a new proclamation declaring that the Fourteenth Amendment had been adopted as part of the Constitution.

Frank Blair, the Democrats' vice presidential candidate, publicly advocated revisiting the issue of ratification after the 1868 election. But he and Horatio Seymour lost to the Republican ticket of Ulysses S. Grant. With their defeat the question of legality was settled. Constitutional battles end when the losers cease fighting them, and the Democrats acquiesced. The 1872 reelection of Grant passed the Fourteenth Amendment into history. Then, a year later in the *Slaughter-House Cases*, the first to be decided under the Fourteenth Amendment, all nine justices accepted the amendment's validity without question. By now the Fifteenth Amendment prohibiting racial discrimination in voter eligibility also had been ratified. But of course there is more than one way to deny an amendment. One can always admit its validity and rely on the Court to decimate it through malevolent interpretation, as we shall see.

Settling the Wartime Constitutional Questions

The Court returned to *McCardle* after the 1868 election and ruled that the repealing statute had stripped it of jurisdiction. Therefore McCardle's petition had to be dismissed. The Court offered a closing caveat, however, that it "seem[s] to have [been] supposed, if effect be given to the repealing act . . . [,] that the whole appellate power of the court, in cases in habeas corpus, is denied. But this is an error."[24] At the Court's next term, in another habeas case involving a Mississippi newspaper editor who killed an army officer, the Court followed its *McCardle* hint and held that it had jurisdiction under a provision of the first Judiciary Act. The Court also looked back at *McCardle* and opined that "legislation of this character is unusual and hardly to be justified except upon some imperious public exigency."[25] Apparently protecting congressional Reconstruction and facilitating the ratification of the Fourteenth Amendment qualified as just such an "imperious public exigency." The editor was released from custody without the Court ruling on the merits.

McCardle had been the third case in which the constitutionality of Reconstruction had come before the Court. In the other two, states had attempted to invoke the Court's original jurisdiction to enjoin first Johnson and then the secretary of war from enforcing the Reconstruction Acts. The Court deemed the questions political and accordingly dismissed them. Once congressional Reconstruction was complete, however, the Court's views on its constitutionality no longer mattered, so it offered them anyway in *Texas v. White.* As it turned out, the Court conceded that Lincoln and the Republicans had been right all along: a state could simultaneously be in the Union and out as well. Secession was void because the "Constitution, in all its provisions, looks to an indestructible Union composed of indestructible States."[26] But Texas's rights as a member of the Union had been suspended because of the rebellion. Article IV imposed the duty on Congress to guarantee to each state a republican form of government, and it was for Congress to choose the means to repair the suspension of relations between the state and the Union.

Having approved the Republican theory of Reconstruction, the Court turned to the one remaining war issue: legal tender. Chase, as secretary of the treasury, had concluded that however undesirable greenbacks were, they were "indispensably necessary" to the Union's finances.[27] He nevertheless remained, as he had been as a young politician, a hard-money man. In *Hepburn v. Griswold,* in peace, he attempted to slay his wartime program. He proceeded in two parts. First, there was no express power that authorized Congress to make paper money legal tender, and he rejected inferring it under the war power. Almost all powers of the government involve money, and perhaps that showed why Congress could regulate the currency. Chase nevertheless went the other way, believing that such an argument proved too much. Besides, he concluded, issuing greenbacks had not been necessary because, contrary to what he had believed when he decided to authorize greenbacks during the war, they did more harm than good. Since Congress lacked the power to issue greenbacks, forcing creditors to accept them would violate the "spirit" of the Constitution. In identifying that "spirit" Chase referred to the constitutional provisions against both impairment of contracts (which states, but not the federal government, are expressly prohibited from doing) and deprivation of property without due process by authorizing payment at less than full value.

Miller, for the Court's three Republicans—Chase now clearly being a Democrat—went back to the arguments made during the war and to *McCulloch v. Maryland.* Legal tender was necessary "to the further borrowing of money and maintaining the army and navy."[28] This was done reluctantly, only after its necessity had become imperative. Miller also wanted nothing to do with Chase's conclusions about the spirit of the Constitution. The concept was just "too vague," especially since so many acts of government may adversely affect property values.[29]

Whatever else might be said about *Hepburn,* Chase, always angling for a presidential nomination, had badly overplayed his hand, probably in the hopes of being the hard-money choice of the Democrats in 1872. The decision was 4–3 at a time when Congress had upped the number of justices again to nine. Chase tried to vote Grier, who retired after the opinion was written but before it was delivered, to claim that he had five votes. That would not wash, because the internal evidence shows that Grier was very confused about his votes in the case. Furthermore, he was so incompetent that the other seven told him it was time to retire—hardly a solid fifth vote.

Grant had sent his nominees to the Senate in late 1869. One was confirmed but died before he could be sworn in; the other was rejected. The next two nominees—William Strong, a former state supreme court judge and now a wealthy Philadelphia lawyer, and Joseph Bradley, a very able railroad lawyer—were solid Republicans, and their nominations were sent to the Senate on the day that *Hepburn* came down. Once confirmed, they quickly voted with the dissenters to rehear the legal tender issue.

Hepburn was law for only fifteen months until it was reversed, 5–4, in *Knox v. Lee.* This stands as a testament to Marshall's wisdom in the 1830s about never handing down a constitutional decision with less than a majority of the full Court.

Strong's majority opinion easily made the point that, under the circumstances of the war, greenbacks were necessary. While citing *McCulloch* again and again, Strong went even further than Marshall would have dared in holding that the Constitution contains unenumerated powers, "neither expressly specified nor deducible from any one specified power, or ancillary to it alone, but which grew out the aggregate of powers conferred upon the government, or out of the sovereignty instituted."[30] In effect, the states' rights ideals of Jefferson, Spencer Roane, the Confederacy, and *Hepburn* were dead.

Bradley concurred, offering a similar view and expressing the Northern conclusion that the compact doctrine "should be regarded as definitely and forever overthrown."[31] It was "self-evident" that the national government is invested with all powers which are "generally considered to belong to every government as such, and as being essential to the exercise of its functions."[32]

The number of Republicans on the Court grew, with new appointments replacing Samuel Nelson in 1872 and Chase two years later (on Grant's seventh try!). A decade later in 1884, with Republicans firmly in control of the Court, the justices upheld an 1878 statute keeping greenbacks in circulation. The question of the expediency of greenbacks as legal tender, whether for convenience or necessity, was for Congress to decide.[33] Field, the lone Democrat, dissented. No one dissented when the Court upheld the Civil War income tax in *Springer v. United States.* The tax was not a forbidden direct tax because, as *Hylton v. United States* had concluded eighty-five years earlier, those were limited to head taxes and land taxes.

The *Slaughter-House Cases*

The nationalist vision of *Knox v. Lee* went blind in 1873 in the Court's first encounter with the Fourteenth Amendment. Louisiana's Reconstruction government created a monopoly in slaughtering animals in New Orleans. It was part health measure, part effort to attract the Texas cattle trade, and part Louisiana graft with legislators lining their pockets. Everyone agreed that prior to the Reconstruction amendments a state had the power to implement such a law, but the disfavored butchers sued, claiming that their rights under the Thirteenth and Fourteenth amendments were being violated. The butchers argued that the amendments transformed protections for fundamental rights, such as the right to pursue a trade, from the states to the federal government. They lost 5–4.

According to Justice Miller, the history of the amendments "is fresh within the memory of us all . . . almost too recent to be called history."[34] But Miller's version of history was truncated: the Civil War, Emancipation, the Thirteenth Amendment, the efforts to subjugate freedmen through the Black Codes, and therefore the Fourteenth Amendment. The Republican politicians who drafted that amendment spoke of all the prewar instances in which the South had demanded it get its way, including its lock on the presidency and the Court. Prior to the war John Bingham, the most important of the Framers of the Fourteenth Amendment, offered a list of offenses committed by the South against the Union. The list ran from Texas, to the demand for annexation of Cuba, to approval of the slave trade, to Bleeding Kansas, to denials of free speech and a free press. For Republicans—and they were the ones providing the votes—the Fourteenth Amendment was about putting the South in its place and eradicating the seven decades of Southern dominance in the federal government. As Justice Swayne stated in his dissent, the Reconstruction amendments marked "an important epoch" and "trenched[ed] directly upon the power of the States, and deeply affect[ed] those bodies."[35] According to Swayne, they should have been construed accordingly.

Miller believed that the amendments protected the freedmen but did little else. He refused to believe that they were "so great a departure" from the 1787 Constitution that they would "fetter and degrade the State governments by subjecting them to the control of Congress, in the exercise of powers heretofore universally conceded to them."[36] He would not accept that they "radically change[d]" the relations of nation and state, without express language so stating,[37] although what language would say this better than the Fourteenth Amendment's is unclear. In concluding that the amendment did not radically change things, Miller parsed each clause of Section 1 separately. "Privileges and immunities" had a portentous ring to it, and everyone knew it was the key clause, so Miller spent most of his time construing it—to death.

Miller noted that there were two types of citizenship, state and national, and two types of privileges and immunities, also state and national, with the national in both instances being protected against state abridgement. Fifty years earlier, on circuit, Bushrod Washington had held that state privileges and immunities were the fundamental rights of the citizen: protection from harm, the right to acquire property, the pursuit of happiness. It was here that Miller's conclusion that the Fourteenth Amendment did not radically change things came into play, as he asked whether it could be the purpose of the Fourteenth Amendment to transfer protection of these fundamental rights from the states to the federal government. He was sure the answer was no.

Miller recognized that in holding that fundamental rights were not protected by the Privileges and Immunities Clause, he nevertheless had to find some rights that *were* protected by the clause. He began with the right to travel to the seat of government, then suggested the right of protection in a foreign land or on the high seas, then the privilege of the writ of habeas corpus, and ended with rights secured by treaties. Even a Democratic congressman from Kentucky acknowledged that the Privileges and Immunities Clause protected all the guarantees of the Bill of Rights.[38] But Miller's only reference thereto was to the rights of peaceable assembly and petition for redress.

The right to travel to the seat of government had been protected by the Court in 1867, before ratification of the Fourteenth Amendment, so the amendment could not affect it, and exactly how a state would abridge an American citizen's rights in France or on the high seas is unclear. The Arkansas navy perhaps? Finally, rights under treaties were already protected by the Supremacy Clause. In other words, Miller's effort to show that fundamental rights were left completely under state control was shameful. Bradley's dissent holding that the amendment was intended "to provide National security against violation by the States of the fundamental rights of the citizen"[39] was exactly right, as was Field's trenchant observation that if privileges and immunities meant only what Miller held, then "it was a vain and idle enactment, which accomplished nothing, and most unnecessarily excited Congress and the people."[40]

As for the butchers' due process argument—that the legislation deprived them of their property interest in their trade—it was quickly rejected by the assertion that no construction of due process that the

Court had seen, or that the Court deemed admissible, could bring the claim within the Due Process Clause. This was not accurate either. *Dred Scott* had presented just such an argument, although perhaps it was fair to ignore *Dred Scott* after the war. But *Hepburn* also used a due process argument, and it was only two years old. To be sure, it had been overruled, but that did not mean that the justices had never seen the argument, as Miller claimed. What he meant was that the argument was so far off base it was an instant loser.

Finally, Miller dismissed the equal protection claim with the conclusion that the clause protected only the freedmen. That it protected freedmen was undoubtedly true, but the origins of the clause were in Jackson's bank veto message, where Jackson had used equal protection in an antimonopoly sense, against the state's granting special favors to its friends. This was precisely what the butchers were arguing.

The dissenters were better at showing what was wrong with the majority opinion than at explaining why the butchers should prevail. Field cited both Adam Smith and the Declaration of Independence, and Bradley referenced Magna Carta, as did Swayne, who thought the meanings were so self-evident that "[t]here is nothing to construe."[41]

Initial Fourteenth Amendment Interpretations

The same day it decided the *Slaughter-House Cases,* the Court held that the practice of law was not a privilege and immunity of national citizenship. The Illinois Supreme Court had denied a license to Myra Bradwell even as it acknowledged that she was well qualified to practice law. The fact that she was a she was reason enough to bar her, according to Illinois. For the *Slaughter-House* dissenters, however, there was a problem, since they thought that the right to practice a chosen occupation was protected. Nevertheless, that did not extend to women in all professions, because their "paramount destiny" was "to fulfill the noble and benign offices of wife and mother. This is the law of the

Creator."[42] The Court made it the law of the Fourteenth Amendment, too.

A year later, in *Minor v. Happersett,* the Court held that the right to vote also was not inherent in citizenship. White women had always been citizens, but states were free to deny any citizen the right to vote, except as prohibited by the Fifteenth Amendment. Susan B. Anthony, Elizabeth Cady Stanton, and other advocates of women's suffrage had opposed the Fourteenth Amendment because Section 2 had introduced the word "male" into voter qualifications. They had also opposed the Fifteenth Amendment because it, too, had rejected women's suffrage.

It is surprising, and perhaps perverse, that none of the initial cases under the Fourteenth Amendment involved the freedmen. This may also explain why each claim lost, although the better explanation for the grudging construction of the amendment is its questionable Article V pedigree.

Limiting the scope of the Fourteenth Amendment continued in the economic sphere. Railroads made it possible for Western farmers to access Eastern markets, but the need for access also left farmers at the mercy of the railroads and grain elevators. Organized in the Grange, initially a social organization for farmers, and with more votes than railroads, farmers in Illinois, Iowa, Minnesota, and Wisconsin had obtained legislative relief in the form of rate regulation. The railroads and grain elevator operators thought such interference with the way they did business had to be unconstitutional. But only the Fourteenth Amendment offered solace, and the *Slaughter-House* holding took that away.

Lacking any arguments save those already rejected, the lawyers made them again, only to have them rejected even more decisively in 1877, by a 7–2 vote, in *Munn v. Illinois.* Grant's chief justice, Morrison Waite, explained that the police power included rate regulation "when such regulation becomes necessary for the public good."[43] Private property is subject to regulation when it is "affected with a public interest," and it is "clothed with a public interest when used in a manner to make it of public consequence, and affect the community at large."[44] Waite acknowledged that the power to set rates could be abused, but for any remedy "people must resort to the polls, not to the courts."[45]

Field dissented with Strong joining. He asserted that the majority had placed all property in a state "at the mercy of the majority of its legislature,"[46] and he denied that "property loses something of its private character when employed in such a way as to be generally useful."[47]

The Contracts Clause remained the most significant limitation on state power, by precluding retroactive impairment of contracts, but the Court fashioned a new limitation on it in *Stone v. Mississippi*. The state had chartered a lottery for twenty-five years and promised not to interfere with it. Shortly thereafter, though, it changed its mind and banned lotteries. The Court held that states could not legislate away by contract the police power on matters affecting public health or public morality.

Stone signaled that the glory days of the Contracts Clause limiting state agreements were coming to an end. Thus the victors in the *Slaughter-House Cases* saw their privileged position vanish when a new company was chartered to compete against them, even though they still had more than a decade left in their monopoly grant. Citing *Stone*, the Court ruled that the public health part of the police power could not be bartered away.[48]

The End of Reconstruction

The Court may have been sure that the Reconstruction Amendments were about the freedmen, but white Southerners were intent on taking control of their state governments at almost any cost. The Ku Klux Klan, initially formed as a social club, had swiftly become a terrorist organization. In 1868 the Klan, operating as the military arm of the Southern Democratic Party, began targeted assassinations of politicians, as well as indiscriminate killings of freedmen in what today might be called an insurgency. Despite new Force Acts, only the army could protect the freedmen and the new Republican governments, which simply lacked the forces to deal with the Klan.

Although Grant won a decisive reelection in 1872, Reconstruction was on the defensive. Then the Panic of 1873 wrecked the economy and caused Northern voters to turn decisively to the Democrats in 1874, effectively placing Reconstruction on its last legs. In the South counterrevolutionary terrorism worked to delegitimize the new governments as unable to protect their citizens. Local power in the governments was always weak, and in the words of a carpetbagger, they could survive only with "steady unswerving power from without."[49] Instead violence always escalated during election season. Decades later Senator "Pitchfork" Ben Tillman of South Carolina proudly declared that "[w]e had to shoot negroes to get relief from the galling tyranny to which we had been subjected."[50] Tillman claimed that "bloodshed and a good deal of it" was essential, and he knew whereof he spoke.[51] Some three thousand freedmen and their white allies were murdered, often brutally, to overthrow the most democratic governments the South had ever seen. Through terror, voter fraud, and a Northern electorate weary of policing the South and depressed by economic woes, plus administration scandals, the South was "redeemed."

The early returns in the 1876 election had Democrat Samuel Tilden besting Rutherford B. Hayes. Florida, Louisiana, and Mississippi, which still were under Republican control, invalidated enough votes from Tilden districts to give Hayes the states and a one-vote margin in the Electoral College, even though Tilden had clearly won the popular vote nationwide. Democrats challenged the results, and rival electoral certificates were sent to Washington. There was talk of a renewed civil war, and politicians searched for an extraconstitutional compromise.

The first step was congressional creation of a fifteen-man electoral commission to canvass the ballots of the three Southern states, as well as those of Oregon. The commission was composed of five House members and five senators, split evenly between the parties. The statute then named four Supreme Court justices, also split evenly by party. They in turn were to name a fifth, who everyone assumed would be David Davis, a former Republican but now an independent. But the Illinois legislature unexpectedly intervened and elected Davis to the Senate. With only Republicans left on the Court, the commission necessarily afforded Republicans a one-vote advantage—precisely reflected in the series of 8–7 votes which found that Hayes had won each of the contested states and therefore the presidency.

There were more negotiations before the Democrats conceded. These involved money for Southern railroads and, most important, the withdrawal of federal troops from the South. A year later Congress guaranteed the solution in the Posse Comitatus Act of 1878, which prevented the use of federal troops for domestic law enforcement. In the end, the Compromise of 1877 put a Republican in the White House, but it left the freedmen in the hands of Southern Democrats, who now controlled all the states of the former Confederacy.

One result of the continuing Republican presidency was a further securing of Republican control of the Court. Hayes made two appointments from the South. The first was John Marshall Harlan, formerly a slaveholding Kentucky Unionist who had opposed Emancipation and the Thirteen and Fourteenth amendments, and had voted for the Peace Democrat George McClellan in 1864, but who nonetheless appears to have undergone a genuine political conversion to the Republican Party (and then shown the wisdom to shift Kentucky's support to Hayes at the Republican convention). A deeply religious man— a colleague claimed he went to bed at eight with the Bible in one hand and the Constitution in the other and slept the sleep of the righteous and just—Harlan, over the next decade and a half, would join with

Miller, Field, and Bradley in forming a strong but factious Court. Harlan became the great dissenter of the century.

Hayes's second appointee, William B. Woods, was a former Union general from Ohio who stayed in the South and served as a federal judge for the Southern Circuit. Later James Garfield had one appointment during his brief tenure, and his successor had two, leaving Field as the lone Democrat. In addition to this rejuvenation of the Court, Congress reached back to the repealed Judiciary Act of 1801 and expanded federal jurisdiction to include all cases relying on a federal claim, as well as generous rights of removal for cases involving nonresidents, including corporations, from state to federal courts. In other words, with the federal judiciary stacked with Republicans, a Republican Congress expanded federal jurisdiction to protect Republican interests.

Civil Rights

Despite the claim of *Slaughter-House* that the Fourteenth Amendment was about protecting the freedmen, the justices, like their Northern Republican brethren, were effectively abandoning the freedmen to their white Democratic neighbors. The Court had already reversed convictions stemming from the Colfax Massacre in Louisiana, where over a hundred perpetrators had left dozens of freedmen dead on Easter Sunday. There were no state charges and only three federal convictions. But these were overturned because of a faulty indictment, and because the Court had concluded that rights under the First and Second amendments were not protected against state action.[52] The Court concluded that the Colfax Massacre implicated only violations of state law and not federal civil rights. This boded ill for future protections of the freedmen.

In both 1880 and 1883 the Court returned to civil rights, dealing with juries, interracial fornication, and the last civil rights act passed by the

Republicans. Its overall conclusion was that the Fourteenth Amendment barred states from formally discriminating against Negroes, but otherwise the amendment changed nothing.

Strauder v. West Virginia dealt with a state's formal discrimination against Negroes, holding that a state statute limiting jury service to white adult males was unconstitutional. The Court offered two separate rationales for its holding. First, the purpose of the Fourteenth Amendment was to protect the freedmen from "unfriendly legislation" by the states. Second, the law discriminated on a racial basis. If the law had excluded "all naturalized Celtic Irishmen" it would have been equally unconstitutional.[53] There was an obvious tension between the two rationales. The first protected only Negroes. The second protected anyone subjected to unjustified discrimination regardless of race.

Strauder closed by noting that while the state could not discriminate on the basis of race, of course it could confine jury service to males, between certain ages, and "to persons having educational qualifications."[54] Naturally, such a reworking of the limitations on jury service did not help Negroes because few could meet the required educational qualifications. This ruling was seconded by companion cases coming from Virginia, which did not have a racial limitation in its statute. Moreover, the Court held that a mixed jury is not required in any particular case, and so all-white juries did not violate the rights of a black defendant.[55] In these ways the South was able to keep its juries lily white for decades.

Interracial sex, once it became consensual, looked different than it had during slavery. Hence Alabama criminalized it in 1867. Subsequently Tony Pace was convicted of interracial fornication (or adultery; the case is not clear) and was sentenced to two years at hard labor under a statute authorizing up to seven years for a first offense. Had the woman been of the same race, the maximum penalty would have been six months.[56] In a terse three-paragraph decision Field rejected Pace's equal protection claim as frivolous. According to the Court, the laws treated whites as badly if they slept with Negroes as it treated Negroes if they slept with whites. The differential punishment is directed against the offense, not against people of a particular color. The Court never bothered to inquire as to why Alabama would penalize one kind of fornication more heavily than another.

By far the most important of the post-Reconstruction cases were the five collectively known as the *Civil Rights Cases* which invalidated the Civil Rights Act of 1875. In contrast to the pre–Civil War years, when the Court formally invalidated federal statutes twice, this marked the eleventh time since the war that the Court had done so.

With depression, scandal, and waning enthusiasm surrounding Reconstruction and hampering Republicans, the Democrats had retaken the House in the 1874 elections. The Republicans in the lame-duck session gave the recently deceased Charles Sumner a posthumous present by enacting a law he had so dearly wanted. At the end of the debate Senator George Edmunds, a Vermont Republican, stated "that there lies in this Constitution, just as in Magna Carta and in the bills of rights of all the States, a series of declarations that the rights of citizens shall not be invaded . . . on the pretense that a man is of a particular race."[57] The Civil Rights Act of 1875 was a sweeping law forbidding racial discrimination in places of public accommodation such as inns, transportation, and theaters.

This was the last possible time a civil rights act could pass. Democrats had always opposed civil rights, and the Republicans' enthusiasm was flagging as they were becoming the party of big business. Eight years later the *Civil Rights Cases* struck down the law by an 8–1 vote. Bradley authored the majority opinion, rejecting claims that the act was valid under both the Thirteenth and Fourteenth amendments despite the fact that the last section in each authorized Congress to enforce the amendment by appropriate legislation. Harlan dissented on both points. Bradley worked from the text of the amendments, Harlan from their spirit.

Just as it had in the *Slaughter-House Cases,* the Court noted that there would be no legal issue but for the Reconstruction amendments. Before 1865 congressional power to pass a civil rights law did not exist. Bradley's opinion stuck with a rigid distinction between racial wrongs committed by private individuals and racial wrongs committed under the authority of the state. The former were individual wrongs to be handled under state law. The latter were constitutional violations subject to the increasingly moribund Fourteenth Amendment. According to Bradley, the power to enforce in Section 5 was the power to enforce only the prohibition on state action. "An individual cannot deprive a man of his right to vote, to hold property, to buy and sell, to sue in the courts, or to be a witness or a juror; he may, by force or fraud, interfere with the enjoyment of the right in a particular case," but unless the state acts to shield him, these are "simply . . . private wrong[s]."[58] Again, harking back to *Slaughter-House,* the Court concluded that if Congress could pass a public accommodations law such as the one at hand, it could "with equal show of authority enact a code of laws for the enforcement and vindication of all rights of life, liberty, and property."[59] According to the Court, that would be absurd.

Turning to the Thirteenth Amendment, which textually lacks the state action problem of the Fourteenth, Bradley denied that racial discrimination was a badge of slavery: "It would be running the slavery argument into the ground to make it apply to every act of discrimination."[60]

Harlan began his dissent by accusing the majority of sacrificing the substance and spirit of the amendments "by a subtle and ingenious verbal criticism."[61] He then turned to the Thirteenth Amendment. As a former slaveholder, he knew that "that institution rested wholly upon the inferiority, as a race, of those held in bondage."[62] Their freedom therefore was guaranteed by protecting them against all discrimination in regard to civil rights. Harlan also found that the Fourteenth Amendment was applicable because Congress was protecting the affirmative rights of citizenship—just as the earlier quotation from Edmunds illustrated. Harlan asserted that the majority had treated the amendments as "splendid baubles, thrown out to delude those who deserved fair and generous treatment at the hands of the nation."[63]

The *Civil Rights Cases*, like *Slaughter-House* before them, treated the amendments as if they had not changed all that much with regard to national power. But unlike *Slaughter-House*, the *Civil Rights Cases* involved race, the sine qua non of the Reconstruction amendments. As a result, as long as the states remained formally neutral on the treatment of race, their private citizens and corporations were free to discriminate racially as they pleased. The only remedy to that discrimination was for the freemen to look to the Southern state governments. That meant saying good-bye to Reconstruction protections.

In his *Slaughter-House* dissent Bradley was passionate about the Fourteenth Amendment and protecting the rights of butchers. "The amendment was an attempt to give voice to the strong National yearning . . . in which American citizenship should be a sure guarantee of safety, and in which every citizen of the United States might stand erect on every portion of its soil, in the full enjoyment of every right and privilege belonging to a freeman, without fear of violence or molestation."[64] But that was before Bradley had been substituted for David Davis on the electoral commission and had become the tie-breaking vote that placed Hayes in the White House. When it was a case of freemen, not butchers, he concluded that "there must be some stage in the progress of [the freedman's] elevation [from slavery] where he takes the rank of a mere citizen, and ceases to be the special favorite of the laws, and when his rights as a citizen, or a man, are to be protected in the ordinary modes by which other men's rights are protected."[65] There it was, the judicial seal of approval on the national abandonment of Negroes in the Compromise of 1877.

Prigg v. Pennsylvania and *Dred Scott* had shown how far the Court would go to protect slavery. After slavery was gone, the *Civil Rights*

Cases showed how far the Court would go to ignore the changed constitutional regime. The Republican justices had adopted the traditional Democratic skepticism about exercises of federal power—when it came to protecting Negroes. Albion Tourgee, a prominent carpetbagger, concluded that "[i]n all except the actual results of the physical struggle, I consider the South to have been the real victors in the war."[66] More precisely, the South, despite losing the Civil War, had won the peace.

· VI ·

Industrializing America

THE POST-RECONSTRUCTION PARTIES were both pro-business with strong sectional roots. Republicans and Democrats were split largely over tariffs (with the Republicans wanting protectionism and the Democrats wanting just enough revenue for federal needs); beyond that the federal government didn't seem to do much except swing between minting only gold and also minting silver. These factors explain the rise of third-party efforts either to tame or to replace the capitalism that seemed to work only for the rich. In no other era has the party affiliation of the justices meant so little.

The membership of the Court was in constant flux. In the twenty-four years beginning with 1888, seventeen justices were appointed: William Howard Taft nominated five, Grover Cleveland and Benjamin Harrison four each, and Theodore Roosevelt three, although William McKinley had but one appointment. Demonstrating both national reconciliation (at least among whites) and Southern support for Democrats, two of Cleveland's appointees, Lucious Q. C. Lamar and Edward D. White, were ex-Confederates. None of this affected the stature of the Court. Only once in a quarter century—the 1896 election—was the

Court an issue, and the attacking Democrats were routed. The Court always had solid Republican support as well as that of a significant wing of the Democratic Party. This granted the Court a freedom not enjoyed in decades to create constitutional doctrine without fear of political pushback.

With the exception of John Marshall Harlan, who lasted well into the Taft presidency, the former giants passed from the scene during Harrison's presidency (1889–1893). Samuel Miller and Joseph Bradley died, and Stephen Field hung on, senile but with the (successful) goal of breaking John Marshall's longevity record. He was finally pushed off the Court at the beginning of McKinley's presidency. The new dominant justices were Republican David Brewer of Kansas, who happened to be Field's nephew, and Democrat Rufus Peckham of New York.

For two decades after the first postwar depression, the Panic of 1873, Jefferson's yeomen farmers, always subject to adverse weather, were being squeezed by falling prices for their crops, while railroad rates to bring the crops to market moved erratically, but with an upward trend. Worse, their debt had grown, and so it took more production to stay even.

The free labor ideology promulgated by antebellum Republicans—that Northern wages were depressed by Southern slavery—proved disastrously wrong. As America industrialized after the war, wages and working conditions so deteriorated that workers had never had it so bad. Pay was low, hours were long, and working conditions deplorable; Karl Marx's daughter thought them worse than in England in the 1840s. Some unemployment each year was likely. The economy went into recession in the mid-1880s and into its worst depression to that time in 1893, when unemployment reached 30 percent. With the depression there was both talk of revolution and real fears of insurrection. There never could be any doubt about where judges' commitments would be, especially insofar as they did not comprehend the mismatch between constitutional traditions and assumptions and the changed conditions of industrializing and urbanizing America.

The Police Power

Upper-middle-class Democrats and Republicans, including politicians and judges, all agreed that the sole valid goal of legislation was to be of general applicability and to promote the general welfare by being neutral among classes. Thus Grover Cleveland vetoed drought relief for Texas by insisting that aid should be "properly related to public service or benefit,"[1] and only farmers in Texas would benefit from the aid. The governor of New York explained why no public projects for the unemployed were created in the aftermath of the Panic of 1893: "In America, the people support the government; it is not the province of government to support the people."[2] Class legislation, based, in the words of Justice Henry Brown, on "the desire of one class to better itself at the expense of the other,"[3] was arbitrary. Therefore, as the *Civil Rights Cases* observed, it was "obnoxious to the . . . Fourteenth Amendment."[4] Property enjoyed primacy, for, as Field remarked, "[i]t should never be forgotten that protection to property and to persons cannot be separated. Where property is insecure, the rights of persons are unsafe."[5] If legislation was general and neutral, then it was a valid exercise of the state's police powers. Thus *Plessy v. Ferguson* sustained the doctrine of "separate but equal" on the ground that the law promoted racial harmony and the public safety. To avoid the conclusion that Jim Crow laws constituted class legislation, the Court denied that segregation imposed a badge of inferiority on African Americans.

The police power was well illustrated in *Mugler v. Kansas*, sustaining the state's ban on alcohol. Harlan stated that everyone knew "that the public health, public morals, and public safety, may be endangered by the general use of intoxicating drinks."[6] Analogizing to the new

Contracts Clause doctrine, the Court reaffirmed that the Fourteenth Amendment did not "impose restraints upon the exercise of . . . powers for the protection of the safety, health, or morals of the community."[7] Even though prohibition rendered breweries worthless, no compensation was required—a point on which Field dissented.

The aftermath of *Mugler* offered lessons on the intersection of various constitutional doctrines. The Court sustained Iowa's prohibition on manufacturing alcohol against a Commerce Clause challenge which claimed that the alcohol would be manufactured for interstate export. The Court was having none of it. In *Gibbons v. Ogden,* Marshall equated commerce with intercourse; here, in *Kidd v. Pearson,* the Court separated commerce from manufacture. Two reasons were offered. One was that everyone agreed with the distinction. The other was that otherwise "Congress would be invested, to the exclusion of the States, with power to regulate, not only manufactures, but also agriculture, horticulture, stock raising, domestic fisheries, mining—in short, every branch of human industry."[8] Such a conclusion, the Court believed, was absurd. It also reflected how far the Court had strayed from *Cooley v. Board of Wardens,* where almost four decades earlier it had concluded that powers to regulate need not be exclusive in either the national or state governments.

Kansas and Iowa were dry islands, with thousands of citizens thirsty for beer and whisky, surrounded by seas of booze. Prohibition or no, saloons flourished because federalism allowed willing suppliers to exist in Wisconsin, Illinois, and Missouri, to name just three. Furthermore, the Constitution, at least initially, offered an end run around the state laws. *Kidd* may have held that the Commerce Clause was no bar to prohibiting manufacturing, but dormant Commerce Clause doctrine dating from John Marshall's era held that states could not bar the importation of goods still in their original packages.[9] Thus in *Leisy v. Hardin,* Chief Justice Melville W. Fuller ruled that Iowa could not prevent cases and kegs of beer from being shipped into the state and purchased in their original packaging (which turned out to be increasingly small).

The consequences of *Leisy* were twofold. Very quickly "original package houses" and "supreme court saloons" sprang into existence. Four months later the activist Republican Fifty-first Congress passed the Wilson Act, which treated arriving intoxicants identically to those already within the state; that is, it overturned *Leisy*'s result and made the importation illegal. *Leisy* had invited Congress to act if it wished, and a year later, Fuller sustained the Wilson Act.[10]

A similar rationale to *Mugler* allowed dairy states to heavily regulate and even prohibit the use of oleomargarine. The Court accepted at face value the claims that margarine was unhealthy and that consumers might be misled into thinking it was butter.[11]

Challenges to the Railroads

Railroads were a ubiquitous and frequent presence before the Court, although the cases reflect no coherent body of law. By the early 1880s four transcontinental railroads were operating, and the railroads had become national symbols of progress and power, as well as greed and corruption. They moved people, raw materials, cattle, crops, and finished products far more swiftly than the canals and steamboats they supplanted. By the 1890s they were the country's largest employer, as well as its primary culprit in killing and maiming workers, passengers, and bystanders alike. They were a magnet for communities that hoped to grow (as all did) and for legislatures that sought to tame their power. People were cheerleaders before a railroad was built and critics afterwards. Railroads were constantly going into bankruptcy, and states and municipalities, particularly in the South and Midwest, repudiated the bonds that had been issued for their construction, raising Contracts Clause issues.

Although a quarter of all constitutional challenges to state action were based on the Contracts Clause, the chances of success dwindled to about one in five—which still was much better than the chances of success under the Fourteenth Amendment. Increasingly the defendants in these cases were governments attempting to repudiate their agreements, especially agreements to pay interest and principal on bonds. The South went to extraordinary lengths to repudiate bonds issued during Reconstruction and was generally successful since states simply refused to appropriate money. Only Virginia was out of luck, because it had promised not only to repay but also to accept interest coupons as payment for taxes; it could find no way to avoid its debts successfully.[12] Eventually, in *Hans v. Louisiana,* the Court through Bradley gave the South an even better avoidance mechanism when it concluded that the Eleventh Amendment extended beyond its textual prohibition of suits against states by out-of-staters to preclude all suits against states without their consent. Essentially Bradley concluded that regardless of what the text of the amendment said, its purpose was to restore the assumption of 1787 that the judicial power of the United States did not extend to private suits against a state. This was an added and surprising benefit to the Compromise of 1877.

Regulating railroad rates had been allowed in *Munn v. Illinois,* but by the 1890s, on the longer, typically interstate routes, increased competition often drove prices so low that they did not cover fixed costs. Smaller communities were generally served by a single line that could set its own rates, and Western farmers were perennially angered by rates that were cheaper for a long haul than a shorter one. This discrimination made no sense to them, and they wanted it ended.

Illinois acted to eliminate short-haul/long-haul discrepancies, such as the rate from Peoria to New York City, which was fifteen cents per hundred pounds, while the rate from Gilman (eighty-six miles closer to New York, through which the Peoria train traveled) was twenty-five cents per hundred pounds. In *Wabash Railway* the Court held that the law ran afoul of the dormant Commerce Clause because it regulated

rates for interstate shipment. If Illinois could regulate a transaction between Gilman and New York, then so could New York and Indiana,
Ohio, and Pennsylvania as well. It was to preclude "just such a case
that the commerce clause of the Constitution was adopted."[13] States
might regulate internal transactions, but transportation through the
country "is essential in modern times to that freedom of commerce
from the restraints which the State might choose to impose upon it."[14]

Congress immediately filled the regulatory vacuum with the Interstate Commerce Act, creating the Interstate Commerce Commission.
The act prohibited short-haul/long-haul discrimination, rebates, and
rate-fixing agreements, and required "reasonable and just rates," without specifying what those were. The ICC was empowered to issue
cease and desist orders for violations of the act. With this, its first statute designed to regulate interstate commerce, Congress entered a new
era. Three years later the most activist non-wartime Congress passed
the Wilson Act, as well as the Sherman Antitrust Act, the Sherman Silver Purchase Act, and the highly protective McKinley Tariff.

In the handful of rate regulation cases that the Court decided before
1895, *Munn* was reaffirmed over a very angry dissent by Brewer, joined
by Field and Brown.[15] Still, the Court also first glimpsed the possibility
that regulation might take from A (the railroad) and give to B (the
shipper). As the quintessential nineteenth-century constitutional violation, such rates would be barred by the Due Process Clause: "Under
pretence of regulating fares and freights, the State cannot require a
railroad corporation to carry persons or property without reward."[16]

In *Reagan v. Farmers' Loan and Trust,* the Court, through Brewer,
unanimously invalidated a rate as being so low as to be confiscatory.
The Court perceived the situation as class legislation whereby property "without compensation [is] wrestled from him [one party] for the
benefit of another, or the public," and thus "one class . . . [is] compelled to suffer loss that others may make gain."[17] The insight that

rates could be too low would mean a lot of extra work for federal courts.

The Three Important Decisions of 1895

Because of the business-oriented, "me too" nature of both Republicans and Democrats (complete with a modest pro-silver wing in each party), farmers in the South and West searched for alternatives that would address their colonial exploitation by forces they could not control. The vehicle was the People's Party (or Populists, because calling someone a "People's" did not parse), which advanced an income tax and easy-money policies plus antitrust rhetoric supporting government ownership of railroads, telephone, and telegraph. The Populists enjoyed initial success in 1892, when they won a million popular votes and twenty-two electoral votes for president, three governorships, and twelve seats in Congress. Nevertheless, the Democrats, for the first time since before the Civil War, captured the presidency and both Houses of Congress—just in time for the Panic of 1893. In the ensuing midterm elections the Democrats were routed, and the House went from 218–127 Democratic to 244–105 Republican (with Populists counted as Democrats). Four-fifths of all non-Southern Democrats were replaced by Republicans. But during their two years of control Democrats drastically cut the McKinley Tariff, even though revenue was down generally because of the depression.

Congress needed added revenue once the tariff was reduced, and Populists demanded an income tax as their price for cooperating to lower the tariff. Sympathetic Democrats agreed, but not a single Republican voted for the bill. The tax was a 2 percent levy on all income in excess of $4,000, thus exempting well over 99 percent of the population. In addition to being class legislation, the tax was also purely sectional, solidly supported in the South and West and functionally applying only in New York, New Jersey, Pennsylvania, and Massachusetts. Cleveland let the measure become law without his signature, while Senator David Hill, a Democrat from New York, expressed the views of the wealthy: "[T]he times are changing; the courts are changing, and I believe that this tax will be declared unconstitutional. At least I hope so."[18]

In the most controversial decision since the *Legal Tender Cases,* Hill's hopes were fulfilled. *Springer v. United States* had held the Civil War income tax constitutional; earlier cases declared that only those taxes which could be apportioned among the states according to their population—quintessentially a head tax—were direct, and an income tax could not be apportioned because there is no correlation between a state's population and its citizens' incomes (whether from land or wages). In *Pollock v. Farmers' Loan & Trust,* Fuller, for a 6–2 Court, held that part of the tax which covered rents from land (as well as taxes on municipal bonds) unconstitutional and announced that the Court was split 4–4 on other parts. The case was reargued when the absent Howell Jackson returned. He voted to uphold the tax, but someone, probably George Shiras, flipped, and the tax was held unconstitutional.

Fuller was animated by fear of "an attack upon accumulated property by mere force of numbers."[19] His reasoning went from the obvious, that a tax on land was direct, to finding that a tax on rent from land was too. Then he concluded that a tax on income from personal property should be treated similarly. Coming finally to income from wages, Fuller ruled that these provisions could not be severed from those already held invalid.[20] Fuller's view protected both states and private property by limiting the power of the national government; *Springer* was distinguished as a product of national emergency.

Fuller opined that the decision had nothing to do with the desirability of an income tax, and suggested that a constitutional amendment would allow time "for the sober second thought of every part of the country."[21] It was a nice kick to the gut of the Democrats and Populists, strongly implying a lack of that sober second thought, as well as the sectional nature of the tax's support. Furthermore, Congress had passed to the Republicans, who wanted no part of the tax.

Field, who hoped to rush the decision for fear that he might die and thus not be able to save the country by his vote, saw the tax as a dangerous opening move: "It will be but the stepping-stone to others, larger and more sweeping, till our political contests will become a war of the poor against the rich; a war constantly growing in intensity and bitterness."[22]

Each of the four dissenters wrote separately. Harlan, who privately thought the decision was the Court's worst, defended the tax as preventing the wealthy from "evad[ing] their share of responsibility for the support of the government."[23] Brown seconded Harlan, seeing the case as "nothing less than a surrender of the taxing power to the moneyed class."[24] The Court split not on party lines but, like the Congress, on sectional lines. Four of the majority justices—Fuller, Field, Horace Gray, and Shiras—came from states with high per capita wealth. Three of the dissenters—Harlan, White, and Jackson—were Southerners, and thus it is interesting that their position, had it prevailed, would have dramatically strengthened the federal government vis-à-vis the states.

United States v. E. C. Knight turned back the government's first attempt to use the Sherman Antitrust Act. The statute—making contracts, conspiracies, and agreements in restraint of trade that affects interstate commerce illegal—passed the House unanimously and the Senate with but a single dissent. Trusts had been growing and were profoundly unpopular, but there was no consensus on how to deal with them. Furthermore, because every contract or agreement restrains trade to some extent, the act essentially punted national policy first to the executive to initiate prosecutions and ultimately to the courts.

The American Sugar Refining Company, already controlling about two-thirds of the country's refining, entered into agreements to purchase four Pennsylvania companies that would give it control of 98 percent of the market. In holding that the government could not block the acquisition, Fuller noted that while Congress has the power to regulate interstate commerce, such power, as *Kidd v. Pearson* stated, did not reach manufacturing, which precedes commerce. The Court offered instead the idea that Congress might reach internal commerce if it "directly affect[ed] external commerce," but contracts to control domestic manufacture would result in indirect effects.[25] Presumably a local monopoly on transportation could create the necessary direct effects.

Like *Kidd*, *E. C. Knight* was concerned with the constitutional boundaries between state and national power, concluding that both the police power and the commerce power gave the respective governments exclusivity in their spheres. By saying that there could be no overlapping authority, the decisions forced a choice about categorization. The Court acknowledged that this might be "perplexing,"[26] perhaps as a nod to Harlan's dissent that the decision seemed blind to the economic effects of a transaction.

Attorney General Richard Olney did not mind the government's defeat since he had predicted it. Indeed he had fought against the Sherman Act and never initiated a prosecution under it. By contrast Olney cared deeply about the labor injunction that broke the Pullman Strike and was sustained in *In re Debs*.

The Pullman Strike of 1894 was but the latest in a series of actions dating back to the 1870s, as the working conditions that so appalled Marx's daughter led to an increasing number of strikes—some large, many violent. Because of the violence, governors could call out troops to restore order by breaking the strike, an occurrence that exceeded an average of one a month for the decade ending in 1895.

With the depression the Pullman Palace Car Company lost business, laid off a portion of its workforce, and cut the wages of those remaining. It did not reduce rents in its company town as its workers requested, nor would it submit to arbitration. Instead it fired three employees on the committee that asked it to reduce rents. Its workers went out on strike. Eugene Debs, head of the American Railway Union, reluctantly took his workers out on a sympathetic strike, and they refused to work on any train carrying a Pullman car. The strike tied up over forty thousand miles of the national railroad system, especially to the west and south of Chicago. Olney obtained an ex parte injunction (that is, one where the opposing side does not appear before the judge) against inhibiting either interstate commerce or transport of the mails. The injunction was backed with a threat to bring in troops. Debs responded that the "first shot fired by the regular soldiers at the mobs here will be the signal for a civil war . . . [in which] 90 per cent of the people of the United States will be arrayed against the other 10 per cent."[27] There were shots; twenty people died, dozens more were injured, and two thousand railroad cars were destroyed. More troops and Debs's arrest broke the strike.

Debs was tried for contempt, but there were problems. Law and order is a local issue, and Illinois governor John Peter Altgeld, a Democrat who refused to use the state militia to break the strike, adamantly opposed bringing in the army, believing, accurately, that a federal presence would inflame the situation. Debs was nevertheless convicted, as the federal judge rested jurisdiction under the Sherman Antitrust Act.

Debs's prediction of civil war was exactly what David Brewer feared. In a speech a year before the strike he had asked, "Who does not see the wide unrest that fills the land; who does not feel that vast social changes are impending and realize that those changes must be guided in justice to safety and peace or they will culminate in revolution?"[28] He found that the Constitution was up to the task of upholding the injunction.

Not surprisingly, the opinion had nothing to do with the Sherman Act. Applying it to the strike but not the Sugar Trust was out of the question. Instead the opinion rests doubly on the simple proposition that the greater includes the lesser. If the government could send in the army, then it could use the federal courts, too. And if the sovereign states are "impotent to obstruct interstate commerce," then voluntary associations of individuals cannot do so either.[29]

Abandoning the spheres of influence of *E. C. Knight* and *Pollock*, or the idea that restoring order was a local issue (at least without the invitation of the governor), the Court announced that "[t]he strong arm of the national government may be put forth to brush away all obstructions to the freedom of interstate commerce or the transportation of the mails."[30] If the choice was between safety and revolution, as Brewer believed, there never could be any doubt where the judges would come down. Naturally the opinion was unanimous.

The 1896 Election and the McKinley Presidency

Populists and organized labor greeted *Debs* and *Pollock* with outrage—calling it the selling out of the have-nots to the haves. But it would be eighteen months before there would be a chance to rain electoral retribution on the Court, because control of Congress had passed to the Republicans in 1894, and the executive branch was hardly unhappy with the cases. When Howell Jackson died shortly after the second *Pollock* decision, Cleveland replaced him with New York judge Rufus Peckham, who was wholly in sympathy with Field and Brewer. Like them he believed that rate regulation mistakenly authorized "the most frequent opportunity for arraying class against class; and, in addition to the ordinary competition that exists throughout all industries, a new competition will be introduced, that of competition for the possession of government."[31]

At their 1896 convention me-too Democrats suffered a stunning defeat when Populists captured the party with the nomination of William Jennings Bryan of Nebraska. The Populists also nominated Bryan, but his success within the Democratic Party was the death knell for the

Populists as an independent party—and to the extent that winning matters, not good news for the Democrats either.

After the previous five presidential elections between me-too candidates, all close, the voters were given a true choice between Bryan and William McKinley, with the parties split over the income tax, silver, the soulless trusts, and government by injunction. Bryan's famous "Cross of Gold" speech stated that the income tax "was not unconstitutional when it was passed . . . It did not become unconstitutional until one judge changed his mind, and we cannot be expected to know when a judge will change his mind."[32] Silver Democrats also feared a future decision invalidating an inflated currency.

In other words, and Bryan used plenty, the Court was front and center, much as it had been in 1860. *Harper's Weekly,* claiming that "Bryan and his mentor Governor Altgeld want free riots and a Supreme Court that will obey the passions of the multitude,"[33] ran a cartoon depicting the Court under a "Popocratic" administration. It shows a bench made up of prominent Populist politicians including a diabolic Altgeld, Sylvester Pennoyer (who had called for the impeachment of the *Pollock* majority), "Pitchfork" Ben Tillman (with his pitchfork in hand), and the Constitution in tatters.[34] Like all good political cartoons, it carried an element of truth: Bryan did want to pack the Court and reverse *Pollock.* The Populists wished to do even more. By scaring urban America, Bryan, who could not even carry Iowa, Minnesota, the Dakotas, and Kentucky, gave McKinley and the Court a decisive victory.

Debs's assertive national power coincided nicely with new assertions of national power, both internationally and domestically. The Interstate Commerce Commission was given added powers, Congress regulated shipments of adulterated food, the Court eased its grip on the Sherman Act, and in the most significant event of the McKinley presidency, the United States engaged in the "splendid little war" with Spain and acquired Puerto Rico and the Philippines as prizes. Bryan remained the Democratic darling, adding anti-imperialism to free silver and lashing at the soulless trusts in his rematch with McKinley. McKinley, with his war hero vice president, Theodore Roosevelt, bested Bryan by a slightly greater total than in their first match-up. The Court had been driven by fear in 1895, but, like the Republicans, it greeted the new century confidently.

National Powers

The Democrats' position on imperialism was clear. The American Revolution had been fought to free the colonies from overseas rule. While the United States had then acquired significant new territories and become a transcontinental nation, the acquisitions had always been made with an eye to incorporating the territories as states, and *Dred Scott* had stated that new territories had to be admitted as states as soon as possible. Implicit in this history was that the nation could not hold overseas colonies and that any territory acquired had to be headed for statehood. Since everyone agreed that neither the Philippines nor Puerto Rico would ever become states, it therefore followed that the United States could not acquire them. The Democratic argument was neatly summarized in the party's 1900 platform: "[T]he Constitution follows the flag."[35]

With new possessions in hand, a majority of the Court, over the dissents of Fuller, Harlan, Brewer, and Peckham, rejected the options of either granting the inhabitants of Puerto Rico and the Philippines full political rights or relinquishing control over the islands. Instead they found that territorial acquisition was an inherent attribute of sovereignty. Therefore Congress could do as it wished, and since Congress wished the islands to be colonies, that was its prerogative. At the time Finley Peter Dunne was writing a newspaper column featuring the satiric observations of a fictional Irish American saloonkeeper, Mr. Dooley. The *Insular Cases* triggered his most famous observation that "no matter whether th' constitution follows th' flag or not, th' Supreme Coort follows th' iliction returns."[36]

The confident recognition of national power in both *Debs* and the *Insular Cases* was matched elsewhere. Distinguishing *Pollock*, the Court upheld an estate tax to help pay for the recent war.[37] The Court opened the door via the Commerce Clause to a general federal police power consonant with the Progressive Era impulse to improve American society. Thus in *Champion v. Ames*,[38] Harlan infused with moralism a holding that Congress could prohibit the interstate shipment of lottery tickets. Fuller, for Brewer, Peckham, and Shiras, saw the legislation as "accomplish[ing] objects not entrusted to the General Government, and to defeat[ing] the operation of the Tenth Amendment."[39] Eight years later, with those dissenters either dead or retired, a unanimous Court held that the federal government had the power to seize mislabeled food even after it was shipped in interstate commerce and had become commingled with local products.[40] In a like vein, the Court held that Congress could tax yellow oleomargarine out of existence.[41] Congress was behaving more like the states, and its actions were almost uniformly sustained.

Antitrust

Just as transportation was the key to a federal police power, it also proved the key to unlocking the Sherman Act; the addition of Peckham as well as those better-conceived targets for prosecution changed the Court's course. Peckham's aversion to rate regulation was grounded in his faith in markets, and that faith encompassed a recognition that price fixing was also rate regulation, artificially high instead of low. The first successful applications of the Sherman Act were to railroad defendants engaging in price fixing.[42] Then Peckham led the Court to apply these decisions to multistate price fixing and market splitting by steel pipe manufacturers.[43]

Even with its resurrection, Roosevelt eyed the Sherman Act warily, though to gain popular approval he used it against a perfect corporate villain. His target was a holding company controlled by railroad magnate James J. Hill and banking tycoon J. P. Morgan that functionally merged the Great Northern and Northern Pacific railroads (the same thing would occur again in 1970), thereby eliminating competition between Chicago and the Pacific Northwest. Roosevelt prevailed 5–4, although there was no majority opinion.[44] One of the dissenters was his first appointee to the Court, the thrice-wounded Civil War veteran and already famous Oliver Wendell Holmes Jr. His dissent proclaimed that "[g]reat cases like hard cases make bad law,"[45] which may be true, but the antitrust law he would have made was terrible. Roosevelt, who trucked no dissent on important matters, supposedly stated that he "could carve out of a banana a judge with more backbone than that," though he truly wanted invertebrates.[46]

Taft elevated Edward White from associate to chief justice when Fuller died, marking the first internal promotion. Over time White, who had dissented from Peckham's early antitrust cases, prevailed. He believed that defendants should be allowed to demonstrate that their actions had been reasonable, and he persuaded a majority to adopt a "rule of reason" test.[47] Henceforth only unreasonable restraints of trade would violate the Sherman Act. Harlan, a leader without followers, dissented vehemently against this "judicial legislation."[48] In this, his last antitrust case, he was again alone, as he had been in *E. C. Knight, Plessy v. Ferguson,* and the *Civil Rights Cases.* The difference was that here he was wrong. The Sherman Act's overly broad language mandated a judicial construction.

Rate Making

The Court's initial reaction to Interstate Commerce Commission orders was icy, with the ICC losing fifteen of sixteen times prior to the 1906 Hepburn Act. When the ICC determined that its power to review the reasonableness of rates included the power to prescribe rates, the Court held that such a power was "never to be implied."[49] Then, when the ICC issued an order to cease charging higher rates for a short haul than for a long haul, the Court ruled that the ICC must take into account the existence of competition on the long-haul route and that reviewing courts were not bound by the ICC's findings of fact.[50] Eventually Congress gave Roosevelt his most prized piece of legislation: the Hepburn Act, granting the ICC power to set rates. Very quickly the Court announced it would not second-guess the ICC on its exercise of this new power.[51]

The nature of no second-guessing was ambiguous because of the Court's conclusion in *Reagan v. Farmers' Loan & Trust* that judicial review of rate decisions was necessary. In *Smyth v. Ames,* Harlan for a unanimous Court offered a laundry list of considerations that were necessary to determine whether a given rate would provide a fair return on the value of the railroad's assets. Application of *Smyth v. Ames* meant that every rate had to be scrutinized by federal courts, for "[e]ach case must depend upon its special facts."[52]

Smyth v. Ames required a very unpleasant job of federal courts, but it also necessitated access to those courts that might be blocked by the Court's Eleventh Amendment jurisprudence. *Ex parte Young* remedied the latter problem. Minnesota passed a law ordering a rate reduction and imposing serious fines and criminal penalties for its violation. The railroad sued the attorney general for an injunction against enforcement. The Court, through Peckham, agreed that the Minnesota law was unconstitutional, on both the rate and the severity of the penalties. But the case's import came from the conclusion that when a state official attempted to enforce an unconstitutional law, he was acting in his personal and not his official capacity. Accordingly the Eleventh Amendment was no bar to the suit. As was becoming typical, Harlan dissented alone, arguing that the decision would "practically obliterate the Eleventh Amendment,"[53] even though he had taken just such a position two decades earlier.[54] *Ex parte Young* was essential to breathe life into *Smyth v. Ames,* but it went further, offering a prophylactic rule to guarantee a federal forum for attacking any unconstitutional state law. Hated by progressives, *Ex parte Young* proved essential to the effort to desegregate the South a half century later.

The Police Power and Liberty of Contract

Unlike in issues of federal power after 1896, the Court stayed its course when dealing with states. Still, as in the issues of federal power, the governments overwhelmingly prevailed. While the Court would not allow states to discriminate against interstate commerce, it continued to sustain legislation designed to protect the public's health, welfare, safety, or morals. Nevertheless, there were two innovations. First, the Court determined that nonracial laws could violate equal protection.[55] More significantly, in *Allgeyer v. Louisiana* the Court recognized a constitutional liberty of contract.

Allgeyer involved a Louisiana law denying state citizens access to the national market by forbidding them to acquire insurance outside the state. That would have violated the dormant Commerce Clause but for a misguided 1869 decision holding that insurance was not part of commerce.[56] Louisiana created an extraterritorial reach by following its citizens as they entered into contracts in other states. Searching for another reason to invalidate this protectionist measure, Peckham, for a unanimous Court, hit on the liberty of contract that, like other liberties, was protected under the Due Process Clause. Liberty "means not only the right of the citizen to be free from the mere physical restraint of his person [but also] to be free in the enjoyment of all his faculties . . . to earn his livelihood by any lawful calling . . . and for that purpose to enter into all contracts which may be proper, necessary and essential."[57] There wasn't a lot of reasoning in the opinion, perhaps because Louisiana's actions were so clearly unconstitutional—contra Holmes, easy cases make bad law—but also because Peckham's construction was hardly novel. It had been only two years since he left the New York

Court of Appeals, and that court, like many other state courts, had enshrined a similar liberty in state constitutional law.

Liberty of contract, like other liberties, was a default sphere that began exactly where the police power ended. In that sense it was like a claimed liberty to be free from laws requiring compulsory vaccination. Holmes easily explained how such a law was a health measure and therefore valid;[58] hence the claimed liberty did not exist. Brewer and Peckham dissented without opinion.

States obviously limit the right to contract: Sunday laws, usury, and prohibitions of lotteries or prostitution come quickly to mind. Therefore *Allgeyer* could not be about a freestanding constitutional right to contract. Thus in *Knoxville Iron Co. v. Harbison* the Court followed the lead of state courts and sustained, over dissents without opinion by Brewer and Peckham, a law requiring a company that pays its employees in its own paper scrip to redeem the scrip (on request) in dollars. The Court quoted extensively from the court below, including its recognition of the unequal bargaining power between employer and employee. *Allgeyer* was also quickly limited to interstate transactions in *Nutting v. Massachusetts*, where the Court allowed Massachusetts to require a license to sell insurance within the state.

Liberty of contract received its most sustained attention in laws setting maximum hours of work for underground miners, bakers, and women. Immediately after *Allgeyer* the Court decided *Holden v. Hardy*, sustaining a Utah law that limited underground miners to eight hours of work per day. The state had an interest in protecting those engaged in "dangerous or unhealthful employments," the Court found.[59] Furthermore, employers and employees have conflicting interests, and the employer in the case was complaining not that his rights to contract were infringed but that the act harmed his employees. The state could thus intervene either where "the public health demands" or "where the parties do not stand upon an equality."[60] Brewer and Peckham again dissented without opinion. Presumably Brewer was unwilling to utter in a judicial opinion what he was willing to say in a commence-ment address: "The police power is the refuge for timid judges to es-cape the obligation of denouncing a wrong in a case where some sup-posed general or public good is the object of the legislation."[61]

Lochner v. New York, involving a law limiting bakers to ten hours a day of work, witnessed a decided lack of timidity on the part of Fuller, Brown, and Joseph McKenna, who along with Brewer joined Peckham's opinion, which marked the first time the Court held that the police power did not justify a law. The opinion simply ignored *Holden's* point about unequal bargaining power with the tart observa-tion that bakers were not "wards of the State."[62]

Instead of beginning by noting that liberty of contract was not ab-solute, *Lochner* began with the "concession" that there is a limit to the police power because otherwise the Fourteenth Amendment "would have no efficacy and . . . the States would have unbounded power."[63] The limit was that the "mere assertion" of a "public health" rationale was insufficient. It had to be real, and the Court did not believe New York—which in fact had codified the law under labor law, not public health (though the opinion did not say so). "[T]he common under-standing of the trade of a baker has never been regarded as an un-healthy one."[64] To sustain this law would be to open the floodgates and authorize the limiting of hours of "doctors, lawyers, scientists, all pro-fessional men, as well as athletes and artisans."[65] That would be absurd. There being no health justification, the act was a labor law, and the as-sertion of the police power was a mere pretext.

Lochner differs from prior cases in finding the police power insuf-ficient and for not explicitly using the language of class legislation. "In-terference with liberty of contract" became the accepted manner of saying "impermissible class legislation."

Harlan for himself, White, and Roosevelt's second appointee, Wil-liam Day, dissented. Relying on a treatise, *Diseases of Workers,* he con-cluded that working as a baker was in fact injurious to health, as demonstrated by the below-average life expectancy of bakers. Since the issue of health was open to honest debate, the Court should defer to the legislature.

Holmes wrote a solo and characteristically pithy dissent that endeared him to progressive reformers. He proclaimed that *Lochner* was "decided upon an economic theory which a large part of the country does not entertain."[66] Then memorably he wrote that "[t]he Fourteenth Amendment does not enact Mr. Herbert Spencer's Social Statics."[67] His claim that a large part of the country disagreed with the Court's theory may have been correct, but the *Nation,* the *Washington Post,* the *New York Times,* and three other New York dailies saluted the decision.

The problem with Holmes's dissent was that it did not join issue with the other eight justices, nor did it explain why their constitutional view that class legislation was improper was in error. He might have explained that in an industrialized nation Jacksonian concepts of neutrality would always benefit the powerful, and that industrialization had rendered classless politics obsolete and likely impossible. But simply noting that the nation "is made for people of fundamentally differing views" and concluding that the Fourteenth Amendment "is perverted when it is held to prevent the natural outcome of dominant opinion" is the cry of judicial abdication. It is hardly a wonder that he was alone.

Lochner was an obscure case when argued, but like *Dred Scott,* it has been hooted down by critics from shortly after it was decided right up to the present day. Yet *Lochner* was so unimportant that it was overruled without citation in 1917 and cited in but a dozen opinions prior to 1937, and the famous pejorative oxymoron for which it stands—substantive due process (as if process could be substantive rather than procedural)—was first mentioned in an opinion in 1944, and in a dissent at that. Again, winners write history, and with Franklin Roosevelt's reelection *Lochner* became a huge loser.

One of those twelve cases citing *Lochner* was *Adair v. United States,* where a railroad discharged an employee for joining a union. That violated an 1898 federal statute forbidding "yellow-dog contracts"—those requiring employees to promise not to join a union. As with state cases, the Court perceived the commerce power operating in one sphere and the Due Process Clause in another. If the act were a valid regulation of commerce—and the Court held it was not because of an insufficient relationship between interstate commerce and membership in a union—then Adair's liberty would not have been infringed. Nevertheless, Harlan took a sweeping view of liberty of contract as he stated, "I[I]t is not within the functions of government . . . to compel any person in the course of his business [to] retain the personal services of another."[68] Again disregarding *Holden,* the Court found that employer and employee "have equality of right, and any legislation that disturbs that equality is an arbitrary interference with liberty of contract."[69] Holmes and McKenna each dissented.

Yet *Adair* was an outlier. Of the almost ten dozen challenges to federal statutes between 1890 and 1911, only eighteen were invalidated on any grounds, and most of these were insignificant ones, like the Oklahoma statehood requirement that the state capital remain in Guthrie until at least 1913.[70]

Shortly after *Adair, Muller v. Oregon* sustained a ten-hour maximum day as applied to women working in any mechanical establishment, factory, or laundry. Brewer's short, unanimous opinion justified the law on the basis of a "woman's physical structure and the performance of maternal functions plac[ing] her at an obvious disadvantage in the struggle for subsistence," as well as history's "disclos[ing] the fact that woman has always been dependent upon man."[71] Thus *Lochner* was easily distinguished. Whether limiting women's hours of work would aid women in their struggle for subsistence—wages and hours are, after all, intertwined—was a policy issue that the Court did not address.

The Bill of Rights

Liberty of contract as found in the Fifth and Fourteenth amendments was one provision of the Bill of Rights that fared well. By contrast the Court acquiesced in Congress's determination to destroy the Mormon Church over polygamy. Even though *Reynolds* held that Mormon polygamy was not protected by the Free Exercise Clause and therefore its criminalization was constitutional, the practice continued. Congress made several attempts to extinguish it, culminating in 1887 with the Edmunds-Tucker Act, which dissolved the church's incorporation and confiscated church property to finance non-Mormon schools in Utah. If the religion was destroyed in the process, that was hardly an unfortunate side effect; indeed, it would be a benefit. Bradley sustained the action because polygamy was "contrary to the spirit of Christianity and of the civilization which Christianity has produced in the Western world," as if that met the claim that Congress was taking property and destroying a church.[72] The president of the church announced receiving a revelation that polygamy was no longer appropriate. He wrote in his diary of "the necessity of acting for the temporal salvation of the church."[73] The Utah Enabling Act granted Utah statehood only on condition of banning polygamy "forever." With church and state conforming to congressional policy, the remaining properties were returned to the church.

Security of property resulted in the Fifth Amendment's Takings Clause being deemed protected by the Fourteenth Amendment's Due Process Clause.[74] But no other provision of the Bill of Rights was similarly treated. The Court rejected claims that freedom of the press, the right to keep and bear arms, grand jury indictment, the privilege against self-incrimination, twelve-man juries, and cruel and unusual punishments were encompassed within either the Privileges and Immunities or Due Process clauses.[75]

Some of the cases were compelling, such as a bootlegger's receiving a few hundred consecutive sentences that cumulatively ran over fifty-four years because he could not pay an enormous $6,600 fine. In addition to rejecting his claim that the Eighth Amendment was part of the Fourteenth, the Court added that he should not have committed so many offenses.[76] Another case involved the jailing, on order of the Colorado Supreme Court, of a Colorado United States senator and publisher of the *Denver Times* and *Rocky Mountain Daily News* because he had editorialized against a judicial coup d'état by that very same court. Holmes explained that the senator would lose anyway because the First Amendment only reached prior restraints and was no bar to punishment for harmful speech.[77] It was the Sedition Act redux.

With the exception of the Second Amendment case, Harlan dissented, taking the historically accurate view that the Fourteenth Amendment bound the states to the guarantees of the Bill of Rights. Once he queried what the Court would do if Utah "should amend its constitution and make the Mormon religion the established religion of the State, to be supported by taxation on all the people of Utah."[78] There being no acceptable answer, no one responded.

Jim Crow

Harlan's most famous dissent, though not nearly his most passionate, was in *Plessy v. Ferguson.* Time vindicated Harlan's opposition to the separate but equal doctrine, but when written, his dissent was quixotic at best.

Two decades after the Compromise of 1877, the Republican Party had some strength in the upper South but not elsewhere, and there was nothing that Northern Republicans could do to revive it in the lower South. Race relations had commenced their long and too often violent downward spiral, and Southern leaders wanted to make sure that there was no renewal of the Republican-Negro voting alliance.

Nine states passed Jim Crow railroad laws between 1887 and 1892, and the ICC had ruled that segregated railroad cars were not an "undue or unreasonable prejudice or disadvantage," as long as the cars were equal.[79] Both imperialism and the wave of immigration from southern and eastern Europe contributed to narrowing Northern and Southern attitudes about race. Everything was conspiring against Negroes in the South, and it was not surprising that the Court was too.

Plessy was decided within the existing police power paradigm, and thus sustaining the Louisiana law requiring separate but equal railroad cars was overdetermined. Everyone—except the Negroes—was for it. A law that promised to minimize racial conflict by minimizing racial interactions looked like a reasonable way of promoting the public safety. The bow to Southern sentiment came with the conclusion that law cannot change attitudes. The Court also granted the states a huge amount of discretion on how to act, noting that in testing reasonableness, the legislature could "act with established usages, custom and traditions of the people, and with a view to promote their comfort, and the preservation of the public peace and good order."[80] Commingling of the races could not be forced. If Negroes thought that the law stamped them with a badge of inferiority, it was only because they chose to put that interpretation forward.

Harlan's solo dissent is memorable for its prescient prediction that *Plessy* "will, in time, prove to be quite as pernicious as . . . *Dred Scott*."[81] He accurately saw that the "destinies of the two races, in this country, are indissolubly linked together, and the interests of both require that the common government of all shall not permit the seeds of race hate to be planted under the sanction of law."[82] He knew that the superficially equal legislation was in fact intended to harm Negroes. Finally, in his most memorable sentence, he proclaimed that the "Constitution is color-blind, and neither knows nor tolerates classes among citizens."[83]

Harlan's last sentiment echoed Senator Chauncey Depew, a New

York Republican, who claimed that the "American Commonwealth is built upon the individual [and] it recognizes neither classes nor masses."[84] Yet even as that idea became dated in the Progressive Era, *Lochner* and *Adair* constitutionalized it to the detriment of workers (and most Americans). When *Plessy* rejected that idea, it was to the detriment of Negroes (and all Americans). The Court's conception of the police power yielded both sets of results. *Plessy*'s conclusion that segregation did not impose a badge of inferiority was essential within the police power framework, because otherwise it would constitute class legislation.

Harlan was also right that worse was still to come. By 1900 there was segregation everywhere in the South, although for the most part it occurred without the need for law. But when law was needed, it was there. The African American leader Booker T. Washington acquiesced because the alternative—which remained all too visible in its use—was white violence. In 1900 alone, 106 Negroes were lynched by hangings, shootings, burnings, and castration. In the words of a Mississippi Negro, white Southerners "had to have a license to kill anything but a nigger. We was always in season."[85] As segregation widened and deepened, lynchings decreased. The police power rationale had something to it once white violence was an accepted fact that could not (and would not) be remedied.

Berea College in Kentucky was one of only two Southern colleges that were integrated. In 1904 Kentucky passed a law forbidding a corporation chartered by the state from offering biracial education. Ignoring both *Lochner*'s freedom of contract and *Plessy*'s statement that commingling of the races had to be "the result of natural affinities . . . and a voluntary consent of individuals,"[86] Brewer sustained the law as part of the state's powers over corporations it has chartered.[87] Harlan dissented, finding that the liberty of those wishing an interracial education had been violated.

At the end of the century and the turn of the next, the South engaged in a massive effort to render the Fifteenth Amendment a nullity. Republicans no longer cared. Since James Garfield's election in 1880, Republicans could win the presidency despite a solid Democratic South.

The South used a variety of methods to disenfranchise Negroes: grandfather clauses, literacy and/or understanding tests, and poll taxes. Both violence and the decline of the Republican Party had already drastically reduced voting by Negroes. Disenfranchisement was a mop-up operation that the Court quickly validated. In *Williams v. Mississippi* the Court unanimously sustained a literacy test because it applied to white and black alike. *Giles v. Harris* was a suit to force the state to register Negro residents who, if not registered, would likely be disenfranchised under a new state constitution going into effect nine months in the future. Holmes declined to grant relief, in no small part because the suit alleged "that the great mass of the white population intends to keep blacks from voting."[88] If that was true—and it was—then "more than ordering the plaintiff's name to be inscribed on a piece of paper will not defeat them."[89] Therefore giving the Negroes their constitutional rights would be an empty gesture, because massive constitutional violations cannot be remedied by courts. Finding Louisiana's separate but equal law constitutional in *Plessy* could have had a similar explanation. Racial subordination was going to be a continuous massive fact regardless of what any court said or did. Harlan, Brewer, and Brown dissented in *Giles*.

Negroes did get relief from a racially neutral Alabama law that conclusively presumed criminal fraud from accepting money and then failing to complete a contract. By criminalizing breach of contract, the statute disproportionately affected Negroes, as they were a majority of agricultural workers, and they habitually needed advances to pay existing debts or fines in order to avoid incarceration for petty crimes.

Alonzo Bailey received a $15 advance on a contract to work for twelve months at $12 per month. After a month and a few days he walked off the job. Since doing so was conclusive proof of fraud, he was not allowed to testify as to his reasons. He was convicted and fined $30 or, in default of that, required to serve 136 days at hard labor. Charles Evans Hughes, the former Republican reform governor of New York and a recent Taft appointee, wrote an opinion finding the Alabama law a Thirteenth Amendment violation: "The State may impose involuntary servitude as a punishment for crime, but it may not compel one man to labor for another in payment of a debt, by punishing him as a criminal if he does not perform the service."[90] Bluntly, the Thirteenth Amendment bars states from using the criminal law to enforce contractual promises—especially in the unacknowledged context of racial subordination.

Putting his *Lochner* dissent in bold relief, Holmes dissented. In *Lochner* he promised to enforce "the natural outcome of a dominant opinion."[91] In *Bailey* that dominant opinion consisted of the white Alabamans' desire, in the absence of slavery, to reduce Negroes to the status of serfs. Holmes was unfazed and kept his promise.

· VII ·

Progressivism, Normalcy, and Depression

THE PROGRESSIVE IMPULSE resulted in the third great wave of constitutional amendments when four new amendments were ratified, two
in 1913 and two in 1920. Like their Reconstruction predecessors, they
emphasized nationalism and equality.

The Sixteenth Amendment authorized an income tax and overturned *Pollock v. Farmers' Loan and Trust*. By 1906 Theodore Roosevelt
had joined the Democrats' call for an income tax, and the question
became whether to accomplish it by a statute or by constitutional
amendment. If by statute, the justices would be faced with the unhappy choice of either admitting that they blew it in *Pollock* or facing
a united and probably angry populace that was increasingly uneasy
with the rich. Seeing that the Court was in a no-win position, Roosevelt's successor, William Howard Taft, fully embraced the amendment
route. The income tax amendment was ratified just before Woodrow
Wilson took office, and a few months later, Congress passed a progressive income tax (which the Court swiftly upheld).[1]

Direct election of senators was a good government idea designed to
clean up corrupt governments (as well as free the Senate from being a
millionaires' club). A majority of states had effectively circumvented

legislative selection of senators by mandating that the legislature ratify a candidate's election victory, and once the Senate let the proposal go to the states, the Seventeenth Amendment was swiftly ratified. With the Sixteenth strengthening the revenues of the national government and the Seventeenth freeing senators from any state legislative accountability, the people, whether consciously or not, had tilted the federal balance decisively toward the national government.

World War I directly produced two long-desired amendments, the Eighteenth, making Prohibition national policy, and the Nineteenth, enfranchising women. Prohibition had become part of the progressive crusade to make better Americans and was decidedly assisted by the fact that all things German—including beer—were under attack during the war. Women's suffrage was promoted by some as yet another means of cleaning up politics. Running as the Republican presidential candidate, Charles Evans Hughes had backed an amendment in 1916, and Wilson eventually promoted suffrage as a recognition that women were partners in the war effort.

In addition to changing the Constitution, a number of Western states adopted recall, initiative, and referendum as ways to get around bosses and legislatures that had sold out to special interests—particularly railroads and utilities. Perhaps understanding that it is easier to buy half a legislature than half the electorate (who by a 10–1 margin had enacted a 2 percent gross receipts tax), Pacific Telephone and Telegraph challenged initiative and referendum as inconsistent with Article IV's requirement of a republican form of government. Copiously quoting from the "absolutely controlling" *Luther v. Borden,* where the Court refused to decide which Rhode Island government was legitimate, Chief Justice Edward White for a unanimous Court ruled that this was a nonjusticiable political question.[2]

Staffing the Court

As the Constitution was being remade, so was the Court. Taft, who had twice declined Theodore Roosevelt's offer to join the Court in hopes of becoming either chief justice or president, placed five new men on the Court as Melville Fuller, John M. Harlan, David Brewer, and Rufus Peckham died and Roosevelt's third appointee retired because of a disabling illness. Taft wanted professional competence, and he appointed men he knew, without regard to party. When the chief justiceship opened up, Taft moved White, who had a good mind but tortured the interminable sentences he composed, to the center seat that Taft so desired for himself. Taft's five other appointments included two more Southern Democrats, Horace H. Lurton and Joseph R. Lamar, as well as New York's embattled reform Republican governor, Charles Evans Hughes, a man of impressive intelligence, and a Republican federal judge from Wyoming, Willis Van Devanter. Taft's proudest achievement as president was reconstituting what had been an aged Court.

Taft also claimed to have told his appointees that if any of them died, he would disown them. Yet during Woodrow Wilson's first term both Lurton and Lamar died, and Hughes resigned when the Republicans chose him as their presidential candidate in 1916. Unlike Taft, who wanted balanced men, Wilson wanted progressives on the Court. He began with his attorney general, the cantankerous, trust-busting Tennesseean James McReynolds. Wilson mistakenly thought that McReynolds's position on trusts was a proxy for progressive beliefs generally. McReynolds instead was a reactionary, whose votes would affect almost a quarter-century of constitutional doctrine. He could have been, but wasn't, a Klansman. Later in his career, when Charles Houston, the first Negro on the *Harvard Law Review* and the NAACP's head of litigation, was arguing, McReynolds turned his chair and faced away from Houston for the entire argument (and then dissented).

To McReynolds's chagrin, the next appointee was a Jew—the highly intelligent, humorless, self-righteous Louis D. Brandeis, who during the presidential campaign had become a principal advisor to the highly intelligent, humorless, self-righteous Wilson. Brandeis was wealthy and public spirited, but very much the Old Testament prophet (as acolytes

Learned Hand and Felix Frankfurter acknowledged by referring to him as Isaiah). Brandeis had amassed an impressive array of enemies, and many of them violently opposed his nomination. Taft, Harvard president A. Lawrence Lowell, former secretary of war and state and current American Bar Association president Elihu Root, former attorney general George Wickersham, and several past presidents of the American Bar Association were just some of those opposing Brandeis. Wilson argued that those who opposed him did so because "he had refused to be serviceable to them in the promotion of their own selfish interests."[3] Brandeis's take-no-prisoners approach to his public interest practice had something to do with it, too—as did raw anti-Semitism. He simply was not clubbable.

From nomination to confirmation took several months and offered the opening salvos of that year's presidential campaign. Although there were an inordinate number of abstentions, those voting did so almost on perfect party lines, and with the Democrats in control of the Senate, Brandeis was confirmed.

Wilson's final choice was a federal judge from Ohio, John H. Clarke, who had taken that job because his progressive candidacy for the Senate had been going nowhere. But with the Republicans removing Hughes from the Court, there was no fight over his replacement. Reflecting on Clarke and Brandeis, *The Call*, a socialist daily in New York, approvingly editorialized about radicals on the bench. Brandeis certainly was different from all his predecessors, a "nightmare" in Taft's estimation.[4]

The New Freedom and Federal Power

Judges, Roosevelt claimed, were "an insurmountable barrier to reform."[5] It didn't appear that way to the Wilson administration, which in its first term adopted the New Freedom, the most far-ranging domestic program since (and probably including) Alexander Hamilton's.

In addition to the new income tax, coupled with the lowering of rates in the Underwood Tariff, Congress created the Federal Reserve system, which gave the federal government control over monetary policy, strengthened the antitrust laws with both the Clayton Act and the creation of the Federal Trade Commission, created worker's compensation for injured federal employees, established an eight-hour day on interstate railroads, and finally, with the 1916 platforms of both parties in support, through the Keating-Owen Act regulated (in such a way as to cripple) the use of child labor. Even labor radical Mother Jones applauded Wilson and the Democrats.

States, too, reformed their economies by protecting women and children. Thirty-eight joined Oregon in limiting the hours of work for women, all but one set a minimum age for child labor (although those of the South were pathetically low), and eight experimented with a minimum wage for women.

Just as Mother Jones praised Wilson, a progressive federal judge expressed satisfaction with the Court. It had "never demonstrated more fully its fitness to apply the Constitution to American life . . . [,] [and] our constitutional government is well adapted to serve the life of the American people."[6] That warm sentiment was especially applicable to the Court's acceptance of the widening congressional powers the progressives were exercising.

The Court had validated a technical rewrite of the Employers' Liability Act that was designed both to encourage railroads to be safer and to provide remedies for injured railway workers. The act imposed greater liability on interstate railroads for the negligence of their workers by repealing the common law fellow servant rule, whereby an employer was not liable for injuries done to one employee by another. A unanimous Court upheld the act, concluding that there is no vested right to a continuation of a common law rule even when the negligent employee was not engaged in interstate commerce, as long as the injured employee was.[7]

In cases involving rate making, the Court first expanded state power and then turned around and approved a stunning extension of federal power. The *Minnesota Rate Cases* upheld state rate orders that had the effect of lowering interstate railroad rates. Hughes noted that there had been no federal regulation of those rates, and a year later, in the *Shreveport Rate Case,* he upheld a federal order overturning rates on routes that were entirely within the state of Texas. The Texas Railroad Commission had set rates from Dallas and Houston to east Texas that were significantly lower than rates from Shreveport to the same destinations, even though the distances were the same. In upholding the Interstate Commerce Commission, the Court held that Congress could reach intrastate activities that affected interstate commerce.

Finally, in *Wilson v. New* the Court upheld the Adamson Act, which limited interstate railroad employees to an eight-hour day and precluded any reduction in pay at least until a commission reported on railway labor issues. The Court easily upheld the eight-hour limitation, finding it "so clearly sustained as to render the subject not disputable."[8] Thereafter, White's opinion is unclear in its reasoning, for it holds that the right of the railroad and the union to fix wages was beyond public control while simultaneously upholding the act as emergency legislation to prevent a paralyzing strike. Four justices dissented because they believed that wage regulation exceeded federal power.

Federal power was even more expansive in the decisions upholding the Mann Act, popularly known as the "White-Slave Traffic Act" (based on the progressives' delusional belief that young white women were being sold into prostitution). Extending the rationale of the Pure Food and Drug Act, Congress made it a crime to transport a woman across state lines for an immoral purpose. The Court recognized that the Mann Act was an exercise of a general police power while rejecting a claim that it invaded the power of the states. "[W]hen rid of confusing and distracting considerations," the power over transportation among the several states "is complete in itself, and . . . Congress . . . may adopt not only means necessary but convenient to its exercise, and the means may have the quality of police regulations."[9] Federal power apparently was complete: with the Pure Food and Drug Act, Congress controlled behavior in the state of origin; with the Mann Act, it reached the destination state.

The Court went even further in its second Mann Act case, where the son of a prominent Democrat and a friend, both married, had taken two women from Sacramento to Reno for some long-term sex. Their defense was that the romp was for pleasure, not money. No matter. When state lines are crossed, *Gibbons v. Ogden* held that commerce was intercourse; almost a century later, *Caminetti v. United States* inverted that equation: nonmarital intercourse was commerce.

It turned out that the Court was more interested in suppressing moral deviants than economic malefactors. Sex may have been an interstate issue, as were most railroads, but child labor was not. Being local, it was beyond the reach of Congress, even when Congress banned shipments across state lines of goods made with child labor. The five-justice majorities that had sustained the Adamson Act and then applied the Mann Act to noncommercial sex vanished in *Hammer v. Dagenhart*, where a father sued on behalf of his two sons, one under age sixteen, the other under fourteen, so that they could keep working in a cotton mill. William Day, an appointee of Theodore Roosevelt, switched sides. He distinguished all the prior cases as "instances [where] the use of interstate transportation was necessary to the accomplishments of harmful results."[10] So much for talk of a police power.

The Court believed that if there was harm with child labor, it resided within the state of manufacture. This blinked at reality, for the harm was also in the economic advantage that manufacturers gained from the low wages paid to children. A majority of the Court rejected this "unfair competition" argument, reasoning that "the Commerce

Clause was not intended to give Congress a general authority to equalize" local conditions that afford one state "an economic advantage over the others."[11] Texas had oil and gas, Minnesota iron ore, West Virginia coal. North Carolina, by luck, had children to exploit. The federal law was "in a twofold sense repugnant to the Constitution. It not only transcends the authority delegated to Congress over commerce but also exerts a power as to a purely local matter to which the federal authority does not extend."[12] Reverting back to *Kidd v. Pearson* and *E. C. Knight,* the Court worried that if Congress could reach activities "entrusted to local authorities . . . [,] all freedom of commerce will be at an end, and the power of the States over local matters may be eliminated, and thus our system of government practically destroyed."[13]

Sustaining state authority over child labor was thus a small price to pay for preserving the Constitution. Holmes, writing a dissent for Joseph McKenna, Brandeis, and Clarke, was hardly persuaded, taking the view that at least since the *Lottery Case,* when state lines were crossed, congressional power was complete. Not too subtly referencing *Caminetti,* Holmes noted that "if there is any matter upon which civilized countries have agreed—far more unanimously than they have with regard to intoxicants and some other matters over which this country is now emotionally aroused—it is the evil of premature and excessive child labor."[14] Had Wilson named anyone other than McReynolds, the odds are overwhelming that the child labor ban would have been sustained.

Progressives were dismayed and angered. The *New Republic* concluded that "[i]n the long run American opinion will not consent to have social legislation invalidated and its social progress retarded by the necessarily accidental and arbitrary preference of one judge in a court of nine."[15] Thinking more of the short run, the *New York Tribune* found it "improbable that such a decision will stand,"[16] and sure enough, eighteen months later, the next Congress slapped the Court by imposing a prohibitive excise tax on goods made by child labor.

State Economic Regulation

During the early years of the New Freedom, state statutes were invalidated when they ran afoul of the dormant Commerce Clause or conflicted with federal legislation (often some aspect of the Hepburn Act or the ICC), but basically that was it—except when the case involved organized labor. The era was one of "government by injunction" as one meaning of *Ex parte Young* became clear. State legislatures might adopt a novel statute, but the affected parties would request a judge to issue an injunction. If, as was typical, he did, the effect of the statute would be delayed for months, or more likely years, until a court declared that it was valid. Thus the fact that the Court was not initially hostile to progressive legislation did not mean that the states could readily gain the benefits of their new legislation.

A further aspect of "government by injunction" was illustrated in *Hitchman Coal & Coke v. Mitchell.* All coal miners in West Virginia were required to sign yellow-dog contracts (whereby employment was conditioned on the pledge never to join a union). Relying on those contracts, coal companies obtained injunctions from a federal judge to preclude the United Mine Workers from even attempting to organize the miners. Over a strong dissent by Brandeis, joined by Holmes and Clarke, the Court upheld the injunction because the UMW was interfering with what the Court believed were the company's property rights in a nonunion workforce. Left unexplained was why it was coercive for a union to threaten to strike over a closed shop, but not coercive for an employer to condition employment on a demand that its employees never join a union. The majority of the justices were so enamored with yellow-dog contracts that unions could not try to organize workers who had signed such contracts even though employment was at will (meaning it could be terminated at any time for any reason), and a yellow-dog contract did not preclude joining a union if the employee then quit his job.

Part of the explanation for "government by injunction" may be found in the Adamson Act, sustained in *Wilson v. New*. The railroad unions had threatened to plunge the nation into economic chaos just two months before a presidential election. The president, Congress, and the Court reluctantly caved. But the lesson and the fear—soon compounded by the Russian Revolution—was cemented. Unions created chaos.

In 1915 the Court reaffirmed that bans on yellow-dog contracts violated due process. Yet the language of *Coppage v. Kansas* was different from that of the seven year-old *Adair v. United States*. Instead of denying the problem of unequal bargaining power, the Court seemed to celebrate it: "[S]ince it is self-evident that, unless all things are held in common, some persons must have more property than others, it is from the nature of things impossible to uphold freedom of contract and the right of private property without at the same time recognizing as legitimate those inequalities of fortune that are the necessary result of the exercise of those rights."[17] Asking what relation the Kansas statute had to "the public health, safety, morals or general welfare," the Court announced, "[W]e are unable to conceive of any."[18] Holmes, Day, and Hughes dissented, believing that the unequal bargaining positions of the employer and employee justified the Kansas ban.

A 5–4 Court was simultaneously struggling with an Oregon law setting a minimum wage of $8.64 per week (with a maximum of fifty hours) for women workers. Brandeis, arguing for Oregon (as he had in *Muller*), tied the law in to the traditional police power rationale by claiming that substandard wages had the result of leaving women ill-fed, poorly housed, or in need of the assistance of some man. The vote was to strike the law, but apparently the opinion wouldn't write. Then, over the summer Lamar took ill, never to return, and Brandeis took his place. The case was reargued with a Court believing 5–4 that the minimum wage was valid—except that Brandeis could not participate, so when the case came down evenly divided, there was no precedent.[19]

That same day in 1917, in *Bunting v. Oregon,* the *Lochner* holding was overruled (although *Lochner* was not mentioned), as the Court sustained a statute mandating a maximum ten-hour workday. *Lochner's* analytical framework nevertheless remained in place. With *Wilson v. New* but three weeks old, the Court had no trouble again recognizing that hours of labor affect workers' health. White, Van Devanter, and McReynolds dissented without opinion.

Later in the year a 5–4 Court struck down a Washington state initiative forbidding employment agencies from collecting a fee from people whom they placed in jobs. In an opinion sparse on reasoning, McReynolds rejected the police power rationale and treated the law as if it prohibited rather than regulated (by forcing the agencies to seek compensation from employers) a business that he characterized as "useful, commendable, and in great demand."[20] The fact that there might be abuses—and there were—"is not enough to justify destruction of one's right to follow a distinctly useful calling in an upright way."[21] It was not clear why—although the word "arbitrary" was thrown around a lot. The case was a bridge between policing class legislation and policing the public interest.

Limiting Jim Crow

Segregation was consolidated in the South, increased in the North, and practiced overtly by the federal government under Wilson, who admitted his belief in the efficacy of the practice. Reflecting Northern acceptance of the Southern interpretation of the Civil War and Reconstruction, D. W. Griffith's *Birth of a Nation* swept the entire country after being shown in the White House with Wilson's warm endorsement as "terribly true."[22] Conditions were so bad in the South that the Great Migration north commenced, and by the end of the decade Detroit's black population was up 600 percent, Cleveland's 300 percent, and Chicago's 150 percent.

Surprisingly, the Court, for the first time since *Strauder v. West Virginia*, declared several explicit limits on discrimination in cases dealing with all the Reconstruction amendments. Even in an era hostile to civil rights and a Court with members unsympathetic to racial justice, some laws went too far in demanding overt discrimination. Unlike in the cases from the prior two decades, this Court required formal compliance with constitutional norms.

Alabama's criminal surety statute allowed employers to pay the fines for those convicted of vagrancy, petty larceny, or other "Negro crimes" and then have the defendant work off the debt (where the alternative was the chain gang). Often there were bidding wars for the defendants, and during harvest season sheriffs initiated vagrancy roundups to create additional workers. Ed Rivers was convicted of petty larceny and fined $15 plus $43.75 in costs. Since he was indigent, he could not pay, so he was sentenced to two months at hard labor. Instead he agreed to a surety contract requiring ten months' work. When he quit after a month, he was convicted of breach of his surety agreement and fined $87.05. He then agreed to a different surety contract, now for over fourteen months. The system was well known for creating virtual slaves (without the ameliorating features of slavery) for white employers at minimal cost, and a unanimous Court, never mentioning race, held it unconstitutional.[23]

Oklahoma required luxury railroad cars for whites but not for Negroes. Hughes tersely demanded equality, rejecting the claim that "the constitutional right [could] depend upon the number of persons who may be discriminated against."[24] (Later, as chief justice, Hughes told the Court's marshal, who had complained about Negroes eating in the cafeteria, to go outside the building and read the words "Equal Justice under Law," warning that he would be replaced if he failed to understand them.) Holmes and the three Southerners (White, Lamar, and McReynolds) refused to go along, concurring in the result, because on a technicality Hughes had denied the successful plaintiffs their requested relief. The decision, while theoretically important, had no practical effect. Railroads did not need to be told by law what they knew from economics. It made no sense to offer luxury cars for which there was no demand.

Louisville, along with too many other cities, decided to promote racial harmony by creating residential segregation. If a city block had more white than Negro residents, then houses could be sold only to white buyers, and vice versa. The ordinance sought to secure a better future while leaving occupancy rights of existing homeowners undisturbed. A unanimous Court in *Buchanan v. Warley* acknowledged that the purpose of the ordinance—racial harmony—was the same as the one the Court had approved from *Plessy* onward, but nevertheless noted that "such legislation must have its limitations,"[25] and declared that such a limitation had been reached here. The reason appeared to be property, which was emphasized again and again as the Court relied on due process rather than equal protection. The racist McReynolds joined the opinion, something he would never do in a true civil rights case (while Holmes, not thinking much of either civil rights or property rights, prepared a dissent that he did not file). Negro newspapers celebrated *Buchanan,* but the *Richmond News Leader* best understood its effect: residential segregation could be maintained by custom, to say nothing of restrictive covenants.

Oklahoma amended its constitution to exempt permanently from literacy requirements anyone descended from a person who would have been eligible to vote in 1866 (when, of course, only whites could vote). *Guinn v. United States* held this grandfather clause unconstitutional, but the case had no real effect in the South. Literacy tests and poll taxes were still valid. Negroes were already disenfranchised, and all the other grandfather clauses had served their purpose and expired.

World War I

The war effort commenced by conscripting men. It soon moved to conscripting minds, and ultimately conscripting property. Constitutional challenges to each failed, because the power to wage war is the power to do so successfully.

A unanimous Court thought that the challenge to the draft was frivolous. Article I gave Congress the power to declare war and to raise an army. The claim that Congress was limited to raising a volunteer army ignored the responsibilities of citizenship. The claim that being drafted was involuntary servitude in violation of the Thirteenth Amendment was "refuted by its mere statement."[26]

The Wilson administration was committed to clamping down on antiwar sentiment. As Attorney General Thomas Gregory stated of those who opposed the war, "May God have mercy on them, for they need expect none from an outraged people and an avenging government."[27] The Court enlisted fully in that righteous crusade, so much so that it affirmed the conviction of Eugene Debs, who had won a million votes as the Socialist Party candidate for president in 1912, for obstructing the draft. Debs, who was not even mentioned by name in Holmes's unanimous opinion, had given a speech about socialism in which he mentioned, with admiration, that he had just visited three socialists convicted of aiding a person in failing to register for the draft. He also condemned "Prussian militarism in a way that naturally might have been thought to be intended to include the mode of proceeding in the United States."[28] He also expressed the socialist view that his listeners were "fit for something better than slavery and cannon fodder."[29]

Holmes concluded that the "jury were most carefully instructed that they could not find the defendant guilty for advocacy of any of his opinions unless the words used had as their natural tendency and reasonably probable effect to obstruct the recruiting service."[30] That done, the First Amendment placed no bar on conviction. If a speech might cause a public harm, then it could claim no constitutional immunity. (Debs was again the Socialist Party's presidential candidate in 1920, and he won almost a million votes while in jail. President Warren Harding pardoned him and invited him to the White House.)

After its summer recess, the Court affirmed convictions of Russian immigrants—"puny anonymities"[31]—who were opposed only to the 1918 invasion of Russia by U.S. troops in support of Russian "Whites" who were resisting the "Red" Russia of the Bolsheviks. The defendants had produced five thousand circulars, some in English, some in Yiddish, some of which were thrown from a window of a building, calling for a general strike. Holmes, with Brandeis as well in dissent, found the defendants' actions protected speech: "[W]hen men have realized that time has upset many fighting faiths, they may come to believe . . . that the ultimate good desired is better reached by the free trade in ideas— that the best test of truth is the power of the thought to get itself accepted in the competition of the market."[32] That, they concluded, was the meaning of the First Amendment. The other seven, through Clarke, disagreed. Reflecting the progressives' disdain for dissent, they affirmed the convictions, reasoning that the speech of the defendants against the Russian invasion might have curtailed wartime production to be used against Germany. The constitutional issue was treated in a single sentence as having been already settled. Speech questioning the war might be acceptable before, and then after, the war, but not during the war itself. Harding also pardoned these defendants, who were in a federal penitentiary, but only on condition that they pay their own way back to Russia—which they did, only to become disillusioned with the regime and move on to Mexico.

Congress responded to the severe housing shortage in the capital immediately after the war by imposing rent controls whereby the tenant could remain in possession after the lease expired by continuing to pay the same rent. The law had a two-year sunset provision, and the owner could regain the premises for self-occupancy. Recognizing an emergency, Holmes stated that "[h]ousing is a necessary of life. All the elements of a public interest justifying some degree of public control are present."[33] He justified the reasonableness of the congressional program by noting that all of the civilized countries of the world made a similar choice. McKenna, for White, Van Devanter, and McReynolds, noted equally that "other things are as necessary [as housing]. May they too be taken from the direction of their owners and disposed of by the Government?"[34] No. The dissenters also expressed concern that "emergency" had trumped a constitutional command and wondered what other constitutional commands further emergencies might trump. (When Congress didn't keep its word and extended the emergency, the Court kept its and unanimously held the extension unconstitutional.)[35]

The Era of Normalcy

With the war many progressives, especially at the *New Republic,* had seen opportunities to improve society further. Conscription was an opportunity to teach citizenship. Laws on sedition fostered unity. The War Industries Board, at least after Congress passed the Overman Act in 1918, gained near dictatorial powers and regulated some 350 industries from asbestos to zinc. There would be a new civic virtue in soldier and citizen alike that would carry over after the peace. It didn't work out that way, however.

Wilson feared and predicted that war would wipe out everything. He was right. He had become president, with a lower percentage of the vote than William Jennings Bryan received in any of his three unsuccessful runs, only because Teddy Roosevelt declared the war of 1912 on Taft. But his first term was so successful, his 1916 slogan—"He kept us out of war"—so compelling, and Hughes's California campaign so awful, that Wilson was reelected, but just barely. Then the midterm elections saw Republicans retake control of Congress, and in 1920, with a return to "normalcy," the Republicans took the presidency as well.

Normalcy meant, for the federal government, a return to the late nineteenth century, an end to regimentation, the end of the progressive impulse to improve everyone and everything. It substituted instead a fear of change heightened by the Russian Revolution. The one exception to normalcy was the Volstead Act's attempted bettering of Americans by criminalizing alcohol.

Prohibition turned millions of Americans into criminals and enriched lawbreakers. It also, like its later descendant, the war on drugs, created a legal atmosphere in which the Court's majority bent over backward to sustain overly aggressive police tactics. *Carroll v. United States* and *Olmstead v. United States* were egregious examples of gutting the Fourth Amendment's warrant requirement. In *Carroll* the Court upheld a warrantless automobile search where the defendants were known bootleggers and the road between the Canadian border and Grand Rapids that they were driving on was the road where bootleg liquor traveled. This, Taft absurdly concluded, constituted probable cause to search the vehicle. In *Olmstead,* over Brandeis's greatest dissent, Taft's majority held that wiretaps were not subject to the Fourth Amendment, thereby sending Roy Olmstead, the major Seattle bootlegger (who ordered his men to avoid guns because no life was worth losing just for money), to the federal penitentiary.

On the conservative side, Taft, Van Devanter, and Edward T. Sanford were consistent in supporting strong enforcement of the Volstead Act (banning transportation of intoxicating liquor, defined as containing more than 0.5 per cent alcohol), because they believed that opposition to it undermined the rule of law. In Taft's case this is especially stark because he had vehemently opposed ratification of the Eighteenth Amendment. He had always believed that immigrants would violate the law but was shocked, he wrote in 1923, by the "spirit of lawlessness among the intelligent and wealthy which now exists."[36] McReynolds, George Sutherland, and Pierce Butler were skeptical here, as elsewhere, about federal power. Holmes and Brandeis typically joined the Taft conservatives to affirm convictions.

Olmstead offered the youthful director of the Federal Bureau of In-

vestigation, J. Edgar Hoover, a tool he would shamelessly use long after Prohibition met its constitutional demise in the Twenty-first Amendment. All in all there were no happy legacies from the "noble experiment" of Prohibition.

Warren Harding received four quick appointments in his abbrevi-
ated term. They began with the death of White. Taft achieved his
dream when Harding tapped him. White's death was followed by three
quick voluntary exits, the shocker being Clarke, leaving after five terms
because he couldn't stand McReynolds and wanted to work for U.S. entry into the League of Nations. He almost lived to see the United Nations, and much as Wilson's misjudgment that McReynolds's trust-
busting meant that he was progressive on other issues affected *Hammer
v. Dagenhart,* Clarke's quixotic quest would fundamentally affect constitutional law during the New Deal. With Taft's assistance, Harding selected men who were, from the perspective of normalcy, very sound:
former Utah Republican representative and senator George Sutherland; Minnesota Democrat (but a Grover Cleveland Democrat) and
railroad lawyer Pierce Butler; and a fifteen-year veteran district judge,
Republican Edward Sanford of Tennessee. Calvin Coolidge subsequently placed his friend Attorney General Harlan Fiske Stone, the Republican former dean of Columbia Law School, on the Court.

Conservative times were matched by a conservative Court. To offer
a corollary to Mr. Dooley: It is easier for the Court to follow the election returns if several justices die or retire shortly after the election.

Review of National Legislation

At the national level the Court generously upheld legislation when it
combined two factors: interstate transportation and a business affected
with a public interest. The Transportation Act of 1920, enacted "to
maintain an adequate railway service for the people of the United
States," subjected the rail system to extensive control. Wisconsin, supported by twenty other states, objected to an ICC order attempting to

ensure the financial health of interstate railroads by preempting intrastate rates on the ground that they were too low. The Court unanimously upheld the ICC: "Commerce is a unit and does not regard state
lines."[37]

The Court embraced an equally expansive view of federal power in
Stafford v. Wallace, sustaining the Packers and Stockyards Act of 1921,
which imposed federal regulation on the subject matter. The stockyards, "great national public utilities," were in "streams of commerce"
connecting "one part of the country to another," just as livestock were
transported to and from them.[38]

When legislation lacked the twin touchstones of transportation and
a business affected with a public interest, its reception depended on
whether the Court approved of its ends. Thus the Court sustained the
National Motor Vehicle Theft Act, which prohibited transporting sto-
len cars across state lines, even though the reasoning of *Hammer* had to
be ignored;[39] but the Court refused to yield on its conclusion that Congress lacked power to legislate on child labor and thus invalidated the
tax on goods made by child workers,[40] even though previous prohibitive taxes on margarine and narcotics had been upheld. A pretext is a
pretext when the Court says so, and allowing Congress to circumvent
the Tenth Amendment's interpretation in *Hammer* would have given
Congress carte blanche to regulate local matters. "The good sought in
unconstitutional legislation is an insidious feature because it leads citizens and legislators of good purpose to promote it without thought of
the serious breach it will make in the ark of our covenant."[41] Child labor was an issue Congress cared about, and a constitutional amendment was authorized and sent to the states for ratification (which then
languished because of the Solid South).

The States' Police Powers

Surprisingly, state experimentation fared poorly, as the Court in the
first half-dozen years of Republican ascendancy invalidated more stat-

utes under the Fourteenth Amendment than it had in the previous fifty years. These results had two principal causes. First, the Court narrowly applied its test of whether a business was affected with the public interest. Second, the Court shifted its perception of its role in government from policing class legislation to placing a limit on the general public interest. Van Devanter, McReynolds, Sutherland, and Butler—eventually dubbed the "Four Horsemen of Reaction" (or "Four Horsemen" for short)—stood adamantly against most economic and social experimentation. This same activism, however, also breathed life into the previously lifeless First Amendment guarantees of free speech and a free press.

Yet not all novel legislation met a hostile Court. When zoning first appeared, the Court upheld it as an exercise of the police power over dissents without opinion by Van Devanter, McReynolds, and Butler.[42] And only Butler dissented from a Holmes opinion upholding involuntary sterilization of the supposedly mentally feeble. Holmes needed but two paragraphs to reject the Fourteenth Amendment claims. He dismissed due process by noting: "We have seen more than once that the public welfare may call upon the best citizens for their lives. It would be strange if it could not call upon those who already sap the strength of the State for these lesser sacrifices."[43] He gave even shorter shrift to equal protection, which he dismissed as "the usual last resort of constitutional arguments."[44] Just as with the Court's rulings on the scope of federal powers, there is no getting around the fact that the Court chose to uphold these laws because it agreed with them on the merits.

Immediately after the war Kansas faced a cold winter with a lack of coal because of a strike. The state responded by mandating compulsory arbitration of labor disputes involving production of food, clothing, and fuel. In *Wolff Packing v. Industrial Court,* Taft, for a unanimous Court, held the statute unconstitutional because the businesses were not affected with the public interest. No matter how important a busi-

ness was—and the Kansas court had referred to the necessities of life—
it had to be something special like railroads, stockyards, or utilities to
be affected with the public interest. Thus in subsequent cases, statutes
limiting theater ticket resales to fifty cents over the ticket price, charges
of employment agencies, and gasoline prices were also held to be beyond state control.[45] Common and ordinary businesses were immune
from price regulation.

While *Wolff Packing* implicitly recognized that unions could aid employees, the Court's hostility to unions continued, epitomized by *Duplex Printing v. Deering* and *Truax v. Corrigan*. Section 6 of the Clayton
Act, supposedly labor's Magna Carta, stated that the antitrust laws did
not apply to unions seeking legitimate objectives. Over a dissent by
Brandeis for Holmes and Clarke, *Duplex Printing* held that a secondary
boycott (where a union threatens customers or suppliers to put pressure on the target employer) was illegal, and therefore the union could
be enjoined for an antitrust violation. *Truax* went further and held
that an Arizona law barring injunctions in labor disputes violated both
due process and equal protection. Taft's opinion for a five-man majority enshrined government by injunction by holding that even peaceful picketing could destroy an employer's property interests in its business. Legislatures are "subordinat[e] to the fundamental principles of
right and justice" which guarantee against such arbitrary actions.[46]
Holmes, Brandeis, Clarke, and Mahlon Pitney vigorously dissented,
with Brandeis a tour de force. It is no wonder that the American Feder-
ation of Labor condemned "a series of adjudications of the highest tribunal of the land, successively destroying a basic right or cherished acquisition of organized labor, each forming a link in a fateful chain
consciously designed to enslave the workers of America."[47]

Just as *Truax* threw the Constitution behind employers, so did *Adkins
v. Children's Hospital*, striking down a minimum wage for women. Sutherland's five-man opinion treated a minimum wage as a subsidy ex-
tracted from the employer in violation of due process. It "arbitrarily

shifts to his shoulders a burden which, if it belongs to anybody, belongs to society as a whole."[48] Even Taft dissented, along with Holmes and Clarke (Brandeis did not participate). *Lochner's* reasoning, if not *Lochner,* was alive and well.

Adkins was class legislation, but in *Jay Burns Baking v. Bryan, Meyer v. Nebraska,* and *Pierce v. Society of Sisters,* the Court expanded due process limitations on the states to regulations that were not intended to protect particular class interests. The former involved a state antifraud law that mandated standardized sizes for fresh loaves of bread. Butler agreed that a state could prescribe minimum weights, but the idea of setting maximum weights—preventing bakers from giving the customer more than anticipated—was simply absurd, imposing an unreasonable burden on a lawful profession. Calling the Court's majority a "super-legislature," Brandeis for Holmes wrote a dissent demonstrating the rationality of the state law.[49]

Meyer struck down a law that prohibited schools from teaching in any language except English. McReynolds expansively defined the liberty protected by the Constitution to include "not merely freedom from bodily restraint but also the right of the individual to contract, to engage in any of the common occupations of law, to acquire useful knowledge, to marry, establish a home and bring up children, to worship God according to the dictates of his own conscience, and generally to enjoy those privileges long recognized at common law as essential to the orderly pursuit of happiness."[50] There was no police power rationale for forbidding teaching in a foreign language. Holmes and Sutherland dissented, finding it not unreasonable that students' instruction in the early school years should be in the nation's language.

Pierce extended *Meyer* to hold that a state could not require children to attend public schools (as mandated by a state law passed by a Ku Klux Klan–dominated Oregon). With an eye on both progressivism and Bolshevism, McReynolds for a unanimous Court wrote that "[t]he child is not the mere creature of the State; those who nurture him and direct his destiny have the right, coupled with the high duty, to recognize and prepare him for additional obligations."[51]

Meyer, with its recognition that constitutional liberty included a right to acquire useful knowledge, led to the realization that protections for freedom of speech and the press were now applicable against the states as well as the federal government. Yet as the World War I cases indicated, the Court did not give those freedoms much scope, and Brandeis, in the best six-word sentence in the United States Reports, summarized their import: "Men feared witches and burnt women."[52] That was the point; as with due process generally, if a legislative concern was reasonable, then the law was constitutional. Thus advocating revolution, like questioning the war, was deemed off-limits no matter how tiresome the speech.

Finding the First Amendment applicable to the states was a start. In the 1930s the Court held that a California law criminalizing the display of a red flag as a symbol of revolution, Huey Long's effort to punish Louisiana's opposition press by discriminatory taxation, and Georgia's conviction for insurrection (by a statute dating from Nat Turner's Rebellion) of a Negro communist for soliciting party membership were all violations of the First Amendment as applied to the states through the Fourteenth Amendment.[53]

Race and Fairness

Southern criminal trials for Negroes, essentially lynching's not-too-distant cousins, typically conducted by kangaroo courts stocked with all-white juries, forced the Court to confront issues of procedural fairness in the enforcement of segregation. The three key cases involved shockingly quick trials that ended in death sentences for Negroes accused of rape or murder.

A rampage by white Arkansans left dozens of Negroes (and one white man) dead. The state prosecuted the surviving Negroes in trials that lasted a couple of hours at most, and jury deliberation took only minutes because a white mob was outside the courthouse threatening to lynch the defendants. This, the Court held over dissents by McReynolds and Sutherland, violated due process.[54]

The trial of the nine Scottsboro Boys for rape was similarly fast, as the defendants were effectively tried without counsel. As the proceedings commenced, the judge appointed all the lawyers in the area to represent the defendants. There was no consultation with the defendants nor any attempt to mount a defense. Sutherland held that denial of counsel was a violation of due process. Butler and McReynolds dissented.[55]

In the final case a Mississippi defendant was twice fake-hanged (which left rope marks on his neck) and then savagely whipped until he confessed. A unanimous Court held that coerced confessions could not be admitted into evidence: "[T]he rack and torture chamber may not be substituted for the witness stand."[56]

Outside the criminal area, the Court did little with respect to race, leaving the promise of the Fourteenth Amendment as elusive as it had been for the previous six decades. It held Texas's all-white primary unconstitutional because of its formal racial discrimination.[57] Texas evaded the decision, however, by deregulating primary elections. Then the state Democratic Party limited its membership to whites only. Thus Negroes were again excluded from primary elections. Lacking state action, this subterfuge unanimously prevailed.[58]

The Great Depression

Two weeks after the crash that ushered in the Great Depression, an ailing Taft wrote to his brother, saying how he dreaded the thought that Herbert Hoover, still seen as a progressive, ultra-competent administrator, might make appointments to the Court: "I must stay on the court in order to prevent the Bolsheviki from getting control."[59] Yet

Hoover filled not only Taft's seat but those of Holmes and Sanford as well. In each case Hoover selected someone more progressive than the man he replaced. For chief justice, Hoover selected Charles Evans Hughes, who had continued his distinguished career after being defeated by Wilson. After sharp debate centering on progressives' forgetting his prior record on the Court and worrying that his profitable representation of corporate clients rendered him a pawn of big business and Southerners, remembering his prior record and therefore concerned that he did not respect states' rights sufficiently, the Senate confirmed Hughes 52–26.

Hoover initially selected circuit judge John Parker to replace Sanford, but labor and civil rights opposition caused his narrow defeat, 39–41. Hoover then selected Owen Roberts, a Philadelphia corporate lawyer and special prosecutor of the Harding administration's Teapot Dome scandal, who was unanimously confirmed. When the ninety-year-old Holmes finally accepted the inevitable, Hoover appointed, to great acclaim, Benjamin Cardozo, the most respected state court judge in the nation.

The deepening depression guaranteed that Hoover would get no further appointments because he would be denied a second term. The nation's industrial production was halved, as was national income. Net investment was negative. Prices were falling yearly. The banking system neared paralysis with over 650 banks failing in 1929, more than double that number a year later, and 2,294 in 1931. In the countryside crops rotted and livestock starved, and farmers faced mortgage foreclosures. Nationwide a fourth of the workforce was unemployed. Two million people were homeless.

Divided government created the opportunity for stalemate, and Democrats in Congress, with their eyes on the presidency in 1932, made obstructionism party dogma. If things weren't bad enough for Hoover in the summer of 1932, his letting Douglas MacArthur use the cavalry on horseback with tanks, machine guns, teargas, and bayonets to rout the Bonus Army, veterans of World War I who had come to the capital to demand an accelerated payment of their promised bonuses, from their squalid Hooverville on the Anacostia Flats was both insensitive and politically maladroit. In November, Hoover carried but six states.

The Democratic nominee, Franklin D. Roosevelt, won the presidency by default. During the absurd five-month interregnum between election and inauguration, during which he survived an assassination attempt that took the life of Chicago's mayor, Roosevelt was urged by some, including Walter Lippmann, to consider a dictatorship. His inaugural address hinted at the possibility. The memorable line "the only thing we have to fear is fear itself"[60] was either vacuous or wrong, but the line that got the most applause was Roosevelt's asking Congress "for the one remaining instrument to meet the crisis—broad executive power to wage a war against the emergency, as great as the power that would be given to me if we were in fact invaded by a foreign foe."[61] With Hitler taking over in Germany, Mussolini holding the reigns in Italy, and Stalin controlling the Soviet Union, applause at such a suggestion was so disconcerting that even Eleanor Roosevelt was troubled. Imagine, then, the reaction of those wedded to the Constitution, especially as it was construed by the Four Horsemen.

A day after the inauguration, Roosevelt declared a four-day bank holiday, halted all transactions in gold, and called a special session of Congress to begin almost immediately. What then followed were the Hundred Days, during which Congress rubberstamped the president by enacting fifteen major pieces of legislation dealing with everything from unemployment relief to banking to agriculture to industry, plus a law legalizing consumption of wine and beer and a proposed constitutional amendment to repeal Prohibition that was ratified by December. The first bill that passed, the Emergency Banking Act, was adopted sight unseen by unanimous shout. Congress also passed a joint resolution authorizing the president to opt for inflation by taking the country off the gold standard, which he did. He indeed looked like a wartime president—albeit an immensely popular one.

The 1934 Cases

The Great Depression came to the Court in a pair of state cases, and Hoover's three appointees joined Brandeis and Stone in opinions that signaled receptivity to the legislative experimentation necessary to deal with the unprecedented economic crisis. The Four Horsemen dissented in each case.

Home Building and Loan Association v. Blaisdell sustained the Minnesota Mortgage Moratorium Law, which offered farmers (especially) temporary relief from their mortgage payments by postponing judicial foreclosure sales and extending redemption periods for the mortgagor. Recognizing that the law impaired the obligation of contract, the Minnesota court nevertheless ruled that what made it constitutional was the emergency created by the depression (as if the Contracts Clause had not been a product of economic hard times). Hughes bluntly rejected history by stating that "full recognition of the occasion and general purpose of the clause does not suffice to fix its precise scope."[62] He also tersely announced that "[e]mergency does not create power," then proceeded to justify the law as an emergency measure because the legislature cannot bargain the police power away, and Minnesota was acting to "safeguard the vital interests of its people."[63] The state could not adopt a policy of destruction of contracts, but this one was only a temporary impairment.

Nebbia v. New York sustained price-setting for milk by turning the class of businesses affected with a public interest into a tautology. If the legislature regulated the business, then it necessarily was one affected with a public interest. As long as regulation was not arbitrary or capricious, the legislature could regulate all matters of a private business: "[T]his court from the early days affirmed that the power to promote the general welfare is inherent in government."[64] The Four Horsemen understood that the majority had made a fundamental shift: "This is not regulation, but management, control, dictation—it amounts to the deprivation of the fundamental right which one has to conduct his own affairs honestly and along customary lines."[65]

Constitutional Crisis

Between *Blaisdell* and *Nebbia*, it looked as if the Court was ready to sustain the whole New Deal program. Both signaled that the fact of the depression mattered and that the Court was ready to pull the plug on the edifice of the previous fifty years. But it didn't. Instead the Court went on a rampage against the New Deal that was without precedent in American history, striking down ten federal statutes—including the National Industrial Recovery Act (NIRA), which Roosevelt deemed the most important statute in American history—in just two years. Furthermore, it did so in a stunning rebuke to Mr. Dooley, for in 1934 the president's party enjoyed by far the most successful midterm election ever as New Dealers were sent to Congress in record numbers.

With reason Roosevelt worried that the Court would declare the decision to abandon the gold standard unconstitutional with respect to federal bond obligations, and such a decision would immediately increase the national debt by $70 billion. At argument, Attorney General Homer Cummings told the justices that the case was of "almost unprecedented importance,"[66] and in anticipation of an adverse decision Roosevelt prepared a Fireside Chat to announce that the people would not abide the decision because it would throw the nation "into an infinitely more serious economic plight than we have yet experienced."[67]

Although eight justices verbally spanked the decision to repudiate bond obligations as unconstitutional—"assum[ing] that the Constitution contemplates a vain promise, a pledge having no other sanction than the pleasure and convenience of the pledgor"[68]—five justices held that it would unjustly enrich the bondholders to repay them in the promised gold, which now had a value of $1.69 to the dollar. McReynolds and the other Horsemen verbally alluded to Nero's Rome while writing, "Loss of reputation for honorable dealing will bring us unending humiliation; the impending legal and moral chaos is appalling."[69] The same five-justice majority relied on the *Second Legal Tender Case* to rather easily sustain voiding gold clauses in private contracts because private parties cannot limit congressional authority over the currency.[70] This marked the last New Deal victory prior to the 1936 presidential election.

In contrast to *Blaisdell* and *Nebbia*, two statutes designed to stabilize the economy were invalidated next. One encouraged older railway workers to retire so that their jobs could go to younger, unemployed men. The other was the cornerstone of the New Deal: the NIRA.

The Railroad Retirement Act was a complex scheme that, like the Transportation Act of 1920, treated railroads as a unitary national system and credited work for any railroad as work for currently operating ones. It required current carriers and employees to contribute to pensions for 2 million past and present employees. Workers were eligible on any one of three bases: age sixty-five, thirty years of employment in the industry, or disability.

Roberts's opinion for the Four Horsemen rejected the entire concept of the act, liberally sprinkling the terms "arbitrary," "gratuitous," and "largess" in finding it a violation of due process as a "naked appropriation of private property."[71] In a single paragraph, perhaps thinking back to the days of his railroad clients, Roberts used "service" five times as a synonym for railroad employment.[72] Having slaughtered the act under due process, Roberts went further and found, despite so many prior railroad cases, that this railroad regulation had nothing to do with interstate commerce. To the claim that pensions would improve morale, Roberts offered a parade of horribles that "seems endless. Provision for free medical attendance and nursing, for clothing, for food, for housing, for education of children, and a hundred other matters."[73]

The Court again used constitutional overkill to strike down the NIRA. *Schechter Poultry* involved a code of fair conduct regulations for the poultry industry where chickens had been transported from Pennsylvania to Manhattan and then resold to a Brooklyn wholesale market. The Court unanimously held that in authorizing the president to issue codes, Congress had unconstitutionally delegated its legislative power. It also held that regulating wages and hours of the Brooklyn slaughterhouse was impermissible because interstate commerce had ceased. The "mere" fact of the constant flow into the state did not mean that the flow continued after arrival.[74] Even Cardozo and Stone, the two justices most supportive of the New Deal, stated that the Commerce Clause problems were "incurable."[75]

Four days later Roosevelt invited reporters into his office, and while thumbing a copy of *Schechter*, he decried the federal government's being denied "powers which exist in the national Governments of every other Nation . . . We have been relegated to the horse-and-buggy definition of interstate commerce."[76] He gave no indications of how he hoped to modernize to remedy the defect, and it would be over a year and a half before he publicly mentioned the Court again. In that period the Greek Revival edifice which still houses the Court opened; a quip in the *New Yorker* called it "a magnificent structure with fine big windows to throw the New Deal out of."[77] As a near-term prediction it was on the money. Roberts and the Four Horsemen invalidated the Guffey Coal Act and the Agricultural Adjustment Act (Hughes agreeing), and reaffirmed that states could not enact minimum wages for women and children.

United States v. Butler scuttled the New Deal's agricultural policy of taxing to create price supports. After embracing Alexander Hamilton's broad vision of the express power to spend for the general welfare,

Roberts concluded that the Agricultural Adjustment Act regulated subjects exclusively left to the states. He denied that farm problems were
national by concluding that this was just "a widespread similarity of local conditions."[78] Agriculture Secretary Henry Wallace retorted that if
agriculture were "truly a local matter . . . half the people in the United
States would quickly starve."[79]

Stone, for Brandeis and Cardozo, dissented with the tart observation that "the only check upon our own exercise of power is our own
sense of judicial self-restraint."[80] That was in short supply with Roberts
and the Horsemen.

The Guffey Coal Act regulated wages and hours in the coal industry with the goal of preventing a large-scale disruption of commerce
by avoiding strikes. In *Carter v. Carter Coal,* Sutherland held that the
act exceeded congressional power under the Commerce Clause, even
though he conceded that a strike might have significant effects on commerce. What mattered was not whether commerce would be harmed
but whether mining was local and prior to any commerce. Between
Carter Coal and *Schechter Poultry,* the Court held that Congress could
not reach industry in the creating state or the consuming state. Congressional power attached only to transportation or businesses, such as
stockyards, that were facilitating transportation—and not always there,
as the Railroad Retirement Act demonstrated.

The coup de grâce and completion of what Roosevelt had called a
"constitutional no-man's land" in the "horse-and-buggy" press conference was *New York ex rel. Morehead v. Tipaldo,*[81] where the five-man majority agreed with the court below that *Adkins* controlled. Many conservative Republicans decried the decision. Roosevelt's own Dutchess
County congressman, Republican Hamilton Fish (the Fish of Roosevelt's slam at obstructionists Martin, Barton, and Fish), was particularly caustic, claiming that it was "a new Dred Scott decision condemning millions of Americans to economic slavery."[82] Subsequently the
Republican Party platform that year backed state minimum wage laws.

It was one thing to check the nationalizing New Deal; it was quite another to check the states, too.

Court-Packing

With the Court seemingly set on dismantling the New Deal, it is astounding that, unlike in 1896, the Court was ignored as a campaign issue as Roosevelt achieved the most overwhelming electoral victory since James Monroe ran unopposed. Undoubtedly the reason for Roosevelt's silence was that he wished to avoid the Republican charge that he wanted a dictatorship unbounded by the Constitution and the rule of law.

During the campaign two journalists published a best-selling book on the Court, *The Nine Old Men*,[83] and the name stuck. It was the oldest Court in American history, and Roosevelt was the first full-term president since Monroe who found himself unable to replace a single justice. (Recall that Harding had four appointments in his twenty-nine months as president.) The Four Horsemen had lasted through his first term. There was nothing to prevent them from tying to do so through his second.

Roosevelt's lengthy coattails created Democratic majorities of 333–102 in the House and 75–21 in the Senate. The majorities were not worth much, however, if the Court declared everything they did unconstitutional, so in secret Roosevelt had his attorney general working on a solution. Just before Christmas, Roosevelt tipped his hand to journalist George Creel when he stated that "Congress can *enlarge* the Supreme Court, increasing the number of justices so as to permit the appointment of men in tune with the spirit of the age," but a magazine article missed the point.[84]

After his inauguration Roosevelt told aide Samuel Rosenman that "[w]hen the Chief Justice read me the oath and came to the words 'support the Constitution of the United States' I felt like saying: 'Yes, but it's the Constitution as *I* understand it, flexible enough to meet any new problem of democracy—not the kind of Constitution your Court has raised up as a barrier to progress and democracy.'"[85] During the inaugural address that followed, Roosevelt stated that the "Constitution of 1787 did not make our democracy impotent." Shortly thereafter, when he said that "the American people will insist that every agency of popular government use effective instruments to carry out their will," Hughes visibly stiffened.[86]

On February 5, 1937, without prior consultation with congressional leaders, Roosevelt unveiled his Court-packing plan designed to achieve his Constitution. For each justice over seventy years old who did not retire, the president would be able to appoint a new justice—and only Stone, Roberts, and Cardozo were under seventy. Six justices attuned to the spirit of the age, plus Stone and Cardozo, would be enough to sustain the New Deal.

A contemporaneous cartoon shows FDR rehearsing his six new smiling justices. He instructs: "Great! Now, once more, all together." The six exclaim "Yes!" in unison. The Constitution and the Scales of Justice are partially visible in a trash barrel.[87]

Roosevelt initially and disingenuously touted the plan as an efficiency measure to help the aged justices keep abreast of their work, thereby taking an implicit slap at two progressive icons—the recently deceased Holmes and the very much alive eighty-year-old Brandeis. There was never a groundswell of support, but with margins of better than 3–1 in Congress, Roosevelt knew he could push it through. In early March he gave a Fireside Chat on the need for new blood "to protect us against catastrophe by meeting squarely our modern social and economic conditions."[88]

While Republicans were aghast at the attack on the independence of the judiciary, the sole institution that could check the constitutional excesses of the New Deal, Democrats were divided on neutering the Court. In light of events in Europe, Court-packing might be a threat to the Court's nascent civil liberties jurisprudence, something Stone explicitly noted in correspondence when he observed that "'judicial reform' might well result in breaking down the guarantees of individual liberty."[89]

Roosevelt held firm, and then the Court intervened. First Hughes, who "look[ed] like God and talk[ed] like God"[90] (or, more moderately, "presided like Toscanini lead[s] an orchestra"),[91] sent a letter, signed also by Van Devanter and Brandeis, to the Senate Judiciary Committee supposedly taking no stand on the plan but noting that the Court was fully abreast of its work and that fifteen justices would make for an unwieldy Court. A week later the first of three major 5–4 decisions came down. Roberts had abandoned the Four Horsemen (although he vehemently denied ever changing, pointing out that his vote to overrule *Adkins* was cast prior to February 5).

West Coast Hotel v. Parrish overruled *Adkins*. Instead of seeing the minimum wage as a subsidy by the employer, Hughes saw the failure to pay a minimum wage as "exploitation" of the "relatively defenseless," requiring the community "to provide what is in effect a subsidy for unconscionable employers."[92] Next the Court upheld the National Labor Relations Act, authorizing unionization and guaranteeing rights to strike. The test case involved a large, completely integrated steel company where a strike in one area would disrupt production everywhere. The Court ignored the government's stream of commerce argument, and instead, on broader grounds, Hughes wrote that government could promote commerce and regulate intrastate businesses where necessary to protect interstate commerce from burdens. Noting that a strike would have serious consequences, the Court said that "interstate commerce itself is a practical conception . . . [and] interferences with that commerce must be appraised by a judgment that does not ignore actual experience."[93] In a companion case the Court sustained the act as applied to a small clothing manufacturer that both obtained most of its materials and sent the finished products out of state.[94] The view that manufacturing preceded commerce—articulated from *E. C. Knight* to *Hammer* to *Carter Coal*—was dead, at least for this year.

Finally, a month later, in a decision gutting *Butler,* the Court sustained the unemployment compensation provisions of the Social Security Act as alleviating national economic distress and therefore a proper exercise under the General Welfare Clause. Even more significantly, Van Devanter announced his retirement. Senators congratulated the majority leader, Arkansas Democrat Joe Robinson, the floor leader of the Court-packing plan and the man to whom Roosevelt had promised the first vacant seat. While they may have thought the plan was dead, Roosevelt wanted it passed. Roberts might switch again, and Robinson was a conservative. "Have we any assurance [about Roberts]?" Roosevelt asked.[95]

Then a majority of the Judiciary Committee issued a scathing denunciation of the plan as an unconstitutional attack on the judiciary. The plan "violates every sacred tradition of American democracy [and] would . . . make this government one of men rather than law."[96]

Roosevelt then offered a compromise that would limit the president to one justice per year for those over age seventy-five (and thus within six months would offer him three). He could have had this compromise in mid-April after *West Coast Hotel* and the sustaining of the National Labor Relations Act. Joe Robinson sent word then that if FDR wanted to compromise, "I can get him a couple of extra justices tomorrow."[97] But in the July heat of Washington, Roosevelt's compromise died when Robinson was found dead in his apartment.

Hugo L. Black

Roosevelt did not take defeat well, and he conceived a nomination to replace Van Devanter that would lash out at his nemeses: economic royalists who backed Republicans, the Senate which had defeated his Court-packing bid, and the Court itself. He found the perfect three-fer in Alabama senator Hugo L. Black, "probably the most radical man in the Senate," unpopular with his colleagues and definitely not one of the "club," and an implacable critic of the Court who had avidly supported FDR's plan and even voted against confirming Hughes.[98] Business would be subject to his rulings; the Senate would have to confirm him because of the absurd custom of "courtesy," whereby a member of the Senate is deemed automatically qualified for any appointive post; and his lack of qualifications and temperament would shame the Court. (Roosevelt had acknowledged that Black was the least able lawyer among the serious contenders.)[99] "Jesus Christ!" Roosevelt's press secretary exclaimed on hearing the news.[100] The *Washington Post* elaborated the next day: "If Senator Black has given any study or thought to any aspect of constitutional law in a way which would entitle him to this preferment, his labors in that direction have been skillfully concealed. If he has ever showed himself exceptionally qualified in either the knowledge or the temperament essential for the exercise of the highest judicial function, the occasion escapes recollection."[101]

Senatorial courtesy brought a confirmation vote of 63–16 with seventeen abstentions, indicating that a lot of his colleagues thought Black was unfit for the Court. Nevertheless, once he was seated, as long as Hughes agreed, the New Deal would be safe even if Roberts reverted to his 1935 views. Then for a moment Black looked insecure when his membership in the Ku Klux Klan was undeniably exposed. With the dictators in Europe and an incipient civil rights–civil liberties jurisprudence at home, the idea of a Klansman on the Court sent a chill down the nation's spine. Black gave a less than satisfying national radio address admitting past membership, claiming he had resigned before joining the Senate, and denying religious intolerance. A day after Black took his seat, the topic decisively changed when Roosevelt gave his "Quarantine" address on the "present reign of terror and international lawlessness," claiming, contrary to the widespread and popular domestic belief, that there was "no escape through mere isolation or neutrality."[102]

· VIII ·

After the New Deal
Constitutional Revolution

"THE WHOLE NEW DEAL really went up in smoke as a result of the Supreme Court fight,"[1] observed FDR's second vice president, Henry Wallace, and only one major New Deal legislative victory—the Fair Labor Standards Act, with its minimum wage provision— was thereafter enacted. But the Court-packing plan gave FDR the Constitution just the way he wanted. Hugo Black was wholly reliable, and Charles Evans Hughes, who never cast a fifth vote to invalidate economic legislation, had, as the *Nation* editorialized, "the acumen to recognize the inevitable, and that is the larger part of statesmanship."[2] With Willis Van Devanter's replacement by Black, the power of the Four—now Three—Horsemen was broken, and every New Deal statute passed constitutional muster. This was the Revolution of 1937.

With their Constitution gone, the Horsemen soon were, too. George Sutherland retired in 1938; Pierce Butler died a year later; and James McReynolds, seeing he could not outlast a three-term president, retired after the 1940 election. Additionally, Benjamin Cardozo died in 1938; Louis Brandeis retired in early 1939; and Hughes retired in 1941. The Court-packing plan had failed, but Roosevelt was nevertheless able to fill the Court with committed New Dealers.

Four of Roosevelt's appointees became giants—and shockingly, one of them was Hugo Black. The three others were all presidential advisors: well-known Harvard professor and Holmes and Brandeis confidant Felix Frankfurter, who replaced Cardozo; forty-year-old former Yale professor William O. Douglas, chairman of the New Deal's showcase agency, the Securities and Exchange Commission, and also a poker-playing companion of the president; and New York friend Robert H. Jackson, a brilliant solicitor general (Brandeis said he should be SG for life) and professional attorney general.

Beyond fealty to the New Deal, the four shared intelligence, confidence, and an ability to write well, with Jackson the best and most candid penman ever to sit. Each, save Frankfurter, who as an immigrant was constitutionally barred, harbored ambitions for the White House.

With the war impending, Roosevelt moved Republican Harlan Fiske Stone to chief justice. The other seats went to New Dealers: Stanley Reed, a competent solicitor general; Frank Murphy, a former Michigan governor and political attorney general; and South Carolina senator James Byrnes. Justice Byrnes lasted only a year and was replaced by an ardent New Dealer, circuit judge and former law school dean Wiley B. Rutledge. Only Stone and Owen Roberts survived from 1936.

The New Deal Revolution

The child labor issue was formally interred in *United States v. Darby* when the Court unanimously sustained the Fair Labor Standards Act, with its wages and hours requirements. The statute prohibited the interstate shipment of goods manufactured except in compliance with the FLSA's requirements and then prohibited manufacture except in compliance. Overruling *Hammer v. Dagenhart,* Stone announced, first, that congressional power was plenary and Congress could exclude from interstate commerce anything it pleased; and second, Congress could regulate intrastate manufacture of goods as a necessary step to the potential preclusion of interstate shipment of any goods not produced in compliance with congressional policy. In the process the Court lopped off the Tenth Amendment as "but a truism that all is retained which has not been surrendered."[3]

The New Deal revolution was sealed in *Wickard v. Filburn* in 1942. At issue was an acreage requirement that Roscoe Filburn had ignored to grow wheat which he fed to animals on his farm. The Court unanimously ruled that Congress could regulate wheat production because the Court accepted the conclusion that lots of similar small intrastate transactions might have an effect on interstate commerce. *Schechter Poultry* held that Congress could not reach a slaughterhouse in Brooklyn which purchased chickens that had traveled in interstate commerce. *Wickard* held that Congress could regulate production even if it had not moved in interstate or intrastate commerce but just on a single farm. The most fundamental issue of constitutional law had gone from 9–0 to 0–9 in just seven years. Attorney General Robert Jackson had written that "[w]hat we demanded for our generation was the right consciously to influence the evolutionary process of constitutional law as other generations have done."[4] Justice Robert Jackson's *Wickard* opinion had helped turn evolution into revolution.

Constitutional issues are settled when the losers give up, and Roberts gave up once the Four Horsemen were gone. Thus Jackson could infuse *Wickard* with the spirit of the New Deal. What was that spirit? Federal economic regulation was constitutional: the Court withdrew from policing the line—if it still existed—between national and local. Governments, if they wished, could bar courts from enjoining labor disputes. Similarly, second-guessing regulatory regimes was over. State economic regulation was constitutional as long as it did not interfere with a federal program or discriminate against or overly burden interstate commerce. The New Dealers, with their emphasis on current needs, had finally and successfully slain the old constitutional order.

Lengthy chapters of American constitutional history closed—to be replaced, as Stone's footnote four in *Carolene Products* suggested, by a more aggressive concern for civil liberties and civil rights.[5]

With the New Deal justices in place, the *Washington Post* offered the conventional wisdom that an era of unanimity was about to wash over the Court. As with its editorial on the appointment of Black, the *Post* was on the mark—but wrong. By the 1943 term, only 42 percent of the cases were decided unanimously, and future numbers headed south. Even when the imperatives of war and national cohesion counseled a single opinion for the Court, the justices had difficulty achieving unanimity. The principal reasons were their intelligence and their personalities. Only Rutledge was liked and respected by the others. Frankfurter thought that there would be general agreement on the Court and because of his teaching at Harvard and his long association with Holmes and Brandeis, he rightly concluded that he knew more than the others. He then wrongly concluded that this entitled him to dominate the others.

The New Deal justices agreed that the old order deserved slaying but disagreed as to why. Had it been wrong because the justices had been too willing to strike down laws or, rather, only because the justices had imposed the wrong values? The New Deal giants displayed deep jurisprudential fissures on the questions. Frankfurter, claiming impartiality, embraced Holmesian restraint with its deference to democratic decision makers. So did the pragmatic Jackson, but to a lesser degree. Black purported to adhere to the views of the Framers as controlling the meaning of the constitutional text and needed no convincing that he was channeling their views. Case-by-case liberalism seemed to be Douglas's initial mode. Underlying each approach were the questions created from the pre-1937 era of how much discretion judges enjoyed and how it might be cabined.

Deep personal animosities exacerbated jurisprudential differences. Black and Jackson eventually feuded, while Frankfurter and Douglas quickly grew to detest each other. During World War II, Frankfurter called Black, Douglas, and Murphy the "Axis." When Douglas tired of hearing Frankfurter speak at length at conference, he would leave the table and lie down on the couch. Neither Douglas nor Black could stomach Frankfurter's condescending attitude, while Jackson believed that both Black and Douglas voted politically.

World War II

Attorney General Francis Biddle, a supporter of the American Civil Liberties Union, was determined that there be no repetition of the hysterical sedition prosecutions of World War I. In this he was successful, perhaps because there was so little dissent over the Good War; the only wartime hysteria befell the Japanese Americans on the West Coast, producing decisions on curfew, relocation, and the rights of loyal citizens to challenge their detention by seeking a writ of habeas corpus. The other major cases arising out of the war effort involved military trials of German saboteurs, treason trials for their collaborators, military trials for war criminals, and the obligatory unsuccessful effort to challenge wartime economic controls.[6] On this last issue Douglas tossed aside objections, stating that a "nation which can demand the lives of its men and women in waging a war is under no constitutional necessity of providing a system of price controls on the domestic front which will assure each landlord a 'fair return' on his property."[7]

In June 1942 eight Nazis put ashore by submarines to sabotage industrial facilities were quickly captured. With input from Frankfurter, Roosevelt ordered them tried by seven generals in secret (the windows of the room were covered by heavy black curtains) with no recourse to courts. Military defense counsel argued that *Ex parte Milligan*, where, after the Civil War, the Court had held that courts-martial could not try civilians while civil courts were open, afforded the defendants the right to be tried before civil courts. After three weeks of trial, but before the inevitable verdict, the Court rushed into a special summer session to hear the case. (The ever injudicious Murphy, who had strenuously lobbied for a commission in the military reserves, reported for duty—oral argument—in his uniform, causing his appalled brethren to force him to recuse himself.) Even though all justices had qualms about the procedure, they unanimously rubberstamped the administration, since Biddle had privately told several members of the Court that Roosevelt would order executions regardless of what the Court held.

The Court rendered its judgment two days after hearing the case; three days later the military commission found the defendants guilty, and within a week six of the eight were executed. Speed on the habeas appeal was demanded by the president and a howling national press (although the Court could not write its opinion anywhere near as rapidly; hence it came down some months later). By deciding the case, however, the Court seemingly vindicated the Constitution, since it necessarily implied that the Court could have decided it the other way and therefore ordered recourse to civil courts.[8] The saboteurs got what they should have expected if captured, but the procedure did not look pretty, despite contemporary flag waving by the press, nicely illustrated by a self-congratulatory editorial in the *New Republic:* "Even in wartime and even toward the enemy, we do not abandon our basic protection of individual rights."[9]

After the war the Court saw a second swift military verdict. General Tomoyuki Yamashita, the "Tiger of Malaya," surrendered on September 3, 1945. His war crimes trial (for atrocities he did not order but which were committed by troops under his command) commenced October 29 and finished six weeks later. His habeas petition reached the Court two weeks after that. The justices heard oral argument the first week of January 1946, they handed down their decision the first week of February, and Yamashita was executed that month. The trial had been a constitutional farce, but it occurred on foreign soil, and Stone, writing for all but Rutledge and Murphy, held in a convoluted opinion that courts retained power to review the decision and that Congress authorized the trial and had not foreclosed the defendant's raising constitutional issues, but any appeal must be taken to military authorities.[10] By some alchemy this was supposed to obviate the need to decide the due process issues. Privately Stone thought that war crimes trials were legalized lynchings by the victors, and he wished that General Douglas MacArthur had simply hanged Yamashita without a trial.

The German saboteurs had had a little American help, and this produced trials for treason in which John Marshall's tough evidentiary standards in Aaron Burr's trial were validated. A majority ruled that the overt acts had to be treasonous in intent so that a jury would find that the accused "actually gave aid and comfort to the enemy."[11] Douglas, writing for four dissenters, thought that the rule made "the way easy for the traitor" and treason all but impossible to prove.[12] He was wrong. Just meeting with an enemy was not enough, but offering shelter, purchasing a car, and arranging for a job in a plant that manufactured bombsights provided the necessary proof.[13]

The relocation of 112,000 people of Japanese descent, most of whom were American citizens, was the biggest single blight on civil liberties in America in the twentieth century. Spurred by public fears after Pearl Harbor, long-standing prejudice against Asians, as well as national newspaper columnists, Roosevelt and then Congress authorized the War Department to declare certain areas military zones, and thereafter the commander of the area could impose curfews and travel restrictions, and even order people excluded entirely from the area.

General John DeWitt, an Alabama friend of Hugo Black who commanded the West Coast, first imposed a curfew on all people of Japanese descent. In an Orwellian twist, the order referred to Japanese American citizens as "non-aliens."[14] DeWitt followed with an order prohibiting those covered by the order from leaving the West Coast. Three weeks later he excluded them from the West Coast. Forbidden to leave, forbidden to stay, they had no other legal option but to leave jobs, homes, and possessions behind (or unload them at distress prices) and report for internment, mainly in the arid West, in one of ten god-forsaken, dust-blown, barbed-wire-fenced camps.

FBI director J. Edgar Hoover told officials that there was no evidence that any Japanese Americans were engaged in sabotage, but California attorney general Earl Warren asserted what too many, including DeWitt, believed—namely, that the fact that no evidence had been found showed how dangerous they were. Biddle and his top aides opposed internment, but they were overwhelmed by the War Department through Assistant Secretary John McCloy. Biddle protested to FDR, but when his legal objections were brushed aside, he washed his hands of the matter and delegated the Justice Department's relocation responsibilities to Tom Clark, a future justice.

The curfew made sense, pending determinations of who was loyal and who was not, but DeWitt had no intention of making that determination. The exclusion order meant that all Japanese Americans would be interred because, as DeWitt so delicately pronounced, "A Jap is a Jap."[15] In that analysis, too, he had plenty of company.

University of Washington senior Gordon Hirabayashi was convicted for violating the curfew and failing to report to a control center. The justices, not wanting to second-guess the military or the president, decided the case as narrowly as possible, limiting themselves to the curfew. Stone asserted that the military and Congress could believe that "there were disloyal members of that population whose numbers and strength could not be precisely and quickly ascertained."[16] Douglas, Murphy, and Rutledge filed concurring opinions indicating concerns about the military action. As Douglas put it: "Detention for reasonable cause is one thing. Detention on account of ancestry is another."[17]

A month before the presidential election, the Court heard oral arguments on the detention involving Fred Korematsu's crime of violating the exclusion order, described by Jackson as "being present in the state whereof he is a citizen, near the place where he was born, and where all his life he has lived."[18] Six justices joined Black's opinion, which, despite some rousing language (racial classifications "are immediately suspect" and must be subject "to the most rigid scrutiny"),[19] justified the detention on the ground that war is hell.

This time there were dissents. Roberts found that the catch-22 of the orders violated due process. Murphy accurately characterized the program as having descended "into the ugly abyss of racism."[20] The most interesting was Jackson's conclusion that courts should abstain from reviewing the constitutionality of military orders because the outcome was foreordained: the pressures of war would cause the courts to validate the orders by "distort[ing] the Constitution to approve all that the military may deem expedient."[21] That had explained the World War I cases as well as those already decided during the current war. Jackson recognized that the military was carrying out a military program, not worrying about the niceties of the Constitution, but "a military order, however unconstitutional, is not apt to last longer than the military emergency."[22] When a court validates the order, it offers "a loaded weapon ready for the hand of any authority that can bring forward a plausible claim of an urgent need. Every repetition imbeds that principle more deeply in our law and thinking and expands it to new purposes."[23]

In the final case, *Ex parte Endo,* the Court ordered Mitsuye Endo, an American citizen whose loyalty the government conceded, released on habeas (as the solicitor general virtually invited). The War Department had already decided to release loyal citizens but had postponed announcing the decision so as not to upset West Coast voters before the election. Frankfurter then leaked the timing of *Endo,* allowing friends at the War Department to beat it by a day with a Sunday announcement that it would begin releasing loyal citizens in two weeks. The last of the camps closed in March 1946.

Preferred Freedoms

With policing the boundaries of appropriate economic legislation at an end, the justices turned to patrolling the boundaries between individuals and their governments. Hughes publicly and pointedly noted the "power of some governments to punish manufactured crime [as] the hand maiden of tyranny" and noted the Court was intent on keeping "the lamps of justice . . . shining brightly here."[24] Civil liberties cases raised three questions: (1) Which individual rights were important? (2) How did the Court know? and (3) How much protection should be given to any individual right?

Palko v. Connecticut rejected a claim that the Double Jeopardy Clause should apply to the states. Cardozo concluded that the prohibition on double jeopardy wasn't all that important but First Amendment freedoms of speech, the press, assembly, and religion were, because "neither liberty nor justice would exist if they were sacrificed."[25] Freedom of expression, he explained, "is the matrix, the indispensable condition, of nearly every other form of freedom."[26]

Cardozo could write as he did because during the 1930s the Court for the first time treated speech and press cases sympathetically. With the importance of the constitutional guarantees recognized, the Court in the 1940s faced tougher issues, propelled by organized labor and Jehovah's Witnesses, about of the scope of these rights.

Longshoreman's Union leader Harry Bridges and the *Los Angeles Times* were each held in contempt of court for out-of-court statements involving separate labor disputes. The *Times* had urged stiff sentences for labor "goons" convicted of assaulting nonunion workers, while Bridges threatened to tie up West Coast ports if a judge enforced an order against one of his locals. Black, for a 5–4 Court, reversed, finding that the First Amendment "command[ed] the broadest scope that explicit language, read in the context of a liberty-loving society, will allow."[27] Working within the "clear and present danger" framework articulated by Holmes and Brandeis but never seriously considered by the Court, he found that the evil must be "extremely serious and the degree of imminence extremely high before the utterance can be punished."[28] Frankfurter, for the dissenters, urged deference to the state courts' balance of the interests of expression and fair judicial administration. Although Frankfurter deemed himself the heir to Holmes and Brandeis, Black's opinion was the one that remained faithful to their legacy.

Jehovah's Witnesses started coming to the Court in the late 1930s, and their results bounced back and forth. The major cases involving the Witnesses involved the compulsory salute to the flag in public schools. While the British were evacuating Dunkirk in June 1940, *Minesville School District v. Gobitis* sustained the salute over the Witnesses' free exercise objection. (They saw the salute as bowing down to graven images in violation of the Second Commandment.) Frankfurter found that promoting national unity through the compulsory pledge was a legitimate end and that the legislature—here a local school board—could balance that end against the free exercise claim the way it had. Stone authored a solo dissent, aptly noting there were alternative ways to instill patriotism that did not trench on religious beliefs. Three years later, in an identical case, *West Virginia v. Barnette*, the Court overruled *Gobitis*. Jackson's *Barnette* is as eloquent a civil liberties opinion as exists, and the Court handed it down on Flag Day as a poignant reminder of what the flag stands for.

Barnette turned the free exercise argument into one over free speech: "To sustain the compulsory flag salute we are required to say that a Bill of Rights which guards the individual's right to speak his own mind, left it open for public authorities to compel him to utter what is not in his mind."[29] In its most frequently quoted language Jackson announced: "The very purpose of a Bill of Rights was to withdraw certain subjects from the vicissitudes of political controversy, to place them beyond the reach of majorities and officials . . . One's right to life, liberty, and property, to free speech, a free press, freedom of worship and assembly, and other fundamental rights may not be submitted to vote; they depend on the outcome of no elections."[30] Frankfurter wrote a bitter dissent, while Roberts and Reed adhered to *Gobitis*.

There are several explanations for the reversal, the simplest of which is that new justices had joined the Court, one of them being Rutledge, who as a newly minted circuit court judge had criticized *Gobitis*. Three justices—Black, Douglas, and Murphy—had concluded that *Gobitis* was wrongly decided. On reflection, they believed that the school districts (backed, of course, by the state) were putting children who took their religion seriously into an untenable position; over two thousand Jehovah's Witness children were expelled from school in the three years after *Gobitis*. Eleanor Roosevelt chastised Felix Frankfurter for his *Gobitis* conclusions. One hundred seventy-five newspapers, including most of the influential ones, editorialized against the decision. Furthermore, some elements in American society thought that *Gobitis* signaled open season on the Witnesses. There were at least 355 violent incidents—including one castration—in forty-four states.

Returning to free exercise a year later, the Court affirmed a child labor conviction of a Jehovah's Witness for encouraging a minor to join her in proselytizing.[31] To the New Deal justices the case presented a labor law issue, not a free exercise issue, but basically the Court left free exercise wedded to the distinction between belief and action articulated sixty years earlier in the first polygamy case, whereby an individual can believe any absurd thing whatsoever but may be punished for any activity the state deems unlawful.

The Court proved more sure about doctrine when, in *Everson v. Board of Education*, it faced the initial Establishment Clause case emanating from the states. All nine justices agreed that the correct principle was found in Thomas Jefferson's metaphor offered in an 1804 letter to the Danbury Baptists: there should be a wall of separation between church and state. All saw the Establishment Clause as the American method for avoiding the religious warfare that erupted in Europe following the Reformation. All believed that the relevant American experience was that of James Madison and Thomas Jefferson disestablishing the Anglican Church in Virginia.

For all the history and concern, the issue in *Everson* was free transportation on public buses to Catholic schools. Black's majority held that this de minimus aid was permissible, while Frankfurter, Jackson, Rutledge, and a Truman appointee, Harold Burton, adopted the Protestant position that any assistance was unconstitutional because it would always lead to the demand for more.

Barnette's mention of "other fundamental rights" may have been an allusion to an unexpected version of the preferred position that flowed from *Skinner v. Oklahoma,* where in a nonracial context the Court nevertheless found an equal protection violation (aided immensely by the situation in Europe). Adopting a three-strikes-and-you're-out policy, Oklahoma decided to sterilize habitual criminals on the assumption that they could pass the traits to their offspring. Anyone convicted of three moral turpitude felonies was to be sterilized. Under Oklahoma law, grand larceny was a felony of moral turpitude but embezzlement was not. Hence a "person [like Skinner] who enters a chicken coop and steals chickens commits a felony; and he may be sterilized if he is thrice convicted," but not so a clerk who takes "over $20 from his employer's till."[32] Douglas's opinion for the Court noted that in "evil or reckless hands [the power to sterilize] can cause races or types which are inimical to the dominant group to wither and disappear."[33] He found that Oklahoma had created an "invidious distinction" affecting "one of the basic civil rights of man" and was subject to "strict scrutiny" and unconstitutional.[34] Not a single mention of reasonableness.

These new concepts, taken at face value, went beyond anything that David Brewer, Rufus Peckham, or the Four Horsemen had claimed.

Frankfurter v. Black

A necessary corollary to preferred freedoms, as Frankfurter lectured his colleagues, was that some rights weren't preferred. *Palko* reasoned that most of the Bill of Rights did not apply to the states because their guarantees were not "implicit in the concept of ordered liberty."[35] While the Court unanimously incorporated First Amendment rights against the states, thereafter it balked. During the 1940s it refused to incorporate the right to counsel for indigents,[36] the privilege against self-incrimination,[37] and the exclusion of evidence seized as a result of an illegal search.[38] The cases produced an extraordinary jurisprudential debate between Frankfurter, holding to the 1908 decision in *Twining v. New Jersey* which rejected incorporation of the Self-Incrimination Clause, and Black, claiming that both proponents and opponents of the Fourteenth Amendment understood it to incorporate the first eight amendments. Both Frankfurter and Black justified their positions on the ground of judicial modesty, and each successfully punctured the other, but without establishing the correctness of his own position.

Black eschewed reliance on the Privileges and Immunities Clause because of his decisions protecting freedom of expression for Harry Bridges and the *Los Angeles Times*. The clause textually applies only to citizens, and Bridges was an alien and the *Los Angeles Times* a corporation. Frankfurter rejoined that it "would be extraordinarily strange for a Constitution to convey such specific commands in such a roundabout and inexplicit way" as due process (which was redundant in the Fifth Amendment).[39] Black's response was that this was what the Framers of the Fourteenth Amendment had done in Section 1 "separately, and as a whole" (whatever that meant).[40]

Black viewed Frankfurter as adopting the discredited natural law position whereby judges "roam at will in the limitless area of their own beliefs as to the reasonableness" of legislation.[41] Not so, claimed Frankfurter; judges do not apply idiosyncratic standards when they conduct "an evaluation based on a disinterested inquiry pursued in the spirit of science, on a balanced order of facts exactly and fairly stated, on detached consideration of conflicting claims . . . [,] duly mindful of reconciling the needs both of continuity and of change in a progressive society."[42] Black believed that limiting judges to the first eight amendments also limited discretion, while Frankfurter thought it imposed an eighteenth-century straitjacket on the states. He noted that there were new abuses which evolving notions of due process could check but the Bill of Rights could reach only by a tortured construction. If the first eight amendments didn't reach them, then Black didn't believe they were constitutional violations.

Although Frankfurter prevailed over Black in results, problems with his view were exposed in *Rochin v. California* and *Irvine v. California,* decided in the early 1950s. On seeing police enter his house, Rochin swallowed two capsules the officers correctly believed were narcotics. They handcuffed him and took him to a hospital, where he was forced to vomit out the capsules. Frankfurter reversed the conviction, saying that the behavior of the police "shocks the conscience."[43] Black concurred, torturing the Fifth Amendment to find that the result of Rochin's vomiting was self-incrimination.

Police broke into Irvine's house four times to move bugs in the bedroom to places where they believed they could better hear him discuss illegal gambling. After a month of listening, they broke in again and ransacked the house. They never tried to obtain a search warrant. Jackson affirmed the conviction, concluding that the Due Process Clause forbade only the introduction of evidence obtained by "coercion, violence or brutality to the person."[44] The police action had been triggered by Irvine's filing a federal gambling tax form, and Black concluded that this violated the privilege against self-incrimination. Frankfurter also issued a dissent based on *Rochin.*

Maybe Frankfurter's approach was correct, but it appeared that only he could apply it. His behavior in the case of Willie Francis's execution suggests, however, that it was too elusive even for him. Following a typically perfunctory trial, a jury convicted the fifteen-year-old Negro of murder after only fifteen minutes of deliberation, on the basis of two confessions which his appointed trial lawyers did not challenge. (They did not put on a defense, nor did they file an appeal). Prison employees, probably drunk, supervised his electrocution in the state's portable electric chair, which malfunctioned, giving Francis a huge shock yet leaving him alive. The question before the Court was whether "if at first you don't succeed, try, try again" constituted cruel and unusual punishment under the Eighth Amendment.[45] Frankfurter voted with the majority to allow Louisiana to go ahead, concluding that to do otherwise would only be enforcing his personal convictions "rather than that consensus of society's opinion"[46]—even though the governor of Louisiana was being deluged (unsuccessfully) with pleas for clemency. Black, too, was one of the five who gave Louisiana the green light.

Organized Labor

Despite being the linchpin of the New Deal coalition as well as its prime beneficiary, labor did not fare as well before the Court as might be expected. In cases under the National Labor Relations Act and the Fair Labor Standards Act, labor unions prevailed because of the Court's deference to agency fact-finding, but to its surprise, labor found itself lumped with business on the losing side of the Court's newly adopted unwillingness to question the constitutionality of any economic legislation. Thus when states forbade a closed shop (where employees must join a union), the Court sustained the laws over liberty of contract and freedom of speech claims.[47]

Labor's high point was reached in 1940 in *Thornhill v. Alabama,* where the Court invalidated on First Amendment grounds a statute forbidding all picketing. "[D]issemination of information concerning the facts of a labor dispute" was encompassed within "the liberty to discuss publicly and truthfully all matters of public concern."[48] The Court began to back away almost immediately, and a decade later a majority allowed a state to enjoin picketing for a lawful objective—to force a self-employed car dealership to close on evenings and weekends. Picketing, the Court ruled, "cannot dogmatically be equated" with freedom of speech.[49]

The two biggest labor cases of the 1940s involved the United Mine Workers but not the Constitution. The first was a portal-to-portal case interpreting whether the workday was triggered when the miners entered the portal of the mine or when they commenced work and whether it ended when they stopped work or exited the mine. Five justices ruled for the miners (portal to portal),[50] but the same Republican Congress that passed the union-curbing Taft-Hartley amendments to the NLRA quickly passed new legislation conforming to the dissenters' views. The Court's decision was consistent with its other decisions expansively interpreting the Fair Labor Standards Act to favor employees.

The second major labor case involved the showdown between the Truman administration and John L. Lewis, leader of the United Mine Workers. Lewis's threats to call a strike in the coal mines, war or no war, had led to the War Labor Disputes Act, which allowed the federal government to operate plants and mines in vital industries. With the war ended, Lewis called a strike in the spring of 1946. The government seized the mines and then negotiated a contract with the union ending the strike. By fall Lewis wanted a better deal and informed the government that he was terminating the contract (under provisions of a preexisting agreement with coalmine operators). Because over 60 percent of America's electricity was coal-powered, a strike in the late fall would have been devastating. Rather than negotiate, Truman went to federal court and secured an injunction. Lewis responded by pulling the miners off the job.

Faced with contempt citations, Lewis and the UMW argued that the court lacked jurisdiction because of the Norris-LaGuardia Act (which stripped federal courts of jurisdiction to issue injunctions in labor disputes). The judge rejected the argument and fined the union $3 million and Lewis $10,000, with additional fines to be added for each day the strike continued. Lewis capitulated after three days.

Bypassing the court of appeals, the Court agreed to hear the case but found itself split on the issues. Frankfurter, who had helped draft Norris-LaGuardia, rejected the government's claim that the law did not apply to the government itself. Five justices in an unpersuasive opinion disagreed. More significantly, seven justices held that even if the district court had lacked jurisdiction to issue the injunction, Lewis and the UMW had to obey it anyway: "There can be no free society without law administered by an independent judiciary. If one man can be allowed to determine for himself what is law, every man can. That means first chaos, then tyranny."[51]

Truman and the Court

By the time of the battle with Lewis, Harry Truman had already made two appointments to the Court, replacing Roberts, who was tired of being alone among New Dealers, and Stone, who died suddenly. This created the most inexperienced Court since the 1790s, with Black, the most senior justice, not yet having served a decade. For Roberts's seat Truman selected the Ohio Republican Senator Harold Burton, a friend of the president's from their days on the Truman Committee investigating defense contracts.

When Stone died a year later, Jackson, who had been promised by

FDR that he would succeed Stone, believed that he was entitled to promotion. He had accepted appointment by Truman as the chief prosecutor at Nuremberg, and when he was passed over for the center seat, he publicly aired the dirty linen of his dispute with Black (over whether Black had wrongly participated in the portal-to-portal case), whom he believed had sabotaged his chance to be chief justice. Instead of Jackson, Truman selected treasury secretary and former Kentucky congressman Fred Vinson. Subsequently in the summer of 1949 Murphy and Rutledge, both in their fifties, died and were replaced with Sherman Minton, a federal judge who had been a Senate friend of Truman's, and Texan Tom Clark, Truman's attorney general. The appointees were cronies, and cronyism is never a recipe for distinction.

While the justices were vindicating an independent judiciary in the UMW case, they were simultaneously enhancing presidential authority. In the spring of 1952, during the Korean War, Truman tested that authority when he ordered the steel mills seized to avert a strike that he claimed would adversely affect defense production. Having taken over the mills, he granted the United Steelworkers their desired wage increases. Truman claimed that the president's executive authority justified his actions and noted that presidents from Lincoln to FDR had similarly exercised such a power. Less than two months later he was stunned and angered when only three justices supported his claims.

Black's majority opinion made short work of Truman's arguments: "The Constitution limits his [the president's] functions in the lawmaking process to the recommending of laws he thinks wise and for vetoing those he thinks bad. And the Constitution is neither silent nor equivocal about who shall make the laws which the president is to execute."[52] A sophisticated concurring opinion by Jackson noted that the president's powers were at their lowest ebb when there was a conflicting legislative policy (as here) and at their highest point when the president was acting pursuant to an express or implied congressional policy. He counseled against leveraging the president's largely unchecked foreign affairs powers into the domestic sphere "by his own commitment of the Nation's armed forces to some foreign venture."[53]

Truman took the defeat badly, in no small part because Vinson had advised him that a majority of the Court would back him and because the two former attorneys general Jackson and Clark had justified seizures while serving in the executive office. Indeed Jackson had gone further and in 1940 approved the excellent, but probably illegal, destroyers-for-bases deal with Great Britain. Yet both voted against Truman in the *Steel Seizure Case*. One of Jackson's law clerks, William Rehnquist, attributed the loss to the related unpopularity of both Truman and the Korean War.

Truman immediately complied with the decision by returning authority to the steel companies, and the union went on a fifty-three-day strike. Defense production was unaffected.

The Cold War Years

Less than a year after the victory in World War II, Winston Churchill gave his "Iron Curtain" speech in Fulton, Missouri. American politicians were already concerned because of what they saw as the Soviet Union's flagrant violation of the promises made at Yalta, especially with respect to free elections in Poland. They saw its actions through a prism well described by Navy Secretary James Forrestal: "The ultimate aim of Soviet foreign policy is Russian domination of a communist world."[54] In the spring of 1947 Truman went before a joint session of Congress to request aid for Greece in its battle against a communist insurgency. That summer Secretary of State George Marshall proposed a massive economic aid program for Europe as a means of forestalling communist takeovers. The Soviet Union and its satellites refused the aid, and nothing forestalled the communist coup in Czechoslovakia in early 1948. Then in April the Soviets cut land access to Berlin, leading to the Berlin airlift to supply the city, as well as the creation of the

North Atlantic Treaty Organization a year later. The same month that NATO was created, Mao Zedong's communists were victorious in the Chinese civil war. In September the Soviet Union detonated an atomic bomb years sooner than American experts had anticipated. In June 1950 the North Korean communists invaded the South, and by the end of November, Chinese communists intervened in the fight against the U.S. forces (fighting under the banner of the United Nations).

Fear of communists abroad inflamed fears of communists at home. Several ex-communists had testified before the House Un-American Activities Committee (HUAC) that communists in America were a fifth column doing the bidding of the Soviet Union. Furthermore, there were allegations (true, as it turned out) that there were highly placed communists in the New Deal administration. Alger Hiss, a State Department official who had been at Yalta, was one who was named, and his trial for perjury (because the statute of limitations for espionage had run out) was a symbolic trial of the New Deal—with Frankfurter, Reed, and Secretary of State Dean Acheson acting unsuccessfully as character witnesses.

Shortly after Hiss's 1950 conviction, Klaus Fuchs, who had worked on atomic weapons for both Great Britain and the United States, confessed in Britain that he had handed over to the Soviets between 1943 and 1947 all the important atomic secrets he could uncover. In August, Julius and Ethel Rosenberg were indicted for conspiracy to commit espionage by passing along atomic secrets. Their conviction a year later sealed the belief that communists were traitors, and there was no crime too great for them to commit. In sentencing the Rosenbergs to death, Judge Irving Kaufman disgracefully blamed them for the deaths of American troops in Korea.

By the time of the Korean War, the federal government had come up with a four-part approach to cripple domestic communism. The initial two steps came from the executive. First, the leadership of the party was decapitated by indictment under the Smith Act in 1948 and conviction a year later of conspiracy to advocate the overthrow of the government. Second, in 1947 Truman issued an executive order establishing a loyalty-security program whereby government workers could be dismissed for membership in, association with, or sympathetic affiliation with any group designated by the attorney general as subversive. Simultaneously, Tom Clark created the "Attorney General's List."

The legislature provided the two other measures of the overall program. One was to drive communists out of their supposed stronghold in labor unions by denying access to the National Labor Relations Board to unions whose officials did not submit an affidavit swearing that they were not communists. The other was to expose communists publicly, and HUAC was a leader in forcing individuals to answer the bingo question "Are you now or have you ever been a communist?" If the answer was yes, then the witness had to name names or be held in contempt. If the answer was no, then a perjury charge loomed. To avoid the dilemma, some witnesses invoked their privilege against self-incrimination, thereby creating the sobriquet "Fifth Amendment communist." An underlying assumption of the program was that communists were different from Republicans or Democrats and that the First Amendment placed no barriers to the program. A further underlying assumption was that those who appeared to be unrepentant communists (or ex-communists) would lose their employment and be shunned in their communities.

The first case at the Court sustained requiring the noncommunist affidavit with a balancing test which concluded that the risks of political strikes to interstate commerce outweighed the speech and associational rights of the unions and their officers.[55] This was a mere preliminary to the First Amendment case of the century, *Dennis v. United States*—the convictions of the party leaders under the Smith Act. They clearly believed in violent revolution but had done nothing to further it. The trial judge had nevertheless instructed the jury that they could convict if the party intended to initiate its attempt to overthrow as speedily as circumstances would permit—that is, at a propitious moment sometime in the future. To justify the convictions Vinson had to gut the clear and present danger test, which he did by holding that Learned Hand's version from the court below was "as succinct and inclusive" as a court could devise.[56] That test, too, was a balancing test (to prove negligence in tort law): "In each case [courts] must ask whether the gravity of the 'evil,' discounted by its improbability, justifies such invasion of free speech as is necessary to avoid the danger."[57] Since the evil was the overthrow of the government and self-preservation was the ultimate value, it virtually went without saying that the balance was for all loyal Americans against the communists. Frankfurter concurred by abdicating: Congress had done all of the necessary balancing when it passed the Smith Act. Jackson also concurred, finding that the conspiracy was entitled to less protection than individuals acting alone.

Black and Douglas dissented, the latter burnishing his New Deal credentials by praising the program for having rendered domestic communists irrelevant. He claimed that their speech was being wrongly "outlawed because Soviet Russia and her Red Army are a threat to world peace."[58] He did not convince the *Washington Post,* which instead was enamored with the Court's able reconciliation of "liberty and security in our time."[59] Just as *Korematsu* shrank due process to meet the needs of the military, *Dennis* shrank the First Amendment to meet the needs of confronting the supposed communist menace, and few Americans seemed to care.

War, even cold war, sets its own rules, as the rush to execute the Rosenbergs illustrated. Requests to review their espionage convictions had been routinely denied until two days after the Court adjourned, when—just two days before their scheduled execution—Douglas granted a stay based on a new claim that the Atomic Energy Act rather than the Espionage Act was the sole applicable law (and that the former precluded capital punishment). Vinson called the Court back into session the next day. Over the dissents of Black, Douglas, and Frank-furter, the stay was lifted and the executions went off as scheduled. The Court explained why the majority thought that Douglas had been in error; it did not—because it could not—explain why the haste had been necessary.[60] One congressman was so angry at the stay that he claimed it constituted "high crimes and misdemeanors" as grounds for impeaching Douglas.

Just before *Dennis,* the Court sustained loyalty discharges and the ability of the government to use the Attorney General's List. This was a 4–4 vote, but as soon as former attorney general Clark ceased be-ing disqualified, he would make a solid fifth vote for the program. That was apparent in state cases that typically, but not exclusively, in-volved loyalty oaths for teachers. The Court believed that in occupa-tions for which a license from the state was necessary, the license con-stituted a privilege which the state could reasonably condition.[61] And taking a loyalty oath was reasonable. Black, Douglas, and Frankfurter dissented.

The virtual carte blanche to hunt communists ended after the De-cember 1954 Senate condemnation of Wisconsin's Joe McCarthy. With Earl Warren at the helm and *Brown v. Board of Education* already on the books, the justices took McCarthy's fall as a signal that the loyalty-security program now could be tested by constitutional standards, and they set about dismantling it. The Court cut back on summary dis-missals from civil service jobs on loyalty grounds by limiting them to employees who had access to sensitive information.[62] More sig-nificant were two state cases, *Pennsylvania v. Nelson* and *Slochower v. Board of Education. Nelson* reversed the sedition conviction of Steve Nelson, the leader of the Communist Party in western Pennsylvania, on the ground that the state law was preempted by the various federal statutes dealing with communists. In *Slochower* the Court invalidated New York's policy of treating the invocation of the right against self-incrimination when questioned about one's employment duties as tantamount to a resignation. Seemingly ending the penalization of Fifth Amendment communists, the Court ruled that because there were innocent reasons for taking the Fifth, a state could not so penalize its use. These decisions provoked outcries from Southerners and national security conservatives but were greeted with satisfaction by civil libertarians as signaling the end of judicial acquiescence to McCarthyism.

The signal was unmistakable in the 1956 term, when the Court decided twelve cases dealing with communists or communism, and the governments lost each time. A couple of the cases were truly significant—such as interpreting the Smith Act to all but preclude further convictions,[63] and lecturing Congress and HUAC that "there is no congressional power to expose for the sake of exposure" (which was all HUAC did in the 1950s).[64] The Court also reversed two decisions by state bar associations that past membership in the Communist Party automatically equated with a lack of good moral character regardless of subsequent facts.[65]

The Eighty-fifth Congress, then in session, proved that just because McCarthy was dead (having drunk himself into the grave in early 1957), it didn't mean that anticommunism was also dead. The 1957 decisions caused the state attorneys general as well as the American Bar Association to join congressional national security conservatives in sharp criticism of the Court. A number of bills were quickly introduced to curb the Court, but in the summer of 1957 little could be done, because Congress was focused almost entirely on what would become the Civil Rights Act of 1957. Thus while Congress was not in a position to do much more than verbally trounce the Court, it nevertheless hurriedly passed the Jencks Act (on defendants' access to FBI interview notes of witnesses testifying against them) at the demand of FBI director Hoover. Although the act basically codified one of the 1957 decisions,[66] it was opposed by the Court's defenders and seen by all as a slap at the Court.

The second session of the Eighty-fifth Congress had time to consider Court-curbing bills even as the Court allowed states again to discharge Fifth Amendment communists—this time on the grounds of incompetence.[67] The House passed measures which created a presumption against finding that a federal statute preempted state counterparts, rewrote the Smith Act provisions on "organizing," and authorized summary discharges of nonsensitive government personnel for security reasons. Senate action focused on William Jenner's proposal to strip the Court of jurisdiction in all the areas where it had interfered with the anticommunist programs. There was too much opposition, and so Senator John Marshall Butler offered an amendment to Jenner's bill that would limit jurisdiction-stripping to admissions to the legal profession, but would also undo the HUAC holding, rewrite the Smith Act on organizing, and change the preemption doctrine.

Senate majority leader Lyndon Johnson tried to prevent any votes on anti-Court measures and was successful until the end of the session neared. Jenner-Butler was ultimately tabled by a 49–41 vote, but that was accompanied by a tremendous amount of anti-Court feeling. Immediately on the heels of that, a motion to table the House proposals failed 39–45. There was pandemonium in the Senate, but Johnson secured a recess until the next day, and between his arm-twisting and that of organized labor, enough votes were changed for the motion to recommit to pass 41–40. Even though no anti-Court measure passed, the Court had been slapped around harder than during the Court-packing fight. Even the state chief justices piled on, adopting by a 36–8 vote a critical report on the Court which claimed "considerable doubt" that the United States was still a government of laws and not of men.[68]

A clear message had been sent, and the Court, or at least a five-man bloc of the Court, got it. Black, Douglas, and two Eisenhower appointees, Chief Justice Earl Warren and William J. Brennan, held firm, but now in dissent.

A year later, in *Barenblatt v. United States,* the Court offered HUAC carte blanche by adopting a balancing test that was a joke. Essentially it pitted the nation's right to survive against the right of the individual to thwart the committee. This test resulted in affirming convictions in 1961 of two uncooperative witnesses who had been called to testify solely because of their opposition to HUAC.[69] The prior bar admission cases were gutted, and the Court ruled that someone who agreed with the Declaration of Independence that "whenever the particular government in power becomes destructive of these [constitutional] ends, it is the right of the people to alter or abolish it and thereupon to establish a new government," could justifiably be asked if he was a communist and be denied admission if he refused to answer.[70] A Smith Act conviction using the membership provisions of the law was affirmed,[71] as was the order of the Subversive Activities Control Board to the Communist Party requiring it to register and list its members.[72]

Congressman Wint Smith had stated that "the Court is simply blind to the reality of our time."[73] The second session of the Eighty-fifth Congress gave it vision. The rout had morphed the jurisprudence of 1961 into that of 1951.

Civil Rights

The other great postwar issue was race. Civil rights litigation had enjoyed unprecedented success from the late 1930s, although many of the decisions had more symbolic than practical significance. The all-white primary, sustained unanimously as late as 1935,[74] was held unconstitutional nine years later in *Smith v. Allwright*. A bitter Roberts, author of that 1935 decision, dissented alone and accused his New Deal brethren of bringing "adjudications of this tribunal into the same class as a restricted railway ticket, good for this day and train only."[75] While the numbers of Negroes registered to vote increased exponentially from the prewar years (when fewer than 5 percent were registered in the South) to the early 1950s, intimidation, especially in rural areas, plus the poll tax continued to keep them from voting. *Shelley v. Kraemer* ruled that racially restrictive covenants were unenforceable in courts. Even more than the demise of the all-white primary, this victory was largely symbolic, as it did not prevent sellers or real estate agents from discriminating. Although the Court declined a request from the attorney general to overrule *Plessy v. Ferguson*, the justices did interpret the Interstate Commerce Act to forbid segregation by railroads.[76]

The Court also extended the coerced confession rule of *Brown v. Mississippi* to situations in which there was no physical torture.[77] After a white man was murdered near Fort Lauderdale in 1933, police rounded up about three dozen Negroes for interrogation. There was no reason to believe that any were involved in the murder. It was simply the way things were done. All were held incommunicado and questioned for a week, deprived of sleep, and threatened with lynching. Three confessed, two pled guilty, and after conviction of the third, all were sentenced to death. A unanimous Court through Black reversed, finding the confessions involuntary. Of course a confession can be involuntary without physical assault, but as with a shock the conscience standard, it is hard to know when the will is overborne. Interrogation is legitimate; too much is not. How much is too much? The Court began to fracture on the question almost immediately. Furthermore, there was nothing inherently Southern about the need to interrogate suspects.

All of the race cases were preliminaries for the attack on separate but equal in public schools because it was the linchpin of the entire Southern way of life and its caste system. The NAACP's litigating arm, under the leadership of Charles Houston and then Thurgood Marshall, was determined to realize the goals enshrined, but heretofore nullified, in the Reconstruction Amendments.

The challenge to *Plessy* began in the 1930s with higher education as the target and in circumstances where the lack of equality was indisputable. Missouri, like most border states and all of the Confederacy, had a law school for whites but not for Negroes. For the latter, the state would pay their tuition, but not their travel or living expenses, to attend a law school in a neighboring state. The Court, through Hughes, reversed in an opinion that was short on reasoning. The case was repeated in Oklahoma after the war and just four days after oral argument, when the Court tersely ordered the state to provide Ada Sipuel with a legal education "as soon as it does for other applicants of any other group."[78] Oklahoma responded immediately by roping off an area in the capitol and assigning professors to teach Sipuel. When the NAACP claimed that this did not comply, the Court, over dissents by Murphy and Rutledge, refused to hear the petition.[79] Implicit in *Sipuel* was what was explicit in the Interstate Commerce Act case: the justices were not yet ready to confront *Plessy* head-on.

Two unanimous opinions by Vinson in 1950 convinced the NAACP it was time to claim that separate but equal was impossible in public education. One was another Oklahoma case, this time involving a graduate program in education; the other was a law school case in which Texas, like Oklahoma, had created a separate law school in the capitol building with (temporary) faculty from the existing white law school at the University of Texas. Oklahoma had initially required sixty-eight-year-old Negro George McLaurin to sit in the corridor outside the classroom, but as the case progressed, he was let inside and allowed to sit in a row reserved for Negroes. His library and meal seatings were improved but also left segregated. He was getting the same education as his white classmates, just in a humiliating way. Heman Sweatt had an easier case. His law "school" lacked a library, permanent faculty, and powerful (indeed any) alumni. Although the Justice Department again urged the Court to overrule *Plessy*, it did not, but Vinson's opinion spoke of intellectual commingling in *McLaurin*[80] and intangibles in *Sweatt*.[81] Thurgood Marshall thought that the opinions offered the NAACP a roadmap to success in the attack on segregation in public schools.

Not only were the Court's new opinions favorable for attacking separate but equal, but so were trends in society as well. After World War II, Jackie Robinson integrated major league baseball, the undisputed national pastime; the Democrats at their 1948 convention joined the Republicans in including a strong civil rights plank; Truman had ordered an end to segregation in the armed forces. Additionally, and significantly, the imperatives of the cold war, in which both the United States and the Soviet Union were trying to woo recently independent nations into their respective orbits, made segregation a huge problem for the State Department, and the Justice Department so informed the Court in a friend of the Court brief.

In the fall of 1952 the Court heard hours of oral argument in cases challenging school segregation in Virginia, South Carolina, Delaware, Kansas, and the District of Columbia. As a matter of conscious strategy, the NAACP did not claim simply that the obviously unequal schools were unequal. The time was ripe, and it was going for a home run. Had Marshall been in the Court's conference room, his hopes might have been dashed. On an issue on which all the justices believed that unanimity was essential, the three border-state justices—Vinson, Reed, and Clark—thought *Plessy* should be reaffirmed. For Black, Douglas, and Truman's two Midwestern appointees, segregation was per se unconstitutional. Frankfurter believed that Marshall had placed the Court in a bind, while Jackson was ambivalent on racial issues, acknowledging that segregation was wrong but not necessarily unconstitutional.

Frankfurter offered a solution to buy time: order the cases rebriefed and reargued on whether the history of the adoption of the Fourteenth Amendment offered guidance to the justices. This would also give the Court a chance to see what the position of the new Eisenhower Justice Department would be (the same as Truman's, as it turned out) and hope for the best.

On September 8, 1953, Vinson died of a heart attack, causing Frankfurter to remark that it was the first indication of the existence of God that he had ever seen. Eisenhower nominated California's popular three-term governor, Earl Warren, to Vinson's seat. Warren radiated integrity; he had grown with every added responsibility, and had been a largely nonpartisan partisan in California politics, where in the cross-filing primaries he had been able to win as both a Democrat and a Republican. He was definitely the latter, having been Thomas Dewey's running mate in 1948, and had hoped that a deadlock between Eisenhower and Robert Taft would give him the 1952 Republican nomination. Neither the deadlock nor the nomination materialized, but Eisenhower had promised him the first seat on the Court, and Ike kept his word.

When Warren spoke at conference after the reargument in *Brown v. Board of Education* and the other four cases, all the justices knew the outcome, since he had just added his voice to the four who believed that segregation was per se unconstitutional. Over the next months he used his exceptional interpersonal skills to achieve unanimity, bringing over Reed, the final holdout, with the observation that he was now alone and had to do what he thought best for the country.

Brown was both short and short on reasoning. Warren avoided claiming that history had decided the case, refusing to turn the clock back to either 1868 or 1896. He did not claim that precedents required the outcome, and he did not say a word about the caste system the South had enshrined. Instead, as in *Sweatt*, he rested his conclusion on intangibles that were closer to those of *McLaurin:* segregation leaves children with "a feeling of inferiority as to their status in the community."[82] *Plessy* had stated that if segregation "stamps the colored race with a badge of inferiority," it did so "solely because the colored race choose to put that construction upon it."[83] *Brown* rid itself of those musings, declaring that "modern authority" backed its contrary conclusions.[84] It then dropped a footnote to six social-scientific studies, including Swedish economist Gunnar Myrdal's mid-1940s classic *An American Dilemma*, which contrasted America's belief in equality with the country's treatment of Negroes.

While the North was satisfied with the outcome, and the Voice of America could trumpet the nation's ability to settle disputes by law rather than mob action or dictatorial fiat, Southern politicians on the Atlantic seacoast south of Virginia roundly condemned it. Richard Russell of Georgia, the most respected member of the Senate, heaped scorn on the justices, labeling them "amateur psychologists."[85] Given the way Warren wrote the opinion, Russell was not off the mark. *Brown* signaled the intended destruction of the "Southern way of life," a societal transformation the likes of which happen only in the aftermath of losing a war. Certainly no court had ever taken on such a task. Everyone was on notice that this Court, under Earl Warren, was ambitious.

At the end of *Brown* the Court ordered yet a new round of briefing and argument, this time on remedy. All the justices knew there would be resistance in the South, and none wanted a decree that would be flouted, so they strove for an opinion and a result that would not upset the region too much. The key phrase in *Brown II* was "all deliberate speed,"[86] by which the Court was acknowledging that it would accept token desegregation later. Still, the *Los Angeles Times* put *Brown II* in a national perspective when it editorialized that the decision would "not suit extremists, but we think most reasonable people will agree with it."[87]

There were few if any reasonable people in positions of power in the South, as every state from the Confederacy except Arkansas, Tennessee, and Texas readied itself at all costs to thwart *any* attempted desegregation, no matter how minimal. Senators Strom Thurmond of South Carolina, Harry Flood Byrd of Virginia, and Russell brought together the Southern Democrats in Congress to issue a frontal attack on the Court. They drafted a "Declaration of Constitutional Principles," quickly shortened to the "Southern Manifesto," issued in March 1956, attacking *Brown* as "a clear abuse of judicial power" and pledging "to use all lawful means to bring about a reversal of this decision which is contrary to the Constitution."[88] Echoing Thomas Jefferson and Spencer Roane, the Southern Manifesto was signed by 101 of 128 Southern Democrats, including all from the Deep South, Virginia, and Arkansas, and all but one from Florida. The politicians understood their voters. Two of the three non-signers from North Carolina lost their primary elections. Massive resistance became Southern orthodoxy—as white Southerners deemed *Brown* void and declared themselves willing to use any means available to nullify it by both laws and private pressure—and old-line race-baiters, virtually extinct in the postwar climate, enjoyed a political comeback.

Eisenhower intentionally avoided nominating a Southerner to the Court, and thus all five of his appointees supported *Brown*. When Jackson died before *Brown II,* Eisenhower selected John Marshall Harlan's grandson and namesake. The second Harlan, a superb Wall Street lawyer and mentor to Attorney General Herbert Brownell, had previously been appointed to the court of appeals. Then, just before the 1956 election, one of Truman's cronies retired, and Eisenhower instructed Brownell to find a conservative Catholic Democratic judge. Checking with the candidate's parish priest to ascertain whether he attended mass regularly, Brownell selected New Jersey Supreme Court judge William J. Brennan. He was a Catholic Democrat all right, but one with a demonstrably liberal record. Like Roosevelt's four great appointments, Eisenhower's first three became giants. (Subsequently Eisenhower would appoint two Midwestern Republicans, Charles Whittaker and Potter Stewart, whom he had previously placed on courts of appeals.)

Massive resistance moved to Arkansas in 1957, when Governor Orval Faubus called out the National Guard to prevent a mere nine Negro students from entering the previously all-white, two thousand–student Central High School in Little Rock pursuant to a court-ordered plan. When a federal judge ordered the Guard removed, their place was taken by a shrieking mob. After three weeks of horrible international publicity, during which time the secretary of state complained to Brownell that Little Rock was ruining American foreign policy, Eisenhower sent in the 101st Airborne—like "Hitler's storm troopers," in Russell's understated words[89]—to enforce the desegregation plan.

Little Rock came to the Court in *Cooper v. Aaron* at a special summer session the next year over the issue of whether the "chaos, bedlam, and turmoil" around Central justified postponing even the limited desegregation for a couple of years.[90] The outcome was overdetermined. If Eisenhower, who Warren (wrongly) thought was opposed to *Brown,* could protect court-ordered desegregation with troops, the Court could not rule that he had acted in vain. Furthermore, to do otherwise would signal to every other Southern state that adopting a policy of violence at the first hint of desegregation was the road to legal salvation. A battered Court (this being immediately after the second session of the Eighty-fifth Congress) ended the opinion with a bravado boast of its own potency. In an unprecedented move, the opinion of the Court listed all nine justices as its authors and for the first time equated the Constitution with its own pronouncements. Thus it claimed that when a public official—like Faubus—took the oath to support the Constitution, the official was duty-bound to support the Court's interpretations.

The *New York Times* cheered the "clear language, understandable even to the most fanatic segregationist."[91] Faubus then ordered the Little Rock schools shut down, and they remained closed for the school year (although Central's reigning state championship football team was allowed to play out its schedule because, as Faubus noted, cancellation would be "a cruel and unnecessary blow to the children").[92] Perhaps that compassion was the reason why a December Gallup poll listing the ten most admired men in the world placed Faubus in the company of Eisenhower, Churchill, Jonas Salk, and Albert Schweitzer.

As part of their massive resistance, Southern states moved to shut down the NAACP—viewing it the way most Americans viewed the

Communist Party. Though ultimately unsuccessful, the effort tied up the organization into the 1960s and was one of the factors contributing to Thurgood Marshall's early retirement from the NAACP Legal Defense Fund.

In the wake of *Cooper* the Court summarily affirmed the validity of Alabama's Pupil Placement Law, a cornerstone of that state's policy of massive resistance. The justices adopted the reasoning of the court below, which opined that the judges could not conclude "in advance of its application, that the Alabama Law will not be properly and constitutionally administered."[93] Actually they could, but Alabama would have ignored any court decision, and Eisenhower wasn't going to send the army in everywhere—indeed anywhere again—in the South. Just as in the domestic security area, the Court was defeated (although instead of reversing itself, it simply pulled out of the school desegregation area). The promise of the Reconstruction Amendments was on hold once more.

· IX ·

Reforming America

THE DOMINANT RED AND BLACK ISSUES from the prior era found resolution in the 1960s. The Civil Rights Act of 1964 and the Voting Rights Act of 1965 enshrined the Court's nondiscrimination principle in statutes where the Southerners filibustered, lost, and verbally acquiesced. The rise of the civil rights movement coincided with the metastasizing of domestic anticommunism into the loony John Birch Society, whose leader thought President Dwight Eisenhower knowingly followed communist orders. Losing its political salience (except in the South, where segregationists saw nondiscrimination as a communist plot), the Court was able to dismantle the domestic security program without the slightest concern over retribution. Indeed, with John Kennedy as president, the Court for the first time since the Taft administration enjoyed the full and public support of the White House. Although lacking the élan of the New Frontier, the justices, like the incoming administration, were supremely confident of their ability to fashion a better world. During this happy interlude of less than a decade, the Court worked harmoniously with political liberals to tackle the nation's problems.

Civil Rights

With the NAACP under attack in the South, the initiative passed to younger activists, who initiated sit-ins and Freedom Rides to call attention to the deplorable conditions there for blacks. At first it didn't work; polling data showed that few Americans thought of civil rights as a priority issue, and most certainly the new Kennedy administration did not. To accomplish anything domestically, the administration had to have Southern votes, and those could only be gotten by ignoring civil rights. For the first two years President Kennedy and his brother, Attorney General Robert F. Kennedy, would not support a civil rights bill as strong as those backed by the Eisenhower administration.

Birmingham, Alabama, in the spring of 1963 changed everything. Beginning with the arrest of Martin Luther King Jr. for a Good Friday march without a permit and his subsequent "Letter from a Birmingham Jail," to chilling pictures of high-pressure fire hoses tumbling bodies down the streets, to electric cattle prods, to the first of the decade's iconic photographs—a white policeman with sunglasses holding a black teenager by the front of his shirt while a German shepherd bites the teen's abdomen—Birmingham moved the North and therefore moved the Kennedys. Before Birmingham, Gallup surveys found that only about 5 percent of Americans thought civil rights was the most important issue facing the country. Shortly afterwards 50 percent did. The aftermath of *Brown v. Board of Education* had brought out the worst in the South. King's genius was in reflecting it northward so the country would demand action.

President Kennedy finally spoke to the nation and demanded a strong civil rights bill "not merely for reasons of economic efficiency, world diplomacy and domestic tranquility—but above all because it is right."[1] Despite the March on Washington, capped by King's "I Have a Dream" speech and the murderous bombing of the Sixteenth

Street Baptist Church in Birmingham in September, Kennedy's bill was stalled in Congress (and still was not the administration's top domestic priority).

Kennedy's assassination in Dallas that fall initiated a decade of shocks to the optimistic nation. The new president, Lyndon B. Johnson, embraced civil rights as the detached Kennedy never had, telling a joint session of a mourning Congress that nothing could better honor the slain president than to enact the civil rights bill quickly. Politically Johnson believed that he could not afford to compromise, because to do so would alienate Kennedy's base. "I had to produce a civil rights bill that was even stronger than the one they'd [have] gotten if Kennedy had lived," he said. "Without this I'd be dead before I could ever begin."[2] The House was easy, passing the bill with an overwhelming bipartisan vote in February 1964. But beginning in the late 1930s, Georgia Democrat Richard Russell had led eleven Senate filibusters, and he had never lost one.

Johnson and the floor leader of the bill in the Senate, Minnesota's Hubert Humphrey, worked tirelessly to woo Senate Republican leader Everett M. Dirksen of Illinois to bring the Republicans to supporting a cloture vote, which needed two-thirds of the Senate to cut off further debate. The Southern filibuster was the longest in Senate history, filling eighty-two days and 63,000 pages of the *Congressional Record*, but eventually Dirksen brought the Republicans to cloture, declaring the Civil Rights Act "an idea whose time has come."[3] Indeed, it received 70 percent of the votes in both Houses. Despite the Republicans' assistance and the fact that the filibuster was spearheaded by Democrats, the Civil Rights Act, followed by the presidential campaign of Barry Goldwater, wedded black voters to the Democratic Party.

Compared to the Southern resistance to *Brown*, the response to the Civil Rights Act was tepid. Russell acknowledged that "as long as it is there it must be obeyed."[4] Therein lies an important datum: on fundamental issues, losers accept a democratic defeat more readily than a judicial one.

The Civil Rights Act eschewed the Fourteenth Amendment and rested on the Commerce Clause instead. Constitutional challenges to the new law didn't have a prayer. The Court had been alone since *Brown*. Now Congress and the president offered assistance. No Court would rebuff that aid.

The cases rocketed to the Court. One was a Justice Department suit against a large Atlanta motel easily accessible from two interstate highways and catering to an interstate clientele. A small family-owned barbeque joint well off the beaten path in Birmingham filed another, claiming the act could not constitutionally reach it. A month after the Democrats' landslide 1964 election victory, the Court unanimously upheld the act. The Atlanta case was easy; Congress could always reach private actors affecting interstate commerce. The Birmingham case might have seemed harder, because any relation to interstate commerce was tenuous, but the consensus after the 1942 *Wickard v. Filburn* decision on homegrown wheat was that Congress could reach anything. That was sufficient. Interestingly, the Court did not rest on the obvious ground that had Congress not prevented discrimination by local businesses, they would have a competitive advantage over their interstate competitors.

Johnson wanted the country to absorb the Civil Rights Act while he used his new two-thirds majorities in both Houses to declare a War on Poverty. But King, fresh off his Nobel Peace Prize, and other civil rights activists demanded immediate action to remedy the decades-old disenfranchisement of Southern blacks. Selma, in the heart of Alabama, was aptly chosen for the demonstrations for both its paucity of registered Negroes and its sheriff, who could instantly explode to violence upon seeing a Negro marching. At one time King would pen a letter accurately asserting "THERE ARE MORE NEGROES IN JAIL WITH ME THAN THERE ARE ON THE VOTING ROLLS."[5]

After the requisite brutality, King called for a march from Selma to the state capital. On the far side of the Edmund Pettis Bridge on the edge of town, the sheriff and his men, with the aid of state troopers on horseback, routed the marchers with tear gas, clubs, and bullwhips. ABC, the only network to get film that Sunday night, interrupted the television premier of *Judgment at Nuremberg* to show footage of the carnage. The juxtaposition of the lawlessness of the Nazis and the violence of Southern police in Selma was perfect. Judgment for the lawless, racist Nazi regime had come at the Nuremberg War Crimes Trials. Judgment for the lawless, racist Southern regimes would come with passage and implementation of a strong voting rights act. Over the two weeks after "Bloody Sunday," Johnson gave the speech of his life to a joint session of Congress (including four justices), and whites streamed to Selma—as they had not to Birmingham—to join blacks in making history. With the full embrace of the national news media, the Voting Rights Act of 1965 was on its way to overwhelming passage in August and its validation by the Court on the first anniversary of "Bloody Sunday."

With the Civil Rights and Voting Rights acts establishing non-discrimination in public accommodations, employment, and voting, the formal legal part of the civil rights agenda was largely complete. Shockingly, less than a week after passage of the Voting Rights Act, a race riot erupted in the Watts section of Los Angeles, leaving thirty-four dead (including a deputy sheriff and a firefighter shot by a sniper), over a thousand injured, and millions of dollars in property damage. A year earlier the first major urban race riot since World War II had broken out in Harlem, and a year later dozens of inner cities burned, a prelude to the huge race riots in Newark and Detroit in 1967. Moreover, some younger civil rights activists were replacing nonviolence with calls for "Black Power," and even King, moving into the North and increasingly concerned about Vietnam, promised to "stir up trouble."[6]

Johnson pondered, "How is it [Watts] possible after all we've accomplished?"[7] So did the Court, which even before Watts had detailed the dangers of mob rule—in a peaceful protest case. The Court had been on the forefront of civil rights issues, but after 1965 it fractured badly and retreated when questions of obedience to lawful authority were presented.

In *Adderly v. Florida* in 1966 the Court affirmed the trespass convictions of black students for peacefully picketing on the grounds of a county jail where a number of other students were being held after having been arrested the previous day for protesting segregation. Hugo Black, for a 5–4 Court, treated the First Amendment claim as if it were one for an unlimited right to protest at any place and at any time, in any manner. With that formulation the claim had to be rejected, even though it would be hard to find a better place to protest unconstitutional arrests than at the local Bastille.

A year later, in *Walker v. Birmingham,* the same majority lectured protesters about the need to respect the law. A presumably unintended irony was that the lecture was directed at King, for violating the injunction against the Good Friday march in Birmingham, rather than to the Alabama judge who issued the unconstitutional injunction. (The Alabama judiciary had been at war with the Court and the Constitution throughout this period.) According to the Court, King had to obey the injunction because "no man can be judge in his own cases, however exalted his station, however righteous his motives," and because "respect for the law is a small price to pay for the civilizing hand of law."[8]

That civilizing hand continued to strike at almost all possible forms of legal discrimination, the exception being prosecutors' preemptive challenges to jurors on racial grounds (a mistake finally corrected in 1986).[9] The most contentious discrimination case was California's Proposition 14, a constitutional amendment passed in 1964 by an even greater margin than that by which Johnson had carried the state. Prop.

14 guaranteed to property owners the right to absolute discretion in selling or leasing property to whomsoever they chose. It both repealed an existing fair housing law and made a constitutional amendment a prerequisite for any future fair housing laws. In an opinion as long on words as it was short on reasoning, a five-man majority in *Reitman v. Mulkey* held that Prop. 14 violated the Fourteenth Amendment because it authorized racial discrimination (as did the common law in every state that lacked a fair housing law—a point conspicuously omitted).

By contrast, the Court in *Loving v. Virginia* had no trouble striking down the commonwealth's law forbidding white people from marrying anyone except other white people (generously excepting descendants of Pocahontas and John Rolfe). Chief Justice Earl Warren held that the law was subject to the "most rigid scrutiny" under the Equal Protection Clause and easily announced that there was no justification whatsoever for the law. Having declared it unconstitutional once, he also found that it burdened marriage, one of the basic civil rights, and therefore violated the Due Process Clause as well.[10]

Domestic Security, Vietnam, and the First Amendment

The domestic security program met its demise because the times had changed—and, vastly more important, the composition of the Court had changed. Both Charles Whittaker and Felix Frankfurter left in ill health in 1962, and Tom Clark was forced off the Court in 1967 by Johnson's elevation of Clark's son Ramsey to attorney general.

Kennedy's first appointee, Byron White, a Rhodes Scholar who had led the NFL in rushing and his Yale Law School class in scoring, was deemed by the president to be the "ideal New Frontier judge."[11] He proved tough on crime, tough on communism, tough on the states, and, over a thirty-year tenure, undistinguished. Kennedy's second appointee, Labor Secretary Arthur Goldberg, provided the liberals—Earl Warren, Hugo Black, William O. Douglas, and William J. Brennan—

a reliable fifth vote. So did his successor, Abe Fortas, after Goldberg was suckered into surrendering his seat for the post of ambassador to the United Nations (and promises of future preferment). This created history's Warren Court—the most liberal Supreme Court ever. The Court's product was so impressive that the Democratic Party abandoned its traditional unease with the judiciary and instead concluded that a Great Society needed a great Court. And fortunately the country had one. Finally, Johnson replaced the conservative Clark with Thurgood Marshall, the twentieth century's most important lawyer, who, since leaving the NAACP in 1961, had been briefly on a federal court of appeals and then solicitor general under Johnson.

It is worth noting how contingency played such a role in creating this liberal Court. Black, who had his own heart problems, might have been the one to leave instead of Frankfurter. President Eisenhower's attorney general Herbert Brownell might have followed Ike's instruction to pick a conservative Catholic Democrat instead of picking Brennan. Or Warren might have turned out to be as conservative as his first term on the Court indicated (and his initial liberal critics feared). If any one of these had occurred, the very liberal Court would not have formed, and its moment would have passed.

Eight opinions by Warren Court liberals demolished both the federal and the remaining state domestic security programs. The most far reaching opinion came in *United States v. Robel,* where Warren struck down a ban on communists' working in defense facilities. The Court invalidated the ban because it reached not only nonsensitive positions but also members of the party who did not share its illegal aims. At an earlier time the Court might have saved the statute through some creative statutory construction, but this Court specifically refused to do so.

The judicial dismantling of the domestic security program was occurring side by side with a protection of wartime dissenters that was unique in American history. The first of the Vietnam cases came when the Georgia senate refused to seat civil rights activist Julian Bond, one of the first African Americans elected to its legislature in the twentieth century. Georgia's action was based on Bond's endorsement of an antiwar statement: he had opposed the war and the draft. If Bond's grandfather had opposed World War I on similar grounds, he could have been prosecuted, and the Court would have found no First Amendment violation. But in *Bond v. Floyd* in 1966 a unanimous Court held that the speech was protected: "The manifest function of the First Amendment in a representative democracy requires that legislators be given the widest latitude to express their views on issues of policy."[12] This state case, fraught with racial overtones that left the Court no options, interred the World War I cases and blocked prosecutions for antiwar speech before they could be started.

Although neither an antiwar nor a communist case, the contemporaneous *Brandenburg v. Ohio* spoke powerfully to both situations as the Court held that speech advocating illegal action could be punished only in circumstances "where such advocacy is directed to inciting or producing imminent lawless action and is likely to incite or produce such action."[13] This is the most speech-protective test ever offered. It was not enough for Black and Douglas, each of whom concurred, demanding more. Douglas acidly attacked the *Dennis* majority, which in 1951 had sustained convictions of Communist Party leaders, as "judges so wedded to the *status quo* that critical analysis made them nervous."[14] Douglas's outspoken criticisms of the Establishment, his flouting of its mores (with four wives, two young enough to be his granddaughters), his environmentalism, and his opposition to the Vietnam War made him a hero to a generation proclaiming that no one over thirty could be trusted, just as he had been a liberal hero at the height of the McCarthy hysteria.

In 1971, two years after Warren retired, the majority of the seven remaining members of the Warren Court decided *Cohen v. California* and the *Pentagon Papers Cases*. Cohen, with his jacket emblazoned with

"Fuck the Draft," was challenging not only the war but also the generation that had engineered it. The F-word was at the time the single most offensive word in the English language; indeed there was no close second. The Court found Cohen's actions in wearing the jacket in a courthouse constitutionally protected. Stunningly, one of the dissenters was Black, adhering to his speech/conduct distinction with the preposterous conclusion that Cohen was engaged in conduct.

The leak of the Pentagon Papers, some forty volumes of highly classified information, was the largest security leak in American history. After the *New York Times* refused to cease publication, the Nixon administration sought an injunction to prevent further publication. While the *Times* was restrained so that the rocket-docket litigation could bolt forward, the *Washington Post* received some of the Pentagon Papers and commenced publishing them. Seventeen days after the first installment appeared in the *Times,* six justices ruled that prior restraints could be issued in only the most extraordinary circumstances, and these cases did not encompass such circumstances. Only the conservative John Marshall Harlan and Richard Nixon's two appointees, Warren Burger and Harry Blackmun, did not stand up to the administration.

Even in time of war, top-secret information, if obtained by the press, could be published (although perhaps subsequently applicable criminal law would be brought to bear on the papers). As Black, in his last opinion, explained: "The press was to serve the governed, not the governors. [It] was protected so that it could bare the secrets of government and inform the people. Only a free and unrestrained press can effectively expose deception in government."[15] Daniel Ellsberg, who leaked the papers, and Nixon's national security advisor Henry Kissinger both thought (from opposite points of view on the war) that publication of the papers would lead to a surge of antiwar sentiment. It didn't happen; nor did the government's prediction that national security would be damaged by publication.

Just as the Court protected antiwar dissent for the first time, it also moved away from its earlier conclusions that neither libel nor obscenity was speech within the meaning of the First Amendment. In the case of obscenity the Court consistently tightened the definition so that less and less was encompassed within the term. The Court began in 1957 by undoing the Victorian underpinnings of obscenity that equated it with sex.[16] The initial goal had been to protect important literature. Then the Court moved to protect all serious literature and did so in a pair of 1964 decisions that produced Potter Stewart's tag line that perhaps he could not define obscenity, but "I know it when I see it."[17] (And he hadn't seen it since World War II.) Within two years the Court went further, causing Governor George Wallace of Alabama to observe, not inaccurately, that the Court couldn't distinguish constitutionally between "smut and great literature."[18] The Court then stumbled on what appeared to be its solution: cease trying to define obscenity and simply protect children and nonconsenting adults from depictions of sex.

Douglas gleefully told a friend that because the Court's obscenity decisions used the legal test of "whether the material arouses a prurient response in the beholder, [t]he older we get[,] the freer the speech."[19] When Richard Nixon got four vacancies to fill in his first term, the Court got younger, and the new justices joined White in attempting to roll back the clock.[20] It was too little, too late. With birth control pills in distribution for over a decade, *Playboy* passing 4 million in circulation per issue (second only to *Reader's Digest*), its publisher, Hugh Hefner, on the cover of *Time,* and a very serious book[21] on sexual research a runaway best-seller, sex had fully entered the mainstream. A cartoon in *Playboy* captured the mood. It shows an elderly couple being interviewed on leaving a theater with *Deep Throat* (the first porno movie to reach a mainstream audience, and one that received a five-page review in the *New York Times*)[22] advertised on the marquee. The woman is saying: "We feel it went beyond community standards of describing sex, nudity and the like; I suppose you might say it appealed to our prurient interest and it was definitely without re-deeming social value. We liked it."[23]

In 1964 the Court took on libel because Alabama used it as one weapon in the state's war to defend segregation. Alabama juries awarded huge verdicts against the *New York Times* and CBS for their re-porting on the state. One result was that the *Times,* which sent fewer than four hundred copies daily to Alabama, pulled its reporter out (as state officials were clearly hoping it would). In *New York Times v. Sullivan* the Court equated criticism of government officials with sedi-tious libel, retroactively held the Sedition Act of 1798 to be unconstitu-tional, and concluded that public officials could prevail in defamation actions only if they could show that the newspaper had printed the materials with reckless disregard for their truth or falsity. The need to protect civil rights from segregationists created a speech-protective rule, just as it would two years later when mixed with antiwar state-ments in *Bond v. Floyd.*

New York Times v. Sullivan quickly spread out of the civil rights area as the Court equated public figures—such as retired army general Edwin A. Walker—with public officials.[24] The Court even flirted with giving the press substantial immunity when reporting on public is-sues,[25] but pulled back in 1974.[26] Nevertheless, the Court had granted the press rights it never had thought possible, freeing it to be a watch-dog instead of a lapdog if it wished. The career of *Washington Post* edi-tor Ben Bradlee—who went from confidant of Kennedy to slayer of Nixon—illustrated the switch.

The Court was seemingly everywhere. If the volumes from John Marshall's thirty-five-year tenure do not fill a bookshelf, those from 1960 to 1974 fill over three and a half shelves.

Black's last words in the *Pentagon Papers Cases,* on the press serving the people, not the government, did more than summarize Black's views; they spoke to what the Court had been doing: (1) protecting those who challenged entrenched authority, (2) removing government

as an intermediary in establishing the acceptable level of style and criticism, and (3) allowing citizen-critics the opportunity to challenge at
will the established truth. The First Amendment in 1971 was close to a
civil libertarian's dream, marred, if at all, by the 1968 decision holding
(over Douglas's solo dissent) that the government could punish draft
card burning.[27] More surprisingly, this consensus had been forged during turbulent times which in the past had found the Court on the side
of governments in their attempts to promote stability.

Religion

The Court's speech cases, with the exception of obscenity, made no
enemies, and its libel cases provided it with influential friends in the
media, who were its beneficiaries. The Court's few religion cases followed the Protestant-Jeffersonian line that a wall of separation between church and state was essential. The first, in 1962, was *Engel v.
Vitale,* invalidating an innocuous twenty-two-word prayer that New
York teachers were required to use to open the school day. Black's
opinion adhered to mainstream Protestant doctrine that religion is private and should be left "to the people themselves and to those the people choose to look to for religious guidance."[28] *Engel* produced more
mail to the Court than any previous case (and few write to say what a
good job the justices are doing). Catholics and Southern Protestants
were particularly shrill in their denunciations of the Court. But the
Court had an important friend. Responding to a planted question at a
press conference, President Kennedy acknowledged that there would
be disagreement, but he hoped that everyone would support the Court
and the Constitution. Affirming a decision like *Engel* was perfect politics for a Catholic president who wished Protestants to see him separate himself from the Catholic Church.

A year later the Court extended *Engel* to ban the Lord's Prayer as
well as Bible reading in public schools.[29] Clark wrote the opinion, and
there were concurring opinions from Douglas, Brennan, and Gold-

berg, causing the *New York Times* to purr about how "the voice of a Protestant, a Catholic, and a Jew on the court spoke up for the princi-ple of church-state separation."[30] It would have been far more interest-ing if one of the justices had been an evangelical Christian. The reac-tion was muted compared to the furor over *Engel,* and when the House Judiciary Committee held hearings on an amendment to overturn the decisions, a veritable who's who of religious groups—the National Council of Churches, the Baptists, Lutherans, Presbyterians, Seventh-Day Adventists, Unitarians, and United Church of Christ—supported the Court (with the Catholic leadership remaining neutral because they had shifted their sights to far bigger game: tax dollars for paro-chial schools). For some years, however, the decisions were widely ig-nored in homogeneous communities in the South and Midwest.

As part of Johnson's Great Society, money began to trickle down to parochial schools. Adopting a child benefit theory, the Court held that if the money benefited parents and children rather than flowing di-rectly to the schools, then it was constitutional.[31] Since money aiding parochial school pupils would inevitably aid the school as well, the child benefit theory was riddled with problems and could be manipu-lated at will either to invalidate or to support any given program.

Simultaneously, the Court breathed life into the moribund Free Ex-ercise Clause by requiring states to justify laws impinging on free exer-cise with a compelling state interest—that is, a policy that is *really* im-portant and cannot be readily achieved by alternative means. As a result, a Seventh Day Adventist obtained unemployment compensa-tion for refusing to work on her Sabbath, and Amish children were al-lowed to abandon education after the eighth grade.[32]

The Political Thicket

Frankfurter believed that the strokes which forced his retirement were caused by *Baker v. Carr,* where, because Tennessee had not redistricted since 1901, the Court ruled that federal courts could evaluate whether the legislative districts met the standards of equal protection—whatever those were. A year later, in 1963, a pair of Georgia cases demanded that congressional districts be drawn on as close to an equal population basis as possible, and that choosing a governor by a system that looked like the Electoral College was unconstitutional. But the key test of *Baker v. Carr* came in 1964, when the Court decided a group of state legislative districting cases.

The operative assumption was that the Court would rule that one house of a state legislature must be composed on an equal population basis but the other house could follow the federal analogy of the Senate and factor in other (likely rural) interests as well. The assumption proved seriously wrong. In *Reynolds v. Sims*, Warren held that both houses of a legislature had to be apportioned on an equal population basis. Because an underlying purpose of the reapportionment decisions was to eliminate rural dominance of the legislative process, it would have been folly to leave one house untouched. The federal analogy was rejected as growing out of "unique historical circumstances" and therefore inapplicable to the states.[33] A companion case ruled that even if the state's voters overwhelmingly approved a plan deviating from one person, one vote (and simultaneously rejecting a perfect apportionment), they were entitled to no deference: "A citizen's constitutional rights can hardly be infringed simply because a majority of the people choose that it can be."[34] Warren myopically believed that if legislatures had been properly apportioned since 1900, the nation's acute racial troubles would have been alleviated.

The Court's entry into the political thicket was awesome, and it implicitly questioned the legitimacy of all the elected branches. In the case of the Georgia governor, the Court rejected the Electoral College analogy and therefore implicitly questioned the presidency. Applying the equal population standard to Congress generally meant that 395 of 435 congressional districts were currently unconstitutional. *Reynolds* expressly rejected the analogy of the Senate in finding that the Fourteenth Amendment mandated one person, one vote. It was as if the only legitimate branch of government was the life-tenured judiciary.

Baker v. Carr was enthusiastically embraced by President Kennedy, who had previously written a piece for the *New York Times Sunday Magazine* condemning malapportioned legislatures—and his Justice Department. There was a mixed reaction to subsequent cases. The public was generally supportive of the Court and indifferent to returning to the old system, while politicians who believed that their jobs were in jeopardy displayed varying degrees of hostility. But it didn't matter, because reapportionment created a self-fulfilling prophecy. Once it was implemented, the new victors had no interest in turning back the clock and relinquishing the offices they had just won.

An unintended aspect of the cases aided the Democratic Party, since most of the reapportionment took place following the Democratic sweep in the 1964 elections. Therefore legislatures controlled by the Democrats drew the new lines, which not surprisingly favored Democrats. Even Nixon's two presidential victories did not dent the Democratic edge in Congress.

The Court believed that one person, one vote, would result in urban problems' receiving needed attention and would curb states and municipalities from looking to Washington for assistance. The justices also believed that legislative races would become more competitive, and gerrymandering would be more difficult. Just as observers' assumptions prior to *Reynolds* did not pan out, the Court's assumptions about its effects didn't either. Frankfurter's fear that the Court would suffer grievously if it entered the political thicket turned out to be wrong, too. Nothing worked out the way anyone predicted.

Criminal Procedure and "Law and Order"

Brown created a solid white South that hated the Court. For a brief period, national security conservatives made the Southern view a majority, but that coalition evaporated when eight Republican senators were defeated by liberal Democrats in the 1958 elections. Nationwide opposition to the Court reemerged in the mid-1960s because the Court, for the first time, was deciding criminal cases whose import was not limited to the South, and this coincided with both an escalating crime rate and summer race riots. The ultimate result was a winning campaign issue that helped place Nixon in the White House.

Only one of the Court's major criminal procedure cases, the 1963 decision in *Gideon v. Wainwright,* was popular. The Court through Black overruled *Betts v. Brady* and held that an indigent defendant must be provided with a lawyer for trial. Everyone understood that if one side has a lawyer and the other does not, it is not a fair fight—and there cannot be a fair trial.

The important shift from Southern to national criminal cases was initiated in 1961 by *Mapp v. Ohio,* holding that evidence obtained without compliance with the Fourth Amendment must be excluded from a criminal trial. Decided two years before *Gideon, Mapp* overruled *Wolf v. Colorado*—a case only twelve years old. Clark justified the overruling by noting that in 1949 two-thirds of the states had rejected the exclusionary rule while now only half did, by claiming that no other solution would deter police misconduct, and by asserting that admitting such evidence impaired judicial integrity. The majority believed that the movement toward the exclusionary rule was inexorable (although in fact only six states had switched in twelve years) and therefore, with history on their side, they were going to help it out. Harlan, for Frankfurter and Whittaker, dissented on federalism grounds, and queried as well whether history was so inevitable. *Gideon* and *Mapp* signaled the rejection of Frankfurter's position that the Fourteenth Amendment did not incorporate the Bill of Rights, although the Court never went as far as Black had wished, to incorporate it all.

A year after *Gideon,* Goldberg authored *Escobedo v. Illinois,* overturning a murder conviction, a case unmatched for its hostility to confessions. Ignoring the fact that some situations, such as murder, may require confessions, the Court suggested that this made the system less reliable and that using "extrinsic evidence independently secured through skillful investigation" was the way to go—as if that were always possible.[35] Additionally Goldberg suggested that confessions were "often" extorted.[36] With reason, White for four dissenters accused the majority of having a "deep-seated distrust of law enforcement officers everywhere" and therefore moving to bar all confessions "whether involuntarily made or not."[37]

Barry Goldwater, soon to be the 1964 Republican presidential nominee, exclaimed that "no wonder our law enforcement officers have been demoralized and rendered ineffective in their jobs."[38] At the Republican convention former president Eisenhower urged delegates "not to be guilty of maudlin sympathy for the criminal who, roaming the streets with switchblade knife and illegal firearms seeking a prey, suddenly becomes upon apprehension a poor, underprivileged person who counts upon the compassion of our society and the weakness of many courts to forgive his offense."[39] During the campaign Goldwater accused courts of contributing to the breakdown of law and order in the cities. But it was to no avail.

Two years later the same 5–4 split (with Fortas having replaced Goldberg) emerged in *Miranda v. Arizona,* one of Warren's most famous opinions, where the majority mandated that before custodial interrogation the police must give a suspect four warnings, beginning with the right to remain silent. Although its tone was not as hostile to confessions as that of *Escobedo, Miranda* produced a volcanic eruption over handcuffing the police and coddling criminals, and it nationalized opposition to the Warren Court in the Republican Party. All of a sudden Republicans had a winning issue—law and order—and in November they reversed their loses from the 1964 elections. The Court could see the riots and read the election results, too, and it moderated its criminal procedure revolution—though it did hold that wiretapping was subject to the Fourth Amendment's warrant requirement. Black, never a fan of the Fourth Amendment, dissented and claimed that in covering wiretapping, the majority was improperly rewriting the Fourth Amendment.

In 1968 Congress passed the Omnibus Crime and Safe Streets Act, which attempted to overrule *Miranda* legislatively. Law and order was the issue that year, and the Democrats lacked a vocabulary to discuss it. Because they were enthralled by the Warren Court and worried about offending black voters, Democrats wished to focus on the root causes of crime. To many Americans this seemed either wasteful spending, a strategy for doing nothing, or a rationale for excusing the criminal. Claims that "enough has been done for those who murder and rape and rob!"[40] resonated better with the electorate, which, by a 57–43 margin, repudiated Democratic presidential nominee Hubert H. Humphrey.

Nixon and Alabama's George Wallace, running as an independent, had both aimed their presidential campaigns against the Court. In his standard stump speech Nixon declared that "some of our courts have gone too far in weakening the peace forces as against the criminal forces,"[41] while Wallace went further, asserting that the Supreme Court was "destroy[ing] constitutional government in the country."[42] Between them, Nixon and Wallace were blaming all the domestic ills of the nation on the Warren Court.

The Court—or at least Warren—had placed itself at issue when, immediately after Robert Kennedy's June 1968 assassination, Warren had announced his retirement. Everyone saw through the unsubtle ploy of giving the chief justiceship to Johnson to fill rather than awaiting the outcome of the November election, and Johnson's choice of Abe Fortas was successfully filibustered in the fall after a summer season of Court-bashing. Subsequently, questionable ethical dealings between Fortas and convicted financier Louis Wolfson were exposed, and with the help of the Nixon White House and a media feeding frenzy, Fortas was forced to resign.

Nixon nominated Warren E. Burger, the leading judicial critic of the Warren Court, to fill Warren's seat. Nixon's first two nominees to replace Fortas were defeated in the Senate—the first on trumped-up ethical charges, the second because he was a segregationist mediocrity. Nixon's third choice, Burger's close friend Harry Blackmun, a court of appeals judge, was then unanimously confirmed by an exhausted Senate. Smarting from his defeats, Nixon ordered House minority leader Gerald Ford to strike out at judicial independence by instigating impeachment proceedings against Douglas, the Court's most liberal justice, basically for being too liberal. A six-month investigation by a House committee exonerated Douglas, and normalcy briefly returned until both Black and Harlan died in the fall of 1971. After toying with the idea of reducing the Court's prestige by nominating two nonentities, California appellate judge Mildred Lillie and Little Rock municipal bond lawyer Herschel Friday, Nixon instead nominated Virginia patrician Lewis Powell and Arizonan William Rehnquist, a Goldwater loyalist. Both were confirmed. A formerly liberal Court now included four Democrats, only three of whom—Douglas, Brennan, and Marshall—were reliably liberal; four country club Republicans (although Powell was nominally a Democrat); and one very conservative Republican.

The newly reconstituted Court faced one more criminal procedure blockbuster that looked more like something from the Warren Court era than a decision by a Court with five Republican justices. Capital punishment had been fading in the 1960s; the last two executions in the United States had been in 1967. After upholding the death penalty over its most serious challenges in 1971, the Court reversed itself a year later, with the five Warren Court holdovers outvoting Nixon's four appointees—who dissented in disbelief, assuming, as did the majority, that capital punishment had effectively been abolished. Instead, "law and order" acquired a further meaning that the Republicans could take to the electorate.

School Busing

Even after the Civil Rights Act of 1964 brought the Justice Department into the issue of school desegregation, the Court stayed out of it. Then, in 1968, it dropped a bombshell on the South by invalidating freedom of choice plans—the South's final hope of avoiding widespread desegregation. The allure of freedom of choice for the South was that no white would ever choose a formerly all-black school, and most blacks could be intimidated into not choosing a formerly all-white school. Brennan's unanimous opinion in *Green v. New Kent County* demanded a plan that would "produce results and that promises realistically to work *now*."[43] There was no way to eradicate all-black schools and achieve results except by an affirmative duty to integrate—a word the justices never put in their opinions but privately had acknowledged was their goal.

The meaning of *Green* was fleshed out in *Swann v. Charlotte-Mecklenburg* three years later. A district judge had rejected the Northern solution of neighborhood schools and had ordered massive busing to achieve racial balance in the Charlotte school system. The appeals court had affirmed the order as to high schools but rejected it for younger children. The Court was split, with Burger, Black, and Blackmun opposed to busing but everyone wishing for unanimity. To rule against busing would have left too much of the urban South looking like it did a decade earlier and would appear to be a reward for Southern intransigence. With six justices favoring busing, the outliers yielded—although achieving unanimity allowed for a mushy opinion by Burger. But the result was to uphold the massive busing order. That meant there would be busing in all the urban areas in the South. *Swann* guaranteed that Southern schools would be considerably more integrated than those in the North.

Although Nixon needed no further help in achieving reelection, as part of his "Southern strategy" of moving white Democrats permanently into the Republican Party he vowed to "hold busing to the minimum required by law" and tried unsuccessfully to block any federal funds for busing.[44] After his reelection, the Court, with Brennan writing in a Northern case, held that if there was proven de jure segregation—such as the siting of new schools or drawing of attendance lines with race in mind—then any segregation anywhere in that system would be presumed also to be de jure. *Keyes v. Denver School District* thus extended the benefits of busing to an unwelcoming North.

Busing rarely enjoyed majority approval from African Americans and always was disliked by whites. It was ordered by judges, was supported by the NAACP and white liberals, and proved impervious to local opposition. White Southerners reluctantly accepted it as punishment for segregation, but in the North—especially in Boston—outcomes were often explosive. In *Keyes,* Powell dissented on busing and Rehnquist dissented on everything.

A year later Powell and Rehnquist were in an all-Republican majority written by Burger in *Milliken v. Bradley* that put busing on a road to irrelevance and hence eventual, albeit lingering, death. Whenever a judge issued a busing order, some whites placed their children in private schools while others moved to the suburbs outside the school district's jurisdiction. Hence a school district under a busing order always saw its white population plummet. (After six years of busing Richmond, Virginia, went from 35 percent to 20 percent white.) In some cities, such as Atlanta and Detroit, it seemed futile to bus the few remaining whites just to spread them around in overwhelmingly black schools. If there was a solution, it was to capture the fleeing whites by attaching urban districts to suburban ones. A district judge in Michigan did just that; indeed, he created a school district the size of Delaware that was 75 percent white—even though it encompassed Detroit, which was but 30 percent white. Burger's majority held that interdistrict busing was appropriate only if the suburban district was responsible for creating segregation in the urban district, an impossible standard to meet.

The four Democratic dissenters were outraged because, between voting with their dollars (for private schools) or with their feet, whites could escape and leave the inner city schools segregated yet poorer as the tax base shrank. There was still the *Green* duty to achieve results "now"; it just had been rendered impossible to accomplish in larger cities. The liberal dream of equality through integrated education remained just that—a dream.

Tackling Poverty

In *Buck v. Bell,* in 1927, Oliver Wendell Holmes claimed that equal protection was "the usual last resort of constitutional arguments."[45] The statement was not accurate then but became so after 1937. By 1960 there was essentially no application of the Equal Protection Clause outside the racial context. Thus Maryland's crazy quilt of exceptions to its Blue Laws (thereby treating various businesses differently) was upheld, as was a Florida statute exempting all women from jury service unless they took specific steps to qualify (which few did).[46] Within a decade the Court, led by Douglas, made equal protection the preferred constitutional doctrine for new initiatives. Legislative apportionment and criminal procedure were the opening wedges, but soon the doctrine spread to the right to vote.

Unwilling to risk derailing the Voting Rights Act of 1965 by dealing with poll taxes for state elections (the Twenty-fourth Amendment having abolished them for federal office), Congress instead directed the attorney general to file suit to test their constitutionality. The outcome, declaring poll taxes unconstitutional, was unexceptional, but what Douglas wrote jumps off the page. Recognizing that poll taxes had previously been sustained, the opinion proclaims that "[n]otions of what constitutes equal treatment for purposes of the Equal Protection Clause *do* change."[47] The Court then offered two rationales for invalidating the $1.50 per year tax. First, voting was a fundamental right. How that was different from a constitutional right and why it mattered were unexplained. Second, in one of the breathtaking statements by the Court, Douglas claimed that "lines drawn on the basis of wealth or property, like those of race, are traditionally disfavored."[48] Where that tradition came from and how it would work in a capitalist society were also unexplained.

Black dissented, claiming history showed that the poll tax, even if not good public policy, was at least rational. Harlan, joined by Stewart, complained that the majority was "rigidly imposing on America an ideology of unrestrained egalitarianism."[49] Perhaps; but Harlan was blind to the fact that the poll tax was part of the Southern effort to prevent African Americans from voting and keep them in their status as second-class citizens. Had Douglas said so, his opinion would have been better grounded, but it also would have lacked its intended nonracial implications.

Douglas used the voting rights context to lay the foundations for a constitutional right to government assistance, although the opinion was equally silent on that. The timing seemed propitious. President Johnson had declared his "War on Poverty" a year earlier, and the nation seemed ready to improve the lot of the least well off. Furthermore, among Democrats (and they controlled everything) there were warm feelings about the Court. Johnson had told historian William Leuchtenburg "that never before have the three independent branches been so productive."[50] He recognized, as did the Court, that it was a full partner in realizing the goals of Kennedy-Johnson liberalism.

In the 1969 decision *Shapiro v. Thompson,* Brennan built on Douglas's foundations. Congress prohibited states from denying welfare to the needy once they had lived in the state for a year, and several states required welfare applicants to have resided in-state for a year before receiving assistance. *Shapiro* held that this residency requirement violated equal protection by distinguishing between the needy who had just arrived and the needy who were longer-term residents. Brennan held that deterring interstate migration was an illegitimate government interest and that protecting the state fisc simply wasn't all that important. Additionally, welfare assistance affects "the ability of families to obtain the very means to subsist—food, shelter, and the other necessities of life."[51] Staying alive was surely as important as the rights of interstate migration or casting a ballot, and Brennan was equating them all as fundamental and protected unless the state could come up with a compelling interest to the contrary. Since no state could ever meet Brennan's standard, concluding that something was fundamental always meant rejection of the state's policy.

Warren dissented, remembering his days as governor at a time when so many Americans were migrating to California, and imagining the problems that giving them immediate welfare would have caused. He knew that state resources were limited and that providing for the newly arrived meant less for those voters already in the state. Black and Harlan dissented as well, with the latter capturing the majority perfectly: "[The decision] reflects to an unusual degree the current notion that this Court possesses a peculiar wisdom all its own whose capacity to lead this Nation out of its present troubles is contained only by the limits of judicial ingenuity in contriving new constitutional principles to meet each new problem as it arises."[52]

A year later in *Goldberg v. Kelly,* Brennan wrote for the Court that welfare assistance could not be terminated before there had been a hearing. The Court was concerned with the accuracy of the determination that someone was no longer eligible, as well as with the respectful treatment of those affected. As a result of *Goldberg,* there would be less money for those who actually needed welfare, as those who should be terminated would continue to receive money until the bureaucracy could hold a hearing. Burger, Black, and Stewart dissented.

Shapiro and *Goldberg* marked the height of the Court's efforts to constitutionalize the welfare state. *Dandridge v. Williams,* decided soon after *Goldberg,* signaled a cutback. Maryland capped the amount of assistance a family could receive regardless of the family's size. Maryland justified the law as a money-saving measure as well as a disincentive to welfare mothers to have more children in order to get more money. Challengers claimed that it unfairly differentiated among needy children and that the remedy was to provide the same amount for each child. Ignoring *Shapiro's* demand for a compelling state interest, the Court concluded that Maryland need not correct all problems at once, and that its imperfect law was good enough.

Douglas, Brennan, and Marshall dissented in *Dandridge* as they would (joined by White) three years later when the five Republicans in *San Antonio Independent School District v. Rodriquez* sustained Texas's reliance on local property taxes to fund public schools. If children lived in a rich property district, the schools had plenty of money. Conversely, poor districts did not. Powell refused to find that education was a fundamental right and claimed that reliance on the district's wealth was not suspect because the Texas approach, like that of most states, was rational; therefore it did not violate equal protection.

The effort to constitutionalize the welfare state was over. The outcome would have been different if Hubert Humphrey had been elected in 1968 and had therefore been the president with four appointments. But the appointments were Nixon's, and that meant elected officials, not federal courts, would decide how money was spent (or not spent) to improve the lives of the less well off. When combined with *Milliken v. Bradley, Rodriquez* meant that minority students were likely to be going to minority schools that had less funding than suburban schools—separate and unequal.

Sex and Gender

Griswold v. Connecticut looked like a throwback to the *Lochner* era. Indeed, dissents by Black and Stewart claimed it was. Patterning itself on Anthony Comstock's Calvinist crusade against pornography, in 1879 Connecticut forbade the use of contraceptives for contraception. In the twentieth century this absurd law could not be repealed because of the strength of the Catholic Church in state politics. As written and applied, the law affected the poor, because any woman who could afford a private physician could have the doctor prescribe contraceptives as a health measure; thereafter they could be used for any purpose desired. As the head of Yale's obstetrics and gynecology clinic observed, "[T]he rich [get] contraceptives and the poor [get] children."[53]

Given the demise of substantive due process in the New Deal revolution, explaining why this silly, outmoded law was unconstitutional was no small task either for an advocate or for the Court. Still, the law was stupid, and the context of the case involved advice given to a married couple. Douglas wrote for a majority, and Goldberg, Harlan, and White each took a shot at explaining the result in separate concurrences.

Douglas created a right of privacy, which the Connecticut law violated. His goal was to show that privacy was based on the text of the Bill of Rights so that he would not have to resort to substantive due process. He reconceptualized due process cases from the 1920s concerning the right to teach in a foreign language and the right to attend private schools as First Amendment cases involving restrictions on knowledge. Citing the First, Third, Fourth, Fifth, and Ninth Amendments, he claimed that the cases "suggest that specific guarantees in the Bill of Rights have penumbras formed by emanations from those guarantees that help give them life and substance."[54] Douglas rightly claimed that marriage and procreation were important, but he was unsuccessful in showing that the right to privacy was textually based.

The three concurring opinions made no effort to claim a textual basis for invalidating the law. Goldberg reached for the Ninth Amendment and its claim that there could be unenumerated rights. But how to find them? Here Goldberg copied Harlan's due process approach demanding a "look to the traditions and collective conscience of our peoples to determine whether a principle is 'so rooted there as to be ranked as fundamental.'"[55] A state could control some sexual behavior, but the intimacy of a husband and wife was something else. Harlan wrote a short opinion relying on an earlier encounter with the Connecticut statute in which the Court had ducked the issue. His expansive view of due process protected the marital use of contraceptives while asserting that the state could prohibit "adultery, homosexuality, fornication and incest."[56] White took a slightly different tack also with due process. Connecticut had argued that the law deterred extramarital sex; White didn't believe it. In their dissents, Black and Stewart had a field day with the majority's efforts. Both were unpersuaded that there was a right to privacy in the Constitution. Black claimed to "like my privacy as well as the next one, but I am nevertheless compelled to admit that government has a right to invade it unless prohibited by some specific constitutional provision."[57]

Persuasive or not, the result in *Griswold* was overwhelmingly popular. Even the Roman Catholic archbishop of Hartford claimed that it was "a valid interpretation of constitutional law."[58] Seven years and a raging sexual revolution later, the Court determined that the marital emphasis of *Griswold* was irrelevant—and indeed unconstitutional (although it did not say so directly). Reversing, on equal protection grounds, a conviction for providing contraceptives to an unmarried person, Brennan stated that "if the right of privacy means anything, it is the right of the *individual*, married or single, to be free from unwarranted governmental intrusion into matters so fundamentally affecting a person as the decision to bear or beget a child."[59] As it had in the obscenity cases, the Court was siding with the ongoing sexual revolution.

The sexual revolution wasn't the only one occurring. Spurred by Betty Friedan's *Feminine Mystique* and aided by the sexism of the civil rights and antiwar movements, women were demanding equal rights—including control over the decision whether to bear or beget a child. Their demands, especially for a constitutional amendment enshrining equal rights—which initially seemed off-the-wall—quickly achieved political ascendancy. Gender equality was, after all, an issue on which politicians (and justices) could be lobbied successfully in their own homes by wives and daughters. It was an upper-middle-class issue, and virtually all elites were solidly supportive (at least in the abstract).

With the backing of both Presidents Johnson and Nixon, the Equal Rights Amendment reached the House floor in 1970, and after an hour of debate in August it passed by a whopping 350–15. But in the Senate questions about whether the ERA meant that women as well as men would be drafted into the armed forces stopped the momentum. This was a serious issue as opposed to the other question: whether separate restrooms would be unconstitutional.

The ERA was reintroduced into the next Congress, and this time it got though the Senate and headed for speedy ratification by the states. On the day it passed the Senate, Hawaii ratified it; the next day three more states did; the following day two more joined; and by the end of January 1973, just ten months after going to the states, the ERA had been ratified by thirty, leaving it with but eight states to go to obtain the necessary three-quarters ratification. And legislatures were in session around the country.

The Court was as much affected by the enthusiasm for gender equality as were Congress and the states. In *Reed v. Reed* in the fall of 1971 the Court reversed an unbroken line of precedents to find for the first time that a statue violated equal protection by treating men and women differently. The law gave husbands a preference over wives in becoming executors of estates of people who died without a will. It was based on the simple historical fact—and resulting stereotype—

that men are more likely than women to have experience in handling finances. In a clear fiction, Burger's unanimous opinion purported to apply existing law to find the preference irrational.

A little over a year after the ERA sailed through Congress, the Court in *Frontiero v. Richardson* considered a federal law giving extra housing and medical allowances to married men in the armed services. By contrast, the law provided the extras to married servicewomen only if they could show that they paid more than half of their husband's living expenses. All but Rehnquist believed the law unconstitutional, but there was a huge split between the Democrats and the country club Republicans. The latter wished to stick with the fiction that the law was unconstitutional because it was irrational.

Brennan bought one argument of Frontiero's lawyer, Ruth Bader Ginsburg, that gender discrimination should be treated exactly like racial discrimination (and was thus as close to per se unconstitutional as it gets). First Brennan analogized gender and race: both are immutable, visible accidents of birth, and both have long been the basis of harmful discrimination. Brennan then turned to the ERA to show that Congress had determined that gender discrimination was "inherently invidious," and respect for a coequal branch of government counseled the Court to do the same.[60]

Brennan was, as Powell recognized, preempting the ratification process of the ERA by concluding that the Fourteenth Amendment already did the job. If the Court follows the conclusions of Congress on what should be in the Constitution, then there is no need for the states to ratify a "proposed" amendment. (As it turned out, the ERA was stalled and would never be ratified, but at the time of *Frontiero* everyone assumed that ratification was just a formality.) The four Democrats, by their actions, demonstrated a belief that the amendment process was a waste of time. A reform Court could do it faster.

There was a similar disdain for politics behind the most controversial decision of the twentieth century, *Roe v. Wade*, which held most abortion laws unconstitutional. The bulk of the opinion is about the history of abortion and the medical profession, which while interesting enough is not particularly relevant to the Constitution. But the Constitution wasn't particularly relevant to the result, either. The Court held that "the right of privacy . . . is broad enough to encompass a woman's decision whether or not to terminate her pregnancy."[61] This had to be qualified, however, because Blackmun, once general counsel to the Mayo Clinic, saw the issue as medical: "[T]he abortion decision, in all aspects is inherently, and primarily, a medical decision, and basic responsibility for it must rest with the physician."[62]

Blackmun's opinion competes successfully as the worst of the twentieth century. Blackmun made no effort to ground the decision in the Constitution's text; he discussed no history of the Fourteenth Amendment nor the federal structure; and he mentioned precedents cavalierly. Even *Griswold*, the most relevant precedent, was but glancingly mentioned (which is just as well; in the years after it came down no one had suggested that it had any potential application to abortion).

Rejecting the claim that life begins at conception, Blackmun noted that the Court could not determine when life begins and then concluded that legislatures couldn't either (even though many thought they had). But at some point during pregnancy, Blackmun conceded, life has begun. Thus having found the right of privacy broad enough, Blackmun proceeded to turn his application of the Constitution into a statute. During the first trimester of pregnancy, the woman's determination controlled. During the second trimester the state had an interest in protecting her health (and thus could regulate facilities). And in the third trimester the state could ban abortions because of its interest in the potential life of the child. Perhaps that is a good statute, but Blackmun was supposed to be engaged in constitutional interpretation. He offered as close to an unreasoned opinion as a justice could produce. But six other justices joined him in it.

At the time of *Roe,* abortion had barely scratched the surface as a political issue. At most the question of updating abortion regulation was six years old, and in Congress it was barely two. A few states, including California under its Republican governor Ronald Reagan, had liberalized their laws, and two states offered abortion on demand. In other states the older law remained in effect either because the issue still lacked salience or because the efforts to liberalize the laws had been unsuccessful owing to religious opposition, largely from the Catholic Church. Elites in both parties were sympathetic to the claims of a right to abortion, but there had been no real national debate on the issue. *Roe* preempted this fledgling debate before average Americans were aware it was going on.

However dated or however misapplied, there was a coherent theory behind *Lochner:* legislation must serve the general public interest. By contrast, there was no coherent theory behind *Roe;* indeed, it appears that there was no theory at all beyond attempting to assert good medical practice. In another comparison, *Griswold* had invalidated a law that existed in a tiny corner of the country and enjoyed no support elsewhere, whereas *Roe* invalidated laws all over the nation that enjoyed significant support everywhere. *Roe* was a result searching for a reason. Perhaps one could be found in a claim that reproductive choice was essential for full citizenship for women. But *Roe* never offered a hint in that direction. It was a case about doctors, with women being their beneficiaries. John Paul Stevens, who came to the Court after *Roe* and solidly supported abortion rights, nevertheless observed that Blackmun had "create[d] a new doctrine that really didn't make sense."[63]

The dissents by White and Rehnquist were low key. None of the nine justices—including the dissenters—anticipated the hostile reaction to *Roe,* which immediately surpassed *Engel*'s banning of school prayer in its production of hate mail. Women's rights groups didn't anticipate the backlash, either. In fact some feared that *Roe* would pass unnoticed because it came down the same day that Lyndon Johnson died (a fate many of the letter writers wished upon the "murderer" Blackmun).

Watergate

The anger over *Roe* was initially counterbalanced by applause over the unanimous opinion in *United States v. Nixon,*[64] ordering the president to turn over tape recordings of White House meetings in the aftermath of the break-in at the Democratic National Committee headquarters in the Watergate complex on June 17, 1972. Within less than three weeks Nixon resigned the presidency.

The taping system in the White House had been discovered on a fluke a year earlier during hearings by a select Senate committee into the break-in and related events. Nixon had been forced to appoint a special prosecutor—Harvard professor and Kennedy solicitor general Archibald Cox—to avoid conflicts of interest in the Justice Department that had occurred during the initial investigation of Watergate. Cox subpoenaed a number of the tapes, but Nixon ordered him to back down, and when he refused, Nixon ordered Attorney General Elliot Richardson, a friend of Cox, to fire him. Richardson resigned instead. Deputy Attorney General William Ruckelshaus then refused to fire Cox and was fired himself. Finally Solicitor General Robert Bork, at the urging of Richardson and Ruckelshaus, fired Cox. These events of October 25, 1973, immediately were dubbed the "Saturday Night Massacre." They inflamed the nation, forced Nixon to appoint a new special prosecutor and turn over some tapes, and, for the first time, placed impeachment on the table. The move for impeachment gained momentum when there turned out to be an eighteen-and-a-half-minute erasure in the middle of one crucial tape.

Everyone demanded the relevant tapes to find out whether Nixon had been involved in the cover-up (as a grand jury eventually believed, having named him an unindicted co-conspirator, a point the special prosecutor brought to the Court's attention). Nixon resisted, but with his popularity wasted, he released edited transcripts of some of the tapes, which created a new national expression—"expletive deleted"— and offered the image of the president at war with his carefully crafted public persona. The federal judge listening to tapes already in his possession concluded that in some places the transcripts had been doctored. With Nixon claiming executive privilege to protect White House confidentiality, the case went to the Court for decision. The Court agreed with John Marshall's willingness to subpoena Thomas Jefferson in Aaron Burr's treason trial: no man, not even the president, is above the law.

Between the Court's decision and the time Nixon released the tapes, the House Judiciary Committee had voted three articles of impeachment supported by all the Democrats and just under half the Republicans. The public had been primed by daily leaks from committee members and staff. The release of the tapes was the final straw, since one tape answered both of Republican senator Howard Baker's oft-repeated questions, "What did the President know and when did he know it?"[65] Baker had asked the questions to create a firewall protecting Nixon, but the June 23, 1972, tape revealed Nixon instructing an aide to have the CIA tell the FBI to stop its investigation. With the "smoking gun" tape, showing he had immediately instigated the cover-up, Nixon's remaining support evaporated, and he resigned on August 9.

After swearing in President Gerald Ford, Burger expressed relief that "it [the system] worked," and *Time* magazine enthusiastically agreed.[66] How myopic they were. If there had been no taping system—or if Nixon had destroyed the tapes (and it remains inexplicable that he did not)—then Watergate would have been a swearing contest between the president of the United States and his youthful former White House counsel John Dean, a man who looked every inch the snake that he was. It would have been no contest; even longtime Nixon haters would not have sided with Dean. Nor did the Court play a great or heroic role. The House Judiciary Committee acted without benefit of the tapes at issue, and the House was sure to follow. What the Court did was revert to what it traditionally does: piling on to facilitate what is already happening.

Vietnam, inflation, the Arab oil embargo, investigations of the Watergate scandal, unhappiness over busing and crime, the assassinations, the general loss of confidence in government, four new justices: the judicial reforming spirit of the astonishing era was spent. The Democratic justices, like the Democratic Party, would have gone further, but except on gender issues and aid to religion—areas where the parties were either in agreement or lacked a position—the explosive spread of the Constitution into American life had ceased. Democrats were a generation away from their next appointment to the Court, and Republicans would not risk another Earl Warren. Powell and Rehnquist were the last appointees who were not already sitting judges.

· X ·

An Uneasy Status Quo

ALTHOUGH THE COUNTRY had been trending conservative, Watergate caused the voters to rain retribution on the Republicans in the 1974 elections—Democrats gained forty-six House seats and four in the Senate—and Jimmy Carter, a Democratic outsider, was elected president two years later. Before his defeat, Gerald Ford appointed a highly regarded federal appeals court judge, John Paul Stevens, who, like Byron White and William Rehnquist, was a former law clerk, to replace William O. Douglas. Douglas, the longest-serving justice ever, had suffered a massive stroke and tried unsuccessfully to outlast the man who had attempted to impeach him. In 1968 there were six liberals on the Court. Eight years later only William Brennan and Thurgood Marshall remained.

The desultory years of the Ford and Carter presidencies—with defeat in Vietnam, oil embargos, soaring inflation, high unemployment, and the Iranian hostage crisis—seemed to cement pessimism as the nation's mood. Yet during these years a newly emergent conservative movement, largely based in the South, gave the Republicans added vitality. The conservatives envisioned a Constitution of small-town 1950s America, but without legally compelled segregation. That is, the Constitution was color-blind, religion could be part of the schools and public life, abortion could be criminalized, and police practices could be largely invisible to judicial scrutiny. The views on religion and abortion enjoyed a special providence. But despite a Court controlled by Republicans, conservatives made little headway on their cherished constitutional agenda. They could not believe it. Then, near the end of Ronald Reagan's presidency, they suffered a huge defeat in one of the most important constitutional incidents of the century when their judicial darling, Robert Bork, was rejected by the Senate after being nominated for the Court. Along with Court-packing and *Brown v. Board of Education*, Bork's defeat was one of the signal constitutional events of the century.

Freedom of Expression

The First Amendment continued to enjoy prominence in the justices' hearts, and with modest recalibrations, the Court continued on the liberal path of the Warren years. The biggest case was an outgrowth of Watergate. In popular parlance "Watergate" symbolized all the illegal domestic activities of the Nixon administration. One had been shakedowns of corporations for campaign contributions, which then were joined with large individual contributions to fund Republican candidates. In 1974 Congress passed comprehensive campaign finance reform. Contributions were limited, as was campaign spending, and public funding of presidential elections (at least for the two major parties) was established.

Because the changes were so fundamental and would affect the 1976 elections, there were immediate challenges to the law. The name of the case that the Court decided, *Buckley v. Valeo*, ignored the names of the real parties in interest. On one side was the American Civil Liberties Union, claiming that money would be spent on putting out a message, and therefore the law restricting money was a restriction on speech and violated the First Amendment. On the other side was a newly formed good government citizens' lobby, Common Cause, which rejected equating money with speech and defended the law on the grounds that it was an important step in cleaning up corruption in the electoral process, and to the extent that it abridged freedom of speech, it did so to enhance the process. The United States, through Solicitor General Robert Bork, filed a true amicus (friend of the court) brief suggesting reasons why the Court might want to decide the case either way.

The Court sustained the contribution limits on the corruption rationale: people might believe that large contributions were purchasing something. The Court then struck down the spending limitations because they did not implicate corruption. The rationale of suppressing some speech in the name of leveling the playing field was emphatically rejected as inconsistent with the premises of the First Amendment. This explained the Court's invalidation of a provision limiting the amount the super-rich— that is, people making their initial run for the Senate—could give to their own campaigns. Finally, the Court sustained public funding despite its near lockout of third parties. Byron White would have sustained everything, while Chief Justice Warren Burger would have done the opposite (as would have the retired Douglas).

Not since before the New Deal revolution had such an important federal law been invalidated. The Court created a solution, perhaps both a constitutional and a commonsense one, that no one had voted for.

Legislative efforts to eliminate corporate money from elections created unusual voting patterns, first displayed in the 1978 case of *First National Bank of Boston v. Bellotti*. Massachusetts forbade corporate expenditures designed to influence ballot measures. Finding the restricted speech "at the heart of the First Amendment's protection," the Court struck down the law, rejecting the claim that corporate money "destroy[ed] the confidence of the people in the democratic process," and responding instead that "the fact that advocacy may persuade is hardly a reason to suppress it."[1] William Brennan, Thurgood Marshall, White, and William Rehnquist dissented. A little over a decade later Harry Blackmun and Stevens joined them to uphold a Michigan statute forbidding corporate expenditures to aid (or defeat) a candidate. Marshall offered a capacious definition of corruption that replaced *Bellotti*'s embrace of persuasion with the mismatch between the amount of advocacy and the amount of "popular support for the corporation's political ideas."[2] How the majority knew the amount of support for the corporation's ideas without a vote was unclear. Nor did the majority explain why once unpopular ideas—like the Nobel laureate Martin Luther King's opposition to the Vietnam War—should, in all other contexts, be allowed to prevail through persuasion and, if necessary, expenditures.

The Court's salute to speech about the democratic process as high-value speech implied that there was lower-value speech (such as obscenity), and the emergence of two novel doctrines pushed this conclusion in different directions. One took commercial speech from the wholly unprotected into a new category offering constitutional protection for most truthful, non-misleading ads. The other attempted to reexpand non-obscene sexual depictions into a new regulated category.

Virginia had forbidden price advertising for prescription drugs. Harry Blackmun's opinion, over a solo dissent by Rehnquist, noted that the public might be more interested in consumer information than in political debate—especially if that information could help alleviate physical pain. Accordingly, some commercial speech was entitled to some constitutional protection.[3] If the state had a sufficient interest in suppressing the information, then it might, but if the requirements of being truthful and not misleading were met, sufficient interests justifying suppression were hard to come by.

The explosion of pornography led to the second novel doctrine. The obscenity settlement had been too little, too late. There was rapid growth in the quantity and quality of sexually explicit material in the marketplace, and despite conservative howls, the American people were not in revolt against an increasingly sexualized culture. Some communities, however, sought new ways to protect those who wished to avoid sexual depictions. Not only did the Court uphold zoning laws (which became increasingly moot as the invention of the VCR moved porn into homes and hotels—where Ronald Reagan watched a porn channel with amusement during the 1984 Republican convention in Dallas),[4] but also a four-justice minority led by Stevens attempted to undo the obscenity settlement through a resurrection and expansion of the idea that some speech was of so little value that no one should worry about its elimination. He famously wrote, "[F]ew of us would march our sons and daughters off to war to preserve the citizen's right to see 'Specified Sexual Activities' exhibited in the theaters of our choice."[5] He did not note that this is equally true of most things protected in First Amendment litigation, as protecting the Klansman Clarence Brandenburg surely exemplified.

The combination of low-value speech and zoning was moved from the land to the airwaves by the Federal Communications Commission when it decided that there were some words that could not be uttered over the air except late at night, when children were supposedly not likely to be in the audience. In a direct slap at *Cohen v. California* and its protection of the jacket with "Fuck the Draft" on its back, *FCC v. Pacifica Corporation* claimed that it would be rare indeed for a speaker to be unable to express an identical thought without using foul language. Stevens said that the opinion was limited to the airwaves by the rationale that a radio purchased, brought home, and then turned on by the listener was an intruder in the house that could be censored before the first utterance. But there was no reason why the rationale could not spread from broadcasting to print to speech, especially since the opinion's efforts to distinguish *Cohen* were transparently thin.

In perhaps the most anticipated speech case of the 1980s, the Court dealt with a suit by the Reverend Jerry Falwell, founder of the Moral Majority, against Larry Flynt, publisher of the vulgar magazine *Hustler.* At a point when the Italian liquor Campari was engaged in a double entendre ad campaign asking, "When was your first time?" *Hustler* parodied both Campari and Falwell by portraying the latter telling an interviewer that his first time was with his mother in an outhouse. A jury voted for Falwell on his claim of intentional infliction of emotional distress. At the Court, Falwell offered an argument echoing *Pacifica,* with its presumption that speech had to be of demonstrated value before it was protected. But Rehnquist's unanimous opinion reaffirmed the traditional rough-and-ready First Amendment that the Warren Court had created by worrying about the prospect of chilling political invective and about the fact that there was no acceptable way of separating the outrageous from the too outrageous.[6]

*Hustler'*s return to the basics of free speech jurisprudence was confirmed when a 5–4 Court, through a preachy opinion by Brennan, held that flag burning was protected expression, inasmuch as the state was regulating the act of flag burning because of the offensive message it sent. Rehnquist wrote a rare impassioned dissent that inadvertently underscored why the majority was correct. He labeled burning the flag "an inarticulate grunt." But he also inconsistently claimed that the "act [conveyed] nothing that could not have been conveyed [in] a dozen different ways,"[7] thereby acknowledging that there was a message—one so powerful it drove Rehnquist to incoherence.

Congress, and especially Republicans, did not take the flag burning decision well. A day after the decision the Senate adopted a resolution 97–3 expressing disappointment in it. President George H. W. Bush, who had run on the flag issue the previous year, went to the Iwo Jima Marine Memorial to call for a constitutional amendment overturning the decision (as if flag burning were a national problem). Democrats, uneasy about both hitting out at the Court and tinkering with the Bill of Rights, instead secured passage of a new statute to bar flag burning. With that the constitutional amendment failed to garner sufficient votes. A year later the same 5–4 majority invalidated the statute, but the pressures for an amendment had dissipated, especially in the Senate.[8]

There is something about flag burning. Reagan appointees Antonin Scalia and Anthony Kennedy were in the majority protecting the act, while Rehnquist was a dissenter. The two cases, like an earlier one from the Warren Court, produced splits along no discernible ideological lines. On all other constitutional issues, however, conservatives stayed conservative and liberals remained liberal. The result was that one or two moderates controlled the outcomes, leaving the Court unhappily treading constitutional water.

The Court of the Carter-Reagan period could compete with any for producing lengthy, ponderous opinions on top of more lengthy, ponderous opinions, necessitating reducing the type size in the *United States Reports*. A contributing factor was the proliferation of law clerks, doubling in number from the 1960s. Opinions were occasionally lightened by Brennan's bewailing a majority's refusal to adhere to precedent—hypocritical words that he never uttered when he was riding high during the Warren era. Nevertheless, with Black, Douglas, and Harlan gone, it became clear that this was a diminished Court, one lacking the intellectual vigor of the past. Only someone whose job required it would read the Court's opinions.

Civil Rights

Republican justices—apart from Rehnquist—accepted, albeit without enthusiasm, the existing consensus on race. But what they were not willing to do, as the Detroit school busing case underscored, was to extend it. Thus in a case not involving busing, *Washington v. Davis*, the Court held that a claim of discrimination under the Equal Protection Clause required a showing of intentional discrimination by the government. By requiring that the discrimination be intentional, the Court rejected the alternative standard of disparate impact (which was the permissible legislative standard of the Civil Rights Act). Disparate impact referred to any government action that on paper looks good and fair (and therefore does not mention race) but nevertheless produces racially disproportionate outcomes and thus would be subject to the highest requirement of justification. The disparate impact test was deemed too radical: the Court noted that the test would have had far-reaching effects and might have led to the invalidation of "a whole range of tax, welfare, public service, regulatory, and licensing statutes that may be more burdensome to the poor and to the average black than to the more affluent white."[9]

A dominant assumption of the era was that a good education leads to good jobs which provide for good homes which lead to good schools. Combined with blocking cross-district busing for school desegregation, *Washington v. Davis* signaled the end to the liberal goal of using the Fourteenth Amendment to create a racially integrated America, a point highlighted by Brennan and Thurgood Marshall, who dissented (though not expressly on constitutional grounds) in isolation. The Court could no longer break the circle. It had no funds to purchase housing, and with these two cases it shut the door on education and jobs. This made affirmative action—giving a bonus based on race in order to achieve more equal outcomes—the essential tool remaining to achieve the liberal ideal.

The nation had made a sudden and virtually seamless transition from the color blindness of the Civil Rights Act of 1964 to the color consciousness of affirmative action. Nixon's labor secretary had initiated the "Philadelphia Plan," which required construction unions in the city to establish goals and timetables to increase their minimal African American membership. The plan had the nifty side effect of pitting the two prime Democratic constituencies, African Americans and organized labor, against each other. Within a year, similar action was required of all federal contractors with fifty or more employees. Then major universities adopted the policy to increase their minority enrollments. It was the policy of the University of California at Davis medical school to reserve sixteen of one hundred places in its entering class for minorities. *Regents v. Bakke,* the first and foremost ruling by the Court on affirmative action, produced a fractured outcome sustaining affirmative action but drawing the line against quotas.

Brennan, Marshall, White, and Blackmun found the Davis quota valid, and despite saying that they were employing some form of heightened scrutiny, they signaled that any affirmative action program was constitutional. Four Republicans found that the program violated the Civil Rights Act (and so they did not reach the Constitution). Lewis Powell split the differences and in the controlling solo opinion found the Davis program unconstitutional, but the need for a diverse student body so compelling an interest that affirmative action programs which avoided a strict quota would be constitutional. In this manner the Court managed to produce a rule governing affirmative action that eight of the nine justices disagreed with!

Until *Bakke* both political parties had embraced some form of affirmative action. But thereafter they split decisively. As the Republican Party became more Southern, it adopted the South's theory of the Fourteenth Amendment. Prior to the Civil Rights Act of 1964, the South claimed that laws could take race into account. Once it decisively lost the national and constitutional battle over segregation, the South switched to adopt a color-blind Constitution. (Interestingly, the NAACP Legal Defense Fund made just the opposite switch at about the same time.) Ronald Reagan's Justice Department adopted pure color-blindness. Democrats, unwilling (and unable) to aid African Americans directly, embraced affirmative action, the cheapest item on the civil rights agenda, with dogmatic rigidity.

The Court's split in *Bakke* continued. In *Richmond v. J. A. Croson,* a majority, over dissents by Brennan, Marshall, and Blackmun, held that

a municipal affirmative action program was subject to strict scrutiny—
a hurdle virtually impossible to overcome. The Richmond program
looked both silly (it included Eskimos, as if the city had ever had the
opportunity to discriminate against them) and greedy, since an African
American–dominated city council had set aside 30 percent of all city
contracts for minorities—in other words, African Americans. A year after *Croson*, Brennan persuaded White and Stevens to switch and uphold Federal Communications Commission policies designed, with
congressional approval, to increase the number of minority broadcast-
ers.[10] Instead of applying strict scrutiny, the new majority stated that a
program could be upheld if it served an important (rather than a compelling) objective. The majority expressly gave the federal government
greater leeway than that accorded to states and municipalities.

O'Connor and Federalism

Following Watergate and Carter's election, Democrats believed that
the unnatural Republican interregnum was over. But Carter became
the only president to serve a full term and never see a vacancy on the
Court. Then, shortly after Reagan's inauguration, Potter Stewart announced his retirement. Reagan had promised to appoint the first
woman to the Court, and he selected Sandra Day O'Connor. There
weren't many Republican women lawyers available, and O'Connor
was the most conservative the administration could find. A former
state legislator and unknown judge on an intermediate Arizona court,
she had graduated third in her (and Rehnquist's) Stanford Law School
class. She shared one trait with Marshall: knowing what it was like to
be on the receiving end of discrimination. Having grown up on a
ranch subject to regulations of the Bureau of Land Management, she
also knew firsthand the incompetence of meddling federal officials.

With her state legislative background as well as her disdain for federal intrusions in and on the states, O'Connor became a willing ally of

Rehnquist, Burger, and Powell in finding constitutional constraints on federal policies that required reluctant states to change. At the extreme this coalition would undo a cornerstone of the New Deal revolution—namely, the federal government's free hand in regulating the economy. In 1975 Rehnquist had fired off a lonely first shot in *Fry v. United States,* when everyone else upheld Nixon's imposition of wage and price controls on state governments as well as the private sector. A year later, in *National League of Cities v. Usery,* Rehnquist created a bare majority opinion to invalidate an extension of the Fair Labor Standards Act and the minimum wage to municipal employees as a violation of state sovereignty. Brennan's dissent accused the majority of a "patent usurpation of the role reserved for the political process . . . [,] a catastrophic judicial body blow at Congress' power under the Commerce Clause."[11] Given the apoplectic nature of the dissent, it is hardly surprising that the dissenters refused to acquiesce.

Then, after O'Connor joined the Court, Blackmun switched sides to write *Garcia v. San Antonio Metropolitan Transit Authority,* overruling *Usery* as "unsound in principle and unworkable in practice."[12] Now it was the turn of those who believed in *Usery* to become apoplectic. Powell thought that the majority, by allowing the federal government to regulate wages and hours of municipal employees, "substantially alter[ed] the federal system embodied in the Constitution . . . [and] emasculat[ed] the powers of the States."[13] Refusing to acquiesce, Rehnquist, Powell, and O'Connor predicted that *Garcia* would be overthrown and *Usery* acknowledged again as correct.

Criminal Procedure and Capital Punishment

As with the efforts to turn back the clock on issues of federalism, the efforts to overturn the Warren Court's criminal procedure decisions proved unavailing. Given four Nixon appointees plus White and O'Connor, this outcome was a shock. The Court steadfastly refused to extend Warren Court decisions, and it carved out many exceptions to those decisions but wouldn't overrule them. Overall, however, the justices seemed willing partners in the various "War[s] on Drugs," and the success rate of prosecutors at the Court was high even as doctrine failed to change much. Postconviction relief was an exception, as the justices placed more faith in their state court counterparts and thus saw less need for federal court supervision of convictions. Thus the Court left convicted defendants where a majority of Americans thought they belonged: in jail and (largely) out of federal courts.[14]

The one area that fundamentally changed was the law of the death penalty. *Furman v. Georgia's* prediction that the nation no longer wished for capital punishment proved disastrously wrong as the decision created its own opposition. Support for capital punishment jumped decisively after *Furman,* reaching far better than 2–1 by 1976. Thirty-five states and the federal government responded to the Court's complaints about the excess of jury discretion in the penalty phase by enacting one of two types of statutes, either making death mandatory for certain crimes or offering guidance, in the form of aggravating circumstances, for the jurors to take into consideration. *Gregg v. Georgia* inaugurated the new era of death penalty jurisprudence by upholding the latter and striking the former, with Stewart, Powell, and Stevens providing the necessary votes for each. There had to be a separate penalty phase that would give individualized consideration to the defendant and his crime. Thus, not only would aggravating circumstances be considered, but so too would mitigating ones.

Marshall wrote a bitter dissent announcing that when he said in *Furman* that Americans were opposed to the death penalty, he had meant informed Americans, and he insisted that still held. By claiming that an informed American would hold the same beliefs he held, Marshall effectively consigned over two-thirds of the nation to the uninformed category.

Because of the increase in the numbers of men—and they were virtually always men—sentenced to death (with the numbers reverting to those of the 1950s), and because of the Court's conclusion that the death penalty was so different that it required heightened scrutiny of the trial, capital cases came to occupy an increased amount of the Court's workload. Its decisions often looked haphazard. It held that death sentences obtained solely through the felony murder rule—whereby all persons involved in a felony are deemed equally responsible for any killing that occurs—were unconstitutional, and then reversed itself when White changed his mind five years later.[15] Similarly, a majority of the Court concluded that evidence of how the victim's death affected others was categorically inadmissible in the sentencing hearing, and then four years later switched, deciding that it may be heard under some circumstances.[16] Whatever the promise of *Furman* and *Gregg* to improve capital sentencing, the results looked pre-*Furman*, especially when the Court concluded that execution was not cruel and unusual punishment for those who committed murders while they were minors,[17] or for the mentally retarded,[18] but that it was unconstitutional to execute the insane.[19]

The biggest change in the law of capital punishment was a huge step toward curing racial discrimination in its application. *Coker v. Georgia* held that it was cruel and unusual to execute someone for rape. Because this was a Southern phenomenon almost exclusively reserved for black-on-white rape, by abolishing it *Coker* offered more racial justice than almost any legislative reform (short of abolition) could.

Relying on the Court's death-is-different approach, the NAACP Legal Defense Fund mounted one last challenge to capital punishment with a strong claim that it was racially discriminatory because juries valued white lives more than others. That is, the race of the victim, not the defendant, was what mattered. The problem with this equal protection argument was *Washington v. Davis* and its requirement of intentional discrimination. While there might be overwhelming statistical proof of racial discrimination in general, the defendant might not be able to prove it existed in his case. As an Eighth Amendment issue, the problem was that racial discrimination could not be limited to the death penalty. This proved dispositive for a five-justice majority by Powell in *McCleskey v. Kemp*, which opined that the Court would not place "totally unrealistic conditions" on the use of the death penalty.[20]

The majority had attempted to advance two irreconcilable positions simultaneously: consistency across cases and individualized determinations. No wonder its death penalty jurisprudence satisfied no one, while nevertheless guaranteeing an extended period of time between conviction and execution despite Burger's outburst that lawyers were "seeking to turn the administration of justice into [a] sporting contest in order to keep their guilty clients alive."[21] Once a death row inmate ran out of appeals, he ran out of luck, too, because an unanticipated consequence of constitutionalizing capital punishment was the virtual elimination of executive clemency. Indeed, Governor Bill Clinton, while running for the Democratic presidential nomination, returned to Arkansas just before the 1992 New Hampshire primary to oversee the execution of Rickey Ray Rector, an African American cop-killer. Clinton wished to show voters that he was a Democrat who was willing to be tough on criminals, even though Ricker had given himself a frontal lobotomy by a gunshot wound to the head, thereby reducing himself to the erratic comprehension of a young child.

Religion

The religion cases of the period were fueled by two separate movements. First, the Catholic Church, in areas where it had substantial political support, tried to alleviate the financial burdens of its parochial schools by securing state aid. Second, conservative Christians, ending their voluntary exile from politics, demanded a greater public embrace of their God. The Court itself was fractured. Brennan, Marshall, and Stevens were almost always ready to reject the religion claims, while

Rehnquist, typically joined by Burger and White, was ready to accept them. That left the others, especially Powell and O'Connor, to control the results. In general, the Catholics were rebuffed, while their Protestant counterparts had a more mixed record.

The Court's analytical framework—if it can be called that—for deciding Establishment Clause cases was the three-part test of the 1971 decision in *Lemon v. Kurtzman.* For a statute to survive Establishment Clause attack, (1) it must have a secular purpose; (2) its primary effect cannot advance religion; and (3) it must not foster excessive government entanglement with religion. Financial aid to parochial schools ran afoul of the primary effects test,[22] so states turned to the next-best thing: in-kind aid. In hairsplitting that only lawyers could love, a majority sustained providing diagnostic services by public employees in the parochial schools, but held that remedial services (by public school teachers) had to be provided off-premises.[23] The majority appeared to believe that secular public school teachers would be transformed upon entering a religious classroom. As armchair sociologists, Brennan and the majority concluded that "the pressures of the religious environment might alter" normal behavior.[24] The necessary supervision to preclude the hypothesized changed behavior would then constitute an excessive entanglement. The dissenters aptly noted that the majority took "advantage of the 'Catch-22' paradox of its own creation."[25]

The move of conservative Christians into political activities had begun in the 1970s, but was given true momentum with the presidential candidacy of Ronald Reagan in 1980 and a Republican Party willing to invoke its faith in God publicly. Reagan's national popularity brought Republicans control of the Senate in 1980, but in the 1982 elections Democrats added twenty-six seats to their existing majority in the House of Representatives. Stymied legislatively—with no likelihood that they would ever take the House—Republicans became committed to controlling the judiciary and legislating their views from the bench. Republicans mistakenly believed that the Democrats had accomplished their goals in the 1960s by controlling the judiciary, and they intended to replicate the feat. Thus Republicans flooded the Court with amicus briefs and hoped to select justices who would favor their agenda.

Both a moment of silence for meditation or prayer and the supplementing of evolution with "creation science" were found to lack secular purposes.[26] But outside the school context, efforts to introduce more religion into the public sphere were successful. *Marsh v. Chambers* sustained by a 5–4 vote the practice of hiring a legislative chaplain. Burger's majority noted that the same Congress that sent the Establishment Clause to the states had hired a chaplain.

Marsh was followed by *Lynch v. Donnelly,* where the same majority approved of Pawtucket, Rhode Island's, sponsorship of a life-sized Nativity scene on private grounds in the shopping district as part of a Christmas display. The crèche was only one element of that display, which included candy-striped poles, reindeer pulling Santa's sleigh, hundreds of lights, and a banner proclaiming "Season's Greetings." Taken together, this demonstrated a secular purpose: shop-till-you-drop for the holidays. Burger believed it would be an overreaction to forbid "this one passive symbol" from the holiday season.[27] Brennan, Marshall, Blackmun, and Stevens correctly stated in dissent that the crèche was a Christian religious symbol designed to commemorate the birth of Jesus. But the majority seemed to have concluded, at least in this area, that the *Lemon* test was a lemon and that a little bit of religion never hurt anyone—even if it was someone else's religion.

At the end of the decade a still badly split Court held unconstitutional a Nativity scene on the main staircase of a county courthouse while simultaneously accepting a Jewish menorah placed next to a Christmas tree at the City-County Building.[28] The latter supposedly alerted viewers to the fact that both religions had winter celebrations. In the former the four dissenters asserted that the majority "reflect[ed] an unjustified hostility to religion" and that the crèche was just a "passive symbol" that coerced no one into doing or believing anything.[29]

O'Connor had suggested that the appropriate way to decide Establishment Clause cases was to determine whether a reasonable observer would find the governmental practice an endorsement of religion. The cases suggested, however, that when it came to religion, there were no reasonable observers.

Gender, Abortion, and Gay Rights through 1987

Oklahoma allowed eighteen-year-old women to purchase 3.2 percent beer but told men to wait three more years (or get a girlfriend). In 1976, in *Craig v. Boren,* Brennan, retreating from his failed effort to anticipate the Equal Rights Amendment and treat gender like race, persuaded a majority to apply something less than strict scrutiny, but nevertheless sufficient to strike Oklahoma's gender distinction, which had been justified by statistics showing that young men eighteen to twenty were ten times (2 percent to 0.18 percent) more likely than young women to drive under the influence of alcohol. The value of the new standard was clear: it would invalidate any existing disabilities placed on women.

The new standard did not, however, eliminate all discrimination based on gender. When Jimmy Carter required young men to register with the Selective Service System, his action was sustained by a majority that believed the deference due the military satisfied *Craig's* standard.[30] The case was litigated by a man and thus was perceived as one that disadvantaged men, but to the extent that military service is an essential element of citizenship, women were discriminated against by the denial of the duties of citizenship. The Court also upheld a statutory rape conviction of a young man aged seventeen and a half- who had sex with a girl a year younger than he, under a law whereby only men could commit the crime.[31] The majority agreed with the state that preventing teenage pregnancy was an interest that satisfied *Craig.*

After O'Connor joined the Court, she created a 5–4 majority that allowed a man who wished to attend an all-female nursing school in his hometown (rather than go to a co-ed one elsewhere in the state) to prevail.[32] She was contemptuous of Mississippi's argument that men were excluded from the nursing school to compensate for discrimination against women. The dissenters worried about the decision's implications for single-sex schools.

Although as written, *Roe v. Wade* had been more about doctors than women, there could be no denying that for its supporters it was part of the movement for gender equality. *Roe* was also the one part of that movement meeting with heavy resistance in many areas of the nation. A number of governments looked for any way they could to undermine the Court's decision: requiring spousal notification or consent, requiring parental notification or consent, denying public funding, denying use of public facilities. Furthermore, the assault on *Roe* grew more intense over time, especially after Republicans became committed to its demise during the Reagan era. *Roe* acted like a cancer on politics. It mobilized conservatives to do something to limit (or better yet kill) it, but then angered them when judges followed the law and struck down their legislative victories. Simultaneously, it confirmed liberal views that abortion was a judicial and not a political issue, so its merits need not be defended politically.

Prior to Reagan's presidency, the only judicial victories for the antiabortion movement involved the upholding of laws that denied financial assistance for an abortion (even as the choice of childbirth was funded).[33] Governments did not have to fund the choice to attend private schools, and they didn't have to fund the choice to have an abortion, either. The fact that a choice was constitutionally protected did not mandate that it be subsidized.

Once O'Connor joined the Court, though, serious questioning of *Roe*'s continued vitality began. White and Rehnquist never acceded to *Roe,* and Burger had been lukewarm at best. Although some Republicans had grumbled during her confirmation proceedings about a pro-abortion legislative vote cast by O'Connor, she questioned *Roe* the first opportunity she had, which was in *Akron v. Akron Center for Reproductive Health* in 1983. Her target was the trimester approach. She noted that it was on a collision course with itself because modern medicine made later abortions safer and earlier births more viable. She did not call for overruling *Roe,* but did advocate replacing the trimester regulation with the question whether a regulation unduly burdens the right to seek an abortion.

Meanwhile, the debate over abortion also impacted gay rights. Michael Hardwick had been caught in his bedroom engaged in consensual sodomy with another man. Although charges were dropped, he brought suit challenging Georgia's sodomy law. To invalidate the law, the Court would have to rely on its right to privacy jurisprudence, which was, because of *Roe,* under attack. A majority of the Court, through White, sustained the law, noting both its ancient roots and the fact that a vast majority of states had outlawed sodomy in 1868 when the Fourteenth Amendment was ratified, that all the states outlawed it as late as 1960, and that twenty-four of them plus the District of Columbia still outlawed it.[34] From this the Court concluded that the right to engage in homosexual conduct could hardly be deemed fundamental. Powell was the fifth vote, having switched from his initial position that the Georgia law was unconstitutional. He explained to one of his clerks that he had never met a homosexual. Ironically that clerk, like many of his predecessors with Powell, was a closeted gay man. Had Powell known this, there is little doubt he would have sided with the four dissenters. But if the dissenters had prevailed, conservatives would have had yet another reason to hate this Court. Those dissenters, in a superb opinion by Blackmun, combined the two rights of privacy—the right to privacy in the home and the right to be let alone—to claim that a person's consensual sexual choices were not the business of government. As *Roe* had come under growing attack, the prickly, always insecure Blackmun increasingly came to vote with the only people who seemed to like his opinion: the Court's liberals.

The Changing Composition of the Court, 1986–1991

The 1984 presidential race had featured the Court for the first time since 1968. The reason was the intertwining of *Roe* with the ages of the justices. The Court had become the oldest in American history; five of the justices had been born during the Roosevelt administration (Teddy's). Both parties predicted constitutional disaster if the other prevailed at the polls and thereby had the opportunity to fill a handful of vacancies. The Democratic presidential candidate, former vice president Walter Mondale, told an audience "that our great cause of justice will be doomed for the lifetime of everyone in this room" if Reagan were reelected[35]—as if justice for Americans could come only through the courts.

The next year, with needed judicial victories still at some temporal distance, Attorney General Edwin Meese opened another Republican front against the Court. His target was *Cooper v. Aaron*, the Little Rock desegregation case, where the Court stated that its decisions were constitutional commands that all elected officials must obey. Harking back to Andrew Jackson, Abraham Lincoln, and Franklin D. Roosevelt, Meese claimed that there was a distinction between the Constitution and the Court's decisions and that only the former was the supreme law of the land. A cascade of anathemas, pronounced by leaders of the bar, prominent academics, and columnists, rained down upon Meese. They all claimed that his position would undermine the rule of law. When he publicly recanted less than three weeks later, the Republicans' option was reduced to taking the Court itself. That process began a year later.

Burger was the first of the octogenarians to leave. Reagan replaced him with Rehnquist and then filled Rehnquist's seat with Antonin Scalia, whom he had earlier placed on the District of Columbia Court of Appeals, as one of several conservative academics auditioning on courts of appeals for a chance at the real thing. Scalia, whose specialty was administrative law, was a devout Catholic, confident, personable, and an outspoken conservative. Functionally, Reagan had replaced Burger with a younger, smarter justice in complete harmony with the conservative social agenda.

The hearings of the Senate Judiciary Committee confirmed the suspicion that the Democrats were brain-dead. Democrats focused their attacks on Rehnquist's pre-Court activities (in a replay of his prior hearings) without understanding that even if they defeated Rehnquist's appointment, he still would be on the Court. As a result, Scalia was essentially given a pass and confirmed 98–0 (compared to Rehnquist's 65–33).

A year later, after Democrats had retaken control of the Senate in the 1986 elections, Powell, well past his prime, became the second octogenarian to retire. Reagan named Robert Bork, another D.C. Circuit judge, who was the darling of the conservatives for his outspoken attacks on Warren Court decisions—especially *Griswold v. Connecticut* and its penumbras and emanations. Unlike Burger, Powell had been the quintessential centrist, and was the fifth vote to protect both *Roe* and affirmative action. Replacing Powell with Bork meant that affirmative action would be found unconstitutional (for it was one of the very few things Bork believed governments were forbidden to do) and abortion could be recriminalized. There could be no doubt that if Bork was confirmed, constitutional law would change. Conservative fundraiser Richard Viguerie exclaimed that conservatives had "waited for over 30 years for this day. This [Bork's nomination] is the most exciting news since President Reagan's reelection."[36]

Liberals went ballistic, none more so than Senator Edward Kennedy. They began a campaign to defeat Bork at any cost. One highly effective weapon was a television ad by People for the American Way, starring Gregory Peck and showing a family on the steps of the Court looking up at its slogan, "Equal Rights under Law." Peck stated that Bork opposed civil rights, privacy, and much free speech protection: "Robert Bork could have the last word on your rights as citizens, but the Senate has the last word on him. Please urge your Senators to vote against the Bork nomination, because if Robert Bork wins a seat on the Supreme Court, it will be for life—his life and yours."[37] The ad had fused two powerful symbols—the family and the Court—and set Bork in opposition to both. It ran a few times and then was picked up as a news story and aired repeatedly, but for free (just as the 1964 Johnson campaign's "Daisy-H-bomb" ad had been transformed from a commercial to news and thus run again and again for free).

Reagan unwittingly gave Democrats needed ammunition when he claimed that Bork was a natural successor to Powell: "[I]f you want someone with Justice Powell's detachment and statesmanship, you can't do better than Judge Bork."[38] Democrats would show that Powell had been mainstream, Bork was not Powell, and therefore Bork was not mainstream—even though his positions on abortion and affirmative action already had four votes among the eight justices.

Surprisingly, conservatives did not mobilize. They had been transfixed at the time by Lieutenant Colonel Oliver North, resplendent with his decorations on his Marine dress uniform, handling his congressional interrogators so well that it appeared that they, not he, were responsible for the illegal actions in the Iran-Contra affair. Conservative activist Phyllis Schafly acknowledged that she had done nothing about Bork because "I've been too busy watching Ollie North."[39] Besides, Bork was so smart that conservatives assumed he would dazzle the Senate and the nation with his testimony.

Like the earlier Iran-Contra hearings, Bork's were televised, and contrary to expectations, Bork often proved to be his own worst enemy. The *Washington Post* television critic summed up his performance by concluding that Bork "looked, and talked, like a man who would throw the book at you—maybe like a man who would throw the book at the whole country."[40]

Bork, as a witness, was followed by William Coleman, Ford's secretary of transportation; Barbara Jordan, the former congresswoman from Texas who had made such an impassioned statement about her belief in the Constitution during the Nixon impeachment hearings; and Andrew Young, the mayor of Atlanta. All were African Americans, and each spoke to what Bork's vision of the Constitution would have meant to their lives. More important, all three brought home Bork's complete lack of empathy for those in need of help.

The nation agreed with the *Post's* television critic: a Gallup poll showed that respondents wanted him defeated by a 51–32 margin. The Senate concurred by a vote of 58–42. Conservatives coined a new verb—"to Bork"—to describe what they believed had happened to him (defeat by character assassination and gross distortion). Amazingly and wrongly, liberals agreed. They justified "Borking" by appealing to the age-old principle that the end justifies the means. And through his subsequent rantings, an unhinged Bork demonstrated that he was temperamentally unfit for the Bench.

Reagan followed the defeat of the fifty-nine-year-old Bork by turning to another former law professor on the D.C. Circuit, forty-one-year-old Douglas Ginsburg. His candidacy was derailed when his use of marijuana as a law professor at Harvard surfaced. Reagan then turned to a fifty-year-old West Coast appellate judge, Anthony Kennedy, who by his own admission led a personal life that was boring. By not talking about abortion and speaking of a Constitution with room for growth, he sailed through without opposition.

With another Republican Catholic on the Court, *Roe* looked ripe for overruling in *Webster v. Reproductive Health Services* in 1989, but O'Connor refused to pull the trigger, slipping comfortably into Powell's centrist role. Instead she concurred separately, providing the fifth vote to uphold significant restrictions on abortion. Kennedy, as expected, voted with Rehnquist, White, and Scalia. A dissenting Blackmun prophesied *Roe*'s demise: "[T]he signs are evident and very ominous, and a chill wind blows."[41]

Blackmun had no idea how chill the wind might be. Brennan and Marshall, the last two liberal icons from the Warren Court, into their eighties and long past their prime, in failing health and believing they could not outlast yet another Republican presidency, retired in 1990 and 1991, respectively. To replace Brennan, President George H. W. Bush selected David Souter, an obscure state court judge recently placed on a federal appeals court. Liberals searched and searched and turned up nothing. It was as if the unmarried Souter had lived in a cave his entire adult life. Democrats were prepared to block him (once floating the idea that because he lacked a wife and children, he did not have the requisite life experiences) unless he made the right promises on future voting behavior. But the Iraqi invasion of Kuwait intervened, and simple politics looked unattractive. Souter had not been asked his views on abortion by Bush, and what he didn't tell the president, he wouldn't tell the Senate. He did, however, say that *Griswold* was correctly decided, that the Due Process Clause did protect an unenumerated right to privacy, and that he respected precedent. Ninety senators voted aye.

Everyone knew that Clarence Thomas would be the nominee to replace Marshall, because Thomas was the most (perhaps the only) prominent African American Republican judge, albeit for only two years. He had a wonderful life story of growing up in poverty (the first nominee since William O. Douglas to do so), but Bush went further and stunningly claimed that he had picked the best man regardless of race—a proposition that no one could believe, given Thomas's thin and undistinguished résumé.

Liberals were outraged that Marshall's seat could go to a conservative African American who had enjoyed the benefits of affirmative action (right up though his nomination) while publicly disproving of the policy. Furthermore, they were sure that he also disapproved of abortion—although he claimed (falsely) that he had never discussed the issue with anyone. He stonewalled the Judiciary Committee on constitutional issues and tried to turn questions to his impressive life story. That appeared to backfire when a former employee, Anita Hill, came forward with charges that Thomas had made inappropriate advances toward her. While she never used the words "sexual harassment," that was how it sounded to everyone, and in the climate of 1991, if Thomas had sexually harassed a subordinate at some point in the past, his nomination was doomed. Thomas flatly denied everything and accused those attacking him of engaging in a "high-tech lynching for uppity blacks who in any way deign to think for themselves."[42] Edward Kennedy, the likely Democratic lead, sat in silence because of his own problems with misogyny, while the Republicans energetically attacked Hill. It worked, though just barely, as a Democratic-controlled Senate confirmed an embittered Thomas by a vote of 52–48. If the Senate were apportioned by population, the nomination would have failed.

Abortion Again

With only Blackmun and Stevens left from the liberal bloc that had been surprisingly successful in the previous decade, liberals braced for Blackmun's "chill wind," while conservatives salivated over their victory. After a decade of trying, the latter now had a Court where every single justice save White had been appointed by a Republican president, and where there appeared to be at least six solid votes to rid the nation of *Roe v. Wade* (and adopt the remainder of the Republican social agenda). Even with O'Connor's defection, there had been four justices ready to gut *Roe*, and Thomas was a sure fifth vote, with Souter seeming a likely sixth.

Souter's appointment had paid an immediate dividend when *Rust v.*

Sullivan sustained a so-called gag rule whereby family planning agencies that receive federal funds were forbidden to discuss the availability of abortion as an option—even when specifically asked about it by a pregnant woman. The lineup, before Marshall's retirement, had a Rehnquist majority with Marshall, Stevens, Blackmun, and O'Connor in dissent. *Rust* looked like a preview of the new split on *Roe*.

From the point of view of abortion advocates, if *Roe* was to go, it would be best to be done quickly—before the 1992 election if possible. That way voters could be energized to support pro-choice Democratic candidates in the election, and with newly replenished Democratic majorities, abortion rights could be protected legislatively. Indeed, abortion rights might be better protected legislatively than they were judicially.

Six days after Thomas was confirmed, a federal court of appeals upheld a twenty-four-hour waiting period and informed consent provisions that the Court had previously ruled unconstitutional. The lower court reasoned that O'Connor's undue burden test was now the law of the land, and its application sustained the restrictions. The losers had until late January to file their petition for review, but they rushed it to the Court in early November in the hope that the Court would grant it in time for argument in the spring and decision four months before the election. Furthermore, they limited their request for review to a single question: Had the Supreme Court overruled the conclusion of *Roe v. Wade* that abortion was a fundamental right? Because the lower court had invalidated a requirement to notify the husband, the state cross-petitioned for review and asked the Court to overrule *Roe* explicitly. Seven justices, but not Rehnquist and O'Connor—perhaps the two most politically astute—agreed to hear the case, *Planned Parenthood of Southeastern Pennsylvania v. Casey,* in the spring.

Contrary to everyone's expectations, *Casey* did not overrule *Roe,* because, in addition to Blackmun's and Stevens's sure votes, O'Connor got Souter and Kennedy (who switched from his *Webster* vote) to join her in claiming that stare decisis—the appropriate respect for precedent—required *Roe*'s survival.

The Republican troika (as they soon came to be labeled), all of whom were as likely to have been struck by lightning as to gain a seat on the Court (an analogy O'Connor explicitly drew), wrote a joint opinion that stood for judicial courage. Taking the high ground, the troika stated that a decision "without principled justification would be no judicial act at all."[43] Yet this was precisely the charge that had been leveled at *Roe*. The troika made no attempt to demonstrate that *Roe* was principled, and if it wasn't principled, then by their reasoning it was "no judicial act at all" and presumably void. They didn't even claim that *Roe* had been rightly decided. They just refused to overrule it "under fire,"[44] as though opposition to *Roe* was sufficient reason to keep the decision alive.

A key argument by the troika was that women make choices in their lives that rely on their ability to terminate an unwanted pregnancy. They elaborated on this unsubstantiated claim by asserting that "for two decades of economic and social developments, people have organized intimate relationships and made choices that define their views of themselves and their places in society, in reliance on the availability of abortion in the event contraception should fail."[45] They noted that "[t]he Constitution serves human values, and while the effect of reliance on *Roe* cannot be exactly measured, neither can the certain cost of overruling *Roe* for people who have ordered their thinking and living around that case be dismissed."[46] One important facet of *Casey* was the key recognition that abortion was a woman's right, not merely a medical issue as *Roe* had suggested. The right came in two distinct parts: a right not to bear children at the risk of the woman's health, and a right not to be forced into the responsibilities of parenthood (where the latter right requires only reasonable timing—prior to viability—to make the decision).

Turning the clock back to earlier contentious times, the troika cele-

brated the New Deal's victory over the old order and *Brown's* overturning of *Plessy* (although the case could have been made that the same
analysis that saved *Roe* could easily have been employed to save *Plessy*,
had the justices so wished). Both of those overrulings were justified on
the ground that there was a new perception of the underlying facts
which necessitated a changed outcome. This allowed the troika to
state that while there had been advances in medical care in the two decades since *Roe*, the new facts went to timing and had no bearing on
what they claimed was *Roe's* "central holding," that abortion prior to
viability is a fundamental right.[47]

Blackmun was celebratory. He noted that after *Webster* "[a]ll that remained between the promise of *Roe* and the darkness of the plural-
ity was a single, flickering flame . . . But now, just when so many expected the darkness to fall, the flame has grown bright."[48] Scalia, for
Rehnquist, White, and Thomas, could scarcely contain himself. His anger was palpable, as he called the troika's arguments "outrageous."[49]
To illustrate, he organized his opinion by sectioning off in bold type a
quotation from the troika and then demolishing it with a vengeance.
He refused to "sit still" for a "lengthy lecture on the virtues of 'con-
stancy'" from two justices who, "in order to remain steadfast, had to
abandon previously stated positions."[50]

Scalia's last point was telling. In reaffirming *Roe*, the troika had
adopted O'Connor's undue burden test, and in application to the Pennsylvania law this resulted in affirming the conclusions of the court below: a twenty-four-hour waiting period was valid, as was a requirement of parental consent for minors, as was a requirement that doctors inform the women of alternatives to abortion. Only the provision
for notifying the husband was invalidated.

The decision was hardly the profile in courage that the troika hero-
ically portrayed it to be. (Kennedy quipped to a reporter just before the
opinion was announced that "[s]ometimes you don't know whether
you are Caesar about to cross the Rubicon or Captain Queeg cut-

ting your own tow line.")[51] The results almost perfectly tracked public opinion. Far from demanding that *Roe* be overruled, Americans overwhelmingly supported abortion before viability. They also did not believe that abortion should be a substitute for birth control. Polling data showed that each of the three provisions upheld was supported by at least a 70 percent popular margin. The troika was following public opinion, perhaps in the hope of influencing election returns.

Only the pro-life minority were angry—and they were furious at Kennedy and Souter, who represented "the emergence on the Court of a Wimp Bloc who are quickly becoming an embarrassment."[52] That proved to be a mild first impression. With eight of the nine justices appointed by Republicans, the party should have been cooing about the Court. Instead Republicans saw the Court as untrustworthy and dangerous. Ironically, this was much the same way Republicans had seen Marshall's all-Federalist Court, the way later Republicans had seen the five Southerners in the *Dred Scott* majority, and the way New Dealers had seen five Republicans and the reactionary James McReynolds in 1936. But it was unprecedented for the party controlling the membership of the Court to view it as a leper.

Casey could not save the Bush presidency. And while *Casey* did save *Roe*, since Clinton got to replace both Blackmun and White, *Roe* remained the gift that keeps on giving—to Republicans.

An Imperial Court

EQUALLY IMPORTANT as *Planned Parenthood v. Casey*'s refusal to over-rule *Roe v. Wade* was what the opinion by Sandra Day O'Connor, An-thony Kennedy, and David Souter said about the role of the Court in American society. According to the troika, the Court could not over-rule *Roe* because to do so would destroy the essential perceptions of the American people about the Court. That would be too traumatic for everyone. The troika claimed that occasionally, as in *Roe,* the Court "decides a case in such a way as to resolve [an] intensely divisive con-troversy."[1] These cases have a "dimension" that a routine case does not, one that is "present whenever the Court's interpretation of the Consti-tution calls the contending sides of a national controversy to end their national division by accepting a common mandate rooted in the Con-stitution."[2]

The troika was doubly wrong. First, abortion was not an "intensely divisive controversy" when *Roe* was decided. In most states it wasn't yet an issue. *Roe* itself created the controversy. Second, and far more significantly, the First Amendment guarantees the right to dissent vig-orously from government policies. The American people decide when the fight over an issue ends. If a decision is not controversial, then it will be readily accepted. But the troika said that if a decision is controversial because so many Americans refuse to accept it, then the Court may not overrule it. The whole point of bringing to the Court's (and the nation's) attention the proposition that the justices have butchered the Constitution is to have the error corrected, not to have it entrenched. The troika essentially presented the nation with a catch-22 scenario: if the people protest, the Court will remain steadfast in adhering to its controversial decisions; and if there is no protest, there would be no need to reconsider the decision.

The troika's opinion did *Cooper v. Aaron* one better. Under assault from the South, *Cooper* held that all public officials were bound by *Brown*. Under assault from Republicans, the troika stated that all Americans must fall in step with the Court and cease fighting over *Roe*. Such an order had no historical pedigree, and pro-lifers refused to quit. But their efforts to overturn abortion through Court-packing came to an abrupt halt when Ross Perot and what appeared to be a continuing recession propelled Bill Clinton into the presidency (with but 43 percent of the popular vote), and he was then immediately rewarded with the retirement of Byron White, who had always opposed *Roe,* and then Harry Blackmun a year later.

Clinton replaced White with Ruth Bader Ginsburg, formerly a leading feminist lawyer for the American Civil Liberties Union and a Columbia Law School professor, whom Jimmy Carter had placed on the District of Columbia Circuit. With Democrats solidly in control of the Senate, she didn't have to hide her warm feelings about women's rights while refusing to offer a hint on how she would deal with issues likely to come before the Court. Like Souter in his hearings, she couldn't (or wouldn't) even say whether the Korean War was a war. Oh, well, Antonin Scalia ducked on a much easier question: whether *Marbury v. Madison* represented a settled principle of law.

Blackmun's replacement was another federal judge, Stephen G. Breyer, who had previously served as general counsel of the Senate Judiciary Committee and as an administrative law professor at Harvard. With the votes of Ginsburg and Breyer, abortion was so secure that the Court even invalidated state restrictions on the controversial procedure known to its opponents as "partial-birth abortion."[3]

No Trespassing

The troika's opinion in *Casey* is the most pretentious in the *United States Reports*. It asserted that the belief Americans hold of themselves as a people who live according to the rule of law "was not readily separable from their understanding of the Court . . . [as] speak[ing] before all others for their constitutional ideals."[4] "Before" meant way above. Thus "[i]f the Court's legitimacy should be undermined, then, so would the country be in its very ability to see itself though its constitutional ideals. The Court's concern with legitimacy is not for the sake of the Court, but for the sake of the Nation."[5] As if the American people (the vast majority of whom can't name two sitting justices) spend their time thinking about the issue. The troika spoke as though to say, "We do it all for you, our people." And despite the contempt of Scalia's dissent, there was no disagreement among the Brethren with regard to the troika's essential position on the role of the Court: "We're number one."

The full Court showed it was serious about its primacy when it struck down federal statutes designed to overrule two 5–4 decisions. One was the 1990 holding in *Employment Division v. Smith* that free exercise claims could be trumped by any law that does not specifically target religion. The other was the Warren Court edict *Miranda v. Arizona* and its notorious Miranda warnings.

Almost immediately after *Smith* was decided, efforts began to return free exercise claims to their former status, and these bore fruit in 1993 with passage of the Religious Freedom Restoration Act. Congress thoroughly vetted the constitutional issues involving Section 5 of the

Fourteenth Amendment and was explicit in its intent to use Section 5 to return to the pre-*Smith* compelling state interest standard. With the support of both religious and civil liberties groups, the RFRA passed the House unanimously and the Senate 97–3.

The RFRA came to the Court when Boerne, Texas, placed a historical zoning designation on a 1923 replica of a mission-style church, preventing a growing Catholic parish from expanding it (and forcing the congregation to hold mass in a school gymnasium). The church sued, but the RFRA, so successful in Congress, could garner at best two votes on the Court in *City of Boerne v. Flores.* Kennedy tersely held that Section 5 gave Congress power to enforce the Fourteenth Amendment, and "[l]egislation which alters the meaning of the Free Exercise Clause cannot be said to be enforcing the Clause. Congress does not enforce a constitutional right by changing what the right is."[6] The RFRA, by protecting religious conduct more generously than *Smith* did, was implementing a congressional policy rather than enforcing the Constitution. Hence the RFRA was beyond congressional authority.

The Court said that because Congress was aware of the decision in *Smith,* it had to know that "the Court will treat its precedents with the respect due them under settled principles, including *stare decisis,* and contrary expectations must be disappointed."[7] The Constitution works best "when each part of government respects both the Constitution and the proper actions and determinations of the other braches."[8] In other words, Congress should know its place and recognize judicial supremacy, and the Court should keep Congress subordinate. Democrats took the message better than Republicans because the former remained ideologically attached to the belief in a Big Court. Republicans, by contrast, were still angry at *Casey* (as well as *Romer v. Evans,* a gay rights case) and continued to be wary of a judiciary they did not fully control.

Meanwhile, *Miranda* had been unpopular with millions of Americans from the instant it was decided. Headlines proclaiming "Confessed Murderer Goes Free"[9] will do that. Summer riots, an escalating crime wave, the quagmire in Vietnam, and an impending presidential election led to the Omnibus Crime Control and Safe Streets Act of 1968, with a provision specifically contrary to *Miranda*. If a judge found that a confession was voluntary, given the totality of the circumstances, then the statute proclaimed it was admissible against the defendant even if no warnings about constitutional rights had been given.

After three decades of nonenforcement, a federal appeals court admitted a suppressed, voluntary, but un-Mirandized confession on the basis of the 1968 law. Rehnquist, O'Connor, and Kennedy were on record as opposing *Miranda's* rule, but the three nevertheless refused to overrule. Rehnquist's opinion in *Dickerson v. United States* bluntly stated that "Congress may not legislatively supersede our decisions interpreting and applying the Constitution."[10] Since *Miranda* applied a constitutional rule, Congress could not overrule it. Rehnquist, O'Connor, and Kennedy didn't like *Miranda* one bit, but they liked the thought of Congress gutting a Supreme Court decision far less. Thus *Miranda* went from 5–4 at the height of the Warren Court to 7–2 (Scalia and Clarence Thomas dissenting) on the Rehnquist Court. If it wasn't for judicial imperialism, such a result simply could not be possible.

The Federalism Revolution

The 1994 elections, fueled by the big government initiatives of the Clintons' failed effort to enact national health insurance and the successful Brady Bill on gun control, created a Republican majority in both the House and the Senate. This provided protective cover for conservative decisions by the Court. Six months after the elections, the Court's willingness to demand limits on congressional power emerged out of nowhere when *United States v. Lopez* struck down one of those symbolic statutes that politicians love: the Gun-Free School Zones Act of 1990. *Lopez* marked the first time since 1936 that the Court found Congress had exceeded its powers under the Commerce Clause.

Alfonzo Lopez, an otherwise lawful high school student, brought a gun to school to give to another student. When the state decided to prosecute him, the feds jumped in too, and he was convicted under a federal statute prohibiting guns within a thousand feet of a school. At oral argument O'Connor asked the solicitor general if he could think of anything Congress could do that would exceed its commerce power. He could not (or would not) offer a single example.

A five-justice majority by Rehnquist created an example for him. It held that Congress could reach activities substantially affecting commerce only when the regulated activity was commercial or economic in nature (such as growing wheat). The four dissenters, Breyer, Souter, Ginsburg, and John Paul Stevens, were beside themselves in disbelief. Not having to worry about being shot at school promoted learning, which in turn facilitated commerce nationwide. Wedded to a status quo that the majority deemed outmoded and unconstitutional, the dissenters were force-fed a basic lesson: no contested constitutional doctrine lasts forever.

Lopez was just a beginning. In the six years after the Republicans took over in Congress, the Court invalidated thirty federal statutes. In comparison, the Warren Court struck down only eighteen in its sixteen years. The Imperial Court was operating at a clip similar to the Four Horsemen's slaughter of the New Deal at the end of FDR's first term. Furthermore, as in the New Deal era, seemingly important statutes—the RFRA, the Brady Bill's requirement of instant background checks by local law enforcement, the Violence Against Women Act, and damage remedies against state governments under both the Age Discrimination Act and the Americans with Disabilities Act—were invalidated. But not one of these had passed a Republican-controlled chamber. Each was the type of statute that Democrats adore—rights-creating (except for the Brady Bill, which was almost as good because it stripped rights from a group Democrats loathe)—and Republicans have a politically difficult time opposing. So the Court did the opposing instead.

Like *Lopez,* the Violence Against Women Act was invalidated because of its lack of connection with interstate commerce. Rehnquist again asserted that congressional authority was not without limits and that it was essential to maintain a "distinction between what is truly national and what is truly local."[11] Thus the Court rejected the voluminous legislative history of the act—arguments that gender-related violence deters travel, harms business, and diminishes productivity—because supposedly it proved too much. Under a similar theory Congress could regulate any crime; indeed it would give Congress the power to rewrite family law, something the Court believed was truly local.

Lopez requires knowing what is economic and what is not. The distinction is elusive, as *Gonzales v. Raich* demonstrated. Angel Raich grew marijuana at home for her personal medical use, as California law authorized. But the federal Controlled Substances Act barred all uses of marijuana. Kennedy's opinion acknowledged that Raich's use was personal; she did not buy marijuana, sell it, or transport any across state lines. Nevertheless, as with congressional regulation of home-consumed wheat, Congress's prophylactic power was upheld because marijuana could be diverted to illicit purposes (and it would be very difficult for the government to prove nonmedicinal uses). Rehnquist, O'Connor, and Thomas, the justices most intent on curbing federal power generally, dissented, aptly noting that similar reasoning—prohibiting guns near schools as part of a necessary effort to prevent sales to minors—could overturn *Lopez.*

Raich helps demonstrate the hollowness of what had been proclaimed as the federalism revolution. The Gun-Free School Zones Act, as well as the Violence Against Women Act, were aimed at harms that the states were already dealing with. The federal government was just piling on. Federalism is about diversity, whereby states can try new ideas and, if successful, demonstrate better ways of governing. That was what California was attempting to do by legalizing medical marijuana; instead Congress, with the Court's blessing, could mandate national conformity. In this respect *Raich* is in harmony with other decisions in which federal law supersedes a conflicting state law: stricter oil tanker safety rules in Puget Sound,[12] tougher air pollution standards in California,[13] and restrictions on tobacco advertising in Massachusetts[14] were all invalidated. The difference with *Raich* is that each of these was a victory for big business.

Federalism did prevail in *Kelo v. New London*, but its strongest supporters dissented. New London, Connecticut, like many other cities in the state, had been in a long-term decline, with double the state's average rate of unemployment and a population that had shrunk to its 1920s level. In an effort to create jobs and increase the tax base, the city condemned a number of private properties (paying what was deemed to be fair market value) so that they could become part of a new private development to revitalize the waterfront area. The issue in *Kelo* was whether that private development constituted a "public use" under the Takings Clause. Deferring to the local legislative judgment, Stevens's majority opinion found that the overall plan for redevelopment constituted a public purpose. If communities wished to use their power of eminent domain to assist private interests, that was their right, as long as the community also benefited. Twenty-one years earlier O'Connor for a unanimous Court had allowed wealthy residents of Honolulu, whose homes were on land covered by long-term leases, to acquire full title to the land through condemnation (even though rental income had been going into a trust to aid native Hawaiians).[15] If that use of eminent domain was a public purpose, New London's action was as well. Without wholly repudiating her earlier opinion, which she now recharacterized as concerning land that imposed an affirmative harm on society, O'Connor wrote the *Kelo* dissent for Rehnquist, Scalia, and Thomas.

Conservatives, who professed to love both judicial restraint and federalism, were outraged. House Republican leader Tom DeLay claimed, "Congress is not going to just sit by—idly sit by—and let an unaccountable judiciary make these kinds of decisions without taking our responsibility and our duty given to us by the Constitution to be a check on the judiciary."[16] His prediction was wrong, although some states reacted by tightening restrictions on eminent domain.

DeLay had already decried an out-of-control judiciary, and Republican senator John Cornyn (a former Texas Supreme Court justice) suggested that recent horrific attacks on judges and their families might have been an effort to make the judiciary more accountable. Cornyn's statement was outrageous and was quickly retracted, but it was a solid representation of conservative resentment since *Casey*.

There never was a federalism revolution. Rather the revolt consisted of random pinpricks to limit what conservative justices saw as an overreaching Congress. The practical effect of the limits was close to nil. It might have been nice to hear that federal power has some limits, but the decisions were either unimportant or easy to circumvent.

Gender and Gay Rights

With the exception of the insistence on judicial supremacy, there was no discernible pattern to the Court's decisions. The reason was that the Court was extraordinarily stable. It went for more than a decade without a new member, and during that period was composed of three very conservative justices (Rehnquist, Scalia, and Thomas) and four pretty reliably liberal ones (Stevens, Souter, Breyer, and Ginsburg). Between the wings, O'Connor and Kennedy controlled the outcome of any case, and they refused to let either wing win consistently. Perhaps the reason was pragmatism; more likely it was that they represented the very definition of a centrist justice. With a preference for balancing tests and a refusal to give either wing a clear-cut win, the two non-movement conservatives ensured that each doctrinal area included victories and defeats for each side. Furthermore, O'Connor seemed uncannily attuned to American public opinion.

Gender equality was the one area where there was a clear direction, since the majority of justices were in harmony with the changed attitudes of elites (like themselves). Virginia funded fifteen public colleges. One, the Virginia Military Institute, was an all-male pre–Civil War institution designed to prepare men for leadership roles in both military and civilian life. VMI was unique in its identity as the sole single-sex college the state funded and in its method of bonding its students through physical and psychological hazing. There was no comparable public institution for women (and the attempt to create one during the litigation failed, as it lacked not just hazing but especially VMI's entrenched old-boy network).

Ginsburg's opinion for the Court came close to achieving her goals as a feminist litigator. The Court viewed VMI's actions with "skeptical scrutiny" that demanded a justification that was "exceedingly persuasive."[17] (No one knows how this differs from strict scrutiny and the compelling state interest test.) Although she followed with a wordy opinion, the case was over when she rightly concluded that VMI was unique and its advantages ran only to men. Scalia alone dissented and because of his close friendship with Ginsburg, the dissent lacked his usual flair.

In a decision that stunned many observers, the Court sustained the Family Medical Leave Act against Nevada's claim of sovereign immunity. William Hibbs, a state employee, needed time off to care for his ailing wife. Before his statutory twelve weeks had been used up, Nevada terminated his employment. Citing historic reliance on "stereotypes about women's domestic roles . . . reinforced by parallel stereotypes presuming a lack of domestic responsibilities for men,"

Rehnquist held that Congress could enact a prophylactic rule without regard to whether a particular state had engaged in past discrimination (against men or women).[18] Kennedy, Scalia, and Thomas dissented.

Just as Americans' views of women's equality had drastically shifted over the previous quarter century, so, too, had their views of homosexuality. In the years after *Bowers v. Hardwick* held that states could criminalize homosexual sodomy, half the states that had such statutes repealed them. Nevertheless, some states passed new anti-gay laws. One was Colorado, whose voters amended the state constitution to bar state and local governments from adopting laws and policies that would protect gay men and women against discrimination. Without citing *Bowers*, Kennedy held that the amendment lacked a legitimate legislative end because its true purpose was to make homosexuals less equal than anyone else.[19] Scalia's bitter dissent for Rehnquist and Thomas accused the majority of siding with elites in a deeply divided cultural debate rather than leaving the issue to the voters. Scalia also wondered why a state could criminalize homosexual conduct but could not authorize discrimination against those most likely to engage in it.

As the dissenters guessed, the Colorado case was a marker on the road to overruling *Bowers*. *Lawrence v. Texas*, like *Bowers*, involved two adult males caught engaging in consensual sex in their home. Placing liberty front and center, Kennedy claimed that it "presumes an autonomy of the self that includes . . . certain intimate sexual conduct" whereby those engaging in it "still retain their dignity as free persons."[20]

Scalia, again dissenting with Rehnquist and Thomas, noted that those justices who had refused to overrule *Roe* in *Casey* were the same ones killing *Bowers*. Scalia accused the majority of being a "product of a law profession culture that has largely signed on to the so-called homosexual agenda, by which I mean the agenda promoted by some homosexual activists directed at eliminating the moral opprobrium that has traditionally attached to homosexual conduct."[21] He also told people to disbelieve the majority's disclaimer that the opinion had any implications for gay marriage. (Later in 2003 the Massachusetts Supreme Judicial Court agreed with Scalia and struck down on state grounds the state's ban on same-sex marriage, thereby giving the Republicans another social issue for the 2004 elections to add to the question of who could best protect America.)[22]

Although virtually no state prosecuted homosexual sodomy, the symbolic victory in *Lawrence* far exceeded defeats in attempting to prevent the Boy Scouts from barring a gay Scout leader and to stop law schools from trying to keep military recruiters out of their buildings. New Jersey applied its antidiscrimination law to the Boy Scouts when Scout leaders revoked the membership of James Dale, a former Eagle Scout, who had publicly outed himself. Rehnquist, for a five-justice majority, held that the Scouts had the right to ban homosexuals as part of their First Amendment right of "expressive association," a new right that allows voluntary groups to maintain their homogeneity.[23] The Scouts claimed that as a group they were exercising their expressive association right to decide that being gay was incompatible with Scout values (expressed in the Boy Scout oath about being "straight" and "clean"). Stevens, for the dissenters, stated that he didn't think the Scouts were as homophobic as they claimed to be.

Most law schools have policies that bar recruiters from using placement facilities unless they sign an antidiscrimination statement. Since the military bans out-of-the-closet homosexuals, the law schools' policies banned military recruiters. Congress responded with the Solomon Amendment, threatening a total cutoff of aid to any university that treated military recruiters differently from others. Seizing on the *Boy Scouts* case, a handful of Northeastern law schools claimed that they had a right of expressive association to bar the military. If the military used placement facilities, the schools declared, the expressive association principle of no discrimination would be undermined. Amazingly, a federal appeals court agreed that law schools were in fact expressive associations. So a unanimous Court restored reality by reversing.[24] The military's presence did not violate the law schools' rights to association regardless of how repugnant they found the recruiters' message. Nor were law schools compelled to say anything against their will. Indeed they were free to demonstrate and speak against the military's "don't ask, don't tell" policy as they pleased. So far, however, there is no indication that law professors are taking up the Court's offer to spend part of their day protesting.

Civil Rights

An overreaching but creative federal judge in Kansas City offered the Court the opportunity to shut down the generation-long experiment with busing schoolchildren for racial balance. Kansas City's busing plan came before the Court twice. Because of the Detroit busing case, the federal judge could not order interdistrict busing. So his goal was to lure whites from the suburbs back into the Kansas City schools (which were less than one-third white and with the numbers dropping yearly). In the first instance, with Brennan and Marshall still on the Court, the justices by a 5–4 vote authorized the district judge to set aside property tax limits so that the school board could raise adequate funds to build the necessary deluxe schools.[25] As a result, even though the voters had defeated proposed tax increases, the school board could impose them anyway; accordingly, per-pupil spending in Kansas City zoomed to among the highest in the nation. In the second case, six years later, the district court had ruled that the tax and spend program would continue until the students in the district achieved their maximum potential (or at least reached the national average, which at best was a long way off in the future). Kennedy's opinion, for a 5–4 majority, reversed the judge and held that the purpose of desegregation was to restore the pupils to where they would have been absent the unlawful conduct. The judge should have limited himself to eliminating the racially identifiable schools (something likely impossible given the city's demographics).[26]

Previously, right after Souter and Thomas were appointed, the Court, in cases from Oklahoma City and Atlanta, pushed judges to get out of the busing business as soon as they could and to cease monitoring areas once they returned them to the schools.[27] Combined with the Kansas City case, these decisions left busing functionally dead. The Court never revisited the grave after the second Kansas City case.

Simultaneously with the Kansas City case, *Adarand Constructors v. Pena* offered the justices their opportunity to give affirmative action a similar burial by adopting the Republican goal of a color-blind Constitution. Adarand was one of three guardrail contractors in Colorado. The other two were minority-controlled, and under the federal program a general contractor received added compensation for being minority-controlled or using minority subcontractors. Thus, even if Adarand was the lowest bidder, it would lose the contract unless the two minority companies got greedy and outbid the federal bonus. O'Connor for a 5–4 majority held for the first time that even the federal government's affirmative action programs had to be tested by strict scrutiny. O'Connor felt that this was necessary to smoke out invidious from benign discrimination, while Stevens in dissent thought the difference was intuitive.

The Court next considered affirmative action in 2003, this time in the context of two separate admissions programs at the University of Michigan. For admission as an undergraduate, an applicant needed to score 100 out of a possible 150 points on a scale of desirable qualities. Minorities were automatically given 20 points. The law school's admissions program was more holistic (largely because there were far fewer applications to read), but it, too, gave minorities an advantage over better-qualified whites, as the law school strove (successfully) to maintain a "critical mass" of minorities in each entering class (with critical mass being two times larger for African Americans than Hispanics). Only O'Connor and Breyer saw a distinction between the programs. They ruled that the law school's program was constitutional,[28] but the undergraduate one was not,[29] even though the law school gave a greater boost to minority applicants. The message seemed to be that the boost should be disguised. Rehnquist, Scalia, Thomas, and Kennedy thought that both programs were unconstitutional, while Stevens, Souter, and Ginsburg would have sustained both.

O'Connor's opinion in *Grutter v. Bollinger* tracked Lewis Powell's twenty-five-year-old opinion in *Bakke*. She found achieving a diverse student body to be a compelling interest. The undergraduate program served that compelling interest, but O'Connor thought that the program was not narrowly tailored to achieve its goal. Finally she asserted that affirmative action should be able to do its job within another twenty-five years, so she sunsetted its constitutionality (although she would not be around to know how successful her assertion would prove to be).

Grutter was probably won at the briefing stage before argument. Normally amicus briefs don't accomplish much more than the gratification of their authors. But two amicus briefs, both cited in the text of O'Connor's opinion, mattered in *Grutter*. One was submitted by a group of Fortune 500 companies asserting the importance of affirmative action in higher education to employment practices in their global operations. The more important one, however, was filed by forty-five retired admirals, generals (some quite well known), and former secretary of defense William Cohen, asserting that affirmative action was essential to West Point, Annapolis, Colorado Springs, and ROTC programs in creating a diverse officer corps in order to ensure the necessary cohesiveness (by eliminating any perception of racial discrimination). "[D]ecades of experience" showed that a "highly qualified, racially diverse officer corps . . . is essential to the military's ability to fulfill its principle [sic] mission to provide national security."[30] The actual function of amicus briefs is to bring to the Court's attention information that it otherwise would not have, and no amicus brief had ever done it better; four justices referenced the brief in the first minutes of oral argument. The solicitor general, arguing against the Michigan programs, conceded that he had not thought about the consequences that ending affirmative action would have on the military academies. Who would have thought that the military would save affirmative action?

Religion

The Court left the rules on prayers at school functions and public religious symbolism where it found them—no on prayer and confused on symbols—but it fundamentally loosened the law on public funding of religion. The key case in the latter move came in 1995 from Thomas Jefferson's University of Virginia. The school subsidized printing costs for a wide variety of student organizations but drew the line at funding religious activities that promoted a particular belief about the deity. UVA's position was simple: the Establishment Clause required it. In *Rosenberger v. University of Virginia,* Kennedy's majority turned the case into one about speech and found that UVA unfairly discriminated between religious speech by students and all other forms of speech. Souter wrapped his dissent, joined by Stevens, Ginsburg, and Breyer, in Jefferson and James Madison, taking no cognizance of the fact that those two were writing before the modern welfare state and its expansive spending for all sorts of social goods.

Rosenberger was followed by the most politically contentious of the religion financial issues: vouchers for students to attend parochial schools. Cleveland's pathetic public school system was the target of an Ohio voucher plan that provided tuition aid to students attending a participating public or private school of the parent's choosing. No suburban public school was willing to participate, but fifty-six private schools did, and forty-six of them were religious. Virtually all participating students—96.6 percent—went to a religious school. There was no doubt the program had the valid secular purpose of improving education, so the question was whether it had the forbidden effect of advancing religion. Because it was a program of parental choice and there were nonreligious options, Rehnquist's majority upheld the program. Souter's dissent harked back to the first state Establishment Clause case, the 1947 decision in *Everson v. New Jersey*, where the justices fought 5–4 over free bus transportation and claimed *Everson*'s demand of "no tax in any amount" was eviscerated.[31] He had a point, but changes dating from the 1960s and 1970s, principally the quelling of anti-Catholic bias over the years following Vatican II and the ending of white flight by the demise of busing, put the issue in a different light.

The Cleveland case established that a state may include religious schools when it is offering funding to other private schools. Did *Rosenberger* signify that a state *must* offer funding to religious programs if it aids secular (private) ones? Rehnquist's opinion in *Locke v. Davey* answered this question in the negative in circumstances in which the state offered a scholarship for study at a religious school but drew the line at majoring in pastoral ministry. Only Scalia and Thomas dissented, with Scalia observing that "[i]n an era when the Court is so quick to come to the aid of other disadvantaged groups [citing the Colorado gay case], its indifference in this case, which involves a form of discrimination to which the Constitution actually speaks, is exceptional."[32]

The Ten Commandments became a contentious issue after Roy Moore, chief judge of the Alabama Supreme Court, placed them in the state supreme court building in the form of a huge monument. Because a 1980 Court decision ruled 8-to-Rehnquist that display of the Commandments lacked a valid secular purpose,[33] a federal court ordered the monument dismantled. After Moore rebuffed the federal court's order, he was removed from office, and the federal order was obeyed.

Although Moore lost (and lost again when he was trounced in the Republican gubernatorial primary), millions of Americans thought he was right and were enraged by the continual attack on any show of public religiosity by government. Legislators in two Kentucky counties ordered the Ten Commandments prominently posted in their courthouses. As litigation progressed, the counties tried to water down their displays by adding, in smaller frames, other historical documents that contained religious references, such as the Declaration of Independence's "endowed by their Creator." Over dissents by Rehnquist, Scalia, Thomas, and Kennedy, a majority by Souter found that an objective observer would conclude that any secular message ascribed to these displays was just a sham and secondary to the obvious religious message.[34]

There was a companion case from Texas, where the Fraternal Order of Eagles had donated to the state a Ten Commandments monument in the wake of the 1950s spectacle *The Ten Commandments,* starring Charlton Heston as Moses. There were sixteen other monuments and twenty-one historical markers displayed in a twenty-two-acre area between the state capitol and the state supreme court building. While eight justices saw no difference between the Texas case and the one from Kentucky, Breyer did. Acknowledging that there would be borderline cases, he thought that judgment based on context and consequences mattered. The key fact was that the Texas monument had been there for forty years without challenge prior to the case.[35]

Capital Punishment

A principal facet of the law of capital punishment remained the procedural maze of federal habeas (after direct appeals are over) as supplemented by the Antiterrorism and Effective Death Penalty Act, a 1996 statute designed to limit state prisoners' access to federal courts. The habeas petitioner must show that his filing was timely and that he has exhausted his state remedies, committed no procedural defaults (or had a very good reason for doing so), and developed an adequate record in state court. If the procedural maze is successfully negotiated, then the federal court determines whether there was constitutional error in applying the law on direct review at the time the conviction became final. No newly developed law may be considered. At the Court, inmates from the West Coast and from Ohio, Kentucky, and Tennessee fared poorly because the justices felt that their appeals courts had been too generous. That was balanced by the opposite conclusion about two of the three courts of appeals covering the South.

Within its framework that the death penalty should be reserved for those most deserving of it, the Court set new limits on who could not be executed by overturning recent decisions upholding the execution of the mentally retarded and those who committed their crimes as seventeen-year-olds. Stevens's opinion in *Atkins v. Virginia* evoked the "evolving standards of decency that mark the progress of a maturing society."[36] Twelve years earlier, when the Court approved executing the mentally retarded, only two states prohibited it, but in the ensuing years sixteen states (and three legislative houses in other states) adopted a ban. The consistency and direction of the change, said Stevens, demonstrated that "a national consensus has developed" against the execution of the mentally retarded, even though a majority of death penalty states had no firm ban in place on such executions.[37] To bolster his claim, Stevens also noted opposition to execution of the retarded by the American Psychological Association, various religious communities, and "the world community."[38] The three dissenters questioned that consensus and claimed that legislatures and juries were "better suited than courts to evaluating and giving effect to the complex societal and moral considerations" of punishment.[39]

Kennedy, for a five-person majority, applied a similar analysis to prohibit the execution of someone aged seventeen at the time of his horrendous crime. The argument for an emerging rejection of the death penalty for juveniles was nowhere near as clear as that in *Atkins* because less had changed. Only five states had abandoned capital punishment for juvenile offenders in the fifteen years since the Court approved it, although no state had gone the other way (and twenty-seven already had a limitation and some no capital punishment for anyone). According to Kennedy, what "is significant" is the "consistency of the direction of change."[40] To bolster his thin data as well as to shame those who disagreed, Kennedy observed that the United Nations Convention on the Rights of the Child prohibits capital punishment for crimes committed by juveniles under the age of eighteen. Only Somalia and the United States refused to ratify the convention. Besides the United States, in the previous fifteen years only seven countries—Iran, Pakistan, Saudi Arabia, Yemen, Nigeria, the Democratic Republic of the Congo, and China—had executed juvenile offenders, and each of those seven had since either abolished capital punishment for juvenile offenders or made a public disavowal of the practice. During the same interval, Texas had carried out almost as many executions for crimes committed by juveniles as had the rest of the world combined.

Scalia's biting dissent stated that "[w]ords have no meaning if the views of less than 50% of the death penalty States [18 of 38] can constitute a national consensus."[41] He also attacked the use of foreign laws as affirming "the Justices' own notion of how the world ought to be, and their diktat that it shall be so henceforth in America."[42]

These cases were supplemented by a case requiring a jury determination (applying the beyond a reasonable doubt standard) of any fact that rendered defendants death-eligible,[43] and by three other cases suggesting a more rigorous enforcement of the right to effective counsel.[44] But there was also the 5–4 decision in *Kansas v. Marsh*[45] upholding a state rule in capital sentencing that said ties go to the state; whenever aggravating and mitigating factors were found by the jury to be in equipoise, death was mandatory. But despite these other cases on other issues, the real action was over innocence.

It is perhaps ironic that in 1993 Rehnquist wrote for a majority that rather cavalierly rejected a habeas petition claiming innocence where there was no way for the inmate to raise the issue under Texas law. The Court saw no need for a state corrective process merely because the state was going to execute the wrong man (although the majority did opine that if an inmate could make a truly persuasive case of innocence, habeas should be available). Less than a decade later, possible innocence was at the forefront of the capital punishment debate, fueled by the identification of wrongfully convicted defendants in Illinois (followed by a moratorium on executions and then three years later by a blanket commutation for the 167 prisoners on Illinois's death row). Whether the public truly supports the death penalty (a bare 3 percent of American counties produce half the capital sentences), it clearly does not support the execution of innocent people. Indeed, worries about the finality of execution for a prisoner who is innocent may offer the basis for the first all-out judicial assault on the death penalty since *McCleskey v. Kemp*, the 1987 case on racial disparities and the death penalty.

The all-out assault, if it occurs, will have four pillars: first, innocence; second, defects in the system both substantive and procedural; third, world opinion; and fourth, Texas. In a 2006 dissent Souter, for Stevens, Ginsburg, and Breyer, wrote that the nation is in a "period of new empirical argument about how 'death is different'" and that the Court's doctrine should take into account the "cautionary lesson of recent experience" with wrongful convictions.[46] Three years earlier Breyer, in a solo opinion, had gratuitously catalogued all the things that were wrong with the death penalty, from wrongful conviction, to its arbitrary imposition, to racial discrimination, to underperforming counsel. Finally there is Kennedy, who worries how his actions will be perceived, loves the adulation of the press, and frequently spends time with his European counterparts in Salzburg. Might not the European experience with abolition, combined with the American experience of wrongful conviction, placed in a context in which half of U.S. executions occur in a single state, Texas, cause him to rethink his support for the jurisprudence of death? If so, there may again be five votes to bring capital punishment to a halt—especially if executions continue to decline and a few states follow New Jersey's 2007 lead and decide to abolish the death penalty.

The second-guessing continued in *Kennedy v. Louisiana*,[47] decided in June 2008, where a 5–4 Court rejected the state's claim (supported by five other states) that there was an emerging view over the previous decade-plus that capital punishment was appropriate in cases of the rape of a child. *Kennedy* also foreclosed the possibility of proving the existence of a new consensus (at least by legislative action) and further questioned the overall jurisprudence of the death penalty by stating that the area remained "in search of a unifying principle."[48] Abolition would be such a principle.

Two years before *Kennedy*, Scalia became so agitated with fear of abolition that he wrote an opinion designed to show that innocent people are never executed. He viewed the subsequent exoneration of those wrongly convicted as evidence that the current system works. A surprising facet of Scalia's opinion was that he (rather than Souter or Kennedy) wrote of world opposition to the death penalty—albeit to charge that Souter's views would play too well with those who "sanctimonious[ly] critici[ze] . . . America's death penalty as somehow unworthy of a civilized society."[49] American jurisdictions have utilized the death penalty, and "[i]t is no proper part of the business of this Court, or of its Justices, to second-guess that judgment, much less to impugn it before the world."[50]

Election Law

Affirmative action intersected with decennial redistricting when the Justice Department of George H. W. Bush demanded creation of safe seats for African American legislators in the South. In North Carolina this resulted in a bizarrely shaped district in the I-85 corridor that caused one legislator to remark that "[i]f you drove down the interstate with both car doors open, you'd kill most of the people in the district."[51] In *Shaw v. Reno*, O'Connor for the conservatives held that the district violated equal protection because there was no rational explanation for its shape except as a way to effect the "deliberate segregation of voters into separate districts on the basis of race."[52]

O'Connor claimed that "appearances do matter," but in fact they didn't, as the same 5–4 majority—this time through Kennedy—soon held that it was the predominant use of race, not the shape of the resulting district, that triggered the constitutional violation.[53] Finally, as she had in other areas, O'Connor retreated, and a five-justice majority by Breyer held that as long as race was not the predominant factor in drawing district lines, its use was constitutional.[54] Thus without turning to strict scrutiny, the Court held that states could consider race— but not too much (however much that was). Given the correlation between race and party affiliation, no state should have future difficulties, causing Thomas for the four dissenters to complain about districts being drawn "based on the stereotype that blacks are reliable Democratic voters."[55]

In 1986 the Court ruled that a gerrymandered legislature could be so extreme as to be unconstitutional.[56] Yet this proved an invitation to unsuccessful litigation, even as gerrymandering became rampant. In states where political control was split between the parties, the goal of decennial redistricting was to create a safe seat for every incumbent. In states where one party controlled the process, that party attempted to gerrymander its way to maximum advantage. Such gerrymandering would be too difficult without computers, but technology enabled almost perfect predictions of electoral outcomes, and incumbent representatives came to enjoy the luxury of choosing their voters. Faced with a particularly successful gerrymander in Pennsylvania, the Court left it alone by a 5–4 vote.[57] Perhaps chastened by a decade of futility with regard to racial gerrymandering, the three conservatives plus O'Connor concluded that a gerrymandering claim was nonjusticiable; that is, no court could rule whether it violated the Constitution. The liberals dissented, each offering a different test to smoke out when a gerrymander went from a reasonable grab to an unconstitutional one. Kennedy voted with the conservatives, but held out the possibility that if someone could offer a better test than the dissenters offered, he would find the area justiciable.

That better test materialized in a Texas case where the Republican legislature, bowing to the demands of House majority leader Tom De-Lay, engaged in mid-decade redistricting to eliminate as many rural white Democratic congressmen as possible and turn the Texas delegation from 17–15 Democratic to at least 21–11 Republican. Despite the unprecedented nature of the mid-decade redistricting, the Court again ducked the constitutional issues (even though its action would allow Texas to redistrict again in 2009 in preparation for redistricting after the 2010 census).[58] Perhaps Texas Democrats were unrealistic in thinking that there was a chance of success. Would a Court (or a majority of the Court) that had placed George W. Bush in the White House really help place San Francisco Democrat Nancy Pelosi in the House Speaker's chair?

The biggest legal, as opposed to practical, change in the law of elections came when the Court upheld the McCain-Feingold campaign finance reform in *McConnell v. Federal Election Commission*. The law expanded federal regulation over both contributions and, significantly, expenditures. Over anguished dissents resting on the First Amendment, the Court wrote a 131-page opinion that read more like government regulation of electric utility rate setting than a decision dampening speech about ongoing political campaigns. Because any limitation on speech was outweighed by the need to avoid the appearance of corruption and to promote fair and informed decision making by the electorate, the majority found the First Amendment no barrier.

The practical effect of *McConnell* was limited. Money in politics, like water everywhere, seeks its own level, and money simply flowed into unregulated outlets: $650 million in 2004. But the theoretical effect of the decision was considerable. There is no logical reason why the majority's rationale could not be applied to limit what the press says—and in the fifteen months leading to passage of McCain-Feingold, the *New York Times* averaged an editorial every three days in favor of campaign finance reform. The decision is also inconsistent with the increased protection of commercial speech over the prior decade. It is almost as if the decision holds political speech to be entitled to less protection than other types of speech. Thus Scalia asked, "Who could have imagined that the same Court which, within the past four years, has sternly disapproved of restrictions upon such inconsequential forms of expression as virtual child pornography, tobacco advertising, dissemination of illegally intercepted communications, [and] sexually explicit cable programming would smile with favor upon a law that cuts to the heart of what the First Amendment is meant to protect: the right to criticize government."[59]

Bush v. Gore

With the 2000 presidential election between George W. Bush and Al Gore hinging on a few votes in Florida, both parties initiated legal challenges, the Republicans first and unsuccessfully in federal court, followed by the Democrats, with better results, in the Democratic Florida Supreme Court. Gore needed manual recounts; because Bush had prevailed in the machine recount, Republicans wanted an end to counting. With the clock ticking toward the moment when the Electoral College would vote, every day that Bush maintained his lead placed him closer to the White House.

Initially the state supreme court extended the date for certification of the election results. After that deadline had passed, the Court vacated the decision and remanded the case so that the Florida court could better explain the legal basis for its decision to change the statutory rules.[60] Pointedly ignoring the remand, a divided Florida Supreme Court ordered a manual recount of all undercounted votes by counties that had yet to complete one. The undercounted votes were ballots on which no vote for president had been registered by the machine count. The Florida court also ruled that results be included from earlier but untimely manual recounts from other counties. It was a huge victory for Gore because it overturned decisions by Florida's secretary of state, a partisan Republican who was also the state co-chair of Bush's Florida campaign.

A day later, with no reservations over entering the ultimate political thicket, a 5–4 Court stayed the Florida order, thereby halting the recount. The stay doomed Gore's chance of prevailing. To grant the stay, the Court had to believe that Bush was likely to prevail on the merits (as he did three days later) and that he would suffer irreparable injury without the stay. But it was Gore who suffered the irreparable injury, because with the manual recount stopped and the clock ticking, he was losing any chance to become president. In an unusual concurring opinion, written because Stevens authored a dissent, Scalia explained how Bush would be irreparably injured without the stay—by casting doubt on the legitimacy of Bush's presidency. Scalia's reasoning was perfectly Orwellian: if the manual recount proceeded, Gore might get the most votes; Americans might therefore think Gore won; this would undermine the legitimacy of Bush's presidency. Hence the recount must be stopped.

Bush v. Gore came down at night, three days after the stay. The five

Republican justices granting the stay—Rehnquist, O'Connor, Scalia, Kennedy, and Thomas—now held that the Florida recount violated equal protection because different counties used different standards to determine the intent of the voter. Their equal protection standard could not be met in Florida, so they did not let the Florida Supreme Court try to create a uniform standard (and therefore possibly continue the vote counting). This sealed Bush's victory, and the next day Gore conceded.

The majority's equal protection standard probably could not have been met by any state in 2000 (or later), so the five solved future problems by saying that the decision was a one-timer, limited "to the present circumstances."[61] Rehnquist, Scalia, and Thomas joined the opinion, but because the three are generally unsympathetic to equal protection claims, especially novel ones, it is likely that they did not really believe the Court's rationale. Instead they indicated that they preferred a rationale based on Article II of the Constitution, providing that the determination of a state outcome in a presidential election is left to the state legislature, not state courts. Then why did they join the equal protection holding? Five justices agreed that Bush had won the election. But six rejected the Article II rationale and seven rejected the equal protection holding. With Bush losing by a majority on each of the two possible rationales for a victory, his presidency might once again look less legitimate. The only way to provide legitimacy was for Rehnquist, Scalia, and Thomas to sign on to a rationale they didn't believe in. In the end Bush won because he split the white male vote and the female vote equally but received 100 percent of the African American vote—meaning, of course, the votes on the Supreme Court.

The result of *Bush v. Gore* was brazen. Could anyone believe that, had all the relevant facts been reversed so that the case was *Gore v. Bush,* the Republican majority on the Court would have used the same rationale to halt the manual recount that might give George W. Bush enough votes to overtake Al Gore's lead? Of course not.

Rehnquist subsequently claimed that the Court's action was necessary to preclude chaos (which meant waiting for the House of Representatives to select Bush). Scalia, and surely others, thought that the Florida Supreme Court was changing the rules on the fly to steal the election for Gore. As between the Florida court and the Court, Scalia had little doubt about who should decide the matter. He also claimed that the Court needed to put an end to the contest, because for the prior three weeks the nation "look[ed] like a fool in the eyes of the world."[62] It was, apparently, one brief shining moment when Scalia cared about world opinion.

In dissent Stevens asserted that it was "perfectly clear [that] the Nation's confidence in the judge as an impartial guardian of the rule of law" had been compromised.[63] But opinion polls showed virtually no change in the public's view of the Court before and after the decision. A *New Yorker* cartoon offers an insight. The cartoon depicts a convict chatting with his cellmate: "I don't know about you, but my confidence in the judge as impartial guardian of the rule of law wasn't that high even before the Supreme Court ruling."[64] Nevertheless, a decision like *Grutter* may have been aided by subsequent buyer's remorse on the part of O'Connor about an administration that offended her.

The Clinton Impeachment

Bush v. Gore was possible only because Al Gore blew the election. He was a terrible candidate, but with the economy booming and no real demand for change, he should have won. Thanks to Clinton's impeachment over his sordid sexual behavior, Gore felt that he had to keep the popular president away from the campaign. This only reinforced Bush's strongest slogan, which indirectly referred to Clinton— the promise to restore integrity to the White House. All of these were unwitting consequences of the unanimous opinion in *Clinton v. Jones*.

Paula Jones filed a sexual harassment suit against Clinton based on alleged actions when he was the governor of Arkansas. He moved to delay the suit until the end of his presidency. The Court rejected his position, noting that giving a deposition would not disrupt his presidency. But it did when Clinton lied about his relationship with a White House intern, Monica Lewinsky.

At this point another Court decision became important. In 1988, over a solo dissent by Scalia, the Court upheld the Ethics in Government Act, which provided for special prosecutors to investigate high-level executive branch wrongdoing.[65] Special prosecutors had worked marvelously well during Watergate, but thereafter the post turned otherwise responsible individuals into monomaniacal fanatics who exceeded any reasonable limits in order to nail their target. Democrats loved them when Republicans were in power and vice versa. The problem was that special prosecutors had unlimited time and money yet no political accountability.

Clinton was already facing a special prosecutor, Kenneth Starr, who was investigating an old Arkansas land deal. Starr received approval to expand his investigation, and in August 1998 Clinton testified (by remote television) to a grand jury. In answers to questions about his deposition in the Paula Jones case, he perjured himself (as he had in that deposition as well). Starr then wrote "the most salacious public document in the history of the republic,"[66] and the House of Representatives, along an almost perfect party-line vote, impeached. With all Senate Democrats voting to acquit, Clinton remained in office, where his popularity was astonishingly high because Starr, a decent man, former federal judge, and solicitor general, and the Republicans had so blatantly overreached. Nevertheless, despite Clinton's continuing popularity, Gore believed that Clinton had to be hidden during the 2000 campaign. Gore went on to lose both his home state of Tennessee and Clinton's Arkansas.

The Court's conclusion in *Clinton v. Jones* that there would be no disruption of the presidency was disastrously wrong. Seventy-five years earlier Chief Justice (and former president) William Howard Taft wrote to incoming justice (and former senator) George Sutherland about the importance of a justice's knowing more than law; a knowledge of politics and of the country was essential, too. If any of the justices deciding *Clinton v. Jones* had been an experienced politician—and Clinton had tried and failed to entice both New York governor Mario Cuomo and Senate majority leader George Mitchell to accept a nomination—maybe the Court would not have been so sanguine. But no justice could have anticipated that Clinton would lie under oath (well, maybe), and Clinton could have solved his problem in any one of three ways: by telling the truth; by not responding to the deposition and thereby suffering a default judgment; or by settling with Jones (as he eventually did).

From 5–4 to 5–4

Because of *Bush v. Gore* there were no retirements in Bush's first term. It would have looked too unseemly for justices who voted with the majority to authorize a president they had selected to select their successors in turn; and those in the minority, needless to say, were not about to hand that president a vacancy to fill. But in the fall of 2004 Rehnquist was diagnosed with the most aggressive form of thyroid cancer. He missed part of the term, and this created expectations of the first vacancy in over a decade. But the term ended, and Rehnquist made no announcement. After checking to make sure she would not upstage any announcement Rehnquist might be planning, O'Connor retired to spend more time with her husband, who was suffering from Alzheimer's.

Bush did not miss on either quality or conservatism with his choice for a replacement. He selected fifty-year-old old federal judge John Roberts, a top Harvard Law School graduate and former Rehnquist clerk, who in both the solicitor general's office and private practice was one of the leading members of the Supreme Court bar. Robert's credentials were the gold standard for possible nominees.

Six weeks later Rehnquist died, and Bush immediately renominated Roberts for the center seat. His hearing before the Senate Judiciary Committee reflected how smart he was and how precisely he knew all the cases. He announced respect for precedent and acknowledged that there is a constitutional right to privacy. He even absurdly analogized a justice to an umpire, as if justices merely apply known rules to recurring situations. Twenty-two Democrats voted no, presumably because they would never support a Republican nominee whose commitment to *Roe v. Wade* was not complete.

Another seat remained to be filled, and with Hurricane Katrina murdering both New Orleans and the aura of competence of the administration, and not only O'Connor and Ginsburg but Laura Bush as well publicly calling for a female appointee, Bush felt that he had no other option. There was a "female Roberts" available, but she had once crossed to the dark side when she argued for Michigan Law School in its affirmative action case. So he selected his own lawyer, Harriet Miers, whose principal qualifications appeared to be gender and unswerving loyalty to Bush. Her nomination outraged conservative activists because she had no developed judicial philosophy and thus might turn out to be a female Souter. When asked who her favorite justice was, she responded Warren—and then had to be prodded to add Burger. After three weeks of public embarrassment and a systematic campaign by the Republican right, she withdrew (even though she probably would have been confirmed).

Bush immediately nominated fifty-five-year-old Samuel Alito, a well-known conservative on a federal court of appeals. Alito, like Roberts, was a Catholic, and after sixteen years of judicial service he had a record that revealed a judicial soft spot for established institutions challenged by individuals. Still, he made the requisite bows to respect for precedent. Democrats on the Judiciary Committee tried unsuccessfully to create so-called "character" issues as a justification for their forthcoming negative votes, and the high (or low) point of the hearings came when Alito's wife broke out in tears at the suggestion that her husband was a closet bigot. Alito was confirmed 58–42, with only four Democrats voting yes.

Despite their obligatory bows to stare decisis in their confirmation hearings, Roberts and Alito, like William Brennan, Lewis Powell, and numerous predecessors, believe most strongly in decisions they feel were correctly decided in the first place. Although no important cases were expressly overruled during their first full term together, in three major areas—abortion, campaign finance, and race—Roberts and Alito voted similarly to Kennedy's previous dissents, thus switching 5–4 decisions to nearly their opposite by a new 5–4 vote. Given the relative ages of the conservatives and the liberals on the Court, the decisions portend a generation of conservative dominance.

The first decision sustained a 2003 congressional ban on so-called partial-birth abortion. The five-Catholic majority opinion by Kennedy accepted the anti-abortion claim that women regret having abortions because an abortion denies the natural love between mother and child. Beyond his concern for the women who change their minds, Kennedy told all women, albeit not as bluntly as Thurgood Marshall told death penalty supporters, that if they were as morally sensitive as he was, they would forgo this gruesome procedure (and, implicitly, choose to give birth). Ginsburg seethed in dissent, comparing the majority's expressions with those of the 124-year-old *Bradwell v. Illinois*. She could not help but interpret Kennedy's opinion as an attack on her entire career. Illustrating how the Court can provide political cover, two prominent Democrats, Senate majority leader Harry Reid and presidential candidate Joseph Biden, condemned the Court for sustaining a statute that both had voted for.

The second decision revisited McCain-Feingold's ban on the broadcasting of so-called "express advocacy" ads mentioning a candidate's name by corporations, whether a General Motors or nonprofits like the American Civil Liberties Union and Wisconsin Right to Life, in the two months (Congress probably wished it had been two years) before an election. Roberts held that only ads explicitly urging a vote for or against a candidate could be prohibited, but otherwise "the tie goes to the speaker, not the censor."[67] The dissenters thought that the majority had made the law's prohibition too easy to circumvent, while a concurring opinion by Scalia, for Kennedy and Thomas, agreed with the dissenters that the Court had overruled part of *McConnell v. FEC* and complained of Roberts's unwillingness to admit it. Scalia noted former House Democratic leader Richard Gephart's assertion that campaign finance reform placed "two important values in direct conflict: freedom of speech and our desire for healthy campaigns in a healthy democracy." Gephart believed that "[y]ou can't have both."[68] Scalia expressed his preference for the Bill of Rights.

The most important of the three decisions concerned school assignment plans in Seattle and Louisville that attempted to forestall resegregation by maintaining some racial balance in each of their schools, doing so by classifying students by race. It was the second time in twenty-five years that the Court faced a voluntary plan by Seattle to overcome the city's de facto residential segregation. The first time, the school district had voluntarily adopted a busing plan. State voters responded by passing a referendum banning the policy. A 5–4 Court held that the referendum ban violated the Equal Protection Clause. Years later, Seattle's new plan used race only in allocating slots to oversubscribed schools. Nevertheless Roberts, for the four conservatives, adhering to the color-blind Constitution Republicans favor, found this modest program unconstitutional. While Kennedy had taken a similar color-blind position in the Michigan affirmative action cases, he moderated his position to something like O'Connor's—that race can be used as a criterion as long as it is not determinative and its effects are disguised in the decision-making process. Thus, while he provided the fifth vote to strike down the programs, Kennedy suggested that attendance zones and school siting could take race into account.

The dissenters were angry, with Breyer making the claim, much repeated by critics of the decision, that it "undermines *Brown*'s promise."[69] He was wrong. It was not the movement conservatives in 2007 who undid *Brown*'s promise; it was the country club Republicans between 1973 and 1976 who ended that promise in *San Antonio Independent School District v. Rodriguez, Milliken v. Bradley,* and *Washington v. Davis.* Subsequent Republican dominance only sealed the deal. Nevertheless, Breyer had a point when one compares the outcomes of the two Seattle cases.

The War on Terror

Beginning in 2004 the Imperial Court faced the imperial presidency in time of war. Traditionally the Court rubberstamps anything the government needs during a war. With the "war on terror" and Americans fighting in both Afghanistan and Iraq, the government claimed to need a lot.

After September 11, 2001, administration lawyers studying legal issues that would be forthcoming agreed unanimously on only one issue—that those captured would be held outside the United States (and therefore, they hoped, outside the law of the United States). Ultimately they decided that captives were not to be considered criminal defendants, thus getting a lawyer and a trial. Nor were they to be prisoners of war, and thereby entitled to the protections of the Geneva Conventions (which White House counsel Alberto Gonzales deemed obsolete, quaint, and inapplicable).[70] Instead they were enemy combatants to be held indefinitely for interrogation.

The initial pair of cases to arise asked (1) whether an American citizen, captured in Afghanistan, could be held as an enemy combatant and denied an opportunity to prove his detention was wrongful, and

(2) whether noncitizens detained abroad had the right to access American courts via habeas corpus to test the legality of their confinement. The same day that arguments were presented for the former, CBS News broke the story of abuses at Abu Ghraib, and while the opinions were being written, the so-called "torture memo" of the Justice Department was released.[71] It claimed that the president had the inherent authority to override a congressional ban on torture. Neither helped the Bush administration.

In *Rasul v. Bush* the Court held that there was preexisting statutory jurisdiction to review the detention of noncitizens held at the Guantanamo Bay Naval Base. Stevens's majority opinion also claimed that the allegations—that those seeking habeas had engaged in neither combat nor acts of terrorism against the United States and were being held in detention without access to counsel or charges of wrongdoing—"unquestionably describe 'custody in violation of the Constitution or laws or treaties of the United States.'"[72]

If noncitizens had a right of access to a federal court, then, a fortiori, citizens, even those detained as enemy combatants (a category defined specifically to fit the facts of battlefield capture), had at least that right also, and *Hamdi v. Rumsfeld* said so. With the exception of Thomas, the justices were unimpressed by the executive's claim that the principles of separation of powers meant that courts should have no role in this aspect of the war on terror.

No opinion garnered a majority of the justices. O'Connor for Rehnquist, Kennedy, and Breyer emphasized that the congressional authorization of the use of force also authorized detention but might not authorize prolonged detention, which "carries the potential to become a means for oppression and abuse."[73] She also concluded that due process required some ability to contest the facts supporting detention. Thus there had to be a fair hearing before a neutral tribunal. Souter, with Ginsburg, found that only a clear expression of congressional intent could justify holding an American citizen without trial, and that the authorization of force was not such a declaration. Scalia, with Stevens, went further and concluded that, to hold an American, the government must either try him criminally or else obtain a statutory suspension of the writ of habeas corpus.

Thomas's lone dissent tracked the Bush administration position—that the judiciary lacked the expertise to second-guess the executive. As long as the executive was acting in good faith to defend the public, it had plenary authority to detain a citizen captured abroad.

Immediately after the decision, the Defense Department created tribunals to review the status of all the detainees at Guantanamo, and the government released Hamdi to Saudi Arabia (once he renounced his American citizenship). After holding him without charges for three years, the government stated that he no longer posed a threat to the United States.

Before the Court heard another war on terror case, two separate developments occurred. First, there were leaks to the news media of heretofore secret and perhaps illegal programs.[74] The second development was passage of the Detainee Treatment Act (DTA) of 2006, which required adherence to the Geneva Conventions but also withdrew jurisdiction of federal courts to hear habeas petitions by Guantanamo detainees. In combination these developments suggested an executive branch that believed it could fight the war on terror without congressional help (or oversight) and a (Republican) Congress that believed the judiciary should keep out of it.

Hamdan v. Rumsfeld was a habeas challenge to the military tribunals created to try detainees. Hamdan, arrested in November 2001 but not charged until after *Hamdi*, challenged the definition of the substantive offense he was charged with—joining an enterprise dedicated to attacking civilians—as well as the structures and procedures of the military commissions. The Court, over dissents by Thomas, Scalia, and Alito (Roberts being disqualified because he had participated in the opinion below anticipating the position of the dissenters), first concluded that the DTA did not apply to Hamdan's case. The majority then held that Congress had not authorized the tribunals, and indeed they were contrary to the Uniform Code of Military Justice and the Geneva Conventions. In an extraordinary declaration the Court stated, "[T]he Executive is bound to comply with the Rule of Law that prevails in this jurisdiction," thereby making clear that the executive was not acting in accordance with the "Rule of Law."[75]

Breyer's concurring opinion twice stated that the president could go to Congress to seek whatever authority he deemed necessary. With his hand forced by *Hamdan,* that is exactly what Bush did, and the supine Republican Congress, abetted by electorally frightened Democrats, responded in barely over three weeks with the Military Commissions Act (MCA) of 2006, giving Bush everything he wanted—including the ability to use evidence obtained by torture prior to December 20, 2005, as well as a specific provision eliminating judicial review except by a single appeal of a verdict by a military commission (limited to issues of law and not fact). Breyer had stated that the Court's "conclusion ultimately rests upon a single ground: Congress had not issued the Executive a 'blank check.'"[76] With the MCA, Congress deposited that check in the executive's account. Some members of Congress knew that they had checked their principles at the door. Senate Judiciary chairman Arlen Specter, for instance, acknowledged that the MCA was unconstitutional and voted aye anyway.

Whether the MCA is consistent with the Constitution is a contested question. If Bush had asked for the MCA in 2003, Congress would have readily handed it to him, and its chances of approval would have been far greater prior to the 2006 elections. Now, however, there are two ways to view *Hamdan.* One is based on separation of powers, a demand that Congress be brought into the process of deciding how to treat detainees. The other is a "Rule of Law" demand that procedures be consistent with the Due Process Clause. After the Court successfully cut Congress in, Congress tried to cut the Court out with the

MCA. Not surprisingly there were challenges to the MCA even before the commissions conducted any trials.

Events undermined the military commission system, beginning with the repudiation of the Republicans in the 2006 midterm elections. In the eighteen months after the Democratic victories, more and more information about the administration's policies on detainees became public. The first challenge to the MCA was denied review over three dissents. Then, almost three months later, after an officer involved with the commissions called the supposed trials a farce, the Court agreed to hear the case, meaning that two justices who had previously voted not to review (Kennedy and Stevens) switched.

Subsequent news reports disclosed that officials at the highest levels of the administration had met in the White House to discuss which detainees to torture and what coercive means should be used. And it appeared that torture may have been widespread. Prosecutors were also told there could be no acquittals (because otherwise how could the years of detention be justified?). All in all, the executive branch had deemed the "Rule of Law" outmoded in a post-9/11 world.

With Roberts able to participate, a 5–4 vote seemed probable, and given Kennedy's switch plus his connections with European jurists, he was highly likely to vote with the liberals. In June 2008 Kennedy indeed authored the 5–4 rebuke to both the administration and the formerly Republican Congress by holding that the denial of habeas in the MCA was unconstitutional and that detainees had a right to a habeas hearing in a federal court.[77] Combat review status tribunals were deemed an inadequate substitute for habeas because a judge can order a prisoner released. This was the ultimate defeat of the administration's legal theory for holding detainees offshore—because the Court ruled that detainees did have rights under the Constitution and federal courts could enforce them.

Roberts's dissent (joined by the other three conservatives) asserted that the decision was premature and accused the majority of judicial triumphalism. The majority felt, however, that after six years of confinement, and with the prospect of lifetime incarceration in case of possible mistaken imprisonment, action now was necessary. (When Hamdan complained that he had won at the Court and yet received nothing for it, the prosecutor rejoined that he had his name and his victory in the law books.) Scalia's dissent claimed that the Court's decision would cost American lives. He didn't consider whether policies toward detainees might also cost American lives.

Republicans and Democrats split completely over the decision. Soon-to-be Republican standard-bearer John McCain proclaimed it among the worst in American history. His Democratic counterpart, Barack Obama, hailed it as a step "toward reestablishing our credibility as a nation committed to the rule of law."[78]

As it had before, the Court left important questions unanswered: What is the substantive standard justifying continued detention? Does the decision affect those whom the government intends to try by military commission? Do the procedures before the commissions comport with due process?

What does not wait for the future is a Court of nine justices, each confident in his or her ability to mold the Constitution in order to solve some of America's contentious issues—although, it must be noted (contra Tocqueville), not the hard ones like dealing with the Wall Street financial crisis, health care, Social Security, trade policy, immigration, the alternative minimum tax, and the deficit, as well as Iraq, Iran, Pakistan, Russia, and North Korea. Yet, however confident and however pretentious, the Court will continue to function as it has for most of its existence—to harmonize the Constitution with the demands of majoritarian politics.

Chronology

1781 Articles of Confederation

1783 Treaty of Paris

1787 Philadelphia Convention

1788 Constitution ratified

1789 First Judiciary Act

1791 Bill of Rights ratified

1793 *Chisholm v. Georgia* (out-of-state citizen v. state)
Neutrality Proclamation

1795 Jay's Treaty ratified

1798 Eleventh Amendment ratification announced
Alien and Sedition Acts
Virginia and Kentucky Resolutions

1800 Jefferson beats Adams

1801 House selects Jefferson over Burr
John Marshall appointed Chief Justice
Judiciary Act of 1801

1802 Judiciary Act of 1802

1803   *Marbury v. Madison* (judicial review)
       Stuart v. Laird (Judiciary Act of 1802)
       Louisiana Purchase

1804   House impeaches Samuel Chase

1805   Senate acquits Chase

1808   Embargo

1810   *Fletcher v. Peck* (Yazoo)

1811   Joseph Story to Court

1812   *U.S. v. Hudson and Goodwin* (no common law crimes)

1816   *Martin v. Hunter's Lessee* (review of state court decisions)
       Bank of the United States rechartered

1819   *McCulloch v. Maryland* (upholding Bank of the United States and
          broad national power)
       Dartmouth College v. Woodward (state charters as contracts)

1820   Missouri Compromise

1824   *Gibbons v. Ogden* (congressional power over interstate commerce)

1825   *The Antelope* (positive law trumps natural law on slavery)

1828   Tariff of Abominations

1830   *Cherokee Nation v. Georgia* (no original jurisdiction for Indian tribes)

1831   *Worcester v. Georgia* (Georgia bound by treaties between U.S. and
          Indians)

1832   Jackson's vetoes rechartering Bank of the United States
       Nullification crisis

1836   Roger B. Taney appointed chief justice

1837   Court expanded to nine justices
       Charles River Bridge v. Warren Bridge (chartering competing bridge not
          a Contracts Clause violation)

1841   Tyler vetoes rechartering Bank of the United States
       The Amistad (freeing African slaves who commandeered Spanish
          ship)

1845   Texas joins Union

1846 Mexican War

1850 Compromise of 1850

1854 Kansas-Nebraska Act

1856 Bleeding Kansas

1857 *Dred Scott v. Sandford* (Missouri Compromise unconstitutional)
Lecompton Constitution

1858 Lincoln-Douglas Debates

1859 John Brown's raid on Harper's Ferry

1860 Lincoln elected president

1861 Civil War

1862 Samuel Miller to Court

1863 *Prize Cases* (presidential blockade constitutional)
Stephen Field to Court

1865 Lincoln assassinated
Thirteenth Amendment ratified

1866 Fourteenth Amendment proposed
Ex parte Milligan (right to be tried in civilian court)
Republicans sweep Northern elections

1867 Military Reconstruction

1868 Andrew Johnson impeached and acquitted
Ex parte McCardle (stripping Court of jurisdiction)
Fourteenth Amendment ratified
Grant elected president

1870 Fifteenth Amendment ratified
Hepburn v. Griswold (first Legal Tender Case)
Joseph Bradley to Court

1871 *Knox v. Lee* (second Legal Tender Case)

1873 Panic of 1873
Slaughter-House Cases (state-granted monopolies and Fourteenth
    Amendment)
Bradwell v. Illinois (barring women from becoming lawyers)

1876   Hayes-Tilden election

1877   Election Commission supports Hayes
Reconstruction ends
John Marshall Harlan to Court
Munn v. Illinois (regulating maximum prices)

1878   *Reynolds v. U.S.* (polygamy)

1880   *Strauder v. West Virginia* (racial discrimination on juries)

1883   Civil Rights Cases (public accommodations)

1887   Interstate Commerce Act

1889   David Brewer to Court

1890   Sherman Antitrust Act

1893   Panic of 1893

1894   Democrats decimated in congressional elections

1895   *Pollock v. Farmers' Loan and Trust* (income tax)
U.S. v. E. C. Knight (Sherman Act)
In re Debs (injunction against Pullman Strike)
Rufus Peckham to Court

1896   McKinley beats Bryan
Plessy v. Ferguson ("separate but equal")

1898   Spanish-American War
Allgeyer v. Louisiana (liberty of contract)

1901   *Insular Cases* (does the Constitution follow the flag?)

1902   Oliver Wendell Holmes to Court

1905   *Lochner v. New York* (limiting hours of work)

1906   Hepburn Act

1908   *Muller v. Oregon* (limiting hours of work for women)

1913   Sixteenth and Seventeenth amendments ratified

1916   Louis D. Brandeis to Court

1917   World War I

1918   *Hammer v. Dagenhart* (child labor)

1919   *Debs v. U.S.* (dissent during war)
         Abrams v. U.S. (dissent during war)
         Prohibition

1923   *Adkins v. Children's Hospital* (minimum wage for women)

1929   Great Depression begins

1930   Charles Evans Hughes appointed chief justice

1932   Roosevelt wins landslide victory

1933   The Hundred Days

1934   *Home Building and Loan v. Blaisdell* (Minnesota mortgage
         moratorium)
         Nebbia v. New York (minimum price controls)

1935   *Schecter Poultry v. U.S.* (National Industrial Recovery Act)

1936   *U.S. v. Butler* (Agricultural Adjustment Act)
         Carter v. Carter Coal (Guffey Coal Act)
         New York ex rel. Morehead v. Tipaldo (minimum wage for women)
         Brown v. Mississippi (coerced confessions)
         Roosevelt wins landslide reelection

1937   Court-packing plan
         West Coast Hotel v. Parrish (minimum wage for women)
         NLRB v. Jones and Laughlin Steel (National Labor Relations Act)
         Hugo Black to Court

1939   Felix Frankfurter and William O. Douglas to Court

1940   *Chambers v. Florida* (coerced confessions)
         Minersville School District v. Gobitis (first flag salute case)

1941   *U.S v. Darby Lumber* (Fair Labor Standards Act)
         Robert Jackson to Court
         World War II

1942   Japanese Exclusion Orders
         Wickard v. Filburn (the "Wheat" case)

1943   *West Virginia v. Barnette* (second flag salute case)
         Hirabayashi v. U.S. (curfew for Japanese Americans)

1944   Smith v. Allright (all-white primary)
        Korematsu v. U.S. (Japanese relocation)

1946   Churchill's "Iron Curtain" speech

1947   Everson v. New Jersey (wall of separation between church and state)

1951   Dennis v. U.S. (Smith Act prosecution of communist leaders)

1952   Youngstown Sheet and Tube v. Sawyer (the Steel Seizure case)

1953   Earl Warren appointed chief justice

1954   Brown v. Board of Education [Brown I] (school desegregation)

1955   Brown v. Board of Education [Brown II] ("all deliberate speed")

1956   "Southern Manifesto"
        William J. Brennan to Court

1957   "Red Monday" (major domestic security policies struck down)
        Eisenhower sends troops to Little Rock

1958   Cooper v. Aaron (Little Rock desegregation)

1959   Barenblatt v. U.S. (House Un-American Activities Committee)

1960   First "sit-in" demonstration

1961   In re Anastaplo (state bar inquiry into communism)
        Freedom Rides begin
        Mapp v. Ohio (the Exclusionary Rule)

1962   Engel v. Vitale (school prayer)
        Baker v. Carr (courts can rule on legislative malapportionment)
        Frankfurter suffers strokes, replaced by Arthur Goldberg

1963   Demonstrations in Birmingham
        Gideon v. Wainwright (right to counsel)
        John Kennedy assassinated

1964   New York Times v. Sullivan (right to criticize government)
        Reynolds v. Sims (one person, one vote)
        Escobedo v. Illinois (confessions)
        Civil Rights Act of 1964
        Lyndon Johnson elected in landslide

1965   Demonstrations in Selma, Alabama
        Griswold v. Connecticut (anti-contraceptive statute)
        Vietnam escalation
        Voting Rights Act of 1965
        Race riot in Watts

1966   *Miranda v. Arizona* (the Miranda warnings)
        Summer race riots

1967   Thurgood Marshall to Court
        Playboy publisher Hugh Hefner on cover of *Time*
        "Long Hot Summer" of race riots

1968   Martin Luther King Jr. assassinated
        Robert Kennedy assassinated
        Green v. New Kent County (freedom of choice desegregation plans)
        Abe Fortas nomination for chief justice filibustered
        Richard Nixon elected president

1969   *Brandenburg v. Ohio* (most speech protective test ever)

1971   *Swann v. Charlotte-Mecklenburg* (busing)
        Pentagon Papers (prior restraints against publication)
        Reed v. Reed (gender discrimination)

1972   *Furman v. Georgia* (death penalty)
        Lewis Powell and William Rehnquist to Court

1973   *Roe v. Wade* (abortion)
        San Antonio Independent School District v. Rodriquez (school
          financing)
        Frontiero v. Richardson (gender discrimination)
        Saturday Night Massacre

1974   *Milliken v. Bradley* (interdistrict busing)
        U.S. v. Nixon (Watergate Tapes case)

1976   John Paul Stevens to Court
        Washington v. Davis (test for Fourteenth Amendment violation)
        Buckley v. Valeo (campaign finance)
        Gregg v. Georgia (capital punishment)

1978   *Board of Regents v. Bakke* (affirmative action in higher education)

1980   Ronald Reagan elected president

1981   Sandra Day O'Connor to Court

1984   *Lynch v. Donnelly* (municipal Nativity scene)

1985   *Garcia v. San Antonio Metropolitan Transport* (federal regulation of municipal wages and hours)

1986   *Bowers v. Hardwick* (homosexual sodomy)
        Rehnquist moved to chief justice, Antonin Scalia to Court

1987   Robert Bork nomination defeated

1988   Anthony Kennedy to Court
        Hustler Magazine v. Falwell (reaffirming expansive speech rights)

1989   *Webster v. Reproductive Health Services* (refusing to overrule *Roe v. Wade*)
        J. C. Croson v. Richmond (affirmative action in city hiring)
        Berlin Wall falls

1990   David Souter to Court
        Iraq invades Kuwait

1991   *Rust v. Sullivan* (abortion gag order)
        Clarence Thomas to Court
        Soviet Union breaks up and the supposed "End of History"

1992   *Planned Parenthood v. Casey* (refusing to overrule *Roe v. Wade*)
        Lee v. Weisman (prayer at graduation)

1993   *Shaw v. Reno* (racial gerrymandering)
        Ruth Bader Ginsburg to Court

1994   Stephen Breyer to Court
        Republicans win congressional elections

1995   *U.S. v. Lopez* (Gun-Free School Zones Act)
        Adarand Constructors v. Pena (affirmative action)
        Rosenberger v. University of Virginia (refusal to fund student religious group)

1996   *Romer v. Evans* (Colorado's Amendment 2)
        U.S. v. Virginia (VMI must admit women)

1997   *City of Boerne v. Flores* (Religious Freedom Restoration Act)
       Printz v. U.S. (use of state officials to implement Brady Bill)
       Clinton v. Jones (presidential deposition in civil suit)

2000   *U.S. v. Morrison* (Violence Against Women Act)
       Dickerson v. U.S. (reaffirming Miranda)
       Bush v. Gore (the 2000 Florida election)

2001   9/11 and the War on Terror

2002   *Zelman v. Harris* (vouchers at religious schools)

2003   *Grutter v. Bollinger* (affirmative action in higher education)
       Lawrence v. Texas (homosexual sodomy)
       McConnell v. FEC (campaign finance reform)

2004   *Locke v. Davie* (refusal to fund pastoral education)
       Vieth v. Jubelirer (gerrymandering)
       Hamdi v. Rumsfeld (access to habeas corpus for Guantanamo Bay
         prisoners)

2005   *Kelo v. New London* (eminent domain)
       Van Orden v. Perry (Ten Commandments)
       John Roberts appointed chief justice

2006   Samuel Alito to Court
       Hamdan v. Rumsfeld (presidential military commissions)
         Military Commissions Act

2007   Democrats retake Congress
       Gonzales v. Carhart (partial birth abortion)
       Federal Election Commission v. Wisconsin Right to Life (issue
         advertisements)
       Parents Involved v. Seattle School Dist. (racial assignments)

2008   *Boumediene v. Bush* (access to habeas corpus for Guantanamo Bay
         prisoners)

Notes

.

1. Very Modest Beginnings

1. Washington to Jefferson, May 30, 1787, in 3 *The Records of the Federal Convention of 1787*, 31 (Max Farrand, ed., 3 vols., 1937).

2. Article 2, Articles of Confederation, in *Basic Documents on the Confederation and Constitution*, 24 (Richard B. Morris, ed., 1970).

3. Article 3, id.

4. Preamble and Article 13, id. at 24, 32.

5. George Mason to Patrick Henry, May 6, 1783, id. at 58 (Mason did not concur with those sentiments).

6. *Dunlop v. Ball*, 6 U.S. (2 Cranch) 180, 182–183 (1804).

7. Article 7 of the Treaty of Paris, in Morris, *Basic Documents*, at 38.

8. Quoted in Richard B. Morris, *The Forging of the Union, 1781–89*, 194 (1987).

9. David Howell to Wm. Greene, July 30, 1782, in 18 *Letters of Delegates to Congress, 1774–1789*, 681 (Paul H. Smith, ed., 1991).

10. Quoted in Morris, *Forging*, at 151.

11. *The Federalist* (J. R. Pole, ed., 2005), No. 10, at 54 (Madison).

12. Washington to Henry Lee, October 31, 1786, in Morris, *Basic Documents*, at 162.

13. 3 Farrand, *Records*, at 14.

14. 1 Farrand, *Records*, at 262.

15. 1 Farrand, *Records*, at 35.

16. Quoted in Morris, *Forging*, at 286.

17. 2 Farrand, *Records*, at 417.

18. *The Federalist* Nos. 13, 15, 22, 23, and 37, at 66, 76, 119, 124, and 193 (4 Hamilton; 1 Madison).

19. 2 Farrand, *Records*, at 299.

20. Id. at 27.

21. Id. at 28.

22. *The Federalist* No. 51 at 281 (Madison).

23. 2 *Elliot's Debates on the Federal Constitution*, 469 (Jonathan Elliot, ed., 1907).

24. *The Federalist* No. 40 at 217 (Madison).

25. Brutus No. 12, in 2 *The Complete Anti-Federalist*, 425 (Herbert J. Storing, ed., 1981).

26. Washington's letter of transmittal, September 15, 1787, quoted in Robert Middlekauff, *The Glorious Cause*, 674 (rev. ed. 2005).

27. Quoted in Ron Chernow, *Alexander Hamilton*, 229 (2004).

28. Quoted in Morris, *Forging*, at 269.

29. Id. at 277. Hamilton put it more quaintly by stating that "had the deliberations been open while going on, the clamours of faction would have prevented any satisfactory result." Chernow, *Hamilton*, at 228.

30. Quoted in Larry Kramer, *The People Themselves*, 82 (2004).

31. *The Federalist* No. 78 at 415 (Hamilton).

32. 2 *Complete Anti-Federalist* at 438.

33. Jefferson to Madison, December 20, 1787, in 12 *The Papers of Thomas Jefferson*, 440 (Julian P. Boyd, ed., 1955).

34. Jefferson to Madison, March 15, 1789, in 14 *Papers of Thomas Jefferson*, 659 (Julian P. Boyd, ed., 1958).

35. Inaugural Address, April 30, 1789, in 1 *Messages and Papers of the Presidents* (James D. Richardson, ed., 1897).

36. 1 *Gales and Seaton's Register of Debates in Congress*, 449 (Joseph Gales Jr., and William W. Seaton, eds., 1856).

37. Id. at 452.

38. Patrick Henry to Richard Henry Lee, August 28, 1789, in *Creating the Bill of Rights*, 289 (Helen E. Veit, Kenneth E. Bowling, and Charlene Bangs Bickford, eds., 1991).

39. Lee to Patrick Henry, September 14, 1789, quoted in Wythe Holt, "'The Federal Courts Have Enemies in All Who Fear Their Influence Upon State Objects,'" 36 *Buffalo Law Review* 301, 339 (1987).

40. Notes for Remarks on Judiciary Bill (June 23, 1789), reprinted in 4 *The Documentary History of the Supreme Court of the United States, 1789–1800*, 416 (Maeva Marcus, ed., 1988).

41. Letter of September 27, 1789, quoted in 1 Charles Warren, *The Supreme Court in United States History*, 31–32 (rev. ed. 1926).

42. Samuel Chase to Hannah Chase, February 4, 1800, in Maeva Marcus, James R. Perry, James M. Buchanan, Christine R. Jordan, and Steven L. Tull, "The Hardships of Supreme Court Service, 1790–1800," in *Yearbook 1984: Supreme Court Historical Society* 118, 124 (1984).

43. Quoted in Walter Stahr, *John Jay*, 279 (2005).

44. Iredell to his wife, Hannah Iredell, May 10, 1790, in Holt, "Federal Courts Have Enemies," at 309.

45. Iredell to Timothy Pickering, June 16, 1798, id. at 308.

46. John Jay, Charge to the New York Grand Jury (April 12, 1790), in 1 *Documentary History* at 25–30.

47. John Jay, Charge to the New York Grand Jury (July 28, 1792), in 2 *Documentary History* at 253–257.

48. James Wilson, Charge to the Massachusetts Grand Jury (June 7, 1793), id. at 396, 400.

49. John Jay, Charge to the Virginia Grand Jury (May 22, 1793), id. at 360.

50. James Iredell, Charge to the Pennsylvania Grand Jury (April 11, 1799), in 3 *Documentary History* at 332, 350.

51. Quoted in William R. Casto, *The Supreme Court in the Early Republic*, 175 (1995).

52. Madison to Henry Lee, April 15, 1792, quoted in Julius Goebel Jr., *Antecedents and Beginnings to 1801*, 562 (1971).

53. 3 *Correspondence and Public Papers of John Jay*, 488 (Henry P. Johnston, ed., 4 vols., 1970).

54. 3 U.S. (3 Dall.) at 16.

55. Kramer, *The People Themselves*, at 4.

56. *The Federalist* No. 81 at 433 (Hamilton).

57. Id.. at 476.

58. Id.. at 479.

59. Quoted in William Swindler, "Mr. Chisholm and the Eleventh Amendment," 1981 *Journal of Supreme Court History* 14, 16.

60. Jay to John Adams, January 2, 1801, in 4 *Jay Correspondence* at 285.

2. The Court in a Two-Party Republic

1. John Marshall, 5 *The Life of George Washington*, 33 (1807).

2. Jefferson to M. Volney, December 9, 1795, in 28 *Papers of Thomas Jefferson*, 551 (John Catanzariti, ed., 2000).

3. 3 U.S. (3 Dall.) 199, 210 (1796).

4. Iredell's Notes of Argument, February 23, 24, and 25, 1796, in 7 *Documentary History of the Supreme Court of the United States, 1789–1800*, 468 (Maeva Marcus, ed., 2003).

5. Id. at 476–477.

6. Oliver Ellsworth had taken his seat after oral argument; Chase was ill; and James Wilson had sat on the court below (where he upheld the tax).

7. *Hylton v. United States,* 3 Dall. at 173 (Chase); there is slightly different language to the same effect in a more extended discussion by Paterson, id. at 178.

8. Message to the Special Session, May 16, 1797, in 1 *Messages and Papers of the Presidents,* 233, 235 (James Richardson, ed., 1897).

9. Message to Congress, March 19, 1798, id. at 264, 265.

10. Jefferson to Madison, March 21, 1798, in 30 *Papers of Thomas Jefferson,* 191 (Barbara B. Oberg, ed., 2003).

11. Quoted in John Morton Smith, *Freedom's Fetters,* 14 (1956).

12. Hamilton to Rufus King, June 16, 1798, in 21 *Papers of Alexander Hamilton,* 490 (Harold C. Syrett, ed., 1974).

13. 1 Stat. 570, 571 (1798).

14. 1 Stat. 596 (1798).

15. *The Federalist* (J. R. Pole, ed., 2005), No. 84, 455 (Hamilton).

16. 8 *Annals of Congress,* 2097 (1798) (Congressman John Allen).

17. Id. at 2112 (Congressman Samuel Dana).

18. Id. at 2146 (Congressman Harrison Otis).

19. Id. at 2167 (Congressman Robert Goodloe Harper).

20. Quoted in Smith, *Freedom's Fetters,* at 229.

21. Francis Wharton, *State Trials of the United States,* 333 (1849).

22. Jefferson to John Taylor, November 26, 1798, in 30 *Papers of Thomas Jefferson* at 588.

23. Third Kentucky Resolution, in 4 *Elliot's Debates on the Federal Constitution,* 541 (Jonathan Elliot, ed., 2nd ed., 1907).

24. 10 *Annals of Congress,* 6th Cong., 952 (1801).

25. Quoted in Geoffrey Stone, *Perilous Times,* 68 (2004).

26. Wharton, *State Trials,* at 676.

27. *United States v. Williams,* id. at 652, 653.

28. *New London Bee,* October 30, 1799, quoted in William Casto, *The Supreme Court in the Early Republic: The Chief Justiceships of John Jay and Oliver Ellsworth,* 153 (1995).

29. Quoted in 1 Charles Warren, *The Supreme Court in United States History,* 163 (rev. ed. 1926).

30. *Federalist* No. 80 at 422 (Hamilton).

31. Jefferson to Gideon Granger, August 13, 1800, in 32 *Papers of Thomas Jefferson,* 96 (Barbara B. Oberg, ed., 2006).

32. St. George Tucker, *Blackstone, Commentaries on the Laws of England,* Appendix E, 380 (1803).

33. Quoted in Warren, *History*, at 167.

34. Adams to Jay, December 19, 1804, in *Correspondence and Public Papers of John Jay*, 284 (Henry P. Johnston, ed., 1890).

35. Jefferson to Madison, June 29, 1792, in 24 *Papers of Thomas Jefferson*, 133 (John Catanzariti, ed., 1990).

36. Jefferson to Madison, December 26, 1800, in 32 *Papers of Thomas Jefferson* at 358.

37. Morris to Robert R. Livingston, February 20, 1801, quoted in 3 Jared Sparks, *The Life of Gouverneur Morris*, 153–154 (1832).

38. Marshall to Charles Cotesworth Pinckney, March 4, 1801, in 6 *Papers of John Marshall*, 89 (Charles F. Hobson, ed., 1990).

39. Jefferson to James Monroe, March 3, 1801, quoted in George L. Haskins and Herbert A. Johnson, *Foundations of Power: John Marshall, 1801–15*, 149 (1981).

40. Jefferson to Benjamin Rush, December 20, 1801, id. at 153.

41. Jefferson to John Dickinson, December 18, 1801, in 9 *The Writings of Thomas Jefferson*, 345 (Paul Leicester Ford, ed., 1905).

42. Quoted in Haskins and Johnson, *Foundations of Power*, at 164.

43. Quoted in Richard Ellis, *The Jeffersonian Crisis*, 57 (1971).

44. Matoon to Timothy Dwight, February 11, 1802, quoted in Bruce Ackerman, *The Failure of the Founding Fathers*, 157 (2005).

45. John Rutledge to James A. Bayard, March 26, 1802, quoted id. at 158.

46. The letter does not survive, but he copied Cushing, whose wife then copied Abigail Adams. Ackerman, *Failure*, at 170.

47. 5 U.S. (1 Cranch) at 162.

48. Id. at 162.

49. Id. at 163.

50. The legal issues are analyzed well in William Van Alstyne, "A Critical Guide to *Marbury v. Madison*," 1969 *Duke Law Journal* 1.

51. "In all Cases affecting Ambassadors, other public Ministers and Consuls, and those in which a State shall be a Party, the Supreme Court shall have original Jurisdiction. In all the other Cases before mentioned, the supreme Court shall have appellate Jurisdiction, both as to Law and Fact, with such Exceptions, and under such Regulations as the Congress shall make."

52. *Stuart*, 5 U.S. (1 Cranch) at 309.

53. Id.

54. *Marbury* is cited on sixty-three different pages in Laurence Tribe's treatise *American Constitutional Law* (1999). *Stuart* is never cited.

55. 5 U.S. (1 Cranch) at 110.

56. 14 *Annals of Congress* at 674.

57. Id.

58. Jefferson to J. H. Nicholdson, May 13, 1803, in 4 *Writings of Thomas Jefferson,* 486 (H. A. Washington, ed., 9 vols., 1854).

59. Quoted in Ackerman, *Failure,* at 201.

60. Marshall to Chase, January 23, 1805 [the letter is misdated as 1804], in 6 *Papers of John Marshall* at 347.

61. Key to J. London, January 4, 1808, quoted in H. G. Connor, "The Granville Estate and North Carolina," 62 *University of Pennsylvania Law Review* 671, 692 (1914).

62. Jefferson to Albert Gallatin, August 11, 1808, in 5 *Writings of Thomas Jefferson* at 336.

63. 2 Stat. 501 (1808).

64. Jefferson to Albert Gallatin, May 6, 1808, in 5 *Writings of Thomas Jefferson* at 287.

65. Caesar Rodney to Jefferson, October 31, 1808, in Warren, *History,* at 336.

66. *United States v. Hoxie,* 26 F. Cas. 397 (C.C.D. Vt. 1808).

67. Jefferson to Thomas Ritchie, December 25, 1820, in 10 *Works of Thomas Jefferson,* 170 (Paul Leicester Ford, ed., 1905).

68. Jefferson to John W. Eppes, May 28, 1807, id. at 413.

69. Jefferson to Madison, October 15, 1810, in 2 *Papers of James Madison,* 581 (Presidential Series, J. C. A. Stagg, Jeanne Kerr Cross, and Susan Holbrook Perdue, eds., 1984).

70. 11 U.S. (7 Cranch) at 32.

71. Id. at 33.

72. *United States v. Burr,* 25 F. Cas. 55, 180 (C.C.D. Va. 1807).

73. Jefferson to Madison, May 25, 1810, in 2 *Papers of James Madison* at 356.

74. Johnson to Jefferson, December 10, 1822, in Donald G. Morgan, *Justice William Johnson,* 182 (1954).

75. Story to Henry Heaton, April 8, 1818, in 1 *Life and Letters of Joseph Story,* 303–304 (William W. Story, ed., 1851).

76. First Inaugural Address, March 4, 1801, in 1 *Messages and Papers* at 321.

3. The States and the Republic

1. Quoted in G. Edward White, *The Marshall Court and Cultural Change, 1815–35,* 603 (1988).

2. Quoted in C. Peter Magrath, *Yazoo,* 22 (1966).

3. 2 Stat. 232 (1803).

4. 10 U.S. (6 Cranch) at 132.

5. Id. at 134.

6. Id. at 131.
7. Id. at 133.
8. Id. at 134.
9. Id. at 135.
10. Id. at 143.
11. 17 U.S. (4 Wheat.) at 644.
12. *Hunter v. Martin*, 4 Munf. at 9 (Justice Cabell).
13. Id. at 58–59 (1815) (all the justices).
14. *Martin v. Hunter's Lessee*, 14 U.S. (1 Wheat.) at 324.
15. Id. at 328.
16. Id. at 381 (Johnson concurring).
17. The Bank Bill, February 2, 1791, in 13 *The Papers of James Madison*, 372, 375, 376 (Charles F. Hobson and Robert A. Rutland, eds., 1981).
18. Id. at 380.
19. Opinion on the Constitutionality of the Bill for Establishing a National Bank, February 15, 1791, in 19 *Papers of Thomas Jefferson*, 275, 276 (Julian P. Boyd, ed., 1974).
20. Id.
21. Jefferson to Edward Livingston, April 30, 1800, in 31 *Papers of Thomas Jefferson*, 547 (Barbara B. Oberg, ed., 2004).
22. Veto Message, January 30, 1815, in 1 *Messages and Papers of the Presidents*, 555 (James Richardson, ed., 10 vols., 1899).
23. 17 U.S. (4 Wheat.) at 402.
24. Id. at 400–401.
25. Id. at 400.
26. Id. at 403.
27. Id. at 408.
28. Id. at 421.
29. Id. at 423.
30. Madison to Spencer Roane, September 2, 1819, in 3 *Letters and Other Writings of James Madison*, 143 (1884).
31. Id. at 431.
32. Veto Message, March 3, 1817, in 1 *Messages and Papers* at 584.
33. 3 Stat. 545, 548 (1820).
34. Marshall to Joseph Story, March 24, 1819, in 8 *The Papers of John Marshall*, 280 (Charles F. Hobson, ed., 1995).
35. Marshall to Bushrod Washington, March 24, 1819, id. at 281.
36. *John Marshall's Defense of McCulloch v. Maryland*, 110 (Gerald Gunther, ed., 1969).

37. Jefferson to Thomas Ritchie, December 25, 1820, in 10 *Works of Thomas Jefferson*, 170 (Paul Leichester Ford, ed., 1905).

38. Johnson to James Monroe, n.d., in 1 Charles Warren, *The Supreme Court in United States History*, 596 (rev. ed. 1926).

39. 19 U.S. (6 Wheat.) at 433.

40. Quoted in White, *Marshall Court*, at 521.

41. 22 U.S. (9 Wheat.) at 190.

42. Id. at 194.

43. Id. at 195.

44. Id. at 196–197.

45. *Houston v. Moore*, 18 U.S. (5 Wheat.) (1820) (militia); *Sturges v. Crowninshield*, 17 U.S. (4 Wheat.) 122 (1819) (bankruptcy).

46. *Register of Debates*, 18th Cong. 2nd sess., 585 (February 15, 1825).

47. Quoted in 2 Robert V. Remini, *Andrew Jackson*, 256 (1981).

48. *Cherokee Nation v. Georgia*, 30 U.S. (5 Pet.) at 8.

49. Story to George Ticknor, January 22, 1831, in 2 *Life and Letters of Joseph Story*, 49 (William W. Story, ed., 1851).

50. *Cherokee Nation*, 30 U.S. at 16.

51. Id. at 15.

52. Id. at 17.

53. Id.

54. *Worcester v. Georgia*, 31 U.S. (6 Pet.) at 561.

55. Story to S. W. Story, March 4, 1832, quoted in 2 *Life and Letters* at 87.

56. Jackson to John Coffee, April 7, 1832, in 4 *Correspondence of Andrew Jackson*, 430 (J. Basset, ed., 1933).

57. Veto Message, July 10, 1832, in 2 *Messages and Papers* at 576, 582.

58. Marshall to Story, September 22, 1832, in 12 *Papers of John Marshall*, 238 (Charles F. Hobson, ed., 2006).

59. Story to S. W. Story, January 27, 1833, quoted in 2 *Life and Letters* at 119.

60. 32 U.S. (7 Pet.) at 247.

61. Id. at 250.

62. Webster to Caroline Webster, quoted in Carl B. Swisher, *The Taney Period*, 34 (1974).

63. Story to James Kent in conversation, March 18, 1835, recorded on the flyleaf of Kent's copy of Story on the Constitution, reported in 5 *American Law Review* 368, 369 (1871).

64. James Kent wrote to Story that the two Western judges were "very feeble lights" and that "I respect it [the Court] no longer." Kent to Story, June 23, 1837, quoted in Swisher, *Taney Period*, at 109 n.27.

4. The Sectional Crisis and the Jacksonian Court

1. Alexis de Tocqueville, *Democracy in America*, 280 (Phillips Bradley, ed., 1948).

2. Story to Harriet Martineau, April 7, 1837, in 2 *Life and Letters of Joseph Story*, 277 (William W. Story, ed., 1851).

3. 53 U.S. (12 How.) at 548.

4. Id. at 598 (dissenting).

5. Story to Kent, June 26, 1837, quoted in Charles Fairman, "The Retirement of Federal Judges," 51 *Harvard Law Review* 397, 413 (1938).

6. 48 U.S. (7 How.) at 38–39.

7. Id. at 39.

8. Id. at 47.

9. Rufus King to J. A. King, February 6, 1820, quoted in 1 Charles Warren, *The Supreme Court in United States History*, 544 (rev. ed. 1926).

10. 3 Stat. 545, 548 (1820).

11. Quoted in Leonard L. Richards, *The Slave Power*, 76 (2000).

12. *Elkison v. Deliesseline*, 8 F. Cas. 493 (No. 4366) (C.C.D.S.C. 1823).

13. *Niles Register*, August 23, 1823, quoted in 1 Warren, *History*, at 625.

14. Marshall to Story, September 26, 1823, in 9 *Papers of John Marshall*, 338 (Charles F. Hobson, ed., 1998).

15. *La Jeune Eugenie*, 26 F. Cas. 832 (No. 15,551) (C.C. Mass. 1822).

16. *The Antelope*, 23 U.S. (10 Wheat.) 66, 120 (1825).

17. Id. at 122.

18. *Congressional Globe*, 33rd Cong., 1st sess., App. 53 (1853) (Joshua Giddings of Ohio recounting the speech some years later).

19. *Groves v. Slaughter*, 40 U.S. (15 Pet.) at 508.

20. Id. at 508

21. 41 U.S. (16 Pet.) at 611.

22. Id. at 613.

23. Id. at 627.

24. Id. at 669.

25. 57 *North American Review* (October 1843), quoted in 2 Warren, *History*, at 86.

26. Story to Ezekiel Bacon, April 1, 1844, in 2 *Life and Letters* at 481.

27. 26 U.S. (1 Pet.) at 542.

28. 2 *The Writings and Speeches of Daniel Webster*, 205 (Edward Everett and William Everett, eds., 1903).

29. June 10, 1844, in 4 *Messages and Papers of the Presidents*, 323 (James Richardson, ed., 10 vols., 1899).

30. May 11, 1846, id. at 442.

31. Third Annual Message, December 31, 1855, in 6 *Messages and Papers* at 2877.

32. 3 Stat. 545, 548 (1820).

33. 2 *Collected Works of Abraham Lincoln*, 355 (Roy Basler, ed., 1953).

34. Grier to Buchanan, February 23, 1857, quoted in Donald Fehrenbacher, *The Dred Scott Case*, 312 (1978).

35. Inaugural Address, March 4, 1857, in 5 *Messages and Papers* at 431.

36. 60 U.S. (19 How.) at 405.

37. Id. at 410.

38. Id. at 407.

39. Id. at 448.

40. Id. at 450.

41. House Divided Speech, in 2 *Collected Works* at 467.

42. Kenneth Stampp, *1857 in America*, 103 (1987).

43. *Congressional Globe*, 35th Cong., 1st sess., 941 (1857).

44. Fehrenbacher, *Dred Scott*, at 430.

45. *The Federalist* (J. R. Pole, ed., 2005), No. 10, 51 (Madison).

46. Hammond to William Gilmore Simms, February 7, 1858, in Fehrenbacher, *Dred Scott*, at 480.

47. *Congressional Globe*, 35th Cong., 1st sess., at 345.

48. *The Lincoln-Douglas Debates*, 106 (Freeport, Ill., August 27, 1858) (Harold Holzer, ed., 1993).

49. 2 *Collected Works* at 465.

50. Id. at 461.

51. Fehrenbacher, *Dred Scott*, at 487.

52. Speech at Chicago, July 9, 1858, in Paul Brest and Sanford Levinson, *Processes of Constitutional Decision Making*, 211 (3rd ed. 1993).

53. Speech at Chicago, July 10, 1858, in 2 *Collected Works* at 495.

54. Speech at Springfield, July 17, 1858, in Brest and Levinson, *Processes*, at 212.

55. Speech at Springfield, July 17, 1858, in 2 *Collected Works* at 516.

56. Id.

57. Id. at 517 (quoting Jefferson to a Mr. Jarvis in 1820).

58. *Ableman v. Booth*, 62 U.S. (21 How.) at 515.

59. Id.

60. Id. at 525.

61. Id. at 519.

62. Third Annual Message, December 19, 1859, in 5 *Messages and Papers* at 552, 554.

5. Civil War and Reconstruction

1. Cooper Union Address, New York City, February 27, 1860, in 3 *Collected Works of Abraham Lincoln*, 522 (Roy Basler, ed., 8 vols., 1953).

2. Seward to Frances A. Seward, December 5, 1860, in 2 Frederick W. Seward, *Seward at Washington, as Senator and Secretary of State*, 480 (1891).

3. First Inaugural Address, March 4, 1861, in 4 *Collected Works* at 264, 365.

4. Id. at 265 (emphasis deleted).

5. Taney to Pierce, June 12, 1861, in 10 *American History Review* 368 (1905).

6. *Ex parte Merryman*, 17 F. Cas. 144 (1861).

7. Quoted in Carl B. Swisher, *The Taney Period*, 848 (1974).

8. *Prize Cases*, 67 U.S. (2 Black) 635 (1863).

9. Id. at 669.

10. George S. Boutwell, 2 *Reminiscences of Sixty Years in Public Service*, 29 (1902) (recounting conversation).

11. *Ex parte Vallandigham*, 28 F. Cas. 874 (C.C.S.D. Ohio 1863).

12. *Ex parte Vallandigham*, 68 U.S. (1 Wall.) 243 (1864).

13. Quoted in Eric Foner, *Reconstruction*, 197 (1988).

14. *Richmond Examiner*, January 9, 1866, quoted in Garrett Epps, "The Antebellum Political Background of the Fourteenth Amendment," 67 *Law and Contemporary Problems* 175, 204 (2004).

15. *Congressional Globe*, 39th Cong., 1st sess., 157 (1866).

16. Quoted in Foner, *Reconstruction*, at 268.

17. *Ex parte Milligan*, 71 U.S. (4 Wall.) 2, 127 (1866).

18. Davis to Julius Rockwell, February 24, 1867, quoted in Charles Fairman, *Reconstruction and Reunion: Part I*, 232 (1971).

19. *Nation*, January 10, 1867, 30.

20. *Cummings v. Missouri*, 71 U.S. (4 Wall.) 277 (1867); *Ex parte Garland*, 71 U.S. (4 Wall.) 333 (1867).

21. Quoted in Foner, *Reconstruction*, at 273.

22. *Congressional Globe*, 40th Cong., 2nd sess., 2062 (March 21, 1868).

23. Proclamation No. 11, 15 Stat. 706, 707 (1868).

24. *Ex parte McCardle*, 74 U.S. (7 Wall.) 506, 515 (1869).

25. *Ex parte Yerger*, 75 U.S. (8 Wall.) 85, 104 (1869).

26. 74 U.S. (7 Wall.) at 725.

27. Chase to William Cullen Bryant, February 4, 1862, in Fairman, *Reconstruction*, at 686.

28. 75 U.S. (8 Wall.) at 634.

29. Id. at 637.

30. 79 U.S. (12 Wall.) at 535.

31. Id. at 555.

32. Id. at 556.

33. *Julliard v. Greenman*, 110 U.S. 421 (1884).

34. 83 U.S. (16 Wall.) at 67, 71.

35. Id. at 125.
36. Id. at 78.
37. Id.
38. *Congressional Record*, 43rd Cong., 1st sess., at 342–343 (1874) (James F. Beck).
39. 83 U.S. (16 Wall.) at 122.
40. Id. at 96.
41. Id. at 126.
42. *Bradwell v. Illinois*, 83 U.S. (16 Wall.) 130, 141 (1873).
43. 94 U.S. at 125.
44. Id. at 126.
45. Id. at 134.
46. Id. at 140.
47. Id. at 139.
48. *Butchers' Union v. Crescent City Co.*, 111 U.S. 746 (1884).
49. A. T. Morgan, *Yazoo*, 323 (1884) (emphasis deleted).
50. "Address delivered to the Red Shirt Reunion," August 25, 1909, quoted in Stephen Budiansky, *The Bloody Shirt: Terror after Appomattox*, 6 (2008).
51. Id.
52. *United States v. Cruikshank*, 92 U.S. 542 (1876).
53. 100 U.S. at 308.
54. Id. at 310.
55. *Virginia v. Rives*, 100 U.S. 313 (1880).
56. *Pace v. Alabama*, 106 U.S. 583 (1883).
57. *Congressional* Globe, 43rd Cong., 2nd sess., 1870 (1875).
58. 109 U.S. at 17.
59. Id. at 14
60. Id. at 24.
61. Id. at 26.
62. Id. at 36.
63. Id. at 48.
64. 83 U.S. (16 Wall.) at 123.
65. 109 U.S. at 25.
66. Quoted in Budiansky, *The Bloody Shirt*, at 9.

6. *Industrializing America*

1. February 16, 1887, in 8 *Messages and Papers of the Presidents*, 557 (James D. Richardson, ed., 1897).
2. Roswell Flower, quoted in James W. Ely Jr., *The Chief Justiceship of Melville Weston Fuller, 1888–1910*, 61 (1995).
3. "The Distribution of Property," 27 *American Law Review* 656, 660 (1893).

4. 109 U.S. 3, 24 (1883).

5. "The Centenary of the Supreme Court," address to the New York City Bar Association, 134 U.S. 729, 745 (1889).

6. 123 U.S. at 662.

7. Id. at 664.

8. 128 U.S. at 21.

9. *Brown v. Maryland*, 25 U.S. (12 Wheat.) 419 (1827).

10. *In re Rahrer*, 140 U.S. 545 (1891).

11. *Powell v. Pennsylvania*, 127 U.S. 678 (1888).

12. *Virginia Coupon Cases*, 114 U.S. 269 (1885).

13. *Wabash, St. Louis and Pacific Railway v. Illinois*, 118 U.S. 557 (1886).

14. Id. at 573.

15. *Budd v. New York*, 143 U.S. 517, 548 (1892).

16. *Railroad Commission Cases*, 116 U.S. 307, 331 (1886).

17. 154 U.S. at 399, 410.

18. 26 *Congressional Record* 6637, 53rd Cong., 2nd sess. (1894).

19. 157 U.S. at 583.

20. *Pollock v. Farmers' Loan & Trust*, 158 U.S. 601 (1895).

21. Id. at 635.

22. 157 U.S. at 607.

23. 158 U.S. at 685.

24. Id. at 695.

25. 156 U.S. at 16.

26. Id. at 13.

27. Quoted in Owen M. Fiss, *Troubled Beginnings of the Modern State, 1888–1910*, 59 (1993).

28. David Brewer, "The Nation's Safeguard," in *New York State Bar Association Proceedings*, 37, 46 (1893).

29. 158 U.S. at 581.

30. Id. at 582.

31. *People v. Budd*, 117 N.Y. 1, 68 (1889).

32. Quoted in 2 *History of American Presidential Elections*, 1847 (Arthur Schlesinger and Fred L. Israel, eds., 1971).

33. Quoted in Alan Westin, "The Supreme Court, the Populist Movement, and the Campaign of 1896," 15 *Journal of Politics* 3, 32 (1953).

34. September 12, 1896, reproduced in *The United States Supreme Court*, Plate A-15 (Christopher Tomlins, ed., 2005).

35. Democratic Party Platform, 1900, in *Political Party Platforms*, 210, 211 (Kirk H. Porter, ed., 1924).

36. Finley Peter Dunne, *Mr. Dooley at His Best*, 77 (1938).

37. *Knowlton v. Moore*, 178 U.S. 41 (1900).

38. 188 U.S. 321 (1903).

39. Id at 365.

40. *Hipolite Egg Co. v. United States*, 220 U.S. 45 (1911).

41. *McCray v. United States*, 195 U.S. 27 (1904).

42. *United States v. Trans-Missouri Freight Assn.*, 166 U.S. 290 (1897); *United States v. Joint Traffic Assn.*, 171 U.S. 505 (1898).

43. *Addyston Pipe and Steel v. United States*, 175 U.S. 211 (1899).

44. *Northern Securities Co. v. United States*, 193 U.S. 197 (1904).

45. Id. at 400.

46. Quoted in Fiss, *Troubled Beginnings*, at 137–138.

47. *Standard Oil v. United States*, 221 U.S. 1 (1911).

48. Id. at 104 (emphasis deleted).

49. *ICC v. Cincinnati, New Orleans, and Texas Pacific Railway Co.*, 167 U.S. 479, 494 (1897).

50. *ICC v. Alabama Midland Railway Co.*, 168 U.S. 144 (1897).

51. *ICC v. Illinois Central Railroad Co.*, 215 U.S. 452 (1910).

52. 159 U.S. at 546.

53. 209 U.S. at 204.

54. *Ex parte Ayers*, 123 U.S. 433 (1887).

55. *Gulf, Colorado, and Santa Fe Railway v. Ellis*, 165 U.S. 150 (1897); *Connolly v. Union Sewer Pipe Co.*, 184 U.S. 540 (1902).

56. *Paul v. Virginia*, 75 U.S. (8 Wall.) 168 (1869).

57. 165 U.S. at 589.

58. *Jacobson v. Massachusetts*, 197 U.S. 11 (1905).

59. 169 U.S. at 386.

60. Id. at 397.

61. David Brewer, "Protection to Private Property from Public Attack," Commencement Address, Yale University, 1891, quoted in Paul Kens, *Judicial Power and Reform Politics*, 110 (1990).

62. 198 U.S. at 58.

63. Id. at 56.

64. Id. at 59.

65. Id. at 60.

66. Id. at 75.

67. Id.

68. 208 U.S. at 174.

69. Id. at 175.

70. *Coyle v. Smith*, 221 U.S. 559 (1911).

71. 208 U.S. at 421.

72. *The Late Corporation of the Church of Jesus Christ of Latter-day Saints v. United States*, 136 U.S. 1 (1890).

73. Quoted in Leonard J. Arrington and Davis Bitton, *The Mormon Experience*, 183 (1980).

74. *Chicago, Burlington, & Quincy Railroad v. Chicago*, 166 U.S. 226 (1897).

75. *Patterson v. Colorado*, 205 U.S. 454 (1907); *Pressler v. Illinois*, 116 U.S. 252 (1886); *Hurtado v. California*, 110 U.S. 516 (1884); *Twining v. New Jersey*, 211 U.S. 78 (1908); *Maxwell v. Dow*, 176 U.S. 581 (1900); *O'Neil v. Vermont*, 144 U.S. 323 (1892).

76. *O'Neil*, 144 U.S. 323 (1892).

77. *Patterson*, 205 U.S. 454 (1907).

78. *Maxwell*, 176 U.S. at 615 (Harlan dissenting).

79. *Council v. Western & Atlantic Railroad*, 1 I.C.C. 638 (1887).

80. 163 U.S. at 550.

81. Id. at 559.

82. Id. at 560.

83. Id. at 559.

84. Quoted in Michael McGeer, *A Fierce Discontent*, 10 (2003).

85. Id. at 187.

86. 163 U.S. at 551.

87. *Berea College v. Kentucky*, 211 U.S. 45 (1908).

88. 189 U.S. at 488.

89. Id.

90. *Bailey v. Alabama*, 219 U.S. 219, 244 (1911).

91. 198 U.S. at 76.

7. Progressivism, Normalcy, and Depression

1. *Brushaber v. Union Pacific Railroad*, 240 U.S. 1 (1916).

2. *Pacific States Telephone and Telegraph Co. v. Oregon*, 223 U.S. 118, 143 (1912).

3. Wilson to C. A. Culbertson, May 5, 1916, in *Nomination of Louis D. Brandeis*, Senate Committee Print, 64th Cong., 1st sess., 7628 (1916).

4. Quoted in Alexander M. Bickel and Benno C. Schmidt Jr., *The Judiciary and Responsible Government*, 1910–21, 378 (1984).

5. Theodore Roosevelt, "Judges and Progress," *Outlook*, January 6, 1912, 42.

6. Charles Amidon to Willis Van Devanter, September 7, 1914, in Bickel and Schmidt, *Judiciary and Responsible Government*, at 414.

7. *Second Employers' Liability Cases*, 223 U.S. 1 (1912).

8. 243 U.S. at 346.

9. *Hoke v. United States*, 227 at 323.

10. 247 U.S. at 271.

11. Id. at 273.

12. Id. at 276.

13. Id.

14. Id. at 280.

15. Quoted in Bickel and Schmidt, *Judiciary and Responsible Government*, at 455.

16. Id.

17. 236 U.S. at 17.

18. Id. at 16.

19. *Stettler v. O'Hara*, 243 U.S. 629 (1917).

20. *Adams v. Tanner*, 244 U.S. at 593.

21. Id. at 594.

22. Quoted in David Pietrusza, *1920: The Year of Six Presidents*, 162 (2007).

23. *United States v. Reynolds*, 235 U.S. 133 (1914).

24. *McCabe v. Atchison, Topeka & Santa Fe Railroad*, 235 U.S. at 161.

25. 245 U.S. at 81.

26. *Selective Service Cases*, 245 U.S. 366, 390 (1918).

27. Quoted in Geoffrey Stone, *Perilous Times*, 153 (2004).

28. *Debs v. United States*, 249 U.S. at 212.

29. Id. at 214.

30. Id. at 216.

31. *Abrams v. United States*, 250 U.S. at 629.

32. Id. at 630.

33. *Block v. Hirsh*, 256 U.S. at 156.

34. Id. at 161.

35. *Chastleton Corp. v. Sinclair*, 264 U.S. 543 (1924).

36. Taft to James R. Sheffield, July 8, 1923, quoted in Robert Post, "Federalism, Positive Law, and the Emergence of the American Administrative State," 48 *William and Mary Law Review* 1, 94 (2006).

37. *Wisconsin Railroad Commission v. Chicago, Burlington & Quincy Railroad*, 257 U.S. at 588.

38. 258 U.S. at 516, 519.

39. *Brooks v. United States*, 267 U.S. 432 (1925).

40. *Bailey v. Drexel Furniture*, 259 U.S. 20 (1922).

41. 259 U.S. at 37.

42. *Village of Euclid v. Ambler Realty*, 272 U.S. 365 (1926).

43. *Buck v. Bell*, 274 U.S. at 207.

44. Id. at 208.

45. *Tyson & Brother v. Banton*, 273 U.S. 418 (1927); *Ribnik v. McBride*, 277 U.S. 350 (1928); *Williams v. Standard Oil*, 278 U.S. 235 (1928).

46. 257 U.S. at 329.

47. Proceedings (1922), quoted in Charles G. Haines, *The American Doctrine of Judicial Supremacy*, 450 (1932).

48. 261 U.S. at 558.

49. 264 U.S. at 534.

50. 262 U.S. at 399.

51. 268 U.S. at 535.

52. *Whitney v. California*, 274 U.S. at 376 (concurring).

53. *Stromberg v. California*, 283 U.S. 359 (1931); *Grosjean v. American Press*, 297 U.S. 233 (1936); *Herndon v. Lowry*, 301 U.S. 242 (1937).

54. *Moore v. Dempsey*, 261 U.S. 86 (1923).

55. *Powell v. Alabama*, 287 U.S. 45 (1932).

56. *Brown v. Mississippi*, 297 U.S. at 285–286.

57. *Nixon v. Herndon*, 273 U.S. 536 (1927); *Nixon v. Condon*, 286 U.S. 73 (1932).

58. *Grovey v. Townsend*, 295 U.S. 45 (1935).

59. Taft to Horace Taft, November 14, 1929, in Henry F. Pringle, *The Life and Times of William Howard Taft*, 967 (1939).

60. First Inaugural, March 4, 1933, in *Inaugural Addresses of the Presidents of the United States*, 269 (Senate Doc. 101–10, 1989).

61. Id. at 271.

62. 290 U.S. at 425, 428.

63. Id. at 424, 434.

64. 291 U.S. at 524.

65. Id. at 554–555 (McReynolds).

66. *New York Times*, January 9, 1935, 1.

67. Quoted in William Leuchtenburg, *The Supreme Court Reborn*, 87 (1995).

68. *Perry v. United States*, 294 U.S. at 351.

69. Id. at 381 (dissent).

70. *Norman v. Baltimore & Ohio Railroad*, 294 U.S. 240 (1935).

71. *Railroad Retirement Board v. Alton Railroad*, 295 U.S. at 348–351.

72. Id. at 348–349.

73. Id. at 368.

74. *United States v. Schechter Poultry*, 295 U.S. at 543.

75. Id. at 554 (concurring).

76. May 31, 1935, in 5 *Complete Presidential Press Conferences of Franklin D. Roosevelt*, 309, 336 (1972).

77. *New Yorker*, September 21, 1935, 30.

78. 297 U.S. at 75.

79. Henry A. Wallace, *Whose Constitution? An Inquiry into the General Welfare*, 93 (1936).

80. 297 U.S. at 79.

81. 298 U.S. 587 (1936).

82. 80 *Congressional Record* 9040, 74th Cong., 1st sess. (1936).

83. Drew Pearson and Robert S. Allen, *The Nine Old Men* (1936).

84. George Creel, *Rebel at Large*, 293–94 (1947). Creel then wrote the article on Roosevelt and the Court appearing in the December 26, 1937, issue of *Collier's*.

85. Samuel I. Rosenman, *Working with Roosevelt*, 144 (1952).

86. Second Inaugural, January 20, 1937, in *The Public Papers and Addresses of Franklin D. Roosevelt*, 2, 4 (1937).

87. Pictured in *Equal Justice under Law: The Supreme Court in American Life*, 93 (Melvin M. Payne, ed., 1965).

88. Fireside Chat, March 9, 1937, reprinted in Robert Jackson, *The Struggle for Judicial Supremacy*, 340, 342 (1941).

89. Stone to Judge Irving Lehman, April 26, 1938, quoted in Alpheus Thomas Mason, *Harlan Fiske Stone: Pillar of the Law*, 515 (1956).

90. Solicitor General Robert H. Jackson to Roosevelt, quoted in Eugene C. Gerhart, *America's Advocate*, 165 (1958).

91. Felix Frankfurter, "Chief Justices I Have Known," 39 *Virginia Law Review* 883, 901 (1953).

92. 300 U.S. at 399.

93. *NLRB v. Jones & Laughlin Steel Corp.*, 301 U.S 1, 41–42 (1937).

94. *NLRB v. Friedman-Harry Marks Clothing*, 301 U.S. 58 (1937).

95. Quoted in Leonard Baker, *Back to Back: The Duel between FDR and the Supreme Court*, 181 (1967).

96. "Reorganization of the Federal Judiciary," *Senate Report No. 711*, 75th Cong., 1st sess., 23 (1937).

97. Joseph Alsop and Turner Catledge, *The 168 Days*, 153 (1938).

98. Id. at 300–301.

99. August 4, 1937, in 2 Harold Ickes, *The Secret Diary of Harold Ickes: The Inside Struggle, 1936–1939*, 183 (1954).

100. Quoted in Leuchtenburg, *Supreme Court Reborn*, at 184.

101. *Washington Post*, August 13, 1937, quoted id. at 187.

102. "Quarantine" Speech at Chicago, October 5, 1937, in *The Public Papers and Addresses of Franklin D. Roosevelt, 1937*, 406, 407, 408 (1938).

8. After the New Deal Constitutional Revolution

1. Quoted in William Leuchtenburg, *The Supreme Court Reborn*, 158 (1995).

2. *Nation*, June 14, 1941, 685.

3. 312 U.S. at 124.

4. Robert H. Jackson, *The Struggle for Judicial Supremacy,* xiv (1941).

5. *United States v. Carolene Products,* 304 U.S. 144, 152 n.4 (1938).

6. *Yakus v. United States,* 321 U.S. 414 (1944).

7. *Bowles v. Willingham,* 321 U.S. 503, 518 (1944).

8. *Ex parte Quirin,* 317 U.S. 1 (1942).

9. "The Sabotuers and the Court," *New Republic,* August 10, 1942, 159.

10. *In re Yamashita,* 327 U.S. 1 (1946).

11. *Cramer v. United States,* 325 U.S. 1 (1945).

12. Id. at 48, 67 (dissenting).

13. *Haupt v. United States,* 330 U.S. 631 (1947).

14. Civilian Exclusion Order No. 34, 323 U.S. at 234.

15. Quoted in Peter Irons, *Justice at War,* 46 (1983).

16. *Hirabayashi v. United States,* 320 U.S. 81, 99 (1943).

17. Id. at 108 (concurring).

18. *Korematsu v. United States,* 323 U.S. 214, 243 (1944) (dissenting).

19. Id. at 216.

20. 323 U.S. at 233 (dissenting).

21. Id. at 244.

22. Id. at 245.

23. Id. at 246.

24. "Address of Chief Justice Hughes to the American Law Institute," 27 *American Bar Association Journal* 334, 335 (1941).

25. 302 U.S. at 326.

26. Id. at 327.

27. *Bridges v. California,* 314 U.S. 252, 263 (1941).

28. 314 U.S. at 263.

29. 319 U.S. at 634.

30. 319 U.S. at 638.

31. *Prince v. Massachusetts,* 321 U.S. 158 (1944).

32. 316 U.S. at 538, 539.

33. 316 U.S. at 541.

34. Id.

35. 302 U.S. at 325.

36. *Betts v. Brady,* 316 U.S. 455 (1942).

37. *Adamson v. California,* 332 U.S. 46 (1947).

38. *Wolf v. Colorado,* 338 U.S. 25 (1949).

39. *Adamson,* 332 U.S. at 63.

40. Id. at 71 (dissent).

41. Id. at 90.

42. *Rochin v. California,* 342 U.S. 165, 172 (1952).

43. 342 U.S. at 172.

44. 347 U.S. at 133.

45. *Louisiana ex rel. Francis v. Resweber*, 329 U.S. 459 (1947).

46. Id. at 471 (concurring).

47. *Lincoln Federal Labor Union v. Northwestern Iron & Metal*, 335 U.S. 525 (1949).

48. 310 U.S. at 101–102.

49. *International Brotherhood of Teamsters v. Hanke*, 339 U.S. 470, 474 (1950).

50. *Jewel Ridge Coal v. Local 6167 UMW*, 325 U.S. 161 (1945).

51. *United States v. United Mine Workers*, 330 U.S. 258, 312 (1947) (Frankfurter concurring).

52. *Youngstown Sheet and Tube v. Sawyer*, 343 U.S. 579, 587 (1952).

53. Id. at 642 (concurring).

54. Quoted in James T. Patterson, *Grand Expectations*, 113 (1996).

55. *American Communication Workers v. Douds*, 339 U.S. 382 (1950).

56. 341 U.S. at 510.

57. Id.

58. Id. at 588 (dissenting).

59. *Washington Post*, June 6, 1951, 12.

60. *Rosenberg v. United States*, 346 U.S. 273 (1953).

61. *Adler v. Board of Education*, 342 U.S. 485 (1952); *Barsky v. Board of Regents*, 347 U.S. 442 (1954).

62. *Cole v. Young*, 351 U.S. 536 (1956).

63. *Yates v. United States*, 354 U.S. 298 (1957).

64. *Watkins v. United States*, 354 U.S. 178, 200 (1957).

65. *Koningsberg v. State Bar*, 353 U.S. 252 (1957); *Schware v. State Bar*, 353 U.S. 232 (1957).

66. *Jencks v. United States*, 353 U.S. 657 (1957).

67. *Beilen v. Board of Education*, 357 U.S. 399 (1958); *Lerner v. Casey*, 357 U.S. 468 (1958).

68. *Report of the Committee on Federal-State Relationships as Affected by Judicial Decisions*, 28 (1958).

69. *Braden v. United States*, 365 U.S. 431 (1961); *Wilkinson v. United States*, 365 U.S. 399 (1961).

70. *In re Anastaplo*, 366 U.S. 82 (1961).

71. *Scales v. United States*, 367 U.S. 203 (1961).

72. *Communist Party v. Subversive Activities Control Board*, 367 U.S. 1 (1961).

73. 104 *Congressional Record* 2011, 85th Cong., 2nd sess. (1958).

74. *Grovey v. Townsend*, 295 U.S. 45 (1935).

75. 321 U.S. at 669 (dissenting).

76. *Mitchell v. United States*, 313 U.S. 80 (1941); *Henderson v. United States*, 339 U.S. 816 (1950).

77. *Chambers v. Florida*, 309 U.S. 227 (1940).

78. *Sipuel v. Board of Regents*, 332 U.S. 631 (1948).

79. *Fisher v. Hurst*, 333 U.S. 147 (1948).

80. *McLaurin v. Regents*, 339 U.S. 637, 641 (1950).

81. *Sweatt v. Painter*, 339 U.S. 626, 634 (1950).

82. 347 U.S. at 494.

83. 163 U.S. at 551.

84. 347 U.S. at 494.

85. 100 *Congressional Record* 6748, 83rd Cong., 2nd sess. (1954).

86. *Brown v. Board of Education*, 349 U.S. 294, 301 (1955).

87. *New York Times*, June 1, 1955, 26 (quoting the *Los Angeles Times*).

88. 102 *Congressional Record* 4515–16, 84th Cong., 2nd sess. (1956).

89. Quoted in Patterson, *Grand Expectations*, at 415.

90. 358 U.S. at 13.

91. *New York Times*, September 30, 1958, 30.

92. Quoted in Elizabeth Jacoway, *Turn Away Thy Son*, 269 (2007).

93. *Shuttlesworth v. Birmingham*, 358 U.S. 101 (1958) affirming 162 F. Supp. 372, 384 (N.D. Ala. 1958).

9. Reforming America

1. Quoted in C. Vann Woodward, *The Strange Career of Jim Crow*, 181 (2nd rev. ed. 1966).

2. Quoted in Doris Kearns Goodwin, *Lyndon Johnson and the American Dream*, 191 (rev. ed. 1991).

3. *New York Times*, June 20, 1964, 11.

4. *New York Times*, July 16, 1964, 13.

5. Quoted in Robert Weisbrot, *Freedom Bound*, 134 (1990).

6. Quoted in Jules Witcover, *The Year the Dream Died*, 7 (1997).

7. Quoted in Goodwin, *Lyndon Johnson*, at 305.

8. 388 U.S. at 321.

9. *Batson v. Kentucky*, 476 U.S. 79 (1986) overruling *Swain v. Alabama*, 380 U.S. 202 (1965).

10. *Loving v. Virginia*, 388 U.S. 1, 11 (1967).

11. Quoted in Benjamin C. Bradlee, *Conversations with Kennedy*, 69 (1975).

12. 385 U.S. at 135–136.

13. 395 U.S. at 447.

14. Id. at 454 (concurring).

15. 403 U.S. at 717 (concurring).

16. *Roth v. United States*, 354 U.S. 476 (1957).

17. *Jacobellis v. Ohio*, 378 U.S. 184, 197 (1964) (concurring).

18. Quoted in Dan T. Carter, *The Politics of Rage*, 425 (1995).

19. Quoted in Harry Ashmore, "Doubling the Standard," 62 *Virginia Quarterly Review* 70, 71 (Winter 1986).

20. *Miller v. California*, 413 U.S. 15 (1973).

21. William Masters and Virginia Johnson, *Human Sexual Response*, (1966).

22. Ralph Blumenthal, "Pornochic: 'Hard Core' Grows Fashionable—and Very Profitable," *New York Times*, January 21, 1973, 272.

23. *Playboy*, May 1973, 230.

24. *Associated Press v. Walker*, 388 U.S. 130 (1967).

25. *Rosenbloom v. Metromedia*, 403 U.S. 29 (1971).

26. *Gertz v. Robert Welch, Inc.*, 418 U.S. 323 (1974).

27. *United States v. O'Brien*, 391 U.S. 367 (1968).

28. 370 U.S. at 435.

29. *Abingdon School District v. Schempp*, 374 U.S. 204 (1963).

30. *New York Times*, June 18, 1963, 1.

31. *Board of Regents v. Allen*, 392 U.S. 236 (1968).

32. *Sherbert v. Verner*, 374 U.S. 394 (1963); *Wisconsin v. Yoder*, 406 U.S. 205 (1972).

33. 377 U.S. at 574.

34. *Lucas v. 44th Colorado General Assembly*, 377 U.S. 713, 736–737 (1964).

35. 378 U.S. at 489.

36. Id. at 490.

37. Id at 498, 495 (dissenting).

38. Quoted in Paul Murphy, *The Constitution in Crisis Times*, 381 (1972)

39. Quoted in Theodore H. White, *The Making of the President, 1964*, 241–242 (1965).

40. Senator Sam Ervin, quoted in *New York Times*, July 23, 1966, 54.

41. Quoted in 2 Stephen Ambrose, *Nixon*, 154 (1989).

42. Carter, *Politics of Rage*, at 339 (quoting *Meet the Press*, June 30, 1968).

43. 391 U.S. at 439.

44. Quoted in Ambrose, *Nixon*, at 204.

45. 274 U.S. 200, 208 (1927).

46. *McGowen v. Maryland*, 366 U.S. 420 (1960); *Hoyt v. Florida*, 368 U.S. 57 (1961).

47. *Harper v. Virginia Board of Elections*, 383 U.S. 663, 669 (1966).

48. Id. at 668.

49. Id. at 686 (dissenting).

50. Quoted in Robert Dallek, *Flawed Giant*, 278 (1998).

51. 394 U.S. at 627.

52. Id. at 677 (dissenting).

53. Quoted in David J. Garrow, *Liberty and Sexuality*, 197 (1994).

54. 381 U.S. at 484.

55. Id. at 487 (concurring).

56. *Poe v. Ullman*, 367 U.S. 497, 552 (1961) (dissenting).

57. Id. at 510 (dissenting).

58. Quoted in Garrow, *Liberty and Sexuality*, at 256.

59. *Eisenstadt v. Baird*, 405 U.S. 438, 453 (1972).

60. 411 U.S. at 688.

61. 410 U.S. at 153.

62. Id. at 166.

63. *New York Times Magazine*, September 23, 2007, 76.

64. 418 U.S. 683 (1974).

65. The expression was so ubiquitous that a chapter of Stanley Kutler, *The Wars of Watergate* (1990), is so named.

66. *Time*, August 19, 1974, 9.

10. An Uneasy Status Quo

1. 435 U.S. at 776, 789, 791.

2. *Austin v. Michigan Chamber of Commerce*, 494 U.S. 652, 659 (1990).

3. *Virginia Board of Pharmacy v. Virginia Citizens Consumer Council*, 425 U.S. 748 (1976).

4. Richard Darmon to Arthur M. Schlesinger Jr., August 31, 1984 (orally), recounted in Arthur M. Schlesinger Jr., *Journals, 1952–2000*, 579 (2007).

5. *Young v. American MiniTheatres*, 427 U.S. 50, 70 (1976).

6. *Hustler Magazine v. Falwell*, 485 U.S. 46 (1988).

7. *Texas v. Johnson*, 491 U. 397, 432, 431 (1989) (dissenting).

8. *United States v. Eichman*, 496 U.S. 310 (1990).

9. 426 U.S. at 248.

10. *Metro Broadcasting v. FCC*, 497 U.S. 547 (1990).

11. 426 U.S. at 858, 880.

12. 469 U.S. 528, 546 (1985).

13. Id. at 557, 572.

14. *Wainwright v. Sykes*, 433 U.S. 72 (1977); *Teague v. Lane*, 489 U.S. 288 (1989).

15. *Tison v. Arizona*, 481 U.S. 137 (1987) overruling *Enmund v. Florida*, 458 U.S. 782 (1982).

16. *Payne v. Tennessee*, 501 U.S. 808 (1991) overruling *Booth v. Maryland*, 482 U.S. 496 (1987).

17. *Stanford v. Kentucky,* 492 U.S. 361 (1989).

18. *Penry v. Lynaugh,* 492 U.S. 302 (1989).

19. *Ford v. Wainwright,* 477 U.S. 399 (1986).

20. 481 U.S. 279, 319 (1987).

21. *Sullivan v. Wainwright,* 464 U.S. 109, 112 (1983).

22. *Committee for Public Education v. Nyquist,* 413 U.S. 756 (1973).

23. *Meek v. Pittenger,* 421 U.S. 349 (1975); *Wollman v. Walter,* 433 U.S. 229 (1977); *Grand Rapids v. Ball,* 473 U.S. 373 (1985).

24. *Grand Rapids,* 473 U.S. at 387.

25. Id. at 420 (in the companion opinion *Aguilar v. Felton,* 473 U.S. 402 (1985)).

26. *Wallace v. Jaffree,* 472 U.S. 38 (1985); *Edwards v. Aguillard,* 482 U.S. 578 (1987).

27. 465 U.S. at 686.

28. *Allegheny County v. ACLU,* 492 U.S. 573 (1989).

29. Id. at 655, 664.

30. *Rostker v. Goldberg,* 453 U.S. 57 (1981).

31. *Michael M. v. Superior Court,* 450 U.S. 464 (1981).

32. *Mississippi University for Women v. Hogan,* 458 U.S. 718 (1982).

33. *Maher v. Roe,* 432 U.S. 464 (1977); *Harris v. McRae,* 448 U.S. 297 (1980).

34. *Bowers v. Hardwick,* 478 U.S. 186 (1986).

35. *New York Times,* January 28, 1984, A8.

36. Quoted in Ethan Bronner, *The Battle for Justice,* 190 (1989).

37. Id. at 154–155.

38. Id. at 196.

39. Id. at 204–205.

40. *Washington Post,* October 9, 1987, B1.

41. 492 U.S. at 560.

42. *Washington Post,* October 12, 1991, A1.

43. 505 U.S. at 865.

44. Id. at 867.

45. Id. at 856.

46. Id.

47. Id. at 860.

48. Id. at 922.

49. Id. at 981.

50. Id. at 997.

51. Quoted in Richard C. Reuben, "Man in the Middle," 12 *California Lawyer* 34 (October 1992).

52. Conservative activist Gary Bauer, quoted in Barbara H. Craig and David O'Brien, *Abortion and American Politics,* 325 (1993).

11. An Imperial Court

1. 505 U.S. at 866.
2. Id. at 866–867.
3. *Stenberg v. Carhart,* 530 U.S. 914 (2000).
4. *Casey,* 505 U.S. at 868.
5. Id. at 868.
6. 512 U.S. at 519.
7. 521 U.S. at 536.
8. Id.
9. Quoted in Fred Graham, *The Self-Inflicted Wound,* 185 (1970).
10. 530 U.S. 428, 437 (2000).
11. *United States v. Morrison,* 529 U.S. 598, 618 (2000).
12. *United States v. Locke,* 529 U.S. 89 (2000).
13. *Engine Manufacturers Association v. South Coast Air Quality Management District,* 541 U.S. 246 (2004).
14. *Lorillard Tobacco v. Reilly,* 533 U.S. 525 (2001).
15. *Hawaiian Housing Authority v. Midkiff,* 467 U.S. 229 (1984).
16. *Washington Post,* July 1, 2005, A1.
17. *United States v. Virginia,* 518 U.S. 515 (1996).
18. *Nevada Department of Human Resources v. Hibbs,* 538 U.S. 721, 736 (2004).
19. *Romer v. Evans,* 517 U.S. 620 (1996).
20. 539 U.S. at 562, 567.
21. Id. at 602.
22. *Goodridge v. Department of Public Health,* 440 Mass. 309, 798 N.E.2d 941 (2003).
23. *Boy Scouts of America v. Dale,* 530 U.S. 640 (2000).
24. *Rumsfeld v. FAIR,* 126 S.Ct. 1297 (2006).
25. *Missouri v. Jenkins,* 491 U.S. 274 (1989).
26. *Missouri v. Jenkins,* 515 U.S. 70 (1995).
27. *Board of Education v. Dowell,* 498 U.S. 237 (1991); *Freeman v. Pitts,* 503 U.S. 467 (1992).
28. *Grutter v. Bollinger,* 539 U.S. 306 (2003).
29. *Gratz v. Bollinger,* 539 U.S. 244 (2003).
30. Id. at 331 quoting amicus brief.
31. *Zelman v. Simmons-Harris,* 536 U.S. 639, 689 (2002).
32. 540 U.S. at 733.
33. *Stone v. Graham,* 449 U.S. 39 (1980).
34. *McCreary County v. ACLU,* 545 U.S. 844 (2005).
35. *Van Orden v. Perry,* 545 U.S. 677 (2005).

36. 536 U.S. 304, 312 (2003).
37. Id. at 324.
38. Id. at 316–317 n.21.
39. Id. at 324 (Rehnquist dissenting).
40. *Roper v. Simmons*, 543 U.S. 551 (2005).
41. Id. at 609.
42. Id. at 628.
43. *Ring v. Arizona*, 536 U.S. 584 (2003).
44. *Williams v. Taylor*, 529 U.S. 362 (2000); *Wiggins v. Smith*, 539 U.S. 510 (2003); *Rompilla v. Beard*, 544 U.S. 374 (2005).
45. 548 U.S. 1016 (2006).
46. 126 S.Ct. at 2545.
47. 128 S.Ct. 2641 (2008).
48. Id. at 2659.
49. 126 S.Ct. at 2532.
50. Id. at 2539.
51. *Shaw v. Reno*, 509 U.S. 630 (1993).
52. Id. at 641.
53. *Miller v. Johnson*, 515 U.S. 900 (1995).
54. *Easley v. Cromartie*, 532 U.S. 234 (2001).
55. Id. at 266.
56. *Davis v. Bandemer*, 478 U.S. 109 (1986).
57. *Vieth v. Jubelirer*, 541 U.S. 267 (2004).
58. *LULAC v. Perry*, 126 S.Ct. 2594 (2006).
59. 540 U.S. at 248.
60. *Bush v. Palm Beach County Canvassing Board*, 531 U.S. 70 (2000).
61. 531 U.S. at 109.
62. Margaret Talbot, "Supreme Confidence," *New Yorker*, March 28, 2005, 43 (quoting Scalia).
63. 531 U.S. at 129.
64. Robert Mankoff, December 25, 2000, in *The Complete Cartoons of the New Yorker* (Robert Mankoff, David Remnick, and Adam Gopnik, eds., 2004), CD-ROM.
65. *Morrison v. Olson*, 487 U.S. 654 (1988).
66. Arthur M. Schlesinger Jr., *Journals, 1952–2000*, 832 (2007).
67. *Federal Election Commission v. Wisconsin Right to Life*, 127 S.Ct. 2652, 2669 (2007).
68. Id. at 2686.
69. *Parents Involved v. Seattle School Dist.*, 127 S.Ct. 2738, 2800 (2007).
70. Memorandum from Alberto Gonzales to President George W. Bush, January

25, 2002, reprinted in *The Torture Papers: The Road to Abu Ghraib,* 119–120 (Karen J. Greenberg and Joshua L. Dratel, eds., 2005).

71. Memorandum from Jay S. Bybee to Alberto Gonzales, "Standards of Conduct for Interrogation," August 1, 2002, reprinted id. at 172.

72. 542 U.S. at 483 n.15.

73. Id. at 530.

74. James Risen, *State of War: The Secret History of the CIA and the Bush Administration* (2006).

75. 126 S.Ct. at 2798.

76. Id. at 2799.

77. *Boumediene v. Bush,* 128 S.Ct. 2229 (2008).

78. *New York Times,* June 13, 2008, A21.

Selected Bibliography

The endnotes reflect the primary, but rarely the secondary, sources that I have consulted. Indeed, many secondary sources consist of books and articles that I have read over the past forty years. Two imaginative lawyer–political scientists have significantly influenced my thinking about the Constitution and the Court and yet receive scant (or no) credit in the endnotes. They are Bruce Ackerman and Mark Graber. Readers familiar with their pathbreaking works will readily note their influences in the preceding pages. In Ackerman's case three books are key: *We the People: Foundations* (1991), *We the People: Transformations* (1998), and *The Failure of the Founding Fathers: Jefferson, Marshall, and the Rise of Presidential Democracy* (2005). In Graber's case two books and two articles were paramount: *Dred Scott and the Problem of Constitutional Evil* (2006) and *Rethinking Abortion: Equal Choice, the Constitution, and Reproductive Rights* (1996); the articles are "The Non-Majoritarian Difficulty: Legislative Deference to the Judiciary," 7 *Studies in American Political Development* 35 (1993), and "Resolving Political Questions into Judicial Questions: Tocqueville's Thesis Revisited," 21 *Constitutional Commentary* 485 (2004). I have also profited from Keith Whittington's "'Interpose Your Friendly Hand': Political Supports for the Exercise of Judicial Review by the United States Supreme Court," 99 *American Political Science Review* 583 (2005), and *Political Foundations of Judicial Supremacy* (2007).

The central theme of this book, that the Court is sensitive to the wishes of political majorities, is a continuation from my previous book, *The Warren Court and American Politics* (2000). Graber's and Whittington's works make a similar point, as do Ran Hirschl, *Towards Juristocracy: The Origins and Consequences of the New*

Constitutionalism (2007), and Paul Frymer, *Black and Blue: African Americans, the Labor Movement, and the Decline of the Democratic Party* (2008).

There are numerous books on the framing of the Constitution. David O. Stewart, *The Summer of 1787* (2007), offers a chronological description of the Philadelphia Convention. This is matched for the Bill of Rights in Richard Labunski, *James Madison and the Struggle for the Bill of Rights* (2006). Jack N. Rakove, *Original Meanings: Politics and Ideas in the Making of the Constitution* (1996); David C. Hendrickson, *Peace Pact: The Lost World of the American Founding*, 2003); Max M. Edling, *A Revolution in Favor of Government: Origins of the U.S. Constitution and the Making of the American State* (2003); and Calvin H. Johnson, *Righteous Anger at the Wicked States: The Meaning of the Founders' Constitution* (2005), offer varying interpretations of the Founding. Forest McDonald's *Novus Ordo Seclorum: The Intellectual Origins of the Constitution* (1986), while slightly older, holds up well. Garry Wills, *Explaining America: The Federalist* (1981), remains the best analysis of the *Federalist Papers*. For the Fourteenth Amendment, Ackerman's *We the People: Foundations*, and Michael Kent Curtis, *"No State Shall Abridge": The Fourteenth Amendment and the Bill of Rights* (1986), are the best sources.

Because my field is the Supreme Court and not American history, I have drawn on my memory of the hundreds of books that I have read as a reviewer over the past two-plus decades for the History Book Club. Specifically, however, I used very well established volumes, biographies, and reference works, especially the published volumes in the superb Oxford History of the United States series.

For the Court, there are two multivolume series available, both defining eras by chief justiceships and both, like any other series, uneven. The Oliver Wendell Holmes Devise History of the Supreme Court volumes are massive tomes intending to be "definitive," as if that were possible. These volumes are far better suited for specialized research than for reading. Thus far they include Julius Goebel Jr., *Antecedents and Beginnings to 1801* (1971); George Haskins and Herbert Johnson, *Foundations of Power* (1981); G. Edward White, *The Marshall Court and Cultural Change, 1815–35* (1988); Carl Swisher, *The Taney Period, 1836–64* (1974); Charles Fairman, *Reconstruction and Reunion, 1864–88, Part One* (1971) and *Part Two* (1988); Owen Fiss, *Troubled Beginnings of the Modern State, 1888–1910* (1993); Alexander Bickel and Benno Schmidt Jr., *The Judiciary and Responsible Government, 1910–21* (1984); and William Wiecek, *The Birth of the Modern Supreme Court, 1941–53* (2006). The volumes by Fairman and White are the best; Goebel's volume is worthless. The thinner but not much more readable South Carolina Press series thus far includes William Casto, *The Supreme Court in the Early Republic* (1995); Herbert Johnson, *The Chief Justiceship of John Marshall, 1801–35* (1997); James Ely, *The Chief Justiceship of Melville W. Fuller, 1888–1910* (1995); Walter Pratt Jr., *The Supreme Court under Edward Douglas White, 1910–21* (1999); William G. Ross, *The Chief Justiceship of*

Charles Evans Hughes, 1930–41 (2007); Melvin Urofsky, *Division and Discord: The Supreme Court under Stone and Vinson, 1941–53* (1997); Michael Belknap, *The Chief Justiceship of Earl Warren, 1953–69* (2004); and Earl Maltz, *The Chief Justiceship of Warren E. Burger, 1969–86* (2000). Casto's and Urofsky's are the most illuminating.

Apart from the multivolume series, Charles Warren's eighty-year-old two-volume study *The Supreme Court in United States History* (rev. ed. 1926) remains useful. Robert McCloskey, *The American Supreme Court* (4th ed. 2005), a 1960 book with subsequent developments updated by Sanford Levinson, remains the best one-volume work on the Court, although McCloskey's emphasis on national economic power is dated. Christopher Tomlins has edited a collection of essays, most arranged by chief justice (but including several broader interpretive essays), *The United States Supreme Court* (2006), which usefully synthesizes material. For quick information on specific references, see the *Oxford Companion to the Supreme Court of the United States* (Kermit Hall, ed., 2nd ed. 2005). Melvin I. Urofsky and Paul Finkelman have authored a two-volume constitutional history, *A March of Liberty: A Constitutional History of the United States* (2nd ed. 2002), that is probably more useful as a reference than a beginning-to-end read.

Those desiring doctrinal analysis of the Court's decisions should consult David P. Currie, *The Constitution in the Supreme Court: The First Hundred Years* (1985), and *The Constitution in the Supreme Court, 1886–1986* (1990). The books are, however, completely ahistorical. Judicial review is helpfully discussed in Robert L. Clinton, *Marbury v. Madison and Judicial Review* (1989), and Sylvia Snowiss, *Judicial Review and the Law of the Constitution* (1990).

I found a handful of histories of particular periods helpful. In chronological order they are James Simon, *What Kind of Nation: Thomas Jefferson, John Marshall, and the Epic Struggle to Create a United States* (2002); Howard Gillman, *The Constitution Besieged: The Rise and Demise of Lochner Era Police Powers Jurisprudence* (1993); William Leuchtenburg, *The Supreme Court Reborn: The Constitutional Revolution in the Age of Roosevelt* (1995); Barry Cashman, *Rethinking the New Deal Court: The Structure of a Constitutional Revolution* (1998); G. Edward White, *The Constitution and the New Deal* (2000); my own *The Warren Court and American Politics* (2000); Mark Tushnet, *The New Constitutional Order* (2003) and *A Court Divided* (2004); Jan Crawford Greenburg, *Supreme Conflict: The Inside Story of the Struggle for Control of the United States Supreme Court* (2007); and Jeffrey Toobin, *The Nine: Inside the Secret World of the Supreme Court* (2007). Finally, the *Journal of Supreme Court History* and *Constitutional Commentary* regularly offers good pieces on various aspects of Supreme Court history.

There are dozens of judicial biographies. Almost no justice was too obscure for someone not to write his (or lately her) biography, although surprisingly there is still no true biography of Robert Jackson, and the many biographies of Felix

Frankfurter suffer from their authors' either loving or loathing him. The judicial biographies I found most helpful for this book were (again in chronological order) Walter Stahr, *John Jay: Founding Father* (2005); Charles Hobson, *The Great Chief Justice: John Marshall and the Rule of Law* (1996); Jean Edward Smith, *John Marshall, Defender of a Nation* (1996); R. Kent Newmyer, *Supreme Court Justice Joseph Story: Statesman of the Old Republic* (1985); Carl Swisher, *Roger B. Taney* (1936); Michael Ross, *Justice of Shattered Dreams: Samuel Freeman Miller and the Supreme Court during the Civil War* (2003); Charles Fairman, *Justice Miller and the Supreme Court, 1862–90* (1938); Paul Kens, *Justice Stephen Field: Shaping Liberty from the Gold Rush to the Gilded Age* (1997); G. Edward White, *Justice Oliver Wendell Holmes: Law and the Inner Self* (1993); Philippa Strum, *Louis D. Brandeis: Justice for the People* (1984); Alpheus Mason, *Brandeis: A Free Man's Life* (1946) and *Harlan Fiske Stone: Pillar of Law* (1956); J. Woodford Howard Jr., *Mr. Justice Murphy: A Political Biography* (1968); John Ferren, *Salt of the Earth, Conscience of the Court: The Story of Justice Wiley Rutledge* (2004); Jim Newton, *Justice for All: Earl Warren and the Nation He Made* (2006); Roger Newman, *Hugo Black: A Biography* (1994); Laura Kalman, *Abe Fortas: A Biography* (1990); John Jeffries Jr., *Justice Lewis F. Powell, Jr.* (1994); Linda Greenhouse, *Becoming Justice Blackmun: Harry Blackmun's Supreme Court Journey* (2005); and Joan Biskupic, *Sandra Day O'Connor: How the First Woman on the Supreme Court Became Its Most Influential Justice* (2005).

The University Press of Kansas has an extensive series on great constitutional cases that is worth consulting (although the formulaic nature of each book is somewhat tired). Additionally, some of the better studies of a single case are C. Peter McGrath, *Yazoo: Law and Politics in the New Republic, the Case of Fletcher v. Peck* (1966); Richard Ellis, *Aggressive Nationalism: McCulloch v. Maryland and the Foundation of Federal Authority in the Young Republic* (2007); Stanley Kutler, *Privilege and Creative Destruction: The Charles River Bridge Case* (rev. ed. 1977); Paul Finkleman, *An Imperfect Union: Slavery, Federalism, and Comity* (1981); Donald Fehrenbacher, *The Dred Scott Case: Its Significance in American Law and Politics* (1978); Sarah Barringer Gordon, *The Mormon Question: Polygamy and Constitutional Conflict in Nineteenth-Century America* (2002); Richard Polenberg, *Fighting Faiths: The Abrams Case, the Supreme Court, and Free Speech* (1987); Richard Cortner, *The "Scottsboro Case" in Mississippi: The Supreme Court and Brown v. Mississippi* (1987); Peter Irons, *Justice at War: The Story of the Japanese Internment Cases* (1983); Maeva Marcus, *Truman and the Steel Seizure Case: The Limits of Presidential Power* (1977); Richard Kluger, *Simple Justice* (1976); Mary L. Dudziak, *Cold War Civil Rights: Race and the Image of American Democracy* (2000); and David Garrow, *Liberty and Sexuality: The Right to Privacy in the Making of Roe v. Wade* (1994). There are numerous studies of *Bush v. Gore*, including Cass Sunstein and Richard Epstein, eds., *The Vote: Bush, Gore, and the Supreme Court* (2001); Howard Gillman, *The Votes That Counted: How the Supreme Court Decided the*

2000 *Presidential Election* (2001); and Richard Posner, *Breaking the Deadlock: The 2000 Election, the Constitution, and the Courts* (2001). Last, but definitely not least, Michael Klarman's *From Jim Crow to Civil Rights: The Supreme Court and the Struggle for Racial Equality* (2004) is indispensable for any understanding of the pre-1964 race cases.

A typical error, especially for lawyers and reporters, is to overstate the importance and influence of the Court. While we say there are three coequal branches of government, the difference in influence between the Court and the Congress and president is one of kind, not degree. A useful corrective is Gerald Rosenberg, *The Hollow Hope* (1991), even if some of his examples are strained.

There is a reason for this truncated bibliography. Sanford Levinson has written an unbeatable bibliographic essay in his updating of McCloskey's *American Supreme Court*. Anyone wanting a complete overview (at least of the books in the field) should consult it. Urofsky and Finkelman in *A March of Liberty* also provide extensive bibliographies.

Index of Cases

General Index